A HISTORY OF
PAKISTAN
AND ITS ORIGINS

A HISTORY OF
PAKISTAN
AND ITS ORIGINS

Edited by
Christophe Jaffrelot

Translated by
Gillian Beaumont

Anthem Press

Anthem Press is an imprint of
Wimbledon Publishing Company
PO Box 9779
London
SW19 7QA

This edition first published by
Wimbledon Publishing Company 2002

© LIBRAIRIE ARTHÈME FAYARD 2000
First published by LIBRAIRIE ARTHÈME
FAYARD, Paris, 2000
as *Le Pakistan*

English translation
© Wimbledon Publishing Company 2002
Afterword © Christophe Jaffrelot 2002

British Library Cataloguing in Publication Data
Data available

Library of Congress Cataloging in Publication Data
A catalog record has been applied for

ISBN 1 84331 030 9 (hbk)

1 3 5 7 9 10 8 6 4 2

CONTENTS

List of Maps   vii
Contributors to This Volume   ix

Introduction   1

PART I
A Country in Search of an Identity   **7**

1 Islamic Identity and Ethnic Tensions   9

2 East Bengal: Between Islam and a Regional Identity   39

3 A Fruitless Search for Democracy   61

PART II
Pakistan's Foreign Policy   **95**

4 Pakistan and the Power Game   97

5 Living with India: Relations between Pakistan and India   112

6 Islam and Foreign Policy: Central Asia and the
  Arab–Persian World   134

PART III
The Economy and Social Structures   **149**

7 The Country and Its People   151

8 Economic Development   163

9 Between Caste and Tribe   189

PART IV
A Plural Culture?   **219**

10 The Many Faces of Islam   221

11 Islam and Politics   235

12 Languages and Education   250

Conclusion: A Country in Crisis   256

Epilogue: Musharraf and the Islamists: from
        support to opposition after September 11   259

Glossary   281
Chronology   285
Notes   295
Index   316

LIST OF MAPS

The Partition of India   3

Pakistan before 1955   22

Kashmir   119

Pakistan   152

CONTRIBUTORS TO THIS VOLUME

France Bhattacharya, Professor at INALCO: Chapter 2.

Gilbert Étienne, Honorary Professor at the Institut universitaire des hautes études internationales, Geneva: Chapters 7 and 8.

Marc Gaborieau, Director of Studies at EHESS and Director of CEIAS: Chapter 11.

Christophe Jaffrelot, Research fellow at the CNRS and Director of CERI: Introduction; Chapters 1 and 3; Conclusion and Epilogue.

Pierre Lafrance, formerly French Ambassador to Pakistan: Chapter 9.

Aminah Mohammad, Research fellow at the CNRS-CEIAS: Chapter 10.

Jean-Luc Racine, Director of Research at the CNRS-CEIAS: Chapters 4 and 5.

Tariq Rahman, Professor at Qaid-i-Azam University, Islamabad: Chapter 12.

Olivier Roy, Director of Research at the CNRS: Chapter 6.

INTRODUCTION

The Partition of British India and the decolonization of southern Asia resulted in the birth of two separate states: Pakistan was born on 14 August 1947. The 'land of the pure' is, then, the outcome of a long historical sequence. Since the beginning of the twentieth century, the Muslims of the Raj – as the subcontinent came to be known during the colonial period – had been preparing themselves to defend their interests against those of the Hindu majority, with the eventual aim of claiming an independent territory. The outcome was in doubt until the very last moment. The standard-bearer of the anticolonial struggle, the Indian National Congress, was always opposed to what it termed 'Muslim communalism', since it wanted to establish a 'plural' nation where all religions could coexist. In May 1944, Gandhi did his best to convince Muhammad Ali Jinnah, leader of the Muslim separatists, that there would be room for a Muslim community in an independent India, where it would enjoy considerable autonomy. Jinnah could not be persuaded. He was all the more resolute since his party, the Muslim League, had won nine-tenths of the seats reserved for Muslims at the expense of the Congress Party at the September 1945 elections. The Congress Party accused him of a criminal obstinacy, that had received the blessing of the British.

Members of the Congress Party even accused the British of fomenting discord between Hindus and Muslims as part of a 'divide and rule' strategy, before withdrawing precipitately under the auspices of a new modus operandi: 'divide and quit'.[1] It was indeed England, exhausted after six years of war, which started the decolonization process in 1946. However, the Cabinet mission sent out by the Attlee government in May 1946 proposed a plan specifically intended to defuse the Muslim League's demands. Independent India was to be a federal union in which overall central government control would be limited to foreign affairs, defence and communications. The provinces, which would assume responsibility for other matters, would be free to form regional groupings. The Punjab and Bengal, the provinces with a Muslim majority, would therefore be able to set themselves up as autonomous states within a truly loose federation. Both the Muslim League and the Congress Party accepted this plan, and their elected representatives prepared to sit together in a Constituent Assembly designated by the provincial assemblies in 1945–6. So the spectre of Partition receded; but on 10 July 1946 Jawaharlal Nehru, the Congress leader, stated that his party did not consider itself bound by any previous

commitments, and that the Constituent Assembly – in which Congress had a majority – would be sovereign in all matters. The Muslim League decided to withdraw
from the constitutional process, and to mobilize its troops for a 'day of direct action'
on 16 August. The demonstration degenerated into riots in Calcutta in which thousands – mainly Hindus – died. The violence intensified across the whole country, and
from that moment Partition seemed inevitable. The viceroy, Lord Wavell, asked
Congress to form a government under Nehru's leadership. Nehru took up his post
of Prime Minister in September, and invited the League to work with him, but they
agreed to do so only in order to cause systematic obstruction. On 20 February 1947
Attlee declared that the British would leave India by June 1948 at the latest, and
appointed Admiral Lord Mountbatten as viceroy with the responsibility of ensuring
the smooth running of this accelerated departure.

As intercommunal riots continued to proliferate, Lord Mountbatten became convinced of the need to separate the Hindus from the Muslims. Considering any
last-minute effort at reconciliation useless, he announced his plan, to be brought into
effect on 3 June: a division of both Bengal and the Punjab, where only areas with a
Muslim majority would become part of Pakistan – the Muslim League, however, had
expected them to be transferred completely. A few weeks later, and in advance of the
due date, the British handed over power to an independent India and an independent Pakistan.[2]

Might Partition have been avoided if the British had acted differently, and Jinnah
had not been head of the Muslim League – or if the parties to the negotiations had
known that he had contracted tuberculosis, and had only a few months to live? The
last years of British rule in India might give the impression that Pakistan was the
product of circumstances, but Jinnah's obstinacy was part of the Muslim League's
long-drawn-out strategy and intercommunal violence reflected the depth of the
chasm between Hindus and Muslims.

An Artificial Construction?

The idea that Partition could have been avoided has led some observers to think of
Pakistan as an artificial construction. It is true that in 1947, the imbalance between
the two countries formed by the Raj was striking. Pakistan represented a mere 23 per
cent of the area, and 18 per cent of the population, of British India. Essentially
rural, it inherited no more than 10 per cent of the industrial potential. Above all, it
was a country of refugees; thousands of Muslims fleeing the intercommunal violence
migrated towards Pakistan. According to the 1957 census, one in every ten Pakistanis
was a mohajir (migrant); this proportion was even higher in West Pakistan than it
was in East Pakistan, where there were 700,000 refugees. During the summer and
autumn of 1947, 4.6 million people fled the eastern Punjab alone. In total, 6 million
Muslims crossed the new frontier. This huge exodus was marked by violence which
claimed 200,000 victims. Some writers, therefore, thought of Pakistan as a slice of
India which had drifted away,[3] led by men who felt that they were embarking on a
dangerous adventure – an adventure they would live to regret. Some even
maintained that the new state would by its very nature prove unviable: not only were

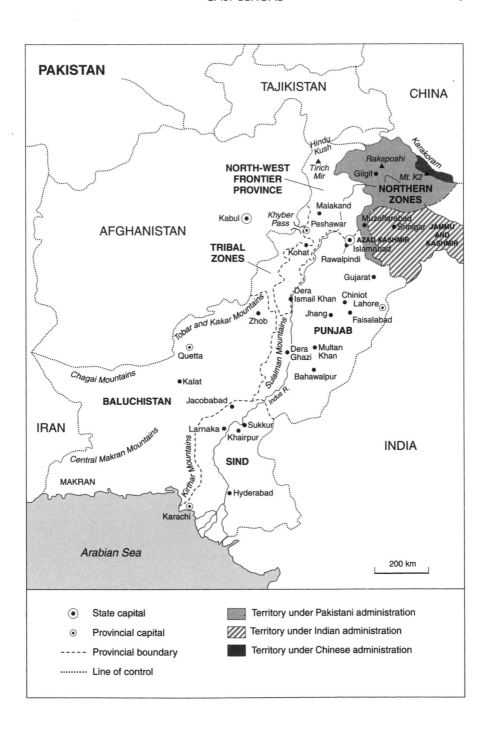

the Princely States of Pakistan integrated more slowly than those in India,[4] but the west of the country was separated from the east by two thousand kilometres of Indian territory – at a time when India became, in effect, Pakistan's Enemy Number One. From this it was easy to conclude that Pakistan was destined to fail – and numerous observers accepted this conclusion readily.

The scepticism which greeted the birth of Pakistan also derived from the widely voiced observation that an 'ideological' state was relying on one fragile basis: the Muslim religion.[5] Islam proved an inadequate cement when East Bengal became the theatre of a separatist movement which resulted in 1971 in the emergence of Bangladesh. Yet the feeling that Pakistan is a mere artificial construction has outlived this second partition, as though this nation has found it impossible to assume an identity of its own. Pakistanis themselves sometimes have difficulty in finding a sense of their history and heritage – even in defining their borders. Some recall the origins of their land before the Christian era: the civilization that flourished in the Indus Valley, or the invasions of Cyrus.[6] Others assert that claiming a separate state for Muslims in southern Asia harks back to the early Muslim expansions – a purely anachronistic concept.[7] This confusion is explained in part by the numerous external influences and changes of rule that the region has experienced throughout history.

Pakistan is situated at the confluence of three areas: South Asia, the Arab–Persian world, and Central Asia. The Mughal Empire, followed by the British Empire, have tied it into the Indian subcontinent. Its South Asian identity is revealed by the use of Urdu (a language with a vocabulary and alphabet of Persian origin, whose syntax is shaped by Hindi) and regional languages, such as Punjabi and Bengali, since the two principal provinces of the Pakistan which first saw the light of day in 1947 are the result of the partition of regions half of which remain Indian. This South Asian base has been institutionalized by Pakistan's adherence to the South Asia Association for Regional Cooperation (SAARC) since the establishment of that association in 1985.

The country's affinities with the Persian world, and beyond that with the Middle East, are no less strong. They derive first from the physical and human geography of the area, for the plateaus of Baluchistan stretch along both sides of the Iranian border, and the tribes inhabiting them belong to the same culture. Besides, Pakistan looks west naturally, because of its Muslim identity. Homeland of the Muslims of the Indian subcontinent, Pakistan quickly established close relations with other nations that shared the Muslim faith, and organized the second international Islamic conference in 1973. This enterprise also led to a military cooperation which allowed Pakistan to show off one of its particular strengths: its army.

Yet Pakistan also has ties with Central Asia. The Pashtuns of the North-West Frontier Province are ethnically the same as the Pashtuns of Afghanistan; this relationship led to strong irredentist sympathies during the colonial period. Since the Soviet invasion of Afghanistan in 1979, Islamabad has been closely involved politically with Kabul – some elements of the Pakistani military have even justified their support for the Taliban as a necessary reinforcement of 'strategic depth'. Beyond Afghanistan, those in power in Pakistan have sought to build a rapprochement with the nations of Central Asia born of the collapse of the USSR, and – along with the two other founder members, Iran and Turkey – welcomed them in 1992 into the heart of the Organization for Economic Cooperation.

The history of this 'crossroads' state has been as divided as its land. It goes back to the Indus Valley civilization (2500–1500 BC), symbolized by the ruins of Mohenjo-Daro. Yet this ancient site has been taken over by other prestigious civilizations. The region was invaded in turn by the Achaemenids between the sixth and fourth centuries BC, and the armies of Alexander the Great (330–324 BC), before the establishment there of short-lived Buddhist kingdoms. One Graeco-Buddhist civilization – that of Gandhara, between the second century BC and the first century AD – was spread on horseback over the entire area of present-day Pakistan and Afghanistan. If we think in terms of centuries, the most significant event was the arrival of Islam in Sind. Its significance grew with the Mongol invasion in the eleventh century, which gave birth to a new civilization that reached its zenith under the Mughal Empire, of which Lahore was the capital at that time. The Great Mughals extended their conquests as far as Bengal, and established the basis of a common destiny, sealed in due course by British colonization.

The temporal and spatial silhouette of Pakistan contrasted sharply with that of India, whose historical continuity was underpinned by its Hindu origins, and produced a world of its own – if only because of its sheer size. These differences should not, however, be exaggerated. Pakistani space may well be fragmented, but everywhere it is dominated by a single river, the Indus, which is in effect the country's jugular vein. The Indus basin is a truly prosperous region, and a channel of communication which has played a crucial role in the integration of this nation throughout the centuries.[8] Despite the many disruptions Pakistan has suffered compared with India, its cultural history has remained unique to itself: Pakistan identifies strongly with its roots in the Indus Valley civilization, and indeed with its roots in Gandhara, source of magnificent art.[9]

With about 140 million inhabitants, Pakistan has the sixth-largest population in the world. Moreover, since 1998 it has been an established nuclear power, and its continually abrasive relations with India could degenerate into a nuclear war. Since 1999 it has been the only state with such capability under a military government.[10] Under these circumstances, the generally nonchalant attitude to this country is all the more astonishing. The pages that follow attempt to compensate for this by presenting Pakistan from four complementary points of view. Part I of the book is devoted to the problem of national identity – particularly with reference to the tension between Islam on the one hand and specific ethnic groups on the other, but also to the stability of Pakistan's institutions, which are grievously dysfunctional in a country where military regimes have alternated with phases of democratic rule with worrying regularity. Part II is concerned with the country's external relations, which – here more than anywhere else – are indissoluble from internal politics. Successive governments – military ones included – have often consolidated their position by gathering support from external sources, in particular from the United States, which has seen Pakistan as a key element in its containment strategy for the Soviet Union; this was clear during the USSR invasion of Afghanistan. Part III, which covers the economy and the structure of society, bears witness to the opening of the country to external influences, since the physical and human geography of Pakistan form the hinge of two worlds: the western half is at one with the Iranian and Afghan world, as much in terms of physical structure as of the tribal organization of the population; while the eastern half is deeply affected by the monsoons of Asia, and shares with India the logic of the caste system. Part IV is devoted to cultural aspects which illustrate, from a different viewpoint, the tension between unity and diversity to which Pakistan has been subject since its inception. Although the country was created specifically for the Muslims of South Asia, Islam in Pakistan presents a very varied picture, and nourishes conflicts which could be considered sectarian. The policy of extending Islamization introduced by different governments has served only to exacerbate old antagonisms. Efforts to promote Urdu as the national language have hardly reduced the influence of ethnic identities; quite the reverse – even if some centrifugal forces have been regulated. Each in its own way, the succeeding chapters build up an assessment of half a century of nation-building in Pakistan, while at the same time placing the country within the context of its relations with the outside world.

PART I

A COUNTRY IN SEARCH OF AN IDENTITY

1

ISLAMIC IDENTITY AND ETHNIC TENSIONS

Muhammad Ali Jinnah, the founding father of Pakistan, wanted to build a strong nation based on the principle of 'one nation, one culture, one language'.[1] All his successors as head of state took their inspiration in the same way from Islam, and in a less formal way from the Urdu culture. The preamble to the first Constitution of 1956 stipulated that citizens 'should organize their lives both as individuals and collectively in accord with the demands and the principles of Islam as laid down in the Koran and in the Sunna [the traditional law of the Prophet].[2]

Although General Ayub Khan, who seized power in 1958, was in favour of some Islamic reform, he had it written into the 1962 Constitution that the laws of the state should never be in conflict with sharia law. Zulfikar Ali Bhutto laid the foundations of a genuine Islamization policy in the 1973 Constitution, which stated bluntly that Pakistan was an Islamic state. This new Constitution also included a reminder that Urdu was the national language of Pakistan, and that measures would be taken for it to replace English as the only official language within fifteen years (Article 251). General Zia, who succeeded Bhutto in 1977 and remained in power until 1988, set in motion a yet more dogmatic Islamization policy. As a defender of Urdu, he strove to enforce its compulsory teaching from the earliest years, threatening to make it the language of several secondary-standard examinations from the beginning of 1989. The last civilian ruler of the country, Nawaz Sharif, strengthened his allegiance to Islamization policy in 1998 when he introduced a fifteenth constitutional amendment, stipulating that the federal state was obliged to apply sharia law.

If these statesmen have taken their inspiration from Islam, it has been far less as a result of their personal religious faith than of their aim to establish a Muslim nation which might transcend ethnic differences. Now this Islamic ideology sprang directly from the struggle waged by the Muslim League in the British era, when they hoped to carve out a 'homeland' for the Muslims from the old Raj. At that time however the League represented above all the Muslims of the provinces where they were in a minority; once they were in power, their ideology failed to erase the sense of ethnic identity of Muslims in other areas.

A Creation of the Muslim 'Minorities' of the Raj

It was the Muslims from the areas in British India where they were in a minority who first showed separatist tendencies, and in particular those who lived in the United Provinces (present-day Uttar Pradesh).[3] At the turn of the century the Muslim elite of this part of India found their status being reduced as the power of the Hindus rose. Aristocratic inheritors of the Mughal Empire they earned the mistrust of the British when they took part in the Indian Mutiny in 1857.[4] At the end of the nineteenth century, their pride suffered when the colonial power decided in 1899 to place both Urdu and Hindi on an equal footing as the official languages of the province.[5] They also were upset by the first stirrings of political democratization: since 1882, native Indians had been able to elect some municipal councillors and in 1909 provinces under direct British rule had been granted legislative councils based on universal suffrage. All these measures reinforced their fears of being in a Muslim minority, for all the demographic forces were against them (according to the 1881census they represented no more than a fifth of the population compared with a Hindu representation of 75 per cent). These small steps towards democratization had an effect on the Muslim elite throughout British India, but they were especially strongly felt in the United Provinces, where they had more to lose, since there, more than elsewhere, they were better represented among the intelligentsia. In 1886 the Muslims, who constituted 13.4 per cent of the population of the area, nevertheless occupied 45 per cent of the administrative positions.[6]

From the School of Aligarh to the Muslim League

The movement that was to become Pakistan was formed in the United Provinces – or, more precisely, in the town of Aligarh. It was there, in the 1860s, that Sayyid Ahmad Khan started his movement for reform, and for the defence of the Muslim community.

Descended from a prominent family at the Mughal court in Delhi, Ahmad Khan chose a career as a lawyer. Having become a judge, he demonstrated his loyalty to the British at the time of the Mutiny. W W Hunter's report on the Muslims of Bengal convinced him that the Muslims were decadent,[7] and he made up his mind to improve the standard of education within his community – already far higher in the United Provinces than it was in Bengal. In 1863 he founded the Aligarh Scientific Society, based on the doctrine that Islam and Western rationalism were not incompatible. He himself maintained that science and nature were both of divine origin. Then, after a visit to England, he set up the Muhammedan Anglo-Oriental College, modelled on Oxford and Cambridge – all with the assistance of the British who found him a site at Aligarh. The MAO College boasted 66 students in 1875 and 457 in 1900, the majority of whom came from the United Provinces, and awarded diplomas to no fewer than 1,184 Muslims between 1882 and 1892.[8] So the 'school of Aligarh' provided the basis for the mobilization of a community spirit, which in turn developed, in the early years of the twentieth century, a political character quite separate from the Indian National Congress, spearhead of the anticolonial movement.

The Congress Party, established in 1885, was in effect the brainchild of the Hindu intelligentsia. The Muslims within it were very much in a minority: they represented no more than 6.5 per cent on average of the delegates to the annual conferences until 1906. That year – with the aim of unloading some local responsibilities, and under pressure from Congress, which was demanding Indianization of the bureaucracy and more democratic politics – the British announced the creation of legislative councils in the provinces. Immediately the Aligarh intelligentsia formed a new interest group, the Muhammedan Educational Conference, in conjunction with the aristocratic elite of East Bengal,[9] with the intention of obtaining protection for Muslims because of their being in a minority. A delegation led by Muhsin al-Mulk, secretary of the MAO College, therefore appeared before the viceroy, Lord Minto, advocating the setting-up of a separate electorate on behalf of the Muslims. Adept at the art of divide and rule, Minto agreed to this demand: he could see value in the establishment of a counter-balancing Muslim force in the face of a Congress that was looking increasingly militant. The Muslims therefore voted within a separate electoral college from the time of the inauguration of the legislative councils in 1909.

The Muslims of the United Provinces, with eleven members, thus became heavily over represented within the delegation which otherwise included seven Punjabis and just one Bengali. Yet it was in Bengal – at Dhaka, the Dhaka of today – that on 30 December 1906, under the auspices of the *nawab*, the Muhammedan Educational Conference became the Muslim League.

The identity of the Muslim League was strengthened after the First World War. The peace treaties – which deprived the Ottoman sultan of his title of caliph, that is, Commander of the faithful – stirred profound emotions among the Muslims of the Indian subcontinent. Several members of the intelligentsia in Aligarh, notably the brothers Muhammad and Shaukat Ali – seeking to put pressure on the British, and party to the peace negotiations – launched a movement in defence of the caliphate. This movement was supported by Gandhi but provoked the hostility of other members of the Congress who, for their part, were involved in encouraging a nationalistic Hindu feeling at the heart of the party, the Hindu Mahasabha. In this way the 1920s saw the crystalization of mutual opposition between Hindus and Muslims. Outbreaks of violence between the two communities became more frequent, particularly in the north of India.[10]

It was in this context that Muhammad Ali Jinnah endeavoured to rejuvenate the Muslim League, which had gradually fallen into a state of disrepair.

Jinnah himself was from an area where Muslims were in a minority: the Bombay Presidency, which included the province of his birth, Sind, until 1936. He was a member of the liberal intelligentsia. He had studied law in England – like so many other men in politics of the period he was a barrister – and had stretched his heterodoxy to the extent of marrying a Parsee.[11] He started his political career in the Congress Party, though he joined the Muslim League in 1913, and even sat on the All India Congress Committee from 1908 to 1920. His respect for institutions however prompted him to leave the Congress in 1920, when Gandhi organized his first campaign of civil disobedience against the British.

At that time the Muslim League was by no means the Muslims' only mouthpiece.

Some supported the Association of Ulemas of India (Jamiyyat-ul Ulama-i Hind), which was dominated by the ulemas of the traditional Deobandi school. Some remained with the Congress movement, which presented itself as the incarnation of the Indian nation rising above the divides between the religious communities. As for the Ali brothers' Central Committee for the Caliphate, it distanced itself from Congress in the name of a more and more strident Muslim nationalism, without going quite as far as the League.

At the end of the 1920s the Muslims strove to reestablish their unity when the Simon Commission was charged by the British government with studying new constitutional reforms. Since there was not a single Indian on the Commission, this initiative provoked violent reactions. The Congress decided to boycott it, and set out a constitution project of its own, associated particularly with Nehru, wherein the principle of separate electorates was dropped entirely on the grounds that this divided the nation. The Muslims, for their part, organized a conference uniting all the different factions (the All-Party Muslim Conference of December 1928), in the course of which they emphasized the strength of their attachment to the principle of separate electorates. Yet they achieved only partial unity. Jinnah himself organized an individual group which was prepared to trade the separate electorates in exchange for a fixed quota of one-third of the seats at the heart of the National Assembly sitting in New Delhi reserved for Muslims. This difference reflected the opposition between the Muslims of those regions where they were in the minority and those regions where they were in a majority; the latter attached less importance to central power.

The reticence of Muslims in 'majority' areas toward the 'theory of two nations'

Jinnah stuck firmly to his guns from the first conference – called the Round Table – in London in 1930, when the British tried to find a constitutional compromise among the various parties in India. In regions where they were in a majority, the Punjab and Bengal, the Muslims wished above all to reinforce the autonomy of these provinces, which they had gained in 1909 and strengthened in 1919, so that they could take advantage of their demographic superiority. The Constitution (the Government of India Act) eventually published by the British in 1935 gave them some satisfaction, since it did represent one more step towards the establishment of a federal system.

The 1937 elections conducted under the auspices of this constitution produced a paradoxical result. For the first time Congress did not boycott them and won a majority in seven provinces (then an eighth in 1938), where it formed the government. For its part the Muslim League collected no more than 5 percent of the Muslim vote, but its defeat set the scene for future victories.

Jinnah was able to exploit this setback to bolster his own interests. Presenting Congress as just a Hindu party, he hammered home the point that a Congress-dominated government would prove a real menace to the Muslim minority once the British left – an event which was steadily approaching. Hindus and Muslims, he maintained, made up two nations which could not live side by side – since they belonged to two different civilizations. Uniting these two peoples within the heart of a single state – the one with a majority, the other in a minority – could not fail to produce an ever-increasing discontentment.[12] To a Congress which claimed to represent all the communities, and to be installing a secularist political regime, Jinnah set out an ethnic concept of the nation, stressing that the Islam of India constituted a separate culture. On the basis of this 'theory of two nations' he demanded a separate state.

Such a project had been expounded since 1930 by Mohammad Iqbal, the philosopher-poet whose writings remain popular in Pakistan. As the president at that time of the Muslim League, Iqbal had called for the creation of a Muslim state comprising the Punjab, Sind, the North-West Frontier Province (NWFP) and Baluchistan. Three years later, in January 1933, a Muslim student at Cambridge, Chaudri Rehmat Ali, had taken up the idea and suggested that the state should be called 'Pakistan', literally the 'land of the pure', the word being formed acronymically: 'P' for Punjab, 'A' for Afghans of the frontier (in fact the Pashtuns of the NWFP), 'K' for Kashmir, 'S' for Sind, and 'tan' for Baluchistan.[13] These proposals became more or less a dead letter. In March 1940 however the Muslim League, in session in Lahore, announced that it was in favour of the creation of two independent states. The name 'Pakistan' was not mentioned but it was specified that 'those areas where Muslims were in the majority, as in the northwest and the east, should be reorganized to form independent states.'[14]

During the 1940s, therefore, the League campaigned invoking the threatening slogan 'Hindu Congress'. The Punjab provided a perfect example of this strategy. Here the Muslim League was in conflict with two political forces. The first of these, Congress, received the support of Hindus in the towns, mostly merchants, professionals and civil servants. The second, the Unionist Party, was supported by the rural population, both Hindu and Muslim. This party founded in 1922, portraying itself as the defender of rural interests, won the 1923, 1926, 1934 and 1937 elections under the guidance of two peasant leaders, one a Hindu named Chhotu Ram; the other a Muslim Fazl-i-Hussain. The intercommunal solidarity represented here did not leave much room for manoeuvre for the Muslim League.[15]

The League, however, benefited from these very circumstances. Fazl-i-Hussain died in 1936 and was succeeded by Sikander Hayat Khan, head of the Unionist government of the Punjab. Hayat Khan was susceptible to Jinnah's blandishments to the point where he was in September 1937 prepared to sign a pact with him, by which he agreed to pledge the support of all Muslim Unionists to the Muslim League. The recent Congress victory in seven provinces of the Raj had led him to fear that central power could fall only to that party, and that they would use it to the detriment of the Muslims of the Punjab, particularly by reducing Muslim representation in the army.[16] Doubtless Hayat Khan also hoped to gain control of the Muslim League in his own province, if not become its overall leader. Above all, he was offering decisive support to a Muslim League which had failed to win more than just a single seat in the Punjab in 1937. Soon after this, the Unionist Party became very unpopular as a result of the participation of the Punjab, breadbasket of India, in the war effort of 1939–45. All this apart, the disappearance from the scene of Sikander Hayat Khan in 1942 and of Chhotu Ram in 1945 reduced its strength considerably. During the 1946 elections the League exploited these handicaps, campaigning on the theme 'Islam in danger'.

Jinnah and most of his lieutenants were not religious, but they used Islam as a focus for an evocation of nationalism, playing on its emotional power to gain the attention of the Muslims in the streets. In the Punjab this strategy was crowned with success as numerous *pir* weighed in to support the idea of a separate state.[17] Thus Islam became a *lingua franca* which allowed the establishment of a front combining the Muslims in 'minority' situations with those in the Punjab. In the 1946 elections the League won a majority in the province with 75 seats compared with just ten for the Unionists.

The Muslim League also managed to win Sind in the same way. There the party had still had to deal with two rival forces: Congress, which gleamed most of its supporters from the mainly Hindu urban districts, and the Sind United Party (SUP), founded in 1936 at the same time as the province itself, on the model of the Punjab Unionist Party. At this time the SUP was closely allied with the major landowners, the *waderas*, a social category of which Shah Nawaz Bhutto, father of Zulfikar Ali Bhutto (who took part in the foundation of the SUP) is a perfect example. From the end of the 1930s the Muslim League succeeded in implanting itself throughout Sind mobilizing the Muslims around a controversial cult site called Manzilgarh, which the League wished to be regarded as a mosque.[18] It can therefore be said to have manipulated Islam before this occurred in the Punjab.

Meanwhile, its leaders were as concerned about the defence of the Sindi identity as they were about the project for an Islamic state – as witness the political journey of G M Syed, who left the Congress Party in 1938 to become the architect of the League of Sind. He was, however, expelled from it in 1946, when he went on record demanding the right of self-determination for all the provinces.[19] Yet the persistence of Sindi nationalist sentiment at the heart of the Muslim League in that region does suggest that the demand for Pakistan was seen above all as the way to free Sind from British and Hindu tutelage, to gain a regional as much as an Islamic identity.

In Bengal, the League had always enjoyed a greater Muslim majority than in its other provinces. Its roots lay less in its ideology than in its capacity to bring to light a separatist tradition of an earlier time, and above all in its exploitation of socioeconomic frustrations. In 1871 the Hunter Report had underlined the poverty of the Muslims of Bengal. This community, composed mainly of a landless peasantry, of tenant farmers and craftsmen, worked for big landowners and industrialists who were, in the main, Hindus. Principally concentrated in the eastern part of Bengal, it wanted this area to be a separate province. In 1905 the British agreed to split the vast Presidency of Bengal into two, but went back on their decision in 1911 under pressure from the Congress. The Muslims of East Bengal continued to labour under a separation which the League had used to its own advantage since its creation in Dhaka (Dhaka) in 1906.

Since the 1930s, like the Punjab and Sind, the League had been confronted with Congress – well established among the Hindu population – and with a rural party which liked to think itself above religious differences, the party of peasant citizens (the Krishak Proja Party). Founded in 1936 by A K Fazlul Huq, this party mainly comprised small Muslim farmers and Muslim agricultural workers. It won 31 per cent of the votes at the 1937 elections, against 27 per cent for the League, which won 39 of the 82 seats. Huq was therefore asked to lead a coalition government with support from the Muslim League. This however was an unnatural partnership, since the League continued above all to represent the Muslim *zamindar* (large landowners) in the province. This discredited the KPP. It lost its traditional supporters and finally took the swift downward route into the arms of the Muslim League, which played to a greater and greater effect the card of Islamic defence. In 1946 the League won 104 of the 111 available seats. Nevertheless the rising popularity of the 'theory of two nations' could not sideline a powerful regional nationalism. In May 1944 a journalist, Abdul Mansur Ahmad, became leader of the Muslim League in Bengal, and presided over the party's annual conference. He declared that the Muslims of Bengal were different not only from the Hindus but also from Muslims from other provinces, because 'religion and culture are not the same thing. Religion transcends geographic frontiers, but culture behaves differently'.[20] It was such pronouncements which sowed the seed for the future Bangladesh back in the 1940s.

The Muslim League's hold was far weaker in the North West Frontier Province (NWFP), a region cobbled together by the British in 1901 as a means of defending the Raj against possible assaults from Central Asia. Although the Pashtuns represented no more than 37 per cent of the population of the province, they formed the dominant ethnic component, with their clan chiefs, the *khans*, wielding absolute local power. 'Pashtun' is the name given to a member of the Pashtun tribe of Pakistan: the same linguistic community extends into Afghanistan on the far side of the Durand Line. Since the 1920s certain Pashtun leaders of the NWFP have delivered a clear irredentist message which chimes with the 'theory of two nations'. They aimed to regroup in a 'Pashtunistan' incorporating ethnically similar people speaking the Pashto language on both sides of the border.

For the NWFP, this ideology was encapsulated by Abdul Ghaffar Khan, a typical representative of the *khan* of intermediate rank who had been able to reinforce his hold with the support of the British. This was the breeding-ground from which Pashtun nationalism had sprung. Abdul Ghaffar Khan published a monthly periodical in the Pashto language, the *Pashtun*, in 1928; the following year he launched a movement called the Khudai Khidmatgar, better known as the 'Red Shirts' from the colour of its members' uniforms. This movement fought hard to defend the Pashto language against the expansion of Punjabi. Impervious to the Muslim League's Islamic message it allied itself with Congress, whose leader, Gandhi, it greatly admired. Abdul Ghaffar Khan was indeed known as the 'Gandhi of the Frontier', since he also was in favour of non-violent protest. This alliance, consolidated during the campaign of civil disobedience launched by Gandhi in 1930, left little room for the Muslim League whose influence was limited to the urban intelligentsia and the – non-Pashtun – district of Hazara. At the 1946 elections to the provincial assembly the League won only 17 seats against Congress's 30.

To sum up: the notion of Pakistan first developed at the heart of the intelligentsia in provinces with a Hindu majority. The Punjab, Sind and Bengal rallied slowly to the idea, without renouncing their regional identity; the North-West Frontier Province took it up even more slowly. This difference between those in majority and minority situations is explained largely by the quasi-federal political system in British India: the Muslim elite in the United Provinces and the Presidency of Bombay wanted to create a state they could govern – this also went for the Muslims in the military – or a market for their industrial businesses;[21] while those in regions where there was a Muslim majority were already in power and had less to fear from the Hindus.

The Muslim League leaders knew that Pakistan would never see the light of day unless all the Muslim regions could be brought together and separated from India. That is why Jinnah – who played only a minor role until the end of the 1930s[22] – sought to intensify the Hindu–Muslim conflict, depicting Congress as the very incarnation of the Hindu menace. From 1937 this strategy was buttressed by the electoral success of the new dominant party. The 'Muslim Mass Contract Campaign' which Nehru organized in 1938 to combat Jinnah's propaganda was a failure. Through his campaigns for the defence of Islam, whose culmination was the 'Direct Action Day'[23] in August 1946, Jinnah succeeded in exacerbating fears of Hindu domination as British withdrawal – precipitated by the Second World War – drew nearer. Thus he was able to create between 1945 and 1947 what Yunas Samad has termed 'a brief moment of political unity,'[24] among the Muslims. At the same time, the Muslim League strove to present the future Pakistan as a loose structure in which each province would enjoy considerable autonomy. The 'Lahore Resolution' of 23 March 1940, created during a session where Jinnah spoke officially for the first time of two independent states, stipulated that their 'constituent units' would be 'autonomous and sovereign'. This was the ultimate concession to the Muslims of the provinces where they already enjoyed majorities, to get them to rally around the project of a Pakistani state.[25] In 1946, during negotiations with the Cabinet Mission, the League replaced the concept of two Muslim states with a single Pakistan but one in which the regions would continue to enjoy considerable autonomy.[26]

For all practical purposes, the League as a political organization – made scant provision for the provinces with Muslim majorities. Its governing body allowed for only a small number of representatives, as the figures show: before reform of the statutes in 1938, Bengal, despite its 33 million Muslims, had only ten seats more than the United Provinces which was home to no more than 7 million Muslims.[27]

The history of the movement for Pakistan in the colonial period allowed the buildup of strong tensions between on the one hand the Muslim League, dominated by an elite from provinces with large Hindu majorities; and, on the other, whole provinces jealous of their cultural identity and of their autonomy.

Islam and Urdu: Forces for Unity or Domination?

The Pakistan which first saw the light of day in 1947 was an Islamic state. For Jinnah, the promotion of Islam should enable the new country to rise above the regional fault-line and go hand in hand with a strong centralized state. Pakistan was not a federal state in the same way as India, where, after the 1950s, the recognition of regionalism resulted in the states of the union orientating themselves along linguistic lines.

The place of Islam in Pakistan, and its political centralization, are both explained by the ethnic make-up of the country. The Muslims of British India who supported the movement for the creation of Pakistan with the utmost determination had never – unlike the Punjabis or Bengalis – had a local base. The state they wanted to create therefore had to have as its base the Islamic ideology of the Muslim League, and a strong centralized power under their command.

Pakistan: A state of immigrants?

From the start Pakistan was the creation of the Muhajirs – literally the migrants. According to the 1951 census there were 7 million Muhajirs in the country – 700,000 of them in East Pakistan. This meant that in West Pakistan there were 6.3 million Muhajirs – a fifth of the total population of 33.7 million.

Once they crossed the border, most Muhajirs made their new home in a similar cultural and linguistic environment: Muslims from the eastern Punjab chose western Punjab, while those from west Bengal made for east Bengal. For the Muhajirs who had fled the Indian provinces with Hindu majorities, however it was a different matter: 100,000 Urdu-speaking Muslims from Bihar migrated into East Bengal, and a million from Uttar Pradesh and Gujarat went to West Pakistan. Soon the label of 'Muhajir' was no longer restricted to their own community. From the start, the Muhajirs' influence in Pakistani politics and society was out of proportion to their simple demographic weight. Since they came from an intellectual, trading elite, they tended to settle principally in the towns of Sind – above all in Karachi, Jinnah's birthplace, which became the capital of the new state.[28] Karachi, despite its numerous commercial enterprises, boasted a mere 360,000 inhabitants in 1941, only half the size of Lahore. In ten years its population had more than tripled, and had exceeded 1.1 million by 1951. At that time the Muhajirs accounted for a fifth of the population of Sind but 57 per cent of the new capital.[29] Other Muhajirs found their homes in Hyderabad and in Sukkur where, according to the 1951 census, they made up 65 per cent and 55 per cent respectively of the population. Thus urban Pakistan became to a large extent a world of migrants. In fact, in 1951, the immigrants formed nearly half the entire population (46 per cent) living in the twelve most important towns.

At the beginning, the Muhajirs acquired a sort of prestige. After all, they had played a decisive role in the establishment of Pakistan, and had given up everything to go and live there. They dominated the state through the Muslim League and its two leaders: Jinnah, the governor general, and Prime Minister Liaquat Ali Khan, who was himself from Uttar Pradesh. They also dominated the public services (95 out of the 101 Muslims in the Indian Civil Service left India, among whom a third were Punjabis and many were Urdu speakers[30]) and the liberal professions. In Sind the careers of lawyer, teacher and businessman had by tradition been filled by Hindus, who left in droves after 1947. The Muhajirs, taking advantage of their abilities in these spheres, took their place to the great satisfaction – which did not last – of the Sindis, who, once Partition had taken place, feared for the continuity of their businesses and public services, and their local government.[31]

Under Muhajir pressure, Urdu was promoted to the rank of official language, even though English remained the natural language of the elite, and therefore of the state. Despite recognizing that English was essential for the smooth functioning of the administration, the government insisted in pressing on with the promotion of Urdu. The organisation charged with defending Urdu, the Anjuman-i Taraqi-i Urdu, saw its budget double between 1948–49 and 1950–51. Meanwhile, the courts and the regional assemblies were strongly encouraged to use Urdu, and in the early 1950s the Committee for the Official Language – established by the government of the Punjab, a province which was very advanced in this matter – invented thousands of Urdu synonyms for English terms where there had been none before.[32] The Punjabis, in fact, played the dominant ideology game the better to indoctrinate the outposts of the new state, and make them abandon their mother tongue in favour of the official language without too much difficulty.

The beginning of Punjabi hegemony

For a long time the Muslims of the Punjab had had reservations about the idea of Pakistan. Nonetheless, from its very inception, they maintained the power they held in their province before independence, and strove to extend it throughout the country. Although they accounted for only a quarter of the population according to the 1951 census, they were heavily over-represented in the army, where they held 80 per cent of the posts, and the military establishment allowed them to reinforce their power during the 1950s.[33] For them service in the army was a revered tradition. The British enlisted many Punjabis during the First World War.[34] For years they had recognized the soldierly skills of the many Muslim clans of the 'country of five rivers', and had recruited them in large numbers as part of their 'Afghan Policy' of establishing a defence against any future Russian incursion into Central Asia.

At the same time, in the 1950s, Punjabis cropped up everywhere in the administration, where they alone occupied 55 per cent of the posts.[35] During the colonial period the Hindus of the province constituted a larger part of the urban population than the Muslims and, by virtue of this very fact, enjoyed a better standard of education. Since 1921 however, Miam Fazl-i Hussain, newly appointed Education Minister in the Punjabi government, had sought to restore some equilibrium by introducing quotas for Muslims in institutions as important as the administration college and the medical faculty.

However, the Punjabis had the benefit of yet a third resource: the land. The great irrigation projects carried out by the British in the Punjab from 1880 onwards had established it as the granary of all sorts of cereal crop – but particularly wheat – for the Raj, and later, of course, for Pakistan, as indeed for India. This prosperity formed the basis for the 'Green Revolution' of the 1960s, the results of which were particularly spectacular in the districts of Lyallpur, Multan and Montgomery. Agricultural production rose by nearly 9 per cent between 1959–60 and 1964–5, almost a doubling of the national rate of growth.[36] Fifteen years later, in the early 1980s, 80 per cent of tractors and 88 per cent of tubewells were to be found in the Punjab.

From the start, then, Pakistan has been dominated on the one hand by Punjabis – dominant in the military and the administration – and on the other by Muhajirs, occupying all the higher positions in the administration and the executive power. The government of Liaquat Ali Khan was formed mainly from members of his own community.[37] Yet the Punjabis and the Muhajirs shared neither the same political culture nor the same interests. The Muhajirs had always thought of the Muslims of South Asia as an ethnic entity on the basis of their culture, and considered Islam to be nothing more than an identifying symbol.[38] In one way their ideology had been overtaken by a process of nationalist secularization. The Punjabi, for his part, had been called to the colours of the state of Pakistan by the cry 'Islam in danger', and his province, which was still very rural, continued to be guided by a conservative social and political ethos.

There was also a socioeconomic side to the opposition between Muhajirs and Punjabis. The former were predominantly urban, while the majority of the latter were tillers of the land, who owed their relative prosperity to the state's policies of financing irrigation work, controlling agricultural markets and protecting the property rights of owner farmers.[39] While the Muhajirs tended towards a liberal outlook, the Punjabis were happy to be part of an interventionist state.[40]

The latent antagonism between Muhajirs and Punjabis was accentuated by Jinnah's death in 1948. Leadership of the Muslim League passed seamlessly to control Liaquat Ali Khan who succeeded Jinnah as head of both government and party. In 1951 however he was assassinated.[41] The post of Prime Minister went to two Bengalis, Khwaja Nazimuddin (1951–53), Muhammad Ali Bogra (1951–55); then to Chandri Muhammad Ali, a leader of the Muslim League born in the eastern Punjab. The post of governor general was occupied first by a Pashtun, Ghulam Muhammad (1951–55), then by Iskander Mirza (1955–58), a Bengali who followed the Punjabi line. He favoured the development of a new party born of a split in the Muslim League, the Republican Party, composed essentially of Punjabis, some of whom had only recently rallied to the movement for Pakistan. The Republicans dismissed the last Muhajir Prime Minister, I I Chundrigar, in 1958, replacing him by a Punjabi, Malik Firoz Khan Noon.

So the Muhajirs did not succeed in integrating themselves with the Pakistani elite as well as they had been led to expect in the fervour of the country's birth. These difficulties were explained partly by the jealousies which underlay the financial success of some of them, notably in Karachi; while others, in relative poverty, had laid claim to land. The government, however, proved unwilling to accede to demands from immigrant farmers for land which had to be taken from wealthy landowners, who made their opposition clear. The Muhajirs of Uttar Pradesh, Bihar and Hyderabad felt especially hard done by, since Pakistan had reached at no compensation agreement with these Indian provinces.[42] They turned for support to the state, but the government of General Ayub Khan, a Pashtun who had seized power from Mirza by means of a a military coup, had no hesitation in pointing out that, in contrast to immigrants from East Punjab and those from West Bengal, the Muhajirs had not suffered the riots of

1947 to provoke their decision to leave. Ayub Khan preferred to give priority to the farmers who had fled East Punjab. To them he gave title to land; this allowed them to take over property abandoned by Hindus and Sikhs.

The military's accession to power sealed the supremacy of the Punjabis – often in alliance with the Pashtuns. The West Punjabis and those arriving from the eastern part of the province – many of them members of Ayub Khan's entourage –therefore tended to constitute a single homogenous group. The Muhajirs' loss of influence was reinforced in 1960 when the capital was transferred from Karachi to Rawalpindi, a Punjabi garrison town. At the end of the 1960s it was again moved a short distance to the purpose-built capital city of Islamabad.

The competition between the ethnic communities was made more bitter by the contrast between their socioeconomic profiles. This is shown especially clearly in the case of East Bengal, where the income level was less than half of that in Baluchistan and a mere seventh of that in Khairpur, one of the Princely States integrated within West Pakistan in 1955.

Table 1.1 Population and income, 1951 (by province)

Provinces	Population (thousands)	%	Income (millions of rupees)	Per capita income (rupees)
The Punjab	18,815	24.9	246.2	12
Sind	4,606	6.1	97	21.1
NWFP	5,865*	7.8	65	20.1
Bahawalpur	1,822	2.4	50.5	27.7
Khairpur	319	0.4	12	37.6
BSA**	552	0.7	5.8	10.5
Baluchistan	602	0.8	not available	not available
Karachi	1,123	1.5	not available	not available
Total for West Pakistan	33,704	44.6	not available	not available
East Pakistan	41,932	55.4	234.5	5.6
Total	75,636	100		

* These figures include the 'North West Frontier Agencies' territories.
** Baluchistan States Union.

Source: Keith Callard, *Pakistan, a Political Study*, London, Allen & Unwin, 1957, p. 156.

The Bengalis of East Pakistan – victims of the underdevelopment of their province but constituting a majority in the country as a whole – demanded, in their turn, a place in the state's institutions.

Political centralization and separatism: From East Pakistan to Bangladesh

By 1951 the population of East Pakistan had reached 41.9 million, but that of West Pakistan amounted to no more than 33.7 million. On these grounds, the people of

East Pakistan demanded at least equal representation in the democratic institutions which the Constituent Assembly was charged to set up.

The provisional Constitution bestowed upon Pakistan in 1947 gave considerable powers to the provinces.[43] The Constituent Assembly also adopted federalistic perspective from the outset, in large measure because its members came with an automatic majority from East Bengal – 44 compared with 22 from the Punjab, 5 from Sind, 3 from the NWFP and 1 from Baluchistan. The Basic Principles Committee (BPC), charged with the establishment of the fundamental principles of the regime, produced its report on 7 September 1950. It recommended a federal system with two chambers: the first would represent the provinces, while the second would be elected under direct universal suffrage. The elected members from the Punjab immediately demanded an equal arrangement, with each wing of the new state allocated the same number of seats in the parliament. For their part those from East Bengal sought the support of the Sindis, Pashtuns and Baluchis in the Assembly in order to gain a clear majority.

From linguistic conflict to a 'One Unit Scheme'

In Karachi, the central authorities thought about passing an act imposing Urdu as a fundamental part of the Pakistani state immediately after independence. The Bengalis, however, were deeply attached to their own language, and continued to venerate its literature, even when its authors had been Hindus of West Bengal. In 1952, when Urdu was elevated to the status of national language, they organized protest movements, and riots broke out. On 21 February 1952, suppression of a strike in support of the national language resulted in several deaths. The event is commemorated each year by a Remembrance Day.

The Muslim League lost the support of Bengali public opinion. It suffered a fresh setback in March 1954, at the time of new elections to the local assembly. The Pakistani government was forced to make some concessions, and in May 1954 a constitutional amendment recognized Urdu and Bengali as national languages of equal status. In October 1954, however just as the Constituent Assembly was preparing a statement on the BPC the governor general, Ghulam Muhammad – a Pashtun from East Punjab, and hostile to any form of Bengali domination – activated his right to dissolve the Assembly and declare a state of emergency. In March 1955 he took upon himself the power to create a single province of West Pakistan, uniting with the Punjab the regions of Sind, Baluchistan and the NWFP to counterbalance East Bengal: this was the 'One Unit Scheme'. A new Constituent Assembly – elected, like the previous ones, by the legislative councils of the provinces in June 1955 – ratified this reform in September 1955. As for East Bengal, it was renamed East Pakistan. By this manoeuvre Karachi was in a better position to hold the Bengalis down just as they had been kept down ever since Partition in a situation of significant socioeconomic disadvantage.

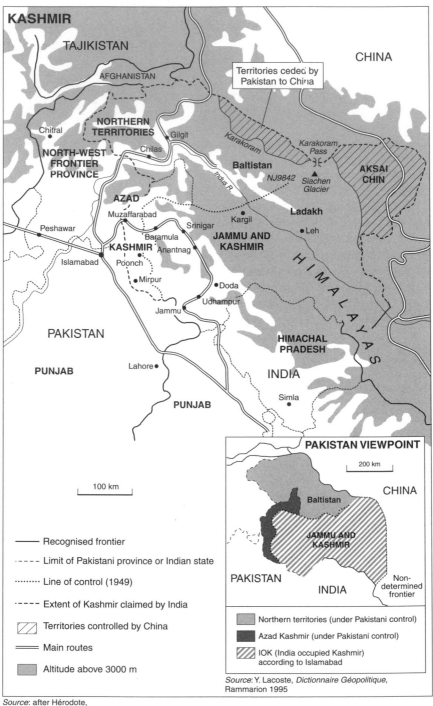

KASHMIR

TAJIKISTAN

AFGHANISTAN

CHINA

Territories ceded by
Pakistan to China

Chitral

NORTHERN
TERRITORIES   Gilgit

NORTH-WEST
FRONTIER   Chilas
PROVINCE

Karakoram   Karakoram
Pass

Baltistan   AKSAI
CHIN

NJ9842   Siachen
Glacier

Indus R.

AZAD

Muzaffarabad   Srinigar   Kargil   Ladakh

Peshawar   Baramula   • Leh

KASHMIR   Anantnag   JAMMU AND
KASHMIR

Islamabad   Poonch

• Mirpur

• Doda

Udhampur

Jammu

PAKISTAN

HIMACHAL
PRADESH

PUNJAB   Lahore •

INDIA

PUNJAB   Simla
•

H
I
M
A
L
A
Y
A
S

100 km

—— Recognised frontier

----- Limit of Pakistani province or Indian state

········· Line of control (1949)

----- Extent of Kashmir claimed by India

▨ Territories controlled by China

=== Main routes

▨ Altitude above 3000 m

PAKISTAN VIEWPOINT

200 km

Baltistan   CHINA

JAMMU AND
KASHMIR

PAKISTAN   Non-
determined
frontier
INDIA

▨ Northern territories (under Pakistani control)

■ Azad Kashmir (under Pakistani control)

▨ IOK (India occupied Kashmir)
according to Islamabad

Source: Y. Lacoste, Dictionnaire Géopolitique,
Rammarion 1995

Source: after Hérodote,
Éditions La Découverte, no. 71, 1993.

The two-economy theory

Of the 95 Muslims in the Indian Civil Service (ICS) who opted for Pakistan, only one or two were from Bengal. From the beginning, therefore, the administration of East Bengal had been in the hands of staff from West Pakistan. After 1949, however Bengalis were allowed an entry quota into the public service: 20 per cent of posts were allotted on merit alone; 40 per cent were allocated to West Pakistan, 23 per cent to the Punjab and Bahawalpur, 15 per cent to a grouping of Sind, NWFP and Baluchistan, and 2 per cent to Karachi. The Bengalis were by no means satisfied with this arrangement.[44] They remained in a tiny minority in the central adminis-tration, where there were only two Bengalis out of 17 high officials in 1964; while on the army list in 1955 only one of 58 generals was from East Bengal.

At the same time the Bengalis were victims of genuine economic exploitation. The hard currency earned from their exports, particularly of jute, was used to finance the industrialization of West Pakistan. Between 1947 and 1962, the eastern region of Pakistan exported goods to the value of 13.08 billion rupees, while the value of exports from the western region reached only 9.9 billion. Similarly, while the value of eastern imports came to no more than 7.9 billion rupees, that from the western wing reached 19.7 billion as it purchased equipment abroad thanks to the favourable bal-ance of trade achieved by East Bengal. The Bengalis complained all the more bitterly since their per capita income at the beginning of the 1960s was about 25 per cent below that of West Pakistan, and the eastern province's growth rate was poorer by a half. Personal incomes had risen by only 17 per cent in East Pakistan between 1959–70, while those in West Pakistan had risen by 42 per cent in the same period.[45] Now the politicization of the Bengali population grew more rapidly as progress in education improved. In 1961, 17.6 per cent of Bengalis were literate, compared with 13.6 per cent in West Pakistan. The economists – of whom there were many among the Bengali intelligentsia – denounced the state of affairs in East Pakistan, suggest-ing that the 'theory of two nations' was being replaced by the 'theory of two economies'.

The Six-Point Programme

Discontent among Bengalis was reflected in the increasing number of opposition parties. Their region had been slow and half-hearted in support of the Muslim League. Fazlul Huq, who had been associated with the League in the 1940s, regained his liberty, and once Independence had been declared he started a new party: the Krishak Sramik Party, the peasants and workers party. A few years later in 1950, H S Suhrawardy created his own party, the Awami League, or the league of the people. These two parties formed an alliance, the United Front, for the 1954 regional elections and won a handsome victory. Huq formed a provincial govern-ment, but two months later he was dismissed on the pretext of separatist intrigues. Similar repression was experienced by the Awami League, and several of its mem-bers hardened their attitude.

At this time, the central government under Ayub Khan blew hot and cold. On the one hand it tried particularly to reduce the development gap between the two halves of the country. The share of development grants for East Pakistan rose from 20 per cent in 1950–55 to 36 per cent in 1965–70 at the expense of West Pakistan, though that province remained the major beneficiary. On the other hand Ayub Khan still showed signs of an authoritarian centralism. The 1962 Constitution maintained the principle of parity between East and West Pakistan, thus negating true federalism. To be sure, the list of headings under which the administration assisted the provinces was lengthened as compared with the 1956 Constitution, but in fact the provinces had no real room for manoeuvre. Executive power was in the hands of governors nominated by Ayub Khan, who were empowered to dismiss regional governments.

Huq demanded greater regional autonomy, which would have left central government with power over foreign affairs and defence only. The Awami League hardened its political attitude further after Suhrawardy's death in 1963. In 1966 their new leader, Mujibur Rahman, announced a six-point programme which amounted to a challenge for power. He demanded in particular that democracy should be restored; that central government should restrict itself to the control of defence and foreign affairs; and that each half of the country should decide its own monetary and fiscal policy (for more details, see Chapter 2 below).

Ayub Khan's response was to arrest Mujibur Rahman on the pretext that he was threatening the integrity of Pakistan. The authorities then ensured that he was discredited by accusing him of accepting arms from India. The 'Agartala trial' – named after the town in India where the alleged transaction took place – opened in 1968 in Dhaka where it provoked a massive mobilization of opponents of the regime. The judges dismissed the charge for lack of proof. The entire episode merely enhanced Mujibur Rahman's popularity.

The mood in Karachi favoured the establishment of a movement for self-government in East Pakistan. Ayub Khan took this on board, but belatedly. In February 1969 he held a conference, called the Round Table, at which he proposed to both sides that the Constitution should be amended in a federalist direction. However, the conference – in which Rahman himself agreed to take part – ended without result. This was largely due to the boycott of this meeting by Zulfikar Ali Bhutto, who had recently set up the Pakistan People's Party (PPP). Ayub Khan then decided to step down in favour of the army's chief of staff, Yahya Khan. His first decision was to abrogate the 1962 Constitution and impose martial law, while at the same time announcing new elections and setting out plans for a federal constitution. Early in 1970 he promulgated a Legal Framework Order, which established a federal regime and gave East Pakistan 169 seats in the 313-strong National Assembly.

The elections took place in December 1970, and resulted in a triumph for the Awami League, which won 160 seats compared with just 81 for the PPP. This ballot sealed the political partition of Pakistan, since the Awami League had contested no seat in the western part of the country while the PPP had contested none in the eastern part. The PPP, though it was led by a Sindi, enjoyed considerable success in the Punjab, with 62 of the 83 seats. This demonstrated the West Pakistanis' willingness to stand up to the Bengalis. Meanwhile Bhutto sought to set himself up as representing the 'real' Pakistan, maintaining that 'Punjab and Sind are the bastions of power in Pakistan. Majority alone does not count in national politics'.[46] His priority was identical to that of the Punjabis: the Bengalis should not be allowed to govern.

Rahman now demanded that the government implement his six-point programme. Yahya Khan seemed to be ready to call a constituent assembly in Dhaka, but Zulfikar Ali Bhutto, the new strong man of West Pakistan, declared that his party would boycott any such move.[47] On 1 March 1971, Yahya Khan announced that the establishment of the proposed constituent assembly would be postponed indefinitely. Rahman's response was to launch a general strike throughout East Pakistan. He demanded the immediate setting up of a confederation in which each half of the country would have its own constitution.

At this, Karachi sent thousands of soldiers and launched a large-scale military operation during the night of 25–26 March 1971. This act of repression had innumerable victims – many struck down in cold blood – and resulted in an exodus towards the Indian border of 10 million Bengalis. New Delhi, in its turn, declared war on Pakistan on 22 November, having taken the time necessary to mobilize its forces, with the declared object of 'liberating Bangladesh'. On 3 December the war spread to West Pakistan, obliging Islamabad to loosen its grip.[48]

The multiple constitutional debates and texts produced between 1947 and the early 1970s revealed the determination of the elites of West Pakistan – whether Muhajirs, Punjabis or Sindis – to keep the Bengalis out of power. The formation of a self-government movement in East Pakistan was, in the main, a direct result of this centralization of the state. In the course of the 1970s, an analogous movement – first for autonomy, later for separation – developed in the North-West Frontier Province and in Baluchistan; while Sind allied itself even more strongly with the Pakistan nation as a result of the electoral successes of the Bhutto family.

The Sindis rise to power

After the secession of East Pakistan, the Punjabis represented nearly 60 per cent of the country's population, and remained overrepresented in the new military, where they filled 70 per cent of the posts.[49] Nevertheless, it was a Sindi, Bhutto, who succeeded Yahya Khan as head of state in 1971. Within the context of martial law, which had been extended, a new constitution – at first sight more favourable to federalism than its predecessors – was promulgated on 12 April 1973. It established a Council of Common Interests where representatives of central government and the four provinces sat as equals. Its responsibility extended over various matters, such as the distribution of river water among the regions. It gave the small provinces equal representation in numbers of seats to that of the Punjab in the Upper Chamber of the parliament. This reform made a limited impact since that chamber had no say in financial affairs. Moreover, the bulk of investment continued to be concentrated in the Punjab.[50] In fact Bhutto – whose PPP, as we have seen, won a great victory in the Punjab at the 1970 elections – conducted a tacit agreement with the Punjabis. An alliance of Sindis and Punjabis seemed set to dominate the country.

The awakening of Sindi nationalism

Bhutto's arrival at the head of the government was accompanied by a political resurgence by the Sindis, who were becoming more and more incensed at the position of the Muhajirs – at least those in Karachi, who still constituted a more prosperous elite than the people of Sindi origin. Their relative success aroused a sense of jealousy which the Sindi nationalist movement exploited.

Before Independence, G M Syed had already set himself up as spokesman for the 'Sindi nation', who, he declared, would reestablish the Indus civilization whose most important vestiges – in particular Mohenjo-Daro[51] – were in their possession. After Partition he denounced the Muhajirs' and Punjabis' grip on Pakistan, criticizing especially the use of Urdu at the expense of Sindi in Karachi. As a result of his militancy he spent a large part of his life under house arrest.

From the beginning of 1972, Bhutto's PPP, which was in charge of the government of Sind, adopted part of the Sindi nationalists' programme. It protested at the meagre representation of Sindis in the army: a mere 2.2 per cent and not one in the senior officer ranks.[52] He also denounced the near monopoly of Punjabis and Muhajirs in the administration – a situation that was partly due to the status of Urdu as the official language. The PPP therefore put through the regional assembly a project to reestablish the Sindi language in the province's schools. This measure provoked demonstrations by the Muhajirs in Karachi, Hyderabad and Larkana, where many riots broke out. Bhutto meanwhile supported the Sindi authorities, whom he had appointed himself – thus pandering to their nationalism. He declared at the National Assembly: 'We have given our lands; we have given our homes, we have given our lives [. . .] to people from all parts, to the Pashtuns, Punjabis, to the Muhajirs living in Sind [. . .] What else can we do to show our loyalty, our love and our respect for Pakistan and for our Muhajir brothers?'[53]

Table 1.2 1973 quotas and community representation in the administration: 1973 and 1983

Provinces	Quotas %	General administration (1973)	Senior public positions (1973)	General administration (1983)	Senior public positions (1983)
The Punjab	50	49.2	53.5	54.9	55.7
NWFP	11.5	10.5	7	13.4	11.6
Urban Sind	7.6	30.2	33.5	17.4	20.2
Rural Sind	11.4	3.2	2.7	5.4	5.1
Baluchistan	3.5	2.5	1.5	3.4	3.1
Northern Areas and FATA	4	2.6	1.3	3.6	3.4
Azad Kashmir	2	1.8	0.5	1.9	0.9
Total	90	100 N=84,749	100 N=6,011	100 N=134,310	100 N=11,816

Source: Charles H Kennedy, *Bureaucracy in Pakistan*, Karachi, Oxford University Press, 1987, p. 194.

In addition, a quota of 11.4 per cent of posts for Sindhi was established in the federal administration to remedy a flagrant imbalance. In 1973 the Muhajirs still occupied 33.5 per cent of the senior public positions, although they represented only 7 per cent of the total population; while the Sindis themselves had only 2.7 per cent.

Bhutto brought about nationalizations which especially penalized the many Muhajirs within the commercial world of Karachi. Furthermore, the vote on the Teaching Promotion and Use of the Sindi Language Bill, introduced in 1972, provoked more demonstrations among the Muhajirs. The law was then amended to establish Urdu as the official language alongside Sindi (speakers of any other language to have had twelve years in which to learn Sindi).

Winning power on the back of Sindi nationalism

Sindi nationalism became even more extreme in 1977 after the dismissal of Bhutto by General Zia, a Punjabi; by his death sentence, meted out by a tribunal composed of a majority of Punjabis;[54] and then by his execution. This made him a Sindi martyr; all the more so as his whole family suffered either exile or life under permanent house arrest.

Once more Zia favoured Punjabis over Sindis. Starting in February 1978, 1,746 civil servants of Sindi origin were sacked from the provincial administration.[55] To cap it all, General Zia tightened controls in the region to subdue the dissidence of any Sindis who denounced his usurpation of power and the 'murder' of Bhutto.

These circumstances explain the success of the Movement for the Restoration of Democracy in Sind. This movement was launched in 1981 by a coalition of the principal opposition parties nationwide, but it found a particular echo in Sind because of the PPP's influence in that province.[56] Over a six-month period, 45,000 soldiers were deployed, and this repression caused around 300 fatal casualties. Pamphlets circulated clandestinely to promote the cause of the 'Sindi Desh' (Sindi Nation). One of the movement's leaders was Mumtaz Bhutto, former governor of Sind and a cousin of Zulfikar Ali. He formulated a programme similar to Mujibur Rahman's Six-Point Programme, demanding a confederation in which Sind would enjoy considerable autonomy.

Benazir Bhutto, returning to Pakistan from years in exile, followed a different strategy.[57] The electoral successes of her father, Zulfikar Ali, especially in the Punjab, had proved that a Sindi could govern Pakistan. This doubtless dissuaded her from promoting too radical a form of Sindi nationalism. Choosing to play her cards within the national political field, she took over the leadership of the PPP shortly before the 1988 elections, which marked the restoration of democracy following the death of Zia, and led the party to victory. Although it won 52 seats out of 113 in the Punjab, the PPP had the air of a Sindi party. It won all the seats in rural areas of Sind and gained a two-thirds majority in the provincial assembly, whereas it won only 94 of the 240 seats at the regional elections to the Punjabi assembly, which were organized to coincide with the general election. The Sindi nationalist parties, on the other hand, did not win a single seat. This reversal – particularly unexpected in the case of the Sind National Front, founded by Mumtaz Bhutto in 1984 – confirmed the recognition of the Sindis within the PPP. The party could be said to have become a pivotal force for their national integration. The fact that Benazir became Prime Minister made the Sindis even more eager to renew their allegiance to the Pakistani state. However, this toing and froing between enthusiasm and defiance in attitudes to a state of according to the ethnic origin of the leader, reveals the weakness of its institutions. The state had not managed to free itself from regional idiosyncrasies. Instead of standing above the throng, it became the stake in a competition between the elites of the different communities. Nevertheless, this political pattern facilitated a national integration of the groups which could hope to gain power – in the event, the Sindis.

Just at the very moment when the Sindis were beginning to lurch away from their old separatist philosophy and support Z A Bhutto's rise to power, two other minorities, the Baluchis and the Pashtuns, felt a rush of nationalist fervour, mainly because of Bhutto's policies.

The Baluchi Self-Determination Movement

Although it is home to a mere 5 per cent of the population of Pakistan according to the 1998 census, Baluchistan covers 42 per cent of the country. It occupies a strategic region bordering both Iran and Afghanistan. The fact is that the Baluchi population extends over several countries – Pakistan, Iran and Afghanistan – and this explains the irredentist nature of their own nationalism within Pakistan.

This nationalism harks back to the realm of Kalat, a principality of the Afghan state. Its eighteenth-century borders coincided roughly with the area over which the ethnic Baluchi population is spread. During the period of British colonization, in 1871, the Goldsmid Line was drawn in the west, ceding a quarter of the zone occupied by Baluchis to Iran. This was followed by the Durand Line, which allocated a further – smaller – area to Afghanistan. In addition, many Baluchi's of colonial India were subjects of various Princely States, of which one was Kalat; while others lived under direct British rule. At the time of Partition the ruler of Kalat opted for independence, but the Pakistani army overcame his resistance in March 1948. The heir to the throne of Kalat then tried to bring together the Baluchi tribal leaders (the *sardar*) in an autonomous state in accordance with the Lahore Resolution of 1940. The Pakistani government, however, succeeded in winning over these chiefs, and two provinces were established – Baluchistan, combining the zones previously under British rule; and the Baluchistan States Union, grouping the former Princely States. The two came together in 1955 under the terms of the 'One Unit Scheme'. However, Baluchistan did not get its first assembly under universal suffrage until 1972.

In the 1950s the Prince of Kalat, Abdul Karim, launched a People's Party which spoke for a Baluchi nationalism based less on language than on an ethnic identity fostered by imagined traditions. In fact Baluchis belong to two linguistic groups; one group speaks Baluchi and the other Brahui, which was accepted as a Baluchi language since Brahui was spoken by the Kalat dynasty itself. The People's Party protested at the underrepresentation of Baluchis in the state apparatus, but interclan rivalries hindered its development.

Baluchi nationalism began to crystallize under the influence of the centralizing zeal of Z A Bhutto. In 1972 a coalition formed by the National Awami Party – whose base was in the NWFP, but which had combined with the People's Party – and the Jamiyyat-ul Ulama-i Islam (JUI), Militant Muslims supported by the *sardar* of Baluchistan – won the elections in both regions. The new governments announced that they were happy to 'indigenize' the administrations of their province, duly replacing civil servants from outside by 'sons of the soil'. However Islamabad disapproved of this 'spoil system' which deprived the national elite – and above all the Punjabis – of attractive opportunities. Redistribution of investments introduced a further point of discord, because Baluchistan and the NWFP, accusing Islamabad of not being sufficiently concerned with development in their territory, wanted control of their own industrialization.[58]

In February 1973 Bhutto, citing separatist intrigues, dismissed the Baluchistan government – at that time under the control of Attaullah Khan Mengal – and the NWFP leader resigned in sympathy. Arms opportunely discovered in the possession of the Iraqi military attaché were said to have been destined for delivery to A K Mengal. Nevertheless, the Baluchi assembly showed strong support for national integration, voting unanimously in favour of Urdu as the province's official language. Such expressions of goodwill evidently did nothing to prevent repression of the Baluchi movement, which was what concerned the capital. However, imprisoning the heads of this movement meant that their subordinates – who, in general were more radical – took their places and organized a guerrilla campaign whose discourse was nationalistic with Marxist overtones. This attracted a number of students and the BPLF (Baluchi People's Liberation Front), together with the BSO (Baluchi Students' Organization), launched an insurrection which led to the mobilization of more than 10,000 fighters over a period of four years.

To put an end to all this, the Pakistani army had to deploy 80,000 men aided by the Shah of Iran, who had no wish to see the troubles boil over into his territory of West Baluchistan.[59] The casualty total for this conflict was heavy: 5,300 victims among the Baluchis and 3,300 in the Pakistani army.[60] The suppression of this insurrection marked a turning point. Before it, the Baluchis simply wanted 'regional autonomy within a confederal Pakistani constitutional framework' but after the hostilities the separatist feelings were 'much intensified'.[61] Once again, state centralism was a key factor in the emergence of self-determination movements. Z A Bhutto has much to answer for in this respect.[62]

General Zia managed to appease one section of the Baluchis by releasing several thousand prisoners and granting an amnesty to those who had sought refuge in Afghanistan or Iran. Some chose to go into exile. One was Ataullah Khan Mengal. He went to London to found the Sind Baluch Pashtun Front with the help of Mumtaz Bhutto and Khair Buksh Marri, who settled in Kabul. Both remained partisans, determined to continue an armed struggle for a confederate regime.

Those who remained in Pakistan adopted a more moderate stance. Former governor Ghaus Bux Bizenjo set up the Pakistan National Party with the aim of exerting pressure on Islamabad to make the authorities respect the federal arrangements inscribed in the 1973 Constitution. An appreciable number of the *sardar* preferred merely to collaborate with central government; which was perfectly happy to accept them.

Baluchi nationalism could hardly look for support from an intelligentsia or a middle class. Neither existed to any great extent in a region where literacy levels were the lowest in the country at 8.5 per cent.[63] Moreover, the province began to lose its relative cultural homogeneity, since so many Baluchis were migrating to other provinces. Of 4 million Baluchis counted in Pakistan in 1981, a third lived in Sind, in the NWFP or in the Punjab, while Baluchistan also received an appreciable number of immigrants. Thus 57 per cent of the inhabitants spoke either Baluchi or Brahui, while 28 per cent spoke Pashto and 8 per cent Sindi.

Among the Pashto speakers were the Pashtuns in the north of the province, a zone which had benefited from a particular effort at development by the British, and a large number of Afghan refugees driven by war to flee their own country. In 1997, out of 1,350,000 Afghan refugees in Pakistan, 352,700 were in Baluchistan.[64] These refugees founded a political party, the Pakhtunkhwa Milli Awami Party, which claimed Pakistani citizenship and the right to vote on their behalf – both of which the Baluchis refused them. Besides, the Baluchi parties had been opposed to orga-nizing a further census for a long time, fearing that it would merely bring out the demographic expansion of Pashtuns in general. In the end this 'enemy within' con-sumed a sizeable portion of their fighting energy, and they no longer blamed Islamabad for all their problems.

The 1988 elections, and those that followed, saw the return to strength of old political factions. In November 1988 the *sardar* Akhtar Mengal had formed the Baluchistan National Movement, which became the majority partner in a coalition government – the Baluchistan National Alliance – whose architect was another Baluchi notable, Nawal Akbar Bugti. Meanwhile on the eve of the 1990 elections, internal strife led to schism. As a result, Bugti created the Jamhoori Watan Party (JWP), which formed an alliance with the Pakistan Muslim League, Nawaz Sharif's party which proceeded to take power in Quetta. This marked a change of strategy by Baluchi political figures, who – rather than associate themselves with other region-alists, as in the days before 1970 – preferred to seek allies among the parties in power in Islamabad. Thus Zulfiqar Ali Khan Magsi led a coalition government in 1996 with the benediction of former Prime Minister Benazir Bhutto: His cabinet included members from the PPP, the Pakistan Muslim League and the Jamiyyat-ul Ulama-i Islami.

In December 1996, the Mengal and Bizenjo factions combined into a new polit-ical party, the Baluchistan National Party (BNP). Yet no regional party managed to win a majority at the 1997 elections. The BNP – with just 10 seats out of the 43 in the Baluchistan assembly – gained the most, but was still very much in a minority. Accordingly, Akhtar Mengal formed a government with the support of four other parties, one of which was the PPP. At the same time, in the National Assembly the BNP was supporting Nawaz Sharif, the Prime Minister from the Pakistan Muslim League.[65] In 1998 however, Mengal resigned, on the pretext that Baluchi honour had been besmirched because the authorities in Quetta had not been kept informed about the nuclear tests carried out in Baluchistan by the Islamabad government. In fact, the main bone of contention between Mengal and Sharif concerned the improper allocation by central governement of funds derived from the exploitation of natural gas in Baluchistan, and the distribution between the provinces of federal subsidies for which Islamabad was responsible. In January 1998 Mengal had questioned the National Finance Commission's annual budget plans. Once again, conflicts of interest fed arguments over identity[66] but at the same time they encouraged a certain degree of pragmatism. This tendency, together with the divisions between the Baluchi leaders, explains their strategy of alliance with the national parties, and the erosion of their natural militancy. The Pashtun movement followed a similar course.

The Pashtuns: From Pashtunistan to Pakhtunkhwa

At the moment of independence, the principal Pashtun leaders were against the integration of their province into Pakistan. Gaffar Khan's 'Red Shirt' movement even called for the formation of a Pashtunistan, and boycotted the referendum which led to the NWFP becoming part of Pakistan.[67] Khan was arrested, and Jinnah dismissed the government.

In the end, Ghaffar Khan went into exile in Afghanistan, but his son, Wali Khan, joined in setting up the National Awami Party (NAP), which agreed to play to the rules of the Pakistani political game. The Pashtun intelligentsia, unlike the elites from Bengal and from Sind, had been educated in Aligarh or in the Punjab. The Pashtuns felt even more at ease than the Baluchis about taking part in the building of the new Pakistan, because of their presence in the army.[68] At the end of the 1960s there were 19 Pashtuns among the 48 highest-ranking officers compared with 16 Punjabis; and three of them – Ayub Khan was one – became chief of army staff. Factors to do with national identity were the main explanations for the mediocre pulling power of Wali Khan's party, which never gained more than 20 per cent of the vote, and only 18 per cent in 1970.[69] It resigned itself to moderating its message for that very reason. In 1969, for example, it accepted the borderline between the NWFP and Baluchistan, part of which Wali Khan had hitherto claimed. The NAP government of 1972 even promoted Urdu to the rank of official language in the province. The government of Baluchistan had passed the same measure, but here it was mainly a reflection of Wali Khan's wish to be seen as a national figure. Furthermore he wanted to compete with Z A Bhutto in presenting himself as a socialist leader on the national political scene.

Pashtun nationalism was, nevertheless supported by propaganda emanating from Kabul. In 1947 the King of Afghanistan had asked the British to allow the NWFP to choose between becoming part of Afghanistan or setting up an independent Pashtunistan. The Afghan authorities pursued this line again after Daud's seizure of power in 1973.[70] The new strong man in Kabul declared that he would work for the establishment of an independent Pashtunistan, on the model of the new Bangladesh, in cooperation with the secretary general of the NAP now in exile in Kabul, Ajmal Khattak. He was evidently altogether more radical than Wali Khan, who had approved of the federal dimension of the constitution set out by Bhutto in 1971. The NAP continued to play its politics the Pakistani way.

This outside support would certainly have been insufficient to relaunch Pashtun nationalism, had it not been revived at that very moment by the centralizing politics of Islamabad. As we have seen, Bhutto dismissed the Baluchi government in 1973, precipitating in turn the resignation of the North West Frontier Province government. The rivalry between Bhutto and Wali Khan intensified, and in 1975 Bhutto used the pretext of the murder of a PPP minister, H M Sherpao, in the NWFP to have Wali Khan arrested and to dissolve the NAP on 9 February. The trial of Wali Khan dragged on until Bhutto's downfall in 1977, at which point the accusations were dropped. The case had never aroused any prolonged violence, and Pashtun nationalism now started to enjoy a modest revival. It is undeniable that the economic position in the NWFP was distinctly improved by the end of the 1970s. Without doubt, after the Punjab, the NWFP was the province that gained most from the rural exodus towards Karachi and the migration of workers to the Gulf States, where between 1976 and 1981, 35 per cent of expatriate workers – some 300,000 – were from Pakistan.

Paradoxically the war in Afghanistan went some way towards reducing Pashtun irredentism, for several reasons. Four-fifths of the some 3 million Afghans, 80 per cent of whom were Pashtuns, who fled to Pakistan between 1980 and 1985, settled in the NWFP, where the population increased by 20 per cent to 16 million, thereby exceeding Afghanistan's population of 14 million. Some Pakistani Pashtun leaders dared to assert that a Pashtunistan had already come into existence *de facto*.[71] The Pashtuns also toned down their most radical nationalistic claims because they saw their priority as aiding General Zia's war effort against the Soviets. In support of the war, Zia promoted a certain number of Pashtuns in the administration and the forces.[72] The influx of so many Afghan refugees was not in itself something that encouraged Pashtun irredentism, given that they provided competition for the local tradesmen and workers, particularly in Peshawar.[73] Wali Khan's party, known thenceforth as the Awami National Party (ANP), finally protested – especially before the 1988 elections – against the costs of the war effort and supporting the swarms of immigrants into the NWFP.[74] The economic argument was indeed pressing, forcing the government in Islamabad to repatriate refugees. According to official sources, 2 million were repatriated in 2000, but that still left 870,000 of them in the NWFP and 457,000 in Baluchistan.[75] Finally, following the Talibanization of Afghanistan, Islam was added to Pashtun tribalism on the identity market of the North West Frontier Province. The new Kabul regime, which relied on an ethnic Pashtun base, therefore found ready recruits among the Pashtuns of Pakistan, as Chapter 6 below demonstrates. Henceforth Islamic militancy tends to prevail over the Pashtun nationalist programme.

All these factors, particularly the relative prosperity of the Pashtuns and their increasing integration into the country's military and administrative elites, explain the weakening of Wali Khan's nationalist programme. It was he, for example, who supported first Zia in 1983, during the Movement for the Restoration of Democracy. As a result, the Pashtun leaders exiled in Kabul returned in 1986. The ANP persisted with this political approach during the 1998 elections, since these elections showed that from now on the mainstream national parties took the front of the political stage in the NWFP. While the ANP and JUI both won 3 seats each, the PPP

gained 7, and Nawaz Sharif's Islami Jamhoori Ittehad (IJI) gained 8. The nationalists therefore decided to collaborate with them. In spring 1989 Wali Khan entered
into an alliance with Nawaz Sharif against their common enemy, the Bhutto family.
This coalition, which sealed the rapprochement between Pashtuns and Punjabis,
provided Sharif with a good way of emasculating Pashtun nationalism; it was to last
nearly ten years.

In 1997 the ANP won 28 of the 83 seats in the NWFP assembly. Its alliance with
Nawaz Sharif's party, the Pakistan Muslim League (N), which had won 31 seats, was
therefore renewed. It formed a new government under a leader of the PML(N). It
broke with Islamabad a year later when Nawaz Sharif rejected a NWFP assembly
resolution, passed on 14 November 1997, to rename the province Pakhtunkhwa.
Sharif has followed this line because the unpopularity of such a change of name
among the non-Pashtuns of the region of Hazara, electoral bastion of the PML.[76]
However, the issue about which the ANP and the PML(N) parted ways reflected the
growing moderation of the Pashtun nationalists. By demonstrating the renaming of
the NWFP, they admitted that they had given up the idea of forming a common
province with the Pashtuns of Baluchistan – that is to say, Pashtunistan. The ANP
accepted the frontier inherited from the British.

In fact one of the principal bones of contention was the Kalabagh barrage project, destined for the NWFP frontier. It had been in the planning stage for some
years. The ANP was against it, arguing that the irrigation waters would benefit
only the Punjab and its agriculture, while there was a risk that the retained water
would cause floods upstream. Once again, economic interests were hidden in the
folds of ideological discussion.[77]

The Growth of a Muhajir Sense of Identity

Of all the communities preoccupied with nationalist feeling, the only one still
inclined towards a violent activism was that of the Muhajirs, yet this movement did
not appear in an obviously separatist light. The Muhajirs became more radical in the
1970s as they reacted to the politicies of Bhutto and the PPP in the province of Sind.
At that time they remained faithful to the Islamic parties and particularly to the
Jamaat-i Islami (JI).[78] Thereafter, looking at themselves as 'more or less imaginary'
victims of discrimination by the state, they tended to define themselves more and
more as a community apart rather than as the spearhead of Islamic ideology. The
Gujaratis and the Urdu speakers minimized their differences and began to 'think of
themselves as Muhajirs'.[79] Once more, a group refashioned its political identity
according to its socioeconomic interests.

Distancing themselves from the JI, the Muhajirs formed their own organization at
the end of the 1970s. Students played a pioneering role in this as they reacted to the
new policy of quotas within the educational system. Some of them – such as Altaf
Hussain, who had just left the Students' Union section of the JI because, in his view
it had been taken over by Punjabis – founded the All-Pakistan Muhajir Student
Organisation (APMSO) in Karachi in 1978. The Muhajirs also demonstrated when
the quotas put in place by Zia were raised again, reserving 10 per cent of civil

service posts for retired soldiers – the army after all being solidly Punjabi. The Muhajirs resented this measure even more than other changes, all to their disadvantage, in the 1980s. The 'Green Revolution' from which Punjabis had benefited since the 1960s had reinforced their hegemony and allowed them to invest in industry even in Karachi.[80] Migrants who wanted to capitalize on the city's dynamism flooded in from all the provinces of Pakistan, not to mention refugees from the Afghan war. In 1981, according to the census figures, the city's population was 61 per cent Muhajir, 16 per cent Punjabi, 11 per cent Pashtun, 7 per cent indigenous Sindi and 5 per cent Baluchi. Finally, the Pashtuns increasing influence in the upper echelons of the army after the Soviet invasion of Afghanistan, further disadvantaged the Muhajirs – just at the very moment when they were losing government posts as a result of the quotas introduced in 1973. Ten years later, the cities of Sind were represented in only a fifth of the higher-ranked civil service posts, compared with a third in 1973. From all this, militant Muhajirs derived grounds for arguing that there was a deliberate pauperization of their community. This point, albeit overstated, was widely taken by groups which – although they still constituted an elite – could not bear to see their privileged positions challenged – very much like the Sikhs in India at about the same time.

In 1984, the leaders of the APMSO – again including Altaf Hussain – formed a political party, the Muhajir Qaumi Mahaz (MQM).[81] This Muhajir National Movement recruited principally among students whose hopes of climbing the social ladder had been dashed by the arrival of so many 'foreigners', notably Pashtuns. The Pashtuns became the first victims of the violence that broke out in the mid-1980s, generally on trivial grounds which the MQM did its best to exacerbate.[82] The MQM had several demands. Its main claims were first, that the Muhajirs should be represented in greater numbers in the University and in the administration, and second, that only those who had lived in Sind at least twenty years should be entitled to vote and buy property within the province. Deep down, they wanted to establish a 'Karachisuba' – a Muhajir province based exclusively on the main city in the land.[83]

This programme, announced in 1987, allowed the MQM to win the municipal elections in both Karachi and the second city of Sind, Hyderabad, during that same year. The party did very well again at the 1998 general elections, – they won 13 seats and the PPP, although it came out on top, failed to gain an absolute majority. As a result, Benazir Bhutto drew up an agreement with the MQM which added enough seats to supply such a majority. In turn the MQM, having thus made an alliance with a national political force, was able to creep up on the other regional parties. The agreement represented a virtual charter for the Muhajir party, but the new Prime Minister was reluctant to keep her promise. Notably she refused entry to the Biharis of Bangladesh, who had wanted for a long time to settle in urban Sind, a move which would have allowed them to reinforce their ranks of the Muhajirs. The Muhajirs' reply was to organize large demonstrations. These degenerated into riots, and the MQM then dissociated itself from the PPP. The violence increased President Ghulam Ishaq Khan's distrust for Benazir Bhutto, who was dismissed from her position for her inability to restore order in Karachi.

With the 1990 elections approaching, the MQM formed a new alliance, this time with the Islam-i Jamhoori Ittehad of Nawaz Sharif, the chief minister of the Punjab, who was able to win a majority in Parliament. Once in power, however, this party proved to be no better disposed towards the Muhajirs than the PPP. In June 1992 the army was called in to 'cleanse' Karachi of its 'antisocial' elements. Operation 'Clean-up', which was meant to last six months, dragged on for two years. Some MQM leaders went underground and some fled the country. Altaf Hussain was already established in London; he is still there in 2002, and controls the movement from a distance.[84] The military operation only reinforced the Muhajir population's allegiance to the MQM. The military themselves left the field in November 1994.

The MQM boycotted the 1993 general election, which saw the return to power of Benazir Bhutto, but participated in the provincial ones in Sind, which were won by the PPP with just 56 seats out of 100 against 27 for the MQM(A); the (A) signified the faction controlled by Altaf Hussain. The MQM had suffered a schism not long before; the other faction, the 'authentic' MQM, was called the MQM Haqiqi. This group seemed somehow seduced by advances made by the army once Operation Clean-up was over. It united a number of dissidents who had been turned away from Altaf Hussain because of his autocratic attitude, and was made up of militants every bit as violent as the MQM(A) – hence the multiple vendettas and bloody settlements of scores – but it had closer links to the local mafia. The death toll due to rioting in Karachi rose to 1,500 in 1995 compared with 600 in 1994. In October and December 1995 the MQM(A) organized two general strikes in response to the murder of two of Altaf's henchmen; paralysing the city.

This violence was part of what came to be called the 'Kalashnikov Culture'. During the Soviet invasion of Afghanistan, the resistance was supplied with arms, particularly Chinese and Egyptian copies of the Kalashnikov and these often came by way of Karachi. The Muhajir movements misappropriated some of this trade, at the same time cementing a relationship between their clients and the gangs involved in other forms of contraband, such as drugs. The armed groups offered them henchmen in exchange for police protection, which they were able to provide periodically when the MQM was in power. The end result was a virtual criminalization of the Muhajir movement.

Far from being irrational, the MQM violence had the aim of 'liberating' some districts of Karachi. Once the army withdrew in 1994, the party worked on reestablishing its authority in the districts lost during Operation Clean-up, particularly those which had passed to the control of the Haqiqi faction. The MQM(A) seemed at times to be involved less in an urban guerrilla operation than in a conquest of territory. It declared that it was prepared to envisage a new partition similar to the one that had given birth to Bangladesh if Islamabad did not satisfy its ambitions.[85] Yet it seemed above all to be looking for an opportunity to go in for illegal trafficking, and levy a sort of revolutionary tax.[86]

Despite its declared separatist aim, the MQM continued to play the electoral game. It even changed its name – but not its acronym – to Mutaheda Qaumi Mahaz (National United Movement) to avoid identification with a particular community and thus be in a position to solicit votes throughout the whole country – especially within the middle class. After the February 1997 elections, though the PPP remained the largest single party, with 36 seats out of 100 in the Sind assembly, it could not head the majority coalition. However, the PML(N) – the Pakistan Muslim League (Nawaz) of Nawaz Sharif – and the Haq Parast group – the political window of the MQM – won 15 and 28 seats respectively. This success prompted Nawaz Sharif and Altaf Hussain to get together and form a more or less majority coalition, with 72 seats of their own and support from small parties and independent candidates. The agreement between the MQM and the PML(N) meant that the former could hold three central government portfolios, the governorship of Sind as well as the presidency of the province's assembly, and a number of ministries similar to that held by PML(N) in the provincial administration. In addition, the 'Biharis' of Bangladesh would be repatriated, while the quota of Muhajirs in the civil service would be raised to 11.5 per cent and the MQM(Haqiqi) disarmed.

Since Nawaz Sharif failed to keep these three promises – least of all the one concerning the MQM(Haqiqi) – the MQM(A) left the Sind government. In autumn 1998, the Prime Minister asked it to hand over the murderer of Hakim Saeed, a former governor who had remained very popular. When the party refused, Sharif declared a state of emergency in the province, whereupon the MQM(A) withdrew its support.

General Musharraf's seizure of power in October 1999 could have been an embarrassment to the Muhajirs. On the one hand, the army had always considered the MQM(A) a terrorist organization, colluding with the Indian secret services in destabilizing the state. This had, after all, been one of the reasons for the extreme violence of Operation Clean-up. On the other hand, for the first time since Liaquat Ali Khan, the strong man of the country was himself a Muhajir, born in Delhi and a member of a family from Uttar Pradesh. But, in fact, the Muhajirs did not consider Liaquat Ali Khan to be one of them. The MQM's militancy is declining for another reason today: the population of Karachi is tired of violence, and is starting to resent its effect on the local economy: although Karachi generates 70 per cent of the state's revenue, it no longer attracts so much foreign investment. This economic situation threatens to influence the development of a movement whose roots were themselves socioeconomic.

No National Integration Yet?

The national integration of Pakistan looked more likely in 2000 than it did in 1970, but it is still far from being achieved, particularly because of the Muhajir problem and the minor provinces' persistent resentment against domination by the Punjab. At the end of the 1990s, under the last civilian government, Prime Minister Nawaz Sharif, President Tarar (elected on 31 December 1997), and army chief Jahangir Karamat were all Punjabis.[87] This province has thereby benefited from ambitious infrastructure schemes, such as the Islamabad – Lahore motorway, construction of which gave Nawaz Sharif the chance to squirrel away considerable sums by way of commission.[88]

The political domination of the Punjabis during the process of democratization was more or less inevitable, since their province has a majority of assembly seats –

115 out of 207 – compared with 46 for Sind, 26 for the NWFP and 11 for Baluchistan. The Punjabis had grave reservations about the organization of the last census, fearing that its results would show a population growth proportionately stronger in the other regions, and that this would result in a fall in its share of the federal budget. Furthermore, the census – which was organized in 1998 seven years late under army supervision – revealed only a modest drop in the comparative weight of the Punjab in favour of Sind where urban growth appeared to have been underestimated. The MQM in particular has denounced the underestimate of the population of Karachi, which must cast doubts on the accuracy of the census.[89]

Such a reaction demonstrates the importance which Pakistanis attach to reports of comparative community strength related to the policy on quotas. The mobilization of the small provinces has taken a new form since October 1998, with the creation of the Movement for the Oppressed Nationalities of Pakistan (PONM). Launched on the initiative of the ANP, this alliance combined the nationalist movements of the NWFP, Sind, Baluchistan, and that part of the Punjab where Seraiki is spoken. The inhabitants of this part of the Punjab consider that they are victimized by other Punjabis.[90]

The leaders of the PONM demanded the creation of a Seraiki province, which, if it split from the Punjab, would mitigate the resentment provoked by its current domination. Their other demands concerned the setting up of a truly federal system, and proportional representation of the provinces in the army and the administration.[91] It was said that General Musharraf, himself of Muhajir origin, had provoked disquiet among Punjabis following an interview he had given to Ajmal Khattak, the Pashtun leader of the PONM. He had also shown his concern for regional minorities by naming ministers within the government from among the Baluchis, the Pashtuns and the Sindis. Such gestures indicated the start of a rebalancing process but required confirmation and amplification so that Punjabi domination might be called into question.

The limits of national integration explain the campaigns against 'others', regularly brought into play by Pakistani leaders in order to weld the unity of the country once more. These campaigns are launched against 'bad Muslims' such as the Ahmadi (see Chapter 10 below) or against the Hindus or the Christians. The Hindus were the victims of planned persecutions, a direct echo of the excesses suffered by the Muslims

Table 1.3 Linguistic groups (%, by province, 1984)

	Punjabi	Pashto	Sindi	Seraiki	Urdu	Baluchi	Other languages
Punjab	78.7	0.8	0.1	14.9	4.3	0.6	0.6
Sind	7.7	3.1	52.4	2.3	22.6	4.5	7.4
NWFP	1.1	68.3	0.1	4	0.8	0.1	25.6
Baluchistan	2.2	25.1	8.3	3.1	1.4	36.3	23.6
Pakistan	48.2	13.1	11.8	9.8	7.6	3	6.5

Source: Government of Pakistan, *Statistical Pocket Book of Pakistan*, 1984, Islamabad, Federal Bureau of Statistics, 1984.

Table 1.4 Population (%, by province, 1981 and 1998 census)

	1981	1998
Punjab	56.7	56
Sind	22.6	23
NWFP	13.1	13.4
Baluchistan	5.1	5
FATA	2.6	2.3

Source: S. Ahmed, 'Centralization, Authoritarianism and the Mismanagement of Ethnic Relations in Pakistan', in M.E. Brown and S. Ganguly (eds), *Government Politics and Ethnic Relations in Asia and the Pacific*, Cambridge Mass., MIT Press, 1997; *Dawn*, 9 July 1998.

in India at the same moment: uprisings in East Bengal in the 1950s, or those that followed the destruction of the mosque at Ayodhya in 1992. This series of violent eruptions has led to a continuing flow of immigration and in 2000 there were fewer than 3 million Hindus in Pakistan, almost all concentrated in Sind.[92] The Christians, often converted Untouchables, have been, and remain, targets and are just as vulnerable.[93] Over and above these scapegoats, those directing the affairs of Pakistan carry on the confrontation with India, systematically invoking the old 'theory of two nations', and all in aid of internal politics. The orchestration of this antagonism is all of a piece with the perpetuation of the conflict over Kashmir. Pakistan, therefore, might well be a case of nationalism without a nation.[94]

2

EAST BENGAL

Between Islam and a Regional Identity

In 1947, the Muslim League – led by M.A. Jinnah, who was struggling to create a single nation incorporating all the Muslims of the subcontinent – gained impressive support in the province of Bengal. Who, then, were these Muslim Bengalis who wanted to join their coreligionists in the north and northwest to form a 'land of the pure'?

Muslim Society in Bengal

At the very beginning of the thirteenth century, an aristocracy, proud of its foreign origins, established itself in Bengal while still retaining its links with the north of India.[1]

Its cultural language was Persian, and Urdu was its vernacular dialect. A political and military elite, it took over great stretches of land during the time of the sultanates and of the Mughal Empire. Nevertheless, by the nineteenth and twentieth centuries these great Muslim landowners had become a minority.[2] They did not speak the local dialect, nor did they feel any particular ties to Bengal. By the end of the period this Muslim elite had admitted high caste Hindu converts to their ranks.

For a long time therefore, the Muslim League had formed a part of the *zamindar* in East Bengal of which the *nawab* of Dhaka constituted a fine example. Khwaja Nazimuddin, who led the first Cabinet of Pakistani East Bengal, came from a family whose forebears had arrived in Bengal from Kashmir early in the eighteenth century, to trade in leathers and pelts. They had acquired widespread landed properties, as a result of their support for the British at the time of the Mutiny, one of them was granted the hereditary title of *nawab*. As Urdu speakers, members of the family had few ties with the people of Bengal. Their luxurious residence in Dhaka, Ahsan Manzil, became the centre for Muslim League activities in Bengal from the time of its foundation, and remained so throughout the Pakistani period.

Alongside this cultural aristocracy with its non-Bengali origins, a second elite grew up. Comprising members of the liberal professions, mostly living in Calcutta – lawyers, journalists and university professors – as well as industrialists and businessmen, for the most part Urdu speakers. Hussain Shaheed Suhrawardy – head of the last government of a unified Bengal, then founder of the Awami League and finally, for a while, Prime Minister of Pakistan – gives us an idea of the social profile of this small but very influential class which claimed, as did the elite described above, the status of *ashraf*.

At the other end of the social scale were the huge majority of Muslim peasantry – illiterate, poor, and speaking only Bengali. These country folk practised a popular Islam largely concerned with the worship of saints and the veneration of Sufi teachers. Throughout the nineteenth century they had been the targets of reformists, who convinced them – with some success – to abandon many practices foreign to the Islam of the Koran, and to maintain their distance from their neighbours, the Hindus.[3] Numerous meetings [*anjuman*] were organized to pass on the instructions of Muslim representatives in the villages. Pious assemblies [*waz mehfils*] in these villages attracted a large number of participants to listen to and pray with a celebrated preacher.[4] All the same, however sincere this piety may have been, the peasantry, long exploited by landowners and moneylenders aspired above all to a betterment of their economic and social condition. In most cases the exploiters belonged to a different religious community and this gave a special edge to the conflicts of interest which partly explained the 'peasants' support for the creation of Pakistan.

Between these extremes – a few aristocrats on the one side, and a numerous impoverished peasantry on the other – an essentially rural middle class arose at the beginning of the twentieth century, thanks to profits from commercial enterprises introduced and developed by the British. Once these Bengali-speaking families of peasant stock had money they sent their sons to study at Dhaka (Dhaka) University, founded in 1921. Many of them were imbued with the liberal culture of the rebirth of Bengal, and a few were attracted by the ideals of the Communist Party of India, established during the 1920s. The influence of the Russian Revolution in October 1917 was always more important in Bengal than in the western provinces of British India, and the students, grouped in syndicates according to their political views, were more activist.[5]

For a long time the Muslim League remained the party of the big property owners, of members of the liberal professions, and industrialists, among whom the most famous were the Ispahani. Only a few years before Partition, it transformed itself into a mass party embracing the great majority of Muslims in the region. Appointed secretary of the League in 1944, Abul Hashim, who was from an educated West Bengal Family, quickly succeeded in selling the party and its ideals to the lower middle class and the peasantry. And so the unity of Muslim society in Bengal was formed around its religious identity. The League seemed to be its guarantor and expression in the face of the Bengali Hindus, who had dominated the political and economic scene ever since the arrival of the British. All the same, the new Pakistani citizens would soon assert with some force the other side of their identity, based this time on their Bengali language and culture.

Nevertheless, the question of the 'national' language of the Muslims of Bengal nevertheless did not arise in a vacuum. It had been the subject of numerous debates throughout the nineteenth century, and the local press had largely echoed these.[6]

Some, in the name of Islam and its culture, centred on the Near and Middle East, defended the place of Urdu and its Arabic alphabet; others, taking due account of the reality and the criterion of numbers, affirmed the preeminence of Bengali. In the end, after much discussion, the Muslim press opted between 1920 and 1930 for Bengali, without taking into account the value of Urdu as a means of communicating with Muslims elsewhere in India. Middle-class intellectuals and university students championed their mother tongue above even the creation of a Pakistani state. To a former vice-chancellor of Aligarh who had suggested that Urdu should become the national language of Pakistan, Muhammad Shahdullah, an eminent linguist at Dhaka University had replied that using Urdu instead of Bengali in the courts and in universities (of their region) would amount to political slavery.[7]

East Pakistan or Bang-I Islam

Nevertheless, Bengali linguistic 'nationalism' had not lessened the rivalries between the Bengali speakers of the two religious communities. In the years preceding Partition, religion had become the salient factor. At the 1946 provincial elections, where the question of Pakistan was at stake, Bengali Muslims elected 113 League candidates out of the 121 seats reserved for Muslims. It can therefore be said that the success of the League, and of its programme, was incontestable. A strong majority of Muslim electors had supported the principle of separation from India, without being sure what the exact position of Bengal in a future Pakistan would be – whether it would be divided, fully included or even remain united and independent. In the very last hours before Partition, a small number of leaders showed a belated burst of Bengali nationalism, but this did nothing to change the fact that the two religious communities were finding it increasingly difficult to live side by side.

Let us recall the circumstances that exacerbated the antagonisms between Hindus and Muslims. Numerous intercommunital disturbances had increased the sense of insecurity between them. The most serious – on the day of direct action 16 August 1946, ordered by the Chief Minister of the government, H.S. Suhrawardy, demanding the creation of Pakistan, caused thousands of deaths in the city of Calcutta alone, especially among the Muslim minority. It was followed by the massacres of Hindus at Noakhali and in Bihar. Ever since 1937 successive governments of the province had been headed by Muslims. Having enjoyed an overall majority in Bengal as a whole since the end of the nineteenth century, they had obtained from the British the agreement that elections should be held according to the principle of separate electorates, so they dominated the political life of the province. A.K. Fazlul Huq, founder of Krishak Praja, the Peasants' Party, was at that time allied with the Muslim League, and he had become the first Chief Minister of Bengal. This gentleman – highly thought of by the peasants of the delta and considered by no one to be 'essentially secular',[8] yet apparently somewhat capricious – had presented an unequivocal resolution for the creation of Pakistan on 23 March 1940, during the League's famous session in Lahore. It stipulated that 'the regions where the Muslims held a numerical majority, as in the northwest and the east of India, should be grouped together to form independent states in which the constituent units should hold autonomous and sovereign status'. This declaration was subject to numerous interpretations; that is why the immediate question arose whether there should be Pakistan in the northwest, Bang-i Islam in the east, and Usmanistan (Hyderabad and Berar) in the centre.[9]

The next year, Fazlul Huq had to leave the League due to differences of opinion with Jinnah who, in his view, did not take the interests of Bengal seriously enough. He then formed a second administration without a single member of the League, but he had to resign from the post of Chief Minister in 1943 under pressure from the governor and following the defection of some European members of the assembly who supported the League. His place was taken by a very influential member of this party and one who was close to Jinnah, Khwaja Nazimuddin. That same year the province suffered a terrible famine which caused 3 million deaths. Then, in March 1946, the elections brought to power Hussain Shaheed Suhrawardy, a lawyer from Calcutta who found himself at the head of the last Cabinet of an undivided Bengal.

It was in this same year, 1946, that an amendment to the Lahore Resolution recommended the creation of a single state for the Muslims of the Indian subcontinent, a state which would include the regions of the northwest and the east, where they were in a majority. On 27 April 1947 however during a press conference, Suhrawardy announced a plan for the founding of a sovereign, united and entirely independent Bengal. He expressed his agreement with the two most important members of Congress at regional level: Sarat Chandra Bose, elder brother of Subhas Chandra Bose: and Kiran Shankar Roy, leader of Congress members in the regional assembly. This was a risk for these politicians, without the prior support of their respective parties. Bose and Roy had distinctly divergent views concerning the direction to be taken by Congress in Delhi. As for Suhrawardy, when he took this initiative he was going against the theory of two nations defended by Jinnah. Nevertheless, Jinnah did not at first seem to be against the plan, but the other important leaders of the League in Bengal, Khwaja Nazimuddin and his friends, reacted against it violently. The majority of the Bengali members of the League still hoped that the whole province would be incorporated in the future Pakistan – including the city of Calcutta, with its factories and its port. Put together late in the day, and against a background of serious intercommunal disturbances, the claim for a unified and sovereign Bengal looked rather like a last-minute proposal by a few Bengali Muslim leaders to prevent the partition of the province and avoid the loss to Pakistan of Calcutta – a loss they dreaded more than anything else, and which seemed inevitable.

Some historians of Bangladesh would like to see in Suhrawardy's declaration the earliest manifestation of a Bengali nationalism destined to grow with the passing years. They recalled the strength with which the Hindus of Bengal had fought the first attempt at partition in 1905 in the name of 'Bengality' at a time when their own dominant position seemed to be assured. In 1947, on the other hand, the Hindus, now in the minority in their province, felt – at least politically – thoroughly weakened. Under the influence of the Hindu Nationalist party, the Hindu Mahasabha and its Bengali leader Shyamprasad Mookerjee, they had no confidence that politicians within the League would defend their interests. The experience of the previous ten years, during which there had been a succession of governments with a Muslim majority in Calcutta, seemed to them to be a proof of impending danger. Encouraged by a press largely in favour of Partition, they therefore preferred to see a separation of their province, even at the price of tremendous displacements of population and the series of painful disasters which would follow in its wake.

In truth, the question of a unified and sovereign Bengal could not be the object of more extensive discussion, because the English wanted to sort out the way in which power might be transferred very quickly, while on the other hand the very powerful leaders of the Congress Party, Jawarhalal Nehru and Sardar Patel, were vehemently expressing their opposition to an independent Bengal. To them, such independence would mean the domination of the country by the Muslim League, and – in either the shorter or longer term – the risk that Bengal, with its majority Muslim population might elect to join Pakistan.[10] Indeed the independence of Bangladesh in 1971 did not give rise to any movement, from either side of the border, in favour of reuniting the Indian State of West Bengal with the new sovereign country. Only a confederation including India and Pakistan might, perhaps, have been able to provide for a unified Bengali nationalism. The question remains to be answered.

The Language Movement

On the morning of 16 August 1947, the Bengalis – for the most part Muslims – in East Bengal therefore woke to find themselves included in a partnership, where due account had been taken of their religion, but where they had the immediate impresson that their political weight did not correspond to the size of their population. Assertion of their identity took the form of claim for an equal status for their language and their culture above all else. Economic and political demands were added later.

The first Cabinet of Pakistani East Bengal was led by Khwaja Nazimuddin, a conservative politician ever loyal to Jinnah. As of 15 September 1947, a mere month after Partition and Independence, a pamphlet circulated in Dhaka proposing that Bengali should be chosen as the language for education, in the courts and in East Pakistan's administration; while Urdu and Bengali should be used jointly at the 'centre' – at that time Karachi. Those who ran the country failed to appreciate the significance of this claim.

As early as September 1947, students at Dhaka University organized themselves in a group known as the Tamaddun Majlis, or Cultural Association, which launched a campaign calling for Bengali to be the language for education and in the courts, but also the language of central government.[11] The following month the Tamaddun Majlis took the initiative by forming an Action Committee in favour of the national language, at first strove to put its point of view in the press and to government officials. Reacting to a decision taken at an education conference held in Karachi, which had accepted Urdu as the state language of Pakistan, the students of Dhaka University gathered on the campus on 6 December 1947 demanding that Bengali should 'take priority in so far as it was a national language of the Pakistani State and at the same time the official language for teaching and the courts in East Pakistan'.[12] The demonstrators were already denouncing what they termed the 'betrayal of Bengali and the people of East Bengal'. After this meeting they marched through the streets of the eastern capital. At the same time, at Sylhet, in the northeast of the country, the partisans of Urdu were apprising the Prime Minister of the province, Khwaja Nazimuddin, of their point of view, but they were very much in the minority and theirs was an isolated action.

The middle class – and particularly the 'vernacular elite'[13] who spoke Bengali naturally felt humiliated by the use of only English and Urdu on banknotes, stamps, coinage, and at the top of governmental papers. When, at the first session of the Constituent Assembly of Pakistan, a Bengali asked for his language to be used in the deliberations on a par with English and Urdu, the Prime Minister, Liaquat Ali Khan, issued a blunt refusal on the pretext of protecting Pakistan unity. This refusal gave rise to vehement protest from the students of the Action Committee: strikes, marches and meetings proliferated. At this time, Bengalis made up 44 million of the total Pakistan population of 69 million. On the basis of numbers alone their language deserved at least equal status with Urdu, mother tongue of no more than 3.5 per cent of the population, according to one 1951 statistic.[14] As for English, its retention as an official language should have been time-limited. As far as Liaquat Ali Khan and the leaders of the League in Karachi were concerned, Urdu was the language of all the Muslims in India, and it had been for those millions that Pakistan had been created at the cost of years of struggle and suffering. This argument was specious on the linguistic level but it did have a certain impact where the Muslims of the north of the subcontinent were concerned, especially for those who had emigrated from the former United Provinces to the new state.

Faced with opposition from the authorities, a fresh action committee of students from all parties except the League was formed in March 1948. It called itself the Action Committee for the National Language, and appealed for a general strike. Its members organized pickets in front of government offices, post offices and courts. The police charged the strikers and demonstrators with lathis, and made numerous arrests. Under pressure from the students, agitation in favour of Bengali gained support in most towns, and was severely repressed in every case. On 15 March 1948 the Prime Minister of East Pakistan, Khwaja Nazimuddin, agreed to receive a delegation from the Action Committee, although he had declared on several occasions that it was made up of communists, enemies of Pakistan. The Pakistani Communist Party did not attract a large number of members at that time but out of 130 deputies to the party's 1948 national congress, 125 were Bengalis and only five from West Pakistan. To men of politics in the West, the influence of East Bengal's communists seemed significant. Besides, some years prior to Independence, several peasant movements – such as the Tebhaga, which had mobilized the tenant farmers to demand a more equitable distribution of revenues from land – had highlighted on the role of communists in the rural north of Bengal. From the start of the campaign for the language, the authorities showed a tendency to throw the leaders of the movement into prison.[15]

Up against the students, Khwaja Nazimuddin signed a document containing eight points under which he undertook to release the imprisoned demonstrators. He also promised that the regional assembly, due to meet in the first week of April, would recognize that Bengali should have the status of the official language of the eastern half of the country once English had been abandoned. Education at all levels should be in the state language; nevertheless in schools and universities the mother tongue of the population concerned could also be used. Under another resolution the regional assembly agreed to recommend to the National Assembly that Bengali should be adopted on an equal status with Urdu as a national language of Pakistan, and the recommendation made it clear that the two languages should have equal status in central government recruitment examinations. Khwaja Nazimuddin probably had no intention of honouring his second promise. Indeed, the question of the national language was never raised by the regional assembly with the authorities in Karachi during his administration. His primary objective was to calm the situation before Qaid-i Azam Jinnah's arrival in Dhaka.

In fact Muhammad Ali Jinnah did come to Dhaka, where he delivered a long speech on 21 March 1948 in the course of which he spoke firmly about the language question. He left to the government and to the elected representatives the job of deciding for themselves what language should be used by the administration, in education and in the courts – for Bengali alone. He vigorously condemned the fomenters of disturbances and was delighted that Khwaja Nazimuddin had been so firm in his efforts to restore order. He considered the promises made by the Prime Minister to the students invalid, saying they had been extorted from him. Moreover, he insisted on the principle that Urdu alone should be the national language of Pakistan, since he saw this as absolutely essential to guarantee the unity of the state. On this occasion, Jinnah – who had no doubt been badly advised – lacked his customary shrewdness. Next day, having agreed to receive a few representatives of the Action Committee, he reiterated his refusal to grant Bengali a status equivalent to that of Urdu.

The resolution adopted by the East Bengal Assembly on 6 April 1948 therefore granted Bengali the status of an official language only within the province and then only once it had been decided to drop English. This was designed to postpone the matter to an uncertain future. Professor Shahidullah, university man and highly regarded linguist, solemnly reaffirmed the 'Bengality' of the province's inhabitants, going so far as to write in the *Daily Azad* of 1 January 1949: 'It is true that there are Hindus and Muslims. But what is transcending is that they are in essence Bengali. This is a reality. Nature with her own hand has stamped the indelible mark of Bengali in such a manner on our appearance and language that it is no longer possible to conceal it.' This declaration by a very respected university man, who was clearly above suspicion as neither a communist nor a foreign agent, marked the beginning of the linguistic and cultural identity of Bengalis, whatever their religious affinity.

The students' activism in defence of Bengali was not entirely disinterested. Thinking of their future careers in the administration they were not unaware of the fact that for many years to come, English alone would give them access to the senior jobs. However they saw the rejection of their own language as an intolerable slur. In their struggle on its behalf they were defending their dignity and they made Bengali the symbol of their identity. The authorities in Karachi failed to understand this.

Not content with refusing Bengali the status of a national language, central government decided, in the name of Pakistan's national unity, to substitute the Arabic-Persian alphabet for the alphabet in which Bengalis had always written their language. Bengali had always been written in an alphabet derived from Brahman writings in the reign of Ashoka in the third century BC, similar to the Devanagari script used for Sanskrit and Hindi. The Pakistan government spent large sums of money establishing centres where adult literacy in Bengali could be taught with the aid of the Arabic alphabet. Inducements in the form of prizes were also given to authors who published their works in Bengali, but in Arabic script. This brutal change of alphabet seemed unacceptable both to students and to intellectuals in the province, since it cut them off from their rich Bengali literature, whose first manifestations went back to the eleventh century. Professor Shahidullah, a member of the Committee for the Reform of the Language of East Bengal, joined the students in condemning this policy. The recommendations of this government committee were not made public until several years later, in the time of Ayub Khan's regime. He proposed the substitution of the Bengali vocabulary, richly embellished with Sanskrit both by borrowing and by derivation, by an Arabic–Persian lexicon which would be shared with Urdu. Bengali grammar was also to be freed from references based on Sanskrit, and the presentation of the language was to be simplified. Finally, the committee hoped for the general acceptance of Urdu as the second language in educational establishments at both primary and secondary level.

Between 1948 and 1952, when the province's economic situation was far from satisfactory, little attention was paid to the subject of language. Some districts had to face conditions of scarcity, aggravated by the deplorable state of all means of communication and the absence of most forms of transport. The peasants expressed their dissatisfaction violently. There were also strikes against rising prices and low wages in the industrial sector, which was still underdeveloped, and indeed by junior civil servants and teachers. During the years following Partition, therefore, popular discontent can be laid at the door of the decisions taken by the government in Dhaka which reacted by imposing strict control on the press, and putting demonstrators in prison. Little by little, popular opinion realized that the regional government was content merely to apply orders from central government and that it really had little room for manoeuvre. Disaffection towards the politicians in the west, members of the League, grew wherever their responsibility for the misfortunes of Bengal was clearly recognized. This discontent was not limited to Communist Party sympathisers: opposition emerged even from the Muslim League of Bengal.

The party known as the Awami Muslim League, which had acted as spearhead of the struggle for autonomy and then independence, had been founded in 1949 by H.S. Suhrawardy, Maulana Abdul Hamid Khan Bhasani and Sheikh Mujibur Rahman, who was twenty-nine at the time. They were all former members of the Muslim League. Later, in 1953, the Awami Muslim League, seeking to show that is was a non-religious party, dropped the word Muslim. This party went on to unite all the nationalists, whether they came from the left, the centre or the right, on a common platform. In fact the Communist Party leaders pushed their members to join the ranks of the new party, where they were less exposed to official repression, and then to work from the inside to get the communist point of view heard. The East Pakistan Youth League, (the Purba Pakistan Yubo League), was set up soon afterwards with the aim of enlisting the young people in the campaigns for the national language and for the propagation of left-wing ideas.

The movement for the defence of the Bengali language was revived once more – and with greater strength after all the frustrations of those who had realized how little importance Karachi attached to the aspirations of East Bengal. In January 1952, Khwaja Nazimuddin, who had become Prime Minister of Pakistan following the assassination of Liaquat Ali Khan, reaffirmed that Urdu alone would be the national language. This declaration was in direct opposition to the promise he had made to the students four years earlier, and was tantamount to snapping his fingers at the previous year's census figures, which had indicated that a majority – 56.4 per-cent – of the Pakistani population declared Bengali to be their mother tongue, while the figure for Urdu had dropped to only 3.37 percent.[16] It provoked a protest campaign which mobilized many outside of the Action Committee for the National Language. The Awami League under its president, Maulana Bhasani, the League of Muslim Students of East Pakistan and other student organizations combined to launch an appeal for a strike. An action committee was formed from all the parties for defence of the national language (the All Parties National Language Action Committee). Meetings and marches followed, and a general strike was called for on 21 February 1952, the Day for the National Language.

The government reacted by absolutely forbidding any meeting or march for a period of thirty days from 20 February. Despite some dithering by the leaders of the movement, the students decided to carry on regardless. They organized meetings and defied the forces of law and order in small groups, leaving the university in pro-cession. The death of three of them, killed by police bullets, gave the movement its first martyrs. Today, 21 February is still commemorated, and celebrations are held around the monument erected to the memory of the students killed defending their language.

These three deaths were followed by several others the day after and the days after that. The importance of those days, particularly of 21 February, also lies in the fact that the death of these students aroused general indignation right out as far as the villages, and it mobilised whole new sections of the population, in both town and country around the status of Bengali and the fight against government decisions. In the days which followed, the Prime Minister of East Bengal, Nurul Amin, accused foreign agents and the communists of fomenting the troubles. Most of the leaders of the Action Committee found themselves in prison.[17]

The 1954 Elections

Encouraged by the Awami League, preparations for the first general elections in March 1954 went ahead with a United Front assembled from all the parties opposed to the Muslim League: the Awami League itself, the Krishak Sramik Party of peasants and workers which the leader AK Fazlul Huq, had put together for the occasion, Maulana Ataha Ali's Nizam-i Islami and the Ganatantri Dal, a party of the left including the communists and led by a former leader of the Tebhaga peasant movement.

This United Front adopted a twenty-one-point programme covering – apart from claims about the adoption of Bengali as one of Pakistan's national languages, and its introduction as the language of education – economic improvements: nationalization of the jute trade, guaranteed prices for this product, abolition without compensation of the *zamindar*, distribution of surplus land among the peasants, and lowering of farm rents. The programme also referred to the Lahore Resolution and insisted that only defence, foreign affairs and finance should remain with central government. Moreover, the Front opposed any military alliance with the United States. This programme was set down as a challenge from the 'vernacular elite' to the 'national elite'.[18] This same elite was prepared to carry the struggle as far as independence. Nonetheless, under pressure from the most left-wing elements of the Front, it was obliged to take into account the demands of the peasants and, to a lesser extent, those of the workers. Thus it succeeded in including in its wish-list something for everyone in East Bengal.

Since the creation of Pakistan, the frustrations of the Bengalis had continued to grow. Politically and economically, they felt that they had been deprived of their share of the benefits of independence. Between 1947 and 1958 the imbalance between the two halves of the country had been strengthened by the effect of structural factors due not only to the weakness of the province's economic framework, but also – and above all – to the partisan policies of central government. Bengalis could not accept that income derived from the export of jute produced by growers in their province should be used largely for the development of the western half of the country. The sharing out of national resources was passing them by. As for foreign aid, it was used mainly to finance projects in West Pakistan. It was to the west, too, that all the imports went. The fact that the country's capital and all the main government departments, including the headquarters of all three military services, were situated in the west exacerbated the discrepancy. Moreover, East Bengal had to buy manufactured goods of mediocre quality from West Pakistan at exorbitant prices in a protected market.

From the earliest years of independence, recruitment into the public administration and armed services favoured the sons of the Punjabi elite. In 1955, only 14 out of 894 high-ranking officers in the Pakistan army were Bengalis. In the navy there were 593 from West Pakistan against seven Bengalis. At that time, not one secretary-general of a ministry was from East Bengal – in a total of 19 all were from the western half of the country.[19] Regional autonomy seemed the only way to reestablish the balance, and put an end to what Dhaka had long called the 'colonization' of East Bengal by Pakistan. The inequality of treatment of the two regions, at least until 1958, was an accepted fact.[20]

All these factors ensured victory for the Front in the 1954 elections in Bengal: 223 seats out of 309. The Muslim League, with only nine, had to admit to a resounding defeat. M.A. Jinnah's party was never given a hearing in the region again. Nurul

Amin, Prime Minister of the province, lost his own seat. The old leader, Fazlul Huq, was therefore called to form a regional Cabinet in which Sheikh Mujibur Rahman, a rising star of the Awami League, was included – rather at the last minute – as Minister for Trade and Industry. This might have been seen as an important portfolio, given that Bengal was suffering such a haemorrhage of its resources. In fact, since independence, important decisions concerning the province had been taken by officials whose upper echelons all originated in the west, and who obeyed orders from the capital. Local ministers really had very little power. A mere six weeks after taking office the minister from the Front had been hounded out of power by central government on the pretext of social problems affecting the Narayanganj jute factories and the Chittagong paper factories. A short while before, Fazlul Huq had been accused – on the basis of remarks made during a trip to Calcutta, repeated in the Pakistani press, – of wanting to dismantle Pakistan. Numerous incidents following strikes gave Karachi a convenient excuse to rid themselves of a Prime Minister who was considered weak. Total power in Bengal was assumed in Bengal by the governor, Iskander Mirza. The Communist Party of East Pakistan was proscribed, and militant members of the Front were imprisoned; Mujibur Rahman among them.

One of the first measures taken by the second Constituent Assembly in July 1955, was to combine the four regions of West Pakistan in a single political and administrative entity. In the parity established between the two halves of the country East Bengal saw only too clearly a negation of its numerical superiority and a ruse to prevent it from seeking to form alliances with Sind or Baluchistan – regions that were equally hostile to Punjabi domination.

In the Constitution of Pakistan which was finally promulgated on 23 March 1956, Bengali was recognized as a national language of equal status with Urdu. This measure came too late to give full satisfaction to the inhabitants of the province. In so far as the symbol of identity was eventually recognized the language had played its part. Other demands now had to pick up the baton.

In September 1956, the governor of East Bengal, A.K. Fazlul Huq, gave Ataur Rahman Khan of the Awami League the task of forming of a provincial government. For some time the Awami League, which had three distinct tendancies – the right led by Suhrawardy; the centre with Mujibur Rahman; and the left, under Maulana Bhasani – had been subject to internal pressures which jeopardized its unity. The presence of Suhrawardy in the government of 1955, led by Muhammad Ali Bogra, was not acceptable to militants of the two other tendancies. It was the same in the following year when Iskander Khan, the new governor general, chose Suhrawardy as Prime Minister of Pakistan. His party demanded that he should introduce regional autonomy, reestablish the division of West Pakistan into four regions, and adopt non-alignment as the basis of his foreign policy. In 1957, the Awami League split. Maulana Bhasani left, and took with him those elements which favoured a more aggressive policy in defence of peasants' interests and more violently hostile to military alliance with the United States, which Suhrawardy supported. His party took the name National Awami Party (NAP), and recruited in both halves of the country without, however, influencing central government policies to any great extent. Maulana's party, wishing to ally Islamism to socialism, played a rather equivocal role in the period preceding the secession of his country in so far as it was drawn towards Ayub Khan's Islamic programme and pro-China policy.

Surhrawardy found himself in a minority after thirteen months in power. He died in 1963, without succeeding in curbing the deterioration in relations between central government and his eastern wing. According to some analysts, he alone would have been able to keep Bengal within Pakistan.[21]

On 7 October 1958, General Ayub Khan's *coup d'état* put an end to hopes for democracy and from the Constitution adopted only two years earlier. The principal leaders of the Awami League, Sheikh Mujibur Rahman among them, were arrested. Liberty of the press and the right of association were severely curbed, and political parties themselves were banned until 1962. When martial law was lifted, the regulations known as the *Public Office Disqualification Order* and the *Elective Bodies Disqualification Order* prevented politicians who had been indicted for acts said to be prejudicial to the state from participating in political life, and further disallowed them from presenting themselves for election for the next eight years. This measure, which removed the principal opposition party chiefs, provoked much criticism in East Bengal. It was the same with the reductions in the electorate defined by the new constitution promulgated in 1962: it reduced to 80,000 'basic democrats' the electorate charged with electing the President – who, meanwhile retained all executive powers including that of dissolving the Assembly. The ensuing protests once more put their leaders, including Mujibur Rahman, in prison. In East Bengal, the opposition against central government, with middle-class university students from rural areas in the vanguard, intensified. Strikes followed strikes. During the academic year 1962–63, there were only 32 days of uninterrupted study.

The Six-Point Programme

Bengalis felt that they were playing a smaller and smaller role in the conduct of their own affairs. As the political pundit Rounaq Jahan wrote: 'Clearly, the Bengalis were marginally represented in the policy-making and political support groups during the Arab period. This nonrepresentation in the elite is a highly elitist system naturally deepened the Bengalis' sense of alienation.'[22]

Ayub Khan came to East Bengal in 1958 to try to win over the province by concentrating on its development in an effort to reduce the disparity between the two halves of the country. Despite some advances under his leadership, only a third of the economic growth went to the eastern province. Middle-class Bengalis therefore felt that separation of the two economies was the only way that East Pakistan could develop using its own resources and exercise the right to manage a favourable financial policy.[23] So the demand for economic autonomy was added the cries for the liberalization and democratization of political life. Opposition to Ayub Khan's regime met with some success: in the January 1965 presidential election Fatima Jinnah, sister of the founder of Pakistan, secured 37 per cent of the votes over the country as a whole, despite government aid to the candidacy of Ayub Khan.[24]

The war between Pakistan and India which broke out in 1965 made the Pakistani Bengalis acutely aware of their extreme vulnerability. Feeling that they were inadequately protected, they added to their list a claim for the establishment of their own military defence force against a possible attack by neighbouring India. In 1965 the Pakistani army had only 300 officers of Bengali origin out of a total of 6,000.[25] The prestige of the army, often presented as invincible, suffered when the terms of the Indo–Pakistani accord signed at Tashkent became known. The next year at Lahore, during a conference attended by all the country's political parties, Sheikh Mujibur Rahman, who was leading the East Bengal delegation, presented a programme of claims involving six points set out by the Awami League:

- a federation based on the 1940 Lahore Resolution, a parliamentary regime with direct universal suffrage for the National Assembly, and legislative supremacy over the executive;
- a federal government with responsibility for defence and foreign affairs, while all other matters would be the concern of the federated states;
- each half of the country to have its own fiscal and financial policies, the two currencies being freely convertible one with the other; or, if a single currency were to be retained, constitutional guarantees to prevent the flight of capital from east to west;
- the federal government to have no right to impose tax, the federated states reserving a fixed proportion of the taxes they themselves levied to cover the needs of central government;
- each half of the country to take separate account of its own currency and the revenues of each to remain there. The foreign exchange needs of central government to be met by each half equally or in predetermined proportions. The products of each half to be available to the other without internal custom tolls, and the Constitution to permit the federated states freely to establish commercial arrangements with foreign countries;
- each federated state to be authorized to set up its own paramilitary and territorial forces.

The declaration of the Six Points reawoke the autonomist agitation in East Bengal. Students belonging to the Awami League united to form the East Pakistan Students' League, and at the same time mobilized to promote the use of Bengali in every walk of public life. They protested against attempts to stop the songs of Tagore being broadcast on radio and television, and against the artificial Islamization of the Bengali language and culture. The workers of Narayanganj joined unions affiliated to the Awami League, and participated massively in demonstrations in defence of the Six Points. At the time, Mujibur Rahman was not against some agreement with central government on the basis of negotiations around the Six Points, and a compromise solution did not seem impossible. Yet the Ayub Khan regime preferred to continue a policy of repression. They had Mujibur Rahman and several other members of the Awami League imprisoned once more, together with some Bengali soldiers and civil servants. Accused of conspiring with India to bring about the destruction of Pakistan, they spent three years in gaol, but eventually the government had to abandon their trial for lack of proof.

This case, known as the 'Agartala Conspiracy Case', further radicalized the movement in favour of the Six Points. In December 1968, students from the various parties regrouped in an All Parties Students Action Committee, which drew up an eleven-point programme, including the Awami League's six, involving the introduction of Bengali at every level in education and the public services, but above all claims of socialist inspiration for the defence of the interests of the lower middle classes and the popular masses. They further demanded the reduction of taxes on the peasants, the nationalization of banks, insurance companies and industry, and the raising of workers' wages. The 'Eleven Points' represented a significant advance on the Six Points which preceded them. Political agitation was no longer limited to student meetings, but spread among the jute workers, and even to the peasants. Repressive measures made numerous victims. The demonstrating students – most of them from families which owned and made their living from land, retained close links with their home areas. Besides, the former occupants of student halls of residence of Dhaka University remained in contact with their successors through associations established in the moderate-sized towns and villages. These factors went some way towards explaining why people rallied to the call from student organizations which, for their part, had ongoing relationships with political parties, as indeed is the case today.

During these troubled times, some Bengali leaders – albeit opposed to the regime – were unwilling to go as far as the Awami League towards autonomy, and sought to find a degree of accord with central government, but no one was prepared to listen.[26] Nurul Amin, former Chief Minister and member of the Muslim League, and founder of the Republican Democratic Party, favoured the re-establishment of democracy, but did not support the claim for complete autonomy in the Awami League programme. Yet other Bengali politicians supported the Karachi regime without reservation; they would pay the price for this later. The governor of East Bengal between 1963 and 1969 – Abdul Monem Khan, who came from Mymensingh – was killed in a guerrilla reprisal operation in Dhaka in June 1971.

The 1971 Elections

The mass movement in favour of the Six Points shook the government; in March 1969 the principal leaders of both halves of the country were summoned to a round-table conference to discuss the constitutional future of Pakistan. Sheikh Mujibur Rahman refused to attend because he was a prisoner on parole. Accordingly he was granted an unconditional release. Once out of prison, he presented his claims – which were refused – and pleaded forcefully for a reduction in the economic disparity between the two regions. As each five-year plan was being outlined, the Bengali economists taking part in the discussions vigorously raised questions about the uneven development of the two regions and the rising discrepancy between the *per capita* incomes of their respective inhabitants, yet their concerns were never acknowledged. After 1962, Ayub Khan certainly made several efforts at restoring equilibrium, but they had never satisfied the Bengalis, who were no longer ready to forego regional autonomy.[27] Participants in the round-table discussions succeeded in reaching agreement on only wo points: the reestablishment of universal suffrage, in stead of an electoral college restricted to 'basic democrats', and the establishment of parliamentary democracy. The government rejected the demand for a federal administration with full autonomy for each region as presented by Sheikh Mujibur Rahman, and the conference ended in failure.

Ayub Khan considered that a strong central authority was indispensable to the survival of Pakistan. This explains why, unable to contain the discontent with his regime, he resigned in favour of the commander-in-chief of the army, General Yahya Khan on 25 March 1969. Taking power while strikes and demonstrations proliferated in the streets, the general reimposed martial law, rekindling the protest movements in East Bengal. The assemblies were dissolved. To resolve the political crisis, Yahya Khan announced that general elections would take place in December 1970 on the basis of universal suffrage, and that the Assembly, once elected, would produce a new constitution. However, he was no more capable than his predecessor of reducing the Punjabis domination in the army and the government. Nevertheless, he did agree to split the western half of the country once more into four provinces, just as it had been until Ayub Khan decided otherwise. At the same time he abandoned the idea of parity between East and West and, giving every adult the right to vote, he accepted *de facto* the numerical superiority of the electors of East Bengal in the Central Assembly. Of its projected 300 seats, 162 deputies would be returned by Bengal.

In that province the electoral campaign was arranged on the basis of the Awami League Six-Point programme. Sheikh Mujibur Rahman, who could not imagine that there could be any other programme, declared several times that the elections must be a referendum for or against the Six Points. The more radical students wanted to go beyond the Six Points towards independence and a socialist regime. All the same, they accepted that they should participate according to the framework set by the powers-that-were at the time. Maulani Bhasani, leader of the pro-Chinese strand of the National Awami League, preferred to ask his candidates to withdraw at the last moment to devote themselves to helping victims of the recent floods.

In fact, once the electoral campaign was in full swing, and after the lifting of all the restrictions imposed on the political parties, a terrible cyclone, followed by a tidal wave and serious flooding, hit the coast of East Bengal on 12 November 1970, causing – according to the international press – 350,000 deaths.[28] Faced with this catastrophe, the Pakistanis of Bengal once again had the feeling that they were being abandoned to their own devices, despite a brief visit by Yahya Khan, who failed to order emergency help on a national scale. International aid was seen as more forthcoming, faster and more efficacious.

The elections took place less than four weeks after this disaster, though some coastal districts were able to delay them by a month. The result was a triumph for the Awami League, which took 160 of 162 seats allotted to the province in the National Assembly and 288 of 300 in the provincial assembly, while the votes for the ten seats reserved for women were never counted.[29] The members elected to the

Dhaka assembly vowed to demand the implementation of the Six and Eleven Points that had already been presented so often. The *fatwa* by 130 Islamic leaders condemning the vote in favour of nationalism as antireligious and socialist had no effect at all. Nurul Amin and the rajah, Tridiv Roy, were returned unopposed by the tribes of the Chittagong Hill Tracts, as the only two elected members who alone did not belong to the Awami League.

According to the election results there is no doubt that Sheikh Mujibur Rahman should have been called upon to head the new central government, since his party won the greatest number of seats. In fact Z A Bhutto's Pakistan People's Party, which came second, won only 81 out of the 138 seats allotted to the western half of the country. Yet neither General Yahya Khan nor Z A Bhutto could face seeing the province of Bengal lay down the law to those who had dominated the national stage since the creation of the state, first from Karachi and later from Islamabad. As for Mujibur Rahman, the position of Prime Minister of Pakistan meant less than the introduction of his Six Points into the Constitution which the Assembly was due to set out. On 1 March 1971, after weeks and months of hesitation and abortive negotiations, Yahya Khan decided to prorogue the National Assembly, this time *sine die*. The session had been due to start in Dhaka two days later. Yahya had decided that the meeting should take place in Dhaka in order to give greater solemnity to the inauguration of a new building designed by an American architect to house the provincial assembly. To justify the prorogation, Yahya Khan used the pretext that Bhutto and members of his party had refused to take their seats in Bengal. The lack of agreement between the Awami League and the Pakistan People's Party on the constitutional status of the country had led the leaders of the PPP to say that they feared for their safety if they set foot in Dhaka. In reality, as soon as the election results were made public, Bhutto had declared that his party would not attend the inaugural session of the Assembly unless he was given the assurance that he would be able to share central power with the Awami League. He had even sworn to get rid of any member of his party who went to Dhaka in answer to the summons.[30] Z A Bhutto's responsibility for the events which ensued is undeniable.[31]

The prorogation of the session brought an immediate response from the East Bengal population: a call for a general strike. A majority of the students, united in the Students of Independent Bangladesh Central Committee for Action, and several politicians, such as Maulana Bhasani and Ataur Rahman Khan, a former chief minister, asked that Mujibur Rahman should declare independence, this he did not do.[32] Hoping to restore order Yahya Khan, replaced the governor general of the province, Admiral Ahsan – whom the Bengalis liked – with General Tikka Khan, who had brutally repressed separatist movements in Baluchistan. The president of the High Court, followed by the other judges, who knew of his reputation, refused to let him swear them in.

Faced with this array of strength, Mujibur Rahman launched a solemn appeal for noncooperation with the authorities. The movement, however was to remain nonviolent. The government of the province was very quickly paralysed: civil servants did not go to their offices, taxes and bills were not paid, banks did not function, communications were cut. Repression, however, was pitiless, and fusillades of rifle fire from the army caused many casualties. The population lost their heads and local feelings boiled over, making victims of 'Biharis', ordinary Muslims from other regions of northern India who had settled in East Bengal at the time of Partition. In 1947, some 500,000 had chosen to make their home in the eastern half of the new state.[33] Remaining loyal to the ideology which had led to Pakistan's creation, and showing little inclination to mix with the indigenous population, they had come to be an unpopular minority. It was they who suffered the backlash of the violence meted out to the Bengalis. Meanwhile, these sporadic uncontrolled assaults provided an army with the excuse to increase the ferocity of its repression.

Throughout March, the students raised the orange and green standard of Bangladesh, while Rabindranath Tagore's song *Amar Sonar Bangla* ('My Golden Bengal') and the slogan 'Joy Bangla' (Victory to Bengal) resonated over the airwaves from Radio Dhaka, which had ceased to use its official title of Radio Pakistan, Dhaka. *Amar Sonar Bangla* had been the students' choice as national anthem for the future Bangladesh. During a passionate address on 7 March, the Sheikh whose nickname was *Bangabandu* (Friend of Bengal) declared: 'Our struggle today is a fight for freedom, a fight for independence'. Representing, as he did, the majority of the electorate of the whole country, and therefore invested with the legitimate authority of the ballot box, he set down in the name of his party four conditions to be laid before the first session of the National Assembly, which was finally scheduled to open on 25 March: the lifting of martial law, the transfer of power to the elected representatives of the people, the announcement of a judicial inquiry into the circumstances leading to the death of so many demonstrators, and finally the army's return to its barracks. There is not the slightest doubt that Sheikh Mujibur Rahman had no firm plan for the dismantling of Pakistan. He would have preferred a confederation which could have freed East Bengal from the tyranny of the soldiers and bureaucrats of central government and allowed it to follow its own political, economic and cultural path. The intransigence of his political adversaries forced him to accept the path of the secessionist movement that geography and cultural differences between the two halves of the country demanded. Despite pressure from radical elements, which had always supported him, and although he defended the centralist position, he was prepared to discuss matters over and over again with those who wanted nothing more than the maintenance of the status quo in relations between central government and the provinces, even if it entailed his own disappearance from the political scene.

On 15 March, General Yahya Khan decided to come with his advisers to Dhaka for negotiations on the basis of the Six Points, to which had been added the demands for the lifting of martial law and transfer of power to the elected representatives. The arrival of Zulfikar Ali Bhutto some days later threw everything back into doubt, although Yahya Khan had already accepted Mujibur Rahman's demands in principle, and an initial draft of a presidential proclamation lifting martial law and transferring power to the majority parties in the provinces had already received the assent of the two main protagonists. Bhutto refused point-blank to endorse the proposed text.[34]

On 23 March the students declared a day of protest against the denial of the transfer of power to those properly elected. In the presence of Mujibur Rahman and an enormous crowd, they hoisted the standard of Bangladesh and refused to raise that of Pakistan alongside it.

A last meeting was again laid on between Yahya Khan and the leaders of the Awami League was still scheduled in an effort to agree a text for the proclamation acceptable to all sides, but on 25 March, Yahya Khan and Z A Bhutto took the plane back to Rawalpindi. In the evening of that same day, the emergency plan prepared long before by General Tikka Khan was put into effect.[35] This was Operation Searchlight, in the course of which the army attacked the campus of Dhaka University, the police barracks, the barracks of the East Pakistan Rifles and the East Bengal Regiment, and areas where there was a Hindu majority. Those Bengali officers and soldiers serving in the army regiments and in the police who managed to escape the massacre rallied to the cause of independence. In Dhaka and Chittagong, and in other towns, the militias who wanted to keep East Bengal within Pakistan, and drew their inspiration primarily from Islam, took part in massacres of intellectuals, teachers, newly elected members of the Assembly and members of the Awami League and important members of the Hindu minority. Those known for their progressive opinions and their attachment to secularism became the first victims. That same night – the night of 25–26 March – Sheikh Mujibur Rahman was arrested, accused of high treason, and thrown into prison in West Pakistan. In a final message, he called on the citizens to sacrifice everything for the true liberation of their country.[36] On 27 March on Chittagong Radio, Major Ziaur Rahman officially proclaimed independence in the name of Sheikh Mujibur Rahman.

The brutal behaviour of the military dealt a fatal blow to the Pakistani nation. Yet had it ever really existed? The national liberation movement had mobilized the popular masses around some thousands of the East Bengal Regiment, the East Pakistan Rifles and the Bengali police, who had received military training. These men were joined by students, farm and factory workers, without weapons or know-how, and constituted the footsoldiers of the army of liberation [*Mukti Bahini*]. Before them stood an organized and disciplined force of several divisions including artillery, tanks and aircraft. The Islamic pro-Pakistani militias, *Razakers, Al Badr* and *Al Shams*, composed essentially of 'biharis' and members of the Islamic Chhatra Sangha, the student wing of the Jamaat-i Islami Party, also played their part in the military operations. This party, opposed to the break-up of Pakistan and in favour of a strong central power, engaged at least some of its 40,000 'associate' members and 425 full members in the struggle, alongside the Pakistani army.[37] With the members of Nizam-i Islami from the Jamiyyat-ul Ulama-i Pakistan and the Jamaat-i Islami, all devoted to the cause of a united Pakistan, the military forces organized councils of peace in towns and villages both great and small; inhabitants were encouraged to act as informers on Hindus and Awami League sympathizers.

On 10 April the principal leaders of the Awami League formed a provisional government, the seat of which, Mujibnagar, was near the Indian border. Colonel MAG Osmany was appointed chief of the army of liberation. Following a period of success, during which the Mukti Bahini took control of a significant part of districts at some distance from the centre, the Pakistan army took a grip on itself, received reinforcements of men and material, and inflicted heavy losses on its enemies. The soldiers occupied the principal towns, and did not hesitate to bombard civilians. Altogether 9.5 million inhabitants of Bengal took refuge in India. Among them were many Hindus but also numerous Muslims, democratic partisans, whose language was Bengali, whose culture was humanist and non-communalist, who had responded to the Awami League's appeal and had some left-wing sympathies. Only a few communists with Maoist leanings condemned this popular uprising. Since it's aim was not a socialist state, the dubbed it a nationalist and petty-bourgeois revolution.

From the start of the armed struggle, India, supplied the fighters of the Mukti Bahini with a refuge, arms and military training. Its frontier forces were ordered to allow anyone who wished to enter India to do so. Its support was vital to the constitution of a special guerrilla force. Nevertheless, considering that its army was not adequately prepared to take on Pakistan on two fronts, and possibly an intervention from China on behalf of its ally Pakistan at the same time, the Indian government decided against launching an immediate military campaign in Bengal. During this period, many important intellectuals and former senior civil servants from East Bengal travelled to Europe and the USA, to make sure governments and public opinion there were aware of the fate of Bangladesh.

On 3 December 1971, war between India and Pakistan broke out, and the Indian army made an incursion into East Bengal. The break-up of Pakistan and the prospect of a friendly government in Dhaka could cause no displeasure in India. Moreover, Indira Gandhi wanted control of operations in East Bengal to remain in the hands of the Awami League, whose political programme was not dissimilar to that of the Congress Party. She was highly distrustful of left-wing movements, which at the time were very active both as guerrillas and as other 'loose cannons'. There was no question of allowing a Maoist revolution on the eastern frontier of India which might, with the help of China, spill over into neighbouring territory. The financial cost of the influx of refugees was also proving a heavy burden on the Indian economy. It was obvious that they would not be going home – at least, not until Bangladesh had become a reality. Reassured about the intentions of Pakistan's allies – the USA and China having made it clear they were adopting a non-interventionist position militarily – Indira Gandhi decided in the end to send troops in on the ground. Several months previously she had signed a peace, friendship and cooperation treaty with the Soviet Union.

The Indian invasion involved seven divisions which attacked the Pakistani forces from west, north and east. Coordination with the Mukti Bahini was excellent. Indian aircraft made quick work of assuring air mastery, and rendered the airports unusable. The fleet blocked the ports. The Pakistan army, unable to get any help from outside, was rapidly demoralized. Only twelve days after the start of operations, on 15 December, General AAK Niazi, commanding the 93,000 Pakistani soldiers stationed in East Bengal, surrendered unconditionally to the Indian General JS Arora. According to the commanders of the units of the Mukti Bahini, the Indian army arrived just when they had almost finished the job.[38] In fact, despite the courage shown by the Bengalis – the majority of whom were under twenty-five – and the efficacy of the guerrilla actions, we must recognize that it was the Indian forces' participation which brought things to a head, and secured a rapid victory for the liberation movement. The number of Bengali victims during the nine months – April to December 1971 – which led to independence has been variously estimated at between one and three million. Whatever the truth, it is certainly justifiable to talk in terms of genocide.[39]

On 10 January 1972, Sheikh Mujibur Rahman, freed from his Pakistani prison, returned to an independent Bangladesh to take up the post of Prime Minister of a parliamentary democracy. In just one year the new state was able to equip itself with a constitution of which the four main fundamental principles were democracy, nationalism, socialism and secularism (equal protection for all religions by the public authorities).

Between 1947 and 1971, the Bengalis had strongly affirmed their linguistic and cultural identity in the face of the Punjabi oligarchy which governed Pakistan. Because of the geographical distance between them, the differences in landscape, climate, diet and clothing customs – to which may be added those of language and culture – only religion could bring the two halves of the country together. Taking as symbols their language and their culture, Bengalis asserted their identity with force, even though their society, in all its variety, found itself dominated once more. This time it was their coreligionists who were to blame.

In this context, the role played by the ideals defended by the writers of the Bengali 'Renaissance', Rabindranath Tagore and Kazi Nasrul Islam – as for example, humanism and love of liberty – should not be underestimated. The idealized image of the socialist revolution also inspired a good number of students and intellectuals of the time. And we must not go away with the idea that the Bangladeshis had forgotten their religion. Indeed, the 'Bengality' of the Muslims of East Bengal did not dilute their attachment to Islam. They are not the only people to possess a plural identity of which the two components are never quite in balance.

Meanwhile, the importance of the Movement for the Defence of the Bengali Language was not restricted to politics alone. Literature and cultural life also had a strong influence. Between 1947 and 1971, at least 1,500 novels were published in East Bengal, many more than in preceding years. The authors of short stories, also very numerous, could find an outlet in the literary magazines which proliferated. Among the principal authors, Saokat Osman (1917–99), Syed Waliullah (1922–71) and Alauddin al-Azad (born 1934) imbued their works with a humanistic and generous message which characterizes the texts of the period. As Badruddin Umar has written:

> 'The language movement has actually laid the foundation not only of a new cultural life of the people but also of a truly non-communal and democratic movement in the country. Muslims of Bengal, during the decades of communal politics almost forgot their national identity. Through the shedding of the martyr's blood the Bengalees began to discover their national identity and their social, cultural, intellectual and political life began to strike roots in the soil of East Bengal.'[40]

During the presidency of Ayub Khan, banning Tagore's songs from radio and television on the pretext that they were inimical to the Islamic ideal only had the effect of making them even more popular – at least with the middle class.

The theatre, too, enjoyed a resurgence at this time. Munier Chowdhury wrote *Kabor* ('The Tomb'), although he was imprisoned in Dhaka for participating in demonstrations against central government policies, and the play was put on by the inmates of the gaol on the eve of 22 February 1952. Dramatic works of the time show an awareness of the hard socioeconomic realities in the rural areas. They mock the superstitions and hypocrisy of the clerics, and they protest against the domination of Bengal by a centralised oligarchy. Actors and actresses were very active during the events of 1971. They put on political plays in the streets and in village squares to keep the national liberation movement alive. Several fine intellectuals were murdered on 25 March 1971. Munier Chowdhury (born 1925), dramatic author and essayist; Moffazal Haider Chowdhury (born 1926) and Anwar Pasha (born 1929), essayists and literary critics, were among those who were killed that day in their homes on the campus of Dhaka University.

Independent Bangladesh and Pakistan

The politicians of Pakistan had the wisdom to return the sheikh to his people and, in so doing, allowed a speedy reconciliation between Pakistan and the newly independent state.

From February 1974, diplomatic relations were established. During the months of struggle, only India and its ally the Soviet Union had supported the future Bangladesh, and they were the first to give it official recognition. The United States and China would have liked to prevent the break-up of Pakistan. During the war, in the name of the peoples' right to self-determination, an appeal for aid from Maulana Bhasani had failed to move Mao Ze-Dong, to whom he addressed himself. All the same, in 1974 Bangladesh could put in an appearance at the Islamic Conference when it met in Lahore. The same year, it participated in the creation of the Islamic Development Bank at Jeddah.

After Mujibur's assassination by the military on 15 August 1975, General Ziaur Rahman seized power. Bangladesh aligned itself more with the Islamic countries and less with India, with which Mujibur had nevertheless signed a treaty of friendship. During the time when first Ziaur Rahman and then General H.M. Ershad were in charge, relations with Pakistan were amicable. The officers of the Bangladeshi army, formed in Pakistan before the secession, had taken no part in the war; many of them had been kept in the west of the country at the time. Their return and the gradual elimination of the chief combatants of 1971 – by putsch, trial or banishment – facilitated a *rapprochement* between the two countries. The religious parties, proscribed at first, later allowed to express themselves freely once again. The amnesty law, promulgated in 1973 by Mujibur Rahman, had allowed a number of the 'collaborators' to regain their rights as citizens and their place in society, even if the Islamic parties were still not officially authorized.

Under the presidency of Ziaur Rahman, the mention of 'secularism' disappeared from the Constitution, to be replaced by the phrase 'absolute trust and faith in Allah, the All-Powerful'; and nationalism was expressed as Bangladeshi rather than Bengali in an effort to underline the difference between the two Bengals. In 1988,

President Ershad, by an amendment to the Constitution, declared Islam to be the state religion, thus aligning Bangladesh more closely with the Muslim countries in general and Pakistan in particular. The geographical position of Bangladesh, encircled by India – not to mention their relatives sizes – leads to contention between the two countries India is readily regarded as a Goliath facing a Bangladeshi David. The division of the water of the Ganges after construction of the Farakka Dam by India at the end of 1974 was resented as a grave injustice. Not until 1996, and the arrival of the government of IK Gujral, could a new, more equitable agreement be signed. Other points of disagreement remain.

Pakistan, separated from East Bengal by 2,000 kilometres of Indian territory, hardly suffers any longer from a negative image. Successive governments have allied themselves ever more closely to the Bangladesh Nationalist Party (BNP), the party of Ziaur Rahman, assassinated by the military in 1981 for – it would seem – personal reasons, and of his widow Begum Khaleda, than with the Awami League of Mujibur Rahman and his daughter, Sheikh Hasina Wajed.

The Awami League, considering itself the only nationalist and workers'party of the liberation, never misses a chance to stress the pivotal role of Sheikh Mujibur Rahman in the independence struggle, Mukti Bahini heroism in the face of the Punjabi soldiers and the atrocities committed by those soldiers upon the people of Bengal. Such talk can serve only to revive antagonism between Dhaka and Islamabad. Nevertheless, for some time now the Awami League has sought to shake off its image as the 'party of India', which gives it no kudos in the eyes of the electorate in general. Its relations with Pakistan will doubtless improve. The BNP, which was again in power between 1991 and 1996, not to speak of the Jamaat-i Islami, the party fundamentally hostile to independence, takes a far less critical line than the Awami League on the Pakistani period of East Bengal.

The problem for Urdu-speaking Biharis – who, having chosen to settle in East Bengal in 1947, today find themselves isolated in a Bangladesh whose citizenship many of them refuse to accept – hardly disturbs the Islamabad authorities, who have no wish to swell the ranks of their Muhajirs. There are still about 250,000. This is the only remaining problem between the two countries, if we ignore deadlocked arguments about the division of possessions at the time of secession. It would seem, rather, that some Pakistani intellectuals are asking themselves whether their country should now be apologizing to the Bangladeshi people for the terrible events of 1971.[41] That would be a moral gesture, albeit one with heavy political overtones.

3

A FRUITLESS SEARCH FOR DEMOCRACY

Since achieving its independence in 1947 Pakistan has had three constitutions and experienced four military coups. This alternation of civil and military regimes, which have succeeded each other at intervals of about ten years, is a striking contrast to the stability of the institutions of its Indian neighbour, which has experienced only one non-democratic interval of eighteen months' duration in 1975–77. How can two states born of the same proto-parliamentary British regime have diverged so much? Yielding to the simplifying charms of culturalism plenty of apologists have maintained the hypothesis that there is an innate incompatibility between Islam and political pluralism.[1]

In fact the shocks and mishaps suffered by democracy in Pakistan have resulted in large part from the heritage bequeathed by the British Raj. The regions united to form Pakistan in 1947 – to start with the Punjab – were submitted during the time of the Raj to more authoritarian regimes than other parts of the Empire. Furthermore, the vice-regal pattern was furthermore a great influence on the father of the nation, Jinnah, who took power into his own hands in 1947 to stress the necessity of building a whole from disparate parts. His successors continued the same methods to the detriment of the political parties which were seen as divisive elements in the fledging nation: those in charge paid no attention to the Muslim League, whose decline deprived the country of a precious link between society and the political establishment. Furthermore, tensions between the various ethnic groups hindered the implementation of a democratic regime. Finally, the obsession with security born of three wars with India explains the influence of the army, ever present in the corridors of power when it was not at the helm itself.

The Priority of State Construction in the Origins of Pakistani Authoritarianism

Quaid-i Azam Jinnah, the New Viceroy?[2]

In 1947 India and Pakistan were elevated by the British to the status of dominions. The Indian Independence Act (July 1947) simply did away with every reference to control by the British Crown given by the Government of India Act (1935), thus fundamentally altering the law of both countries. India drew up its own constitution as early as 1950; Pakistan waited until 1956 to do so. India, like every other dominion in the Commonwealth, appointed as governor general a figure who commanded respect but had no great political authority: C Rajagopalichariar. In Pakistan however, Muhammad Ali Jinnah himself decided to assume this function, despite Lord Mountbatten's lack of enthusiasm. Jinnah, drawing inspiration from the British governors general who bore the title of viceroy, followed the authoritarian and centralizing line bequeathed by the British, while India was more influenced by the parliamentary and federal aspect of the bequest.

Certainly Jinnah declared that he was in favour of an Islamic democracy. Some weeks before Independence, during a Muslim League meeting on 9 June 1947, he proclaimed that the Pakistani Constitution would be 'of a democratic type', and that it would 'embody the essential principles of Islam'.[3] A little later, on 11 August in his inaugural address to the Constituent Assembly, he declared: 'In the course of time, Hindus will cease to be Hindus and Muslims will cease to be Muslims, not in the religious sense because that is personal faith of each individual, but in the political sense as citizens of the State.'[4] Jinnah himself believed, therefore, in liberal democracy. All his successors felt that they must follow in his footsteps – perhaps so as not to be outdone by India. Right from the birth of Pakistan, however, the project of an Islamic democracy on a universalist basis foundered on Jinnah's authoritarianism, which did not leave much room for the religious and linguistic communities.

If Jinnah saw himself as a democrat, he did not conceal his reservations about the parliamentary regime: 'Presidential form of government more suited for Pakistan',[5] he acknowledged as early as July 1947. From the outset he inculcated a forceful personalization of power from which Pakistan has never been able to free itself: as well as acting as a governor general, he was also President of the Constituent Assembly.[6] This amalgamation of these duties remains unique in the history of the British dominions.[7]

The concentration of power instituted by Jinnah went hand in hand with a strong centralization of the state. Certainly he did abrogate Article 93 of the Government of India Act (1935) which gave the viceroy the right to dismiss a regional government but he achieved the same result by invoking Article 51 (5), under the terms of which provincial governors were under the authority of the governor general, who equally had the right to dismiss the government of their constituency. One week after the creation of Pakistan he had the government of the NWFP fired in this way. Its chief was Dr Khan Sahib,[8] who had called for an independent Pashtunistan. Similarly, on 28 April 1948 the governor of Sind dismissed, on his orders, the chief minister, M A Khuhro, who had objected to its capital, Karachi, being placed under direct central government control. Jinnah justified his centralizing authoritarianism by arguing that there was a state to be built[9], an argument we shall examine below. This bad start, however, put a strain on the democracy to which he claimed to aspire.

Liaquat Ali Khan: the Prime Minister who distrusted the party system

Once Jinnah had disappeared from the scene in September 1948, the strong man of the country, Liaquat Ali Khan, became Prime Minister and appointed a new governor general, Khwaja Nazimuddin. Instead of relying on his parliamentary majority and the Muslim League Liaquat Ali Khan immediately adopted the politics of Jinnah. As early as January 1949 he dismissed the Punjabi government on the pretext of mismanagement, although it enjoyed a solid majority in the provincial assembly.[10] Like Jinnah, Liaquat Ali Khan amalgamated posts of responsibility and so took over leadership of the Muslim League in 1950.

The weakness of the Muslim League and the party system therefore appeared to be an insuperable obstacle in the path of parliamentary democracy. Numerous parties surfaced, above all in the provinces – initially expressions of ethnic movements. Dismissed from his job as chief of the NWFP government, Khan Sahib formed the Republican Party, which served as a model for the National Awami Party founded by Wali Khan, the son of Ghaffar Khan, figurehead of Pashtun nationalism. This movement, which was particularly active during the 1950s against the 'One Unit Scheme', soon concluded an alliance with G M Syed, leader of a Sindi organization which changed its name several times. In East Pakistan, too, two regional parties emerged: Suhrawardy's Awami League and the Krishak Sramik Party (peasants' and workers' party), led by Fazlul Huq. Although they claimed to reprenet the will of the people [awami] of Pakistan, none of these political formations was nationwide. The only organizations boasting pan-Pakistani ambitions were, of course, those based on Islam, principally the Jamaat-i Islami (see Chapter 11 below) and the Muslim League. Although the League was roughly the Pakistani equivalent of the Indian National Congress, it was by no means as well structured as that party, which had a whole network of local and regional sections put in place by Gandhi as long ago as the 1920s. For a long time the League had been no more than a small elite group representing a landowning and literate aristocracy, and even by the mid-1940s it had hardly begun to mobilize the Muslim masses. After Independence, Jinnah and Liaquat Ali Khan both used the party as an instrument to wield power. The other leaders of the League never attempted to oppose the executive – even when it fell into the hands of Ghulam Muhammad.[11] On the contrary, they called upon their activists to fall in behind the leaders parachuted in by the executive, all of which threw considerable doubt on the party's credibility. The centralization of power in the hands of the government and the civil service, and the infrequency of elections encouraged the grass-roots workers not to bother to work 'on the ground' but rather to devote themselves to backroom politics and internecine struggles.

Liaquat Ali Khan, a party leader himself, never really admitted the existence of other parties, and spent little time on his own. Pakistan was 'the child of the Muslim League', and in his view those who joined other political formations were the 'enemies of Pakistan who aim to destroy the unity of the people'.[12] The Jamaat-i Islami, determined to participate in the construction of democratic institutions provided they recognized the sovereignty of Allah, was the first to suffer repression. Its leader was arrested in October 1948, and spent many months in gaol.[13]

Liaquat Ali Khan's distrust of politicians was obvious in the Public and Representative Officers (Disqualification) Act (PRODA), voted in on 26 January 1950. This law gave the governor general, the governors of provinces and even ordinary citizens the right to lodge a complaint against a minister or an elected member suspected of corruption, nepotism, favouritism or bad management. The accusations had to be heard by a tribunal composed of two judges nominated by the governor general, and the maximum penalty was exclusion from public duties for a period of ten years. So, rather than holding elections to win support for its responsible politicians, Pakistan had recourse to a new kind of legal action, which would eliminate the most pernicious. Politicians prepared to risk 5,000 rupees – the deposit required to start proceedings – used the PRODA to attack their rivals, giving rise to partisan vendettas which gave a bad name to the whole political class. The Assembly abrogated this law in 1954.

The decline of the Muslim League and the weakness of the party system precluded the establishment of an essential link between government and people. The contrast with the situation in India is striking. On the other side of the border, as election followed election, the state was built gradually with the support of the Congress Party and its network of notables.[14] In Pakistan, those in charge devoted all their energies to establishing a centralized administration which lacked any electoral blessing right down to the local level. In the Punjab, for example, the municipal and district councils – and there were not many – were presided over by a functionary appointed by central government, just as in colonial times. At the end of the 1950s more than half of them were controlled directly by the state, which disdained to organize local elections, since these might reinforce the establishment of party politics.[15] The Pakistani leaders thereby deprived themselves of the links and channels of communication indispensable to the democratic plan which they professed to favour.

The Punjabis reject the law of numbers

The effect of demographic forces placed a further obstacle in the way of constitutional debate. To begin with, democracy was high on the agenda. In March 1949 Liaquat Ali Khan's government submitted to the Constituent Assembly an 'Objectives Resolution' which stipulated that 'the principles of democracy, freedom, equality, tolerance and social justice as enunciated in Islam shall be fully observed.'

The Constituent Assembly was composed of Muslims elected by the assemblies of the regions which constituted Pakistan after Partition. It had a Committee of Fundamental Principles, divided into several subcommittees, whose reports formed the basis of a first draft of a constitution, known as the 'Interim Report'. Liaquat Ali Khan submitted it to the Assembly in September 1950. But this rough outline of a constitution soon gave rise to protestations from Bengali representatives worried both by the elevation of Urdu to the rank of national language and by their underrepresentation in the proposed institutions. Although the Bengalis were in a majority in the country, according to these proposals they would be represented on an equal basis with the other administrative entities of West Pakistan (the Punjab, the NWFP, Baluchistan, Sind and Karachi) in the Upper Chamber. This parity was even more prejudicial to their interests in that the two assemblies would have the same legislative competence. Faced with opposition from the Bengalis and with protestations from the religious groups, who felt that the report gave insufficient emphasis to Islam, Liaquat Ali Khan withdrew it in November 1950.

The difficulty of installing a democratic regime stemmed to a large extent from the power relations of the various linguistic communities.[16] The Bengalis had rejected the Interim Report because of the parity issue, but their position became more difficult after the Punjabis, who were keener on it than any other ethnic group, took power from the start of the 1950s. On 16 October 1951, Liaquat Ali Khan was assassinated during a meeting in Rawalpindi. Khwaja Muhammad then took over as Prime Minister, leaving the post of governor general to Ghulam Muhammad, who was officially appointed by the British Crown on 18 October. This arrangement established the advent of 'the bureaucrats' – as they are traditionally called in Pakistan – at the expense of politicians and the Punjabis at the expense of the Bengalis.

Formerly Finance Minister under Liaquat Ali Khan, Ghulam Muhammad had begun his career in the Indian Civil Service. From his years as a senior functionary of the Raj he had retained his nostalgia for the efficacy of the British 'steel frame' – the colonial administration, a sentiment that was far more thoroughly developed in the Punjab, his home province, than in the others, particularly Bengal. In that region, from the end of the eighteenth century, the British East India Company had in effect established institutions on the British model: the governor general governed in concert with his council in which over the years, Indians had made their appearance little by little. In the Punjab on the other hand, a province conquered as late as 1849, long after Bengal, the administration, and more precisely the administrators within it, were all-powerful; the colonial imagery presented them as strong personalities in direct contact with those they administered. The district magistrates traversed their territory, levying taxes and administering justice. They were the pillars of the state accounting to no assembly for their actions and their prestige, supposedly genuine, arose from their devotion to the public good. At the time of the Raj, this lack of political participation in the Punjab – contrasting with the 'colonial parliamentarianism'[17] prevalent further east – was to be found equally in the other provinces of the northwest, which formed the defensive perimeter of the Indian Empire to contain the Russian thrust into Central Asia.[18]

The arrival of Ghulam Muhammad therefore marks the triumph of a typically Punjabi authoritarian bureaucracy. The new governor general gave the politicians even less confidence than had Jinnah and Liaquat Ali Khan, and distrusted the parliamentary system – its debates, its sources of division and its delays – even more. These reservations about a democratic regime could also be explained by an understandable self-interest: the Punjabis, whom he represented more than any other group, had everything to lose from the development of institutions based on the law of numbers because of their relative demographic weakness. The Bengalis, on the other hand, were drawn to democracy not just because of their constitutionalist tradition but again, and above all, because they represented the majority of the population. Their principal representative was Prime Minister Nazimuddin. He submitted a new report for the Committee of Fundamental Principles to the Constituent Assembly in November 1952, having erased the earlier report's clauses favouring West Pakistan: the Bengalis found that they would henceforth have a majority of seats in the Lower Chamber. The Punjabi Muslim League, however, rejected these proposals, and Ghulam Muhammad was against them too. Nazimuddin withdrew the report on 21 January 1953, and the Constituent Assembly was adjourned *sine die*. On 17 April Nazimuddin was dismissed by the governor general, who also disapproved of the reduction in military expenditure in the report's financial section. (Ghulam Muhammad enjoyed a privileged relationship with the army.) Nazamuddin tried to complain – notably to Queen Elizabeth II – about the unconstitutional nature of his dismissal but he was speedily discouraged by the police pressure to which he found himself subject.

One of the first moves of the new Prime Minister – Muhammad Ali Bogra, another Bengali – consisted of implementing the 'One Unit Scheme', conceived by Ghulam Muhammad to integrate the various provinces of West Pakistan and so assist in restoring the balance with East Bengal. Pakistan would henceforth be made up of more than two administrative entities, corresponding to its two 'wings'. The 'western' Cabinet was entrusted to a Pashtun, Dr Khan Sahib, who had renounced Pashtun nationalism, but this reform clearly illustrated the Punjabis' determination to establish their hegemony over the western 'wing', the better to resist the Bengali majority. The minor provinces – Sind, Baluchistan and the NWFP – protested in vain against this administrative reorganization.

However, Bogra also defended the interest of his own community, the Bengalis. On 7 October 1953 he submitted to the Constituent Assembly the final report to the Committee of Fundamental Principles, which still gave to the Bengalis a majority of seats in the Lower Chamber. As the regional elections of March 1954 approached, the Bengali political class showed its determination by forming a coalition, the United Front, which grouped together the Awami League, Suhrawardy's party, and Fazlul Huq's KSP. This alliance, which campaigned on a 21 point-programme with strong autonomist undertones, won handsomely against the Muslim League, which kept only 11 seats out of 239. Fazlul Huq was soon at the head of the government. Soon afterwards, on 7 May, Bogra had the Assembly pass a motion by which Bengali was to be used as a national language on a par with Urdu, while English remained the official language.

Ghulam Muhammad reacted to the Bengali call to arms by dismissing Huq from his duties as chief minister of Bengal on the pretext that he would be in favour of union with Indian West Bengal. The decisive turning point came six months later. On 21 September 1954, the Constituent Assembly finally approved the report of the Committee of Fundamental Rights against the Punjabi deputies in the chamber. One month later, however, Ghulam Muhammad succeeded in avoiding the adoption of a constitution which would have established a truly parliamentary regime by declaring a state of emergency on the pretext that 'the constitutional machine has broken down'.[19] He imposed press censorship and prevented elected members from taking their seats in the Assembly.

This show of strength was not followed by demonstrations in the streets, even in Bengal, particularly because the governor general had taken care to include in his new government the two principal leaders of the province, Huq and Suhrawardy. The only person to take a stand against the regime's drift towards authoritarianism was the President of the Assembly, Tamizuddin Khan, who, on 8 November 1954, placed before the Sind tribunal a complaint contesting the validity of the measures taken by Ghulam Muhammad. The tribunal ruled unanimously in his favour, considering the Constituent Assembly to be a sovereign body. The government entered an appeal before the Supreme Court, the highest tribunal in the land, which approved the governor general's actions on 21 March 1955. The chief of the Supreme Court, a Punjabi named Munir appointed by the governor general a few months earlier, implicitly agreed with the latter's contention concerning the 'Bengali menace' and justified the state of emergency on the basis of a new doctrine the 'civil law of necessity'.[20]

Once the dissolution of the Constituent Assembly was confirmed, Ghulam Muhammad had a second one elected in 1955. This assembly produced, in record time, a constitution which appeared to have all the attributes of parliamentary government, yet devolved upon the governor general – now rebaptized the president – prerogatives that were incompatible with such a regime, since he could now dismiss the central government as well as those of the provinces. The Constitution was finally promulgated in 1956. Ghulam Muhammad then resigned in favour of Iskander Mirza, who thus became the first President of Pakistan. Mirza, a senior civil servant like his predecessor, was born in Bengal but had been linked with Punjabi bureaucrats throughout his career.

By the mid-1950s therefore parliamentary democracy had foundered on the demographic power relations between Bengalis and Punjabis on the one hand, and between politicians and bureaucrats on the other. Moreover, Ghulam Muhammad and Iskander Mirza, were senior civil servants trained in the tradition of British administration and hostile to political parties whose degree of dysfunction – it must be admitted – did strain their credibility.

The Politics of Factions and 'Feudalism': The 1956 Constitution Fails

The country now had a constitution combining parliamentary and presidential principles but the political parties that could have brought it to life did not exist. A form of multiparty system was certainly confirmed by the decline of the Muslim League, which lost its majority at the elections to the second Constituent Assembly with just 20 seats against 16 for the United Front and 12 for the Awami League, but most of their rivals were either the regional parties – like those mentioned above – or some artificial creations like the Republican Party which emerged in 1956 to act as a screen for Ghulam Muhammad and Mirza. This party, like so many similar tiny groups, was born of the factionalism of the Muslim League.

The factionalism which undermined the political parties of Pakistan, cannot be dissociated from the sway held by tribal chiefs, such as the *sardar* of Baluchistan and the *khan* of the NWFP, and the 'feudal lords' – as they are traditionally called in Pakistan, particularly the big landowners of the Punjab and Sind.[21] The distribution of land was significant: 0.17 per cent of property owners, or about 6,000 people, possessed 7.5 million acres or some 15 per cent of the cultivated land surface, each holding in general to over more than 500 acres. This 'feudal' domination was especially marked in the western area: 28 of the 40 members elected from this region to the second Constituent Assembly were landed property owners.[22] Their hold on political power explains why agrarian reform got bogged down: the Muslim League had made proposals in this direction in July 1949, but they were buried.

The 'feudal' character of Pakistani politics goes a long way to explain the intensity of factional strife. The choice of a leader or of a party was to a great extent dictated by quarrels between tribes, *biradari* or family clans often going back several generations. So in the Punjab the republican party was supported by the Qizilbash, the Noon, the Tiwana, the Gardezi, the Leghari and the Gilani, well-known rural grandees who opposed other 'feudals' who themselves supported the regional boss of the Muslim League, Mian Mumtaz Daultana. The superimposition of 'feudal' politics and factional strife weakened the political parties even more and led to instability in regional governments because of the volatility of their support in the Assembly, a tendency further reinforced by the central government's strategy of 'divide and rule'.

Iskander Mirza was a past master in this art, as his capacity to play Huq off against Suhrawardy in East Pakistan demonstrated.[23] In three years – between 1956 and 1958 – there were three prime ministers, Suhrawardy, I I Chundrigar and Firoz Khan Noon – belonging to three different parties (the Awami League, the Muslim League and the Republican Party). This instability reflected the opportunism of the elected representatives, who were all the more ready to switch allegiances as the dividing lines between the parties were artificial. It also had the effect of introducing antagonism between Prime Minister and President. H S Suhrawardy tried to break free from Mirza's tutelage by seeking a vote of confidence from the Assembly. Mirza, unwilling to recognize the Assembly's power to make and unmake governments, refused to convoke the Assembly, forcing Suhrawardy to resign on 11 October 1957. His place was taken by Firoz Khan Noon, who was no easier to manipulate and took the same line as Suhrawardy.

In fact, Pakistan was facing a problem which it had to confront repeatedly until 1990s. The Constitution wanted parliamentary government but, at the same time, gave the President such prerogatives that he could not bring himself to let his Prime Minister get on with governing. In the case of a conflict, the only solution was to dismiss the government and/or the Assembly, perhaps even suspending the institutions. Mirza chose that last option on 7 October 1958 by proclaiming martial law.

Ayub Khan's Praetorian Rule: From Martial Law to 'Controlled Democracy'

To some extent, Mirza took his decision under the influence of General Muhammad Ayub Khan, commander-in-chief of the army, whose authority symbolized the growing role of the military at the heart of all the institutions.

From its birth, Pakistan had felt threatened by its neighbour, India, and wanted a powerful army.[24] This categorical imperative had been reinforced more strongly still during the first war over Kashmir in 1948–49. Now the troops which Pakistan had inherited at the time of Partition represented only 36 per cent of the British Indian Army (140,000 men out of 400,000), giving New Delhi a considerable advantage.[25] The government therefore made an exceptional financial effort to strengthen the army and modernize its equipment. Between 1947 and 1949 military spending represented on average more than half the annual budget, with a peak of 73 per cent in the fiscal year 1950–51.[26] The country's political economy was clearly dominated by security considerations.[27]

This priority explains why Pakistan joined the Western camp and its network of military alliances in the context of the Cold War. From 1953, American support helped it to finance its armaments effort. Furthermore, it benefited from external support, which was all the more appreciable during times of crisis. It joined the Southeast Asia Treaty Organization (SEATO) and the Central Treaty Organization (CENTO) in 1954–55, two years in the course of which American economic aid rose from 15 million to 114 million dollars.[28] At this stage, Pakistani officers began to go to the United States rather than England for their training courses.[29] So Pakistan formed part of a mechanism of 'containment' directed against the USSR, a continuation of the 'great diplomatic and military game', whose theatre this region had been when Afghanistan and the northern provinces of Pakistan served as a buffer zone for the British. This geopolitical constant had guaranteed the Pakistani military particularly strong American support at the beginning of the Cold War and again after the Soviet invasion of Afghanistan, but it had also reinforced the military in the Punjab and in the North-West Frontier Province.

In 1947, the Pakistan army consisted of 77 per cent Punjabis; Pashtuns represented 19.5 per cent of the troops.[30] Officers were taught that every country tends to organize itself around a 'heartland', loss of which generally leads to the collapse of national resistance – in the case of Pakistan that 'heartland' is, of course, the Punjab. As in many countries, the Pakistani military rather despised the politicians because of their incessant squabbling. Democracy did not appeal to them much either, because it risked giving power to the Bengalis, a community the Punjabis and Pashtuns looked down on. Since colonial times, according to a well-established stereotype, Bengalis had been seen by them – and others as puny, effeminate creatures.[31] The Punjabis and Pashtuns, whom the British had labelled 'martial races', considered that their warrior ethic was necessary to the survival of the country. Whatever might happen, they could not conceive of a situation where the Bengalis gained power over a simple question of demographic power relations.

Ayub Khan, who had been army commander-in-chief since 1951, embodied this military institution better than anyone. His ethnic origin was Pashtun, he was born in the Punjab – like Ghulam Muhammad – and he believed in a centralized state dominated by the Punjab, to which he was keen to rally members of his community.[32] Since his studies at Sandhurst Military Academy in England and years spent under the command of British officers, he had adhered to the notion that soldiers should avoid politics. [33] Yet the failings of the civilian government since 1947 convinced him that Pakistan's survival depended on the army. He then found himself alongside Ghulam Muhammad in 1953–54 when the 'Bengali threat' became a reality and he even agreed to serve as Minister of Defence. This experience, however, strengthened his misgivings about politicians. Mirza, the manipulator, did not seem much of an improvement: having urged him to impose martial law, he forced him to resign on 27 October 1958.

Ayub Khan took over the presidency from Mirza. The 1956 Constitution was abrogated, the governments – that of the centre as well as those of the provinces – were dismissed, the Assembly was dissolved, and political parties were declared illegal. Nearly 150 former ministers, from national as well as provincial governments, and 600 ex-deputies were put on trial for corruption. Among them were Suhrawardy and Firoz Khan Noon. The civil service did not escape the purge, since the commissions of inquiry set up by the new authorities forced the dismissal or premature retirement of 1,662 officials.[34] Finally, in March 1959, Ayub Khan promulgated a decree confirming his willingness to drive politicians from the public sphere: the Elective Bodies (Disqualification) Order (EBDO), under the terms of which those suspected of improper behaviour or corruption had the choice of trial or retirement from political life, the guilty being banned from public office until 31 December 1966. Several important politicians, including Mian Mumtaz Daultana, Firoz Khan Noon and M A Khurho – fell foul of the terms of EBDO. The main political parties lost their leaders.[35]

At the same time, Ayub Khan took several populist measures. A few weeks after seizing power he fixed the price of basic foodstuffs and promised agrarian reform. The 'feudal lords', whom no civilian government had as yet dared to attack, were the first victims of martial law. A commission charged with agrarian reform was appointed from as early as 31 October 1958: it reported on 7 February 1959 and on the basis of this report Ayub Khan's regime limited the maximum individual landholding to 500 acres of irrigated and 1,000 acres of non-irrigated land, allowing the redistribution of 2.2 million acres among 150,000 new property owners. The reform undoubtedly spared the middle-ranking landowners, the main recruitment source of so many Punjabi and Pashtun soldiers, but it was still greeted with approval by the press.

Ayub Khan also emphasized industrial development – as witness his decision to take over the presidency of the Planning Commission. This effort produced a rise in the average annual growth of manufacturing production during the second five-year plan (1960–65). He was popular among businessmen for his firm return to political stability. Nevertheless, only a minority gained from this boom, in particular the 'twenty-two families' who were said to own Pakistan. While this is an exaggeration, it is true that in 1962 four big merchant communities – the Memons, the Chiniotis, the Bohras and the Khojas – controlled two-thirds of the national industrial heritage, though they represented only 0.5 per cent of the population.[36] This trend was confirmed at the end of Ayub Khan's reign: in 1968 two-thirds of industry and 87 per cent of banking and insurance were in the hands of a couple of dozen families. 'These industrial families, together with an estimated 15,000 senior civil servants belonging to approximately 10,000 families, and about 500 generals and senior military officials, formed the core of the regime's bases of support in the urban areas.'[37]

Having achieved economic development, Ayub Khan also forced through the modernization of Islam in Pakistan. The religion seemed to him to be the sole basis of national unity but he took a public stand against the obscurantism of the ulemas, and sought to separate spiritual and temporal spheres.[38] He pressurized the imams in the mosques to open their thoughts to Western science and to reform the Muslim practices which stood in the way of the country's progress, such as divorce by the mere repudiation of wives, and polygamy, itself in part responsible for the country's disturbing demographic growth. To this effect on 15 July 1961 he promulgated the Muslim Family Laws Ordinance (MFLO), establishing a council of arbitration, to which all demands for divorce had to be submitted, which insisted on a three-month period during which the couple had to attempt reconciliation. This procedure conformed to the Islamic tradition of *talaq al-ahsan*, while husbands often preferred pure and simple repudiation of their wives according to *talaq al-bid'a*. This council was also charged with obtaining the first wife's assent when a man wanted to remarry. Should he fail to submit to the council's decision, he was liable to a punishment which might extend to as much as a year in gaol. Finally the MFLO allowed orphans of both father and mother irrespective of sex, to inherit from their grandparents. All these reforms clearly reflected the University of Aligarh's modernizing influence on the young Ayub Khan, before he continued his studies in England. From traditional Islam he extracted a political model, that of the Caliph Omar (634–44), who governed alone, though from time to time he took advice from a consultative committee. Ayub Khan cast the Parliament in this role.[39]

Even if Ayub Khan's speeches were studded with democratic references, (such as 'controlled democracy', of which he was especially fond)[40], his political ideal was reminiscent of the authoritarian paternalism of the Punjabi administration of the British period. The Basic Democracies Order, promulgated to mark the first anniversary of his coming to power, in fact established a political regime very similar to the indirect administration of the Raj. The aim of this political mechanism was to coopt local notables who could form a link with government authority, both local and regional, just like the collaborators whom the British saw as the 'national leaders' of the rural world. There were four levels. At village level, the committee was elected by universal suffrage; but at the *tehsil*, regional and provincial level the 'basic democrats' who served on the committees were elected by indirect ballot. These authorities, as in colonial times, inevitably included a high proportion of members chosen by central government or by those acting in its name – this proportion could be as high as 50 per cent. Moreover, these 'basic democrats' formed an 80,000 strong electoral college, half chosen from West Pakistan and half from East Pakistan, with whom lay the responsibility of electing the President. Ayub Khan, as the only candidate, was thus elected in January 1960 by 75,084 votes to 2,829.

The Constitution was promulgated on 8 June 1962, at the moment when martial law was lifted, and formally sanctioned the rule of Ayub Khan. The presidential right of veto over decisions of the single-chamber Parliament was absolute in all fields except that of finance[41] – even in the event of a two-thirds-majority vote, because the President could always submit the matter for decision by referendum. The National Assembly was clearly within the President's control. It was elected, just as he was, by the electoral college formed by the 80,000 'basic democrats', whose votes he could readily buy or force. Even if members of the opposition managed to get elected – as was the case in April 1962, when Ayub Khan failed to gain a two-thirds majority (necessary where votes on constitutional amendments were concerned) – he found the means to achieve his ends: some rural deputies were threatened with loss of water for their irrigation canals if they voted the wrong way.[42] Moreover, the April 1962 elections took place just when the courts had lost some of their room for manoeuvre, the press were still under censorship,[43] and political parties were still proscribed, thus preventing the formation of parliamentary groups and the mobilization of an opposition.

After martial law had been lifted, the Bengali leaders of the Awami League and the KSP revolted against the ban on political parties in the form of a common announcement on 24 June 1962. Their campaign compelled Ayub Khan to legalize them in July by the Political Parties Act. Suhrawardy then formed the National Democratic Front combining the Awami League, the KSP and the Jamaat-i Islami, the readiest of all to reorganize. Ayub Khan had to admit that political parties were back with a vengeance. As a result he established his own political party, the Muslim Convention League, created in September 1962 out of the debris of a breakaway faction of the Muslim League. Although he disdained to be a party man, Ayub Khan became its president in December 1963. Like Ghulam Muhammad and Mirza's Republican Party, it was no more than a collection of courtiers, a sycophantic coterie without any local connections. The majority of Muslim League veterans did not rally to it, but set up their own Muslim League Council, which, under the presidency of Khwaja Nazimuddin, joined the National Democratic Front.

This return to partisan politics was not complete because many politicians remained disqualified under the EBDO regulations, which still prevented the heavy-weights of Pakistani politics from contesting the 1965 presidential election. Fatima Jinnah, the Qaid-i Azam's sister, therefore stood against Ayub Khan with the support of most of the parties, including the Jamaat-i Islami. Its electoral campaign, under the slogan 'Democracy Against Dictatorship', found a profound echo among the population, as witnessed by the dense crowds attending its meetings in every corner of the country. The 'basic democrats' voted 65 per cent for Ayub Khan, but the confrontation left him weakened.

The military defeat of Pakistan by India in 1965 marked a far more decisive turning point a little later. Pakistan, having gained confidence from India's rout by the Chinese in 1962, took the initiative, but Ayub Khan and his army overestimated the Indian Kashmiris' determination to revolt against New Delhi, while they underestimated the Indian army's capacity to react. Kashmir remained relatively calm, despite the launching in the region of Operation Gibraltar by the Pakistan army; while the Indian air force replied by attacking Lahore and Sialkot on 6 September 1965, to the amazement of the authorities in Islamabad. On 22 September Ayub Khan had to accept a humiliating cease-fire, to the considerable displeasure of his Foreign Minister, Zulfikar Ali Bhutto, who took no part in the negotiations in Tashkent in January 1966, and even resigned from the government in June.

Ayub Khan never recovered from the defeat of 1965, which all the opposition parties were quick to exploit. On 13 January, the leaders of organizations as diverse as the Awami League and the Jamaat-i Islami held a joint press conference in Lahore to denounce the peace of Tashkent. This opposition was considerably strengthened by the creation of the Pakistan People's Party in November 1967 on the initiative of Z A Bhutto, who succeeded in channelling student agitation against the humiliation at Tashkent and the anger of the working class, those who had not benefited from economic growth.[44] The disturbances reached such proportions that on 13 November 1968 Ayub Khan had to put his former foreign minister under arrest for several weeks.

The Bengali question provided the final straw that broke the back of Ayub Khan. Mujibur Rahman's campaign for greater autonomy for East Pakistan led Islamabad to reimpose martial law on 17 March 1969. A few days later, on 25 March, the president resigned himself to stepping down. He invited his military chief, General Agha Muhammad Yahya Khan, to succeed him, thus scorning the constitutional procedures which foresaw the passage of power to the Assembly's president in the case of the president's resignation. Yahya Khan abrogated the Constitution, dissolved the assemblies and banned political parties, just as Ayub Khan had done eleven years earlier.

Democratization and Bengali Separatism

Yahya Khan came to power with no preconceived ideas.[45] Inheriting a delicate situation in which presidential power was being contested more and more, he was in no doubt that some concessions to the opposition were needed, as much in terms of political liberalization as of recognition of ethnic differences. Yet both these two lines of attack were still as unacceptable to the Punjabi elite as they had been in the 1950s. Any democratization – especially if it also meant a significant move towards recognition of the country's cultural diversity – must result in the end in submitting the Punjabis – indeed all of West Pakistan – to domination by the majority Bengalis, whose nationalist feelings had been aroused by decades of repression.[46]

The day after the taking up of duties, Yahya Khan announced free elections and then annulled the 'One Unit Scheme'. He also promulgated, on 30 March 1970, a Legal Framework Order stipulating that the future National Assembly would have 313 seats, of which 169 would go to East Pakistan, and that the provinces would enjoy autonomy under a federal system. Yahya Khan believed he was taking a calculated risk after the secret service had assured him that Mujibur Rahman's Awami League would not gain more than 80 seats.[47]

The 1970 elections and the regionalization of Pakistani politics

From the start of the election campaign the authorities, sticking to a custom that harked back to Mirza's Republican Party, appropriated one party: a Muslim League, whose leadership was entrusted to Abdul Qayyum Khan, former head of the NWFP government, which received significant subsidies. Yahya Khan also supported –

more or less directly – the Islamic parties, the Jamaat-i Islami, the Deobandi JUI and the Barelwi JUP (see Chapters 10 and 11 below). None of these organizations won more than 9 out of the 300 seats available – not only because they had never managed to gain a foothold in East Pakistan, where they had never gained a single seat, but above all because they clashed in West Pakistan with a new rival, the PPP.

Table 3.1 National Assembly elections, 1970 (by party and region)

	The Punjab	*Sind*	*NWFP*	*Baluchistan*	*West Pakistan*	*East Pakistan*	*Total*
Awami League	–	–	–	–	–	*160*	160
Pakistan People's Party (PPP)	62	18	1	–	*81*	–	81
Pakistan Muslim League (Qayyum Khan)	1	1	7	–	*9*	–	9
Convention Muslim League	7	–	–	–	*7*	–	7
Jamiyyat-ul Ulama (H)	–	–	6	1	*7*	–	7
Jamiyyat-ul Ulama-i Pakistan	4	3	–	–	*7*	–	7
National Awami Party (Wali Khan)	–	–	3	3	*6*	–	6
Jamaat-i Islami	1	2	1	–	*4*	–	4
Others	2	–	–	–	*2*	*1*	3
Independents	5	3	7	–	*15*	*1*	16
Total	82	27	25	4	*138*	*162*	300

Source: C. Baxter, 'Pakistan Votes – 1970', *Asian Survey*, 11 (3), March 1971.

The Pakistan People's Party, a new creation of Z A Bhutto, concentrated its efforts in West Pakistan alone, never putting up a candidate in the eastern half of the country. Its programme was more attractive, its leader more dynamic. For months Bhutto held meetings as he toured the whole of West Pakistan in the populist style embodied at the same time in India by Indira Gandhi. Bhutto went to the people to promise them '*roti, kapra aur makan*' (bread, clothes and a house). In answer to this slogan the religious parties could produce only the negative '*Socialism kufir hai: Muslim millat ek ho*' (Socialism is a heresy: let us defend the Muslim people). Bhutto accepted the epithet 'socialist' with good grace, since he claimed it made him the protector of the masses while fending off the implied criticism by qualifying his doctrine as 'Islamic socialism',[48] an idea he associated with *musawat*, the equality of all Muslims as defined by their religion. What was more, the extreme anti-Indian line that he had taken when he was Foreign Minister (and after) had given him a nationalist image that was very attractive to Muhajirs and Punjabis alike. Thus Bhutto overcame the handicaps of being a Shi'a Sindi. The PPP took 81 seats – 62 in the Punjab, where it had contested 82, and 18 out of 27 in Sind. It was the main victor in West Pakistan despite a clear rejection in Baluchistan and the NWFP, two provinces where the Islamic and ethnic parties triumphed, a sign of the growing regionalization of the political game in Pakistan.

This trend, which would have been systematic but for Bhutto's incursions into the Punjab, was even more evident from the tidal wave with which the Awami League swept through East Pakistan. Frustrating the prognostications of the agents of army intelligence, Mujibur Rahman's party took 160 of the 162 seats available in East Bengal. Such a success was unlikely to induce a moderation of his claims for autonomy.

Democratization leads to a second partition

The 1970 elections confirmed West Pakistan's fears: the use of democratic procedures could have only one effect – the transfer of power to the Bengalis as a result of the simple play of demographic forces.

Bhutto did not leave it at that. As soon as the results came out, he declared that the law of the majority was not the only consideration in politics, and that the historic role played by the PPP in the struggle against Ayub Khan gave it the right to share power. Mujibur Rahman replied on 3 January 1971 that the Awami League was now the majority party, and his intention was to endow the country with a new constitution based on his Six-Point Programme. Conversations ensued between Rahman, Yahya Khan and Bhutto, but they were inconclusive; the latter two were adamant that they would not concede the power Rahman claimed. The events that followed have been related in Chapter 2 above.

Yahya Khan put off *sine die* the convocation of the National Assembly. The Awami League then organized demonstrations for 3 March, the day the Assembly had been due to meet. Yahya Khan announced soon after that his deputies would take their seats on 25 March, but Rahman stipulated further conditions for his party's participation, among which were the lifting of martial law and the immediate transfer of power to the Assembly. The conversations continued, but on 23 March, the anniversary of the Lahore Resolution, Rahman announced that he would accept only a Pakistani confederation where central government would retain limited sovereign prerogatives. On the advice of the military, who encouraged him to resort once more to force in order to eradicate the Awami League, Yahya Khan launched Operation Searchlight at midnight on 25 March. Students at Dhaka University, some of Rahman's most faithful supporters, were the first targets – the army's intervention left hundreds of victims strewn about the campus. The soldiers or police employed in the repression were all either Punjabis or Biharis, Urduspeakers who had come from Bihar in 1947, or their descendants.

Mujibur Rahman was arrested, but some of his lieutenants made it to India, where they set up a government-in-exile on 17 April. In total, ten million refugees from East Pakistan found refuge in India. The Indian army lent support to the Mukti Bahini, the liberation army consisting of commandos largely from among the youth, who carried on guerrilla operations in the name of Bangladesh. In November 1971 India launched a full-scale attack which it had been preparing for some time. The war lasted only two weeks, during which the Pakistani forces lost half their fleet, a third of their army and a quarter of their air force.[49] On 16 December Islamabad was forced to sign a humiliating cease-fire under the terms of which India held as prisoners 93,000 soldiers captured in the area around Dhaka.

The rout was such that the army had to persuade Yahya Khan to resign and entrust power to a civilian, Bhutto. It was on 20 December, therefore, that Bhutto became President and the administrator of martial law. The transition to democracy, initiated after the 1965 war, resumed after the conflict of 1971. Unfortunately, it seems that Pakistan lacked the internal resources necessary to consolidate a democratization process that, once again, was prompted by an external crisis.

The Bhutto Years: Democracy's False Dawn

Zulfikar Ali Bhutto found himself faced with the same challenge as his predecessors: he had to assert the primacy of those returned to power over the military and the bureaucrats. In seeking to do so he did hold one personal trump: his extraordinary fighting spirit, and a popularity not seen since the days of Jinnah, to whom he largely owed his social and nationalistic programme. Yet his origins provoked some doubts over his progressiveness: even if he had studied law in England, he remained a *wadera*, a big Sindi property owner, whose lands in Larkana stretched as far as the eye could see. All his biographers have stressed the ambivalence of a man who combined modern values with feudal attitudes.[50]

Bhutto started by showing the military that he was the real captain of the ship. Four months after his accession to power, 29 senior officers had been shown the door, including his chief of army staff, General Gul Hassan Khan, who was replaced by General Tikka Khan.[51] The new President wanted to build a more professional army in the service of the civil government[52] and at first the soldiers approved of his reforms,[53] all the more so as military expenditure remained very high – 59.3 per cent of the budget in 1972–73 and 44.7 per cent in 1976–77.[54] To counterbalance the military influence however, in October 1972 Bhutto created a federal security force under the control of central government, with the duty of helping the police in operations to maintain civil order. The army never accepted this new institution, which soon boasted 18,500 men, seeing it as a force to limit the risk of a putsch. The military had to take an oath never to take part in any political activity, and the crime of high treason was defined as an act seeking to subvert the Constitution by force. Nevertheless, Bhutto brought the army to the front of the political stage involuntarily in 1973, when he dismissed the government of Baluchistan and committed himself to a war that involved 80,000 men in 1977. This deployment of force showed just how dependent the civilian government was on the armed forces.

Nor did Bhutto succeed in freeing himself from the influence of the civil service. Following the example of his predecessors, he certainly indulged in 'spoil system' tactics in his dealings with senior civil servants. He even abolished the Police Service of Pakistan and the Civil Service of Pakistan, the state's aristocracy which was still providing the country's 'steel frame', and absorbed them into a new All-Pakistan Unified Grade.[55] He had to resign himself, however, to restoring something of their old glory to the bureaucrats when the nationalizations in which he indulged in the 1970s demanded the skills of a greater number of them. Other 'socialist' measures, such as agrarian reforms, led him also to rely on the bureaucrats: as defender of an ideology in which the state must be the architect of social progress, Bhutto could not manage without the civil service.

The force Bhutto was able to muster to face the army and the administration was largely the result of the popular legitimacy of his programme, combining as it did democracy and socialism. He was indeed the architect of the first Pakistani democratization that Yahya Khan had only managed to sketch out under pressure of circumstances. Four months after seizing power, on 21 April 1972, he put an end to martial law by promulgating a temporary constitution. This was superseded on 14 August 1973 by Pakistan's third Constitution, which is still in place today, although it has been amended many times. This introduced a truly parliamentary system where power was in the hands of a Prime Minister elected by the Assembly, rather than in those of the President. Article 48, for example, stipulates that the Prime Minister's signature should also appear on presidential decrees.

From the time of the promulgation of the Constitution, Bhutto therefore occupied the position of prime minister, the post of president going to a background figure, Fazlal Elahi Chaudhry. The Constitution reaffirmed the Islamic character of Pakistan – both prime minister and president must be Muslims. It foresaw, as replacement for the Advisory Council on Islamic Ideology, in suspended animation since the mid 1960s (see Note 38), the nomination by the president of a Council on Islamic Ideology. This body, whose role was to be no more than consultative, was charged with 'the total Islamization of Pakistan', due to be completed by the 1980s.[56]

The new government's socioeconomic reform programme started with a fresh launching of agrarian reform. The limit for large landowners was reduced to 150 acres of irrigated and 300 acres of non-irrigated land. All the same, this measure did not lead to a very substantial redistribution in favour of the most deprived, because the land thus acquired was often of low quality. Furthermore, the title to property could be transferred within a family, and the owners of tractors and drilled wells had the right to additional areas Bhutto admitted the limited success of this reform quite frankly during the 1977 election campaign, promising the further reduction in ceilings for holdings to 100 and 200 acres respectively. For the workers, Bhutto announced a range of measures on 10 February 1971: the unions gained influence thanks to the introduction of labour courts to which their disputes with bosses could be submitted. In the factories, workers' representatives had to be elected, and businesses were under an obligation to distribute between 2 per cent and 4 per cent of their profits to the workforce.[57]

As far as the economic reforms were concerned, the nationalizations were the main achievement. From January 1972 Bhutto transferred to the public sector more than 30 large organizations in a dozen industrial sectors, ranging from the iron and steel industry to petrochemicals, and including electrical materials. It was a matter of bringing into line the so-called '22 families' who still controlled the Pakistani economy. Nationalizations extended into the financial sector – life insurance, then certain banks by early 1974. Between 1973 and 1976 Bhutto completed his plan for the nationalization of companies producing or distributing goods for direct consumption, such as rice and cotton, but this alienated a number of small entrepreneurs and merchants who had supported him since the 1970 elections.

Apart from a weakening of power due to these sector-based measures and to failure to keep his promises, Bhutto was suffering two major handicaps on the eve of the 1977 elections. First of all his party, the PPP, which did not have a particularly solid foundation, had sunk into a sort of lethargy ever since its leader had been preoccupied with governmental matters. Bhutto made an effort to reorganize it in December 1976, in view of the forthcoming general elections, but he put in as leaders faithful friends of no great calibre. This only reinforced the centralization and personalization of power – indeed the PPP experienced the same process of deinstitutionalization as which Indira Gandhi's party was suffering at the same time. Secondly, Bhutto had not yet completed his programme of social reforms, as his agrarian reforms show, and just before the 1977 elections he did not hesitate to go against this for the sake of mere opportunism, nominating to his party a number of property owner.

The elections, organized in March, saw a vigorous opposition campaign. Bhutto waited until January to announce them, to put his adversaries at a time disadvantage, but by 11 March nine opposition parties had grouped under the banner of the Pakistan National Alliance (PNA). This coalition ranged from traditional religious bodies to leftist groups, including various fractions of the Muslim League. Most observers were of the opinion that the PPP would definitely suffer in the face of a unified opposition.[58] The results, giving 155 seats out of 200 to the PPP against 36 to the PNA, were therefore regarded with suspicion abroad, and denounced by the opposition as the inevitable result of fraud on a grand scale. The PNA organized demonstrations in which two social groups which had supported Bhutto in the past – the students and the small traders – also joined. Repression of the demonstration resulted in 200 deaths over a 14-day period, and this only reinforced the opposition. Lahore, Karachi and Hyderabad had to be placed under martial law.

Bhutto called for support from the army, which lost no opportunity to denounce the negligence of corrupt politicians and justify a new *coup d'état*. This initiative was taken by General Zia ul-Haq, whom Bhutto had appointed head of the army a little while before, imagining that he had acquired the services of a docile man. The military seized power – bloodlessly, even gently – on 5 July 1977. Zia immediately announced that new elections would take place in 90 days. The leaders of the PPP, including Bhutto, and of the PNA were arrested, but released after three weeks. However, Zia did assume the title of administrator-in-chief of martial law and, going back on his promises, submitted the country to a long and repressive military regime, though not without regular announcements of impending elections.

The Zia Era: A Military Regime
in the Service of Islam

General Zia had been appointed head of the army by Bhutto in spring 1976, thus bypassing a dozen more senior officers on the grounds of 'his great piety, his patriotism and his professionalism'.[59] In Pakistan, 'patriot' is often a synonym for 'anti-Indian'. Zia's hostility towards India was indeed particularly vehement – so much the more so because, born in East Punjab in 1924, he had had to emigrate with his family in 1947, and remained haunted by this trauma. His professionalism and his piety were to lie at the heart of his political project: the careful construction of an authoritarian regime in the name of Islamic ideology.

An authoritarian regime reinforced by the war in Afghanistan

Bhutto was the Zia's first victim. He was arrested once more on 3 September 1977, accused of being behind an attempt on the life of one of his PPP rivals in 1974. His wife, Begum Nusrat, whom he had appointed to head his party, contested the constitutionality of the Prime Minister's detention in court. The Supreme Court dismissed her case on the grounds of the doctrine of 'State necessity', which was previously invoked in 1954. The judges further confirmed Zia in his position of administrator-in-chief of martial law, and therefore his powers to legislate and to amend the Constitution. The Punjab tribunal declared Bhutto guilty, and condemned him to death on 18 March 1978. Zia remained deaf to international pressure for a presidential pardon, and Bhutto was hanged on 3 April 1979.

Zia did not wait for Bhutto's execution to lay the foundations for his dictatorial regime. Although there had been no abrogation of the Constitution, and although right up to the early 1980s he presented himself as only a temporary director of operations who wanted to hold early elections, he ruled with a rod of iron, supported by the army. Unlike Ayub Khan, he retained his position as Chief of Army Staff (COAS) thanks to a constitutional amendment, and combined it with that of President from 1978. The Council of Advisers he set up on 14 January 1978 was directed by officers and bureaucrats: thus 10 per cent of civil administrative posts were reserved for the military, and a large number of officers were brought out of retirement to take up positions as governors of provinces or as ambassadors.[60] Meanwhile, Zia managed to coopt politicians from the Muslim League, the first being Muhammad Khan Junejo, who entered the government in a ministerial reshuffle marking the first anniversary of the putsch. Once again, members of the Muslim League did not hesitate to compromise themselves with the military regime. All the same, Zia banned parties and political meetings on 16 October 1978, when censorship had also been reinforced. He completed his project at the end of 1981, when he appointed 350 members of a purely consultative assembly, the Majlis-i Shura, whose principal role was to guide the Islamization policy, the regime's grand design.

General Zia cemented his authority in a favourable context, that of the war in Afghanistan. The Soviet invasion launched on 28 December 1979 led in effect to the United States supporting Pakistan in its efforts to contain communist expansion – a policy which Zia knew how to milk for all he was worth. Not only did he receive a \$3.2 billion hand-out from Washington over a period of six years, but he also escaped American pressures – indeed, western pressures more widely – in favour of a return to democracy and the defence of human rights. Zia occupied too strategic a position to be upset by interference in the internal affairs of his country. Pakistan could even pursue a nuclear programme without the United

States taking any action except protestations and the customary warnings,[61] although it had vigorously criticized Bhutto's launching of the programme.[6] The army also profited from the conflict in Afghanistan in financial terms. In 1981, military expenditure represented 6.9 per cent of Gross National Product and 29.1 per cent of the total budget.[63]

Islam as state ideology

Zia typified a new social background to the Pakistan army. Officers now came more and more from the Punjabi middle class, known for their conservative and orthodox religious attitudes. In his first televised address, he declared with conviction: 'Pakistan, created in the name of Islam, will only survive if it continues to adhere to Islam'. First he enforced Islamization of the economy, forbidding the charging of interest [riba] in 1979 as required by the precepts of Islam. Another financial measure followed on 20 June 1979 in the form of a charity tax in line with the Islamic tradition of zakat, whereby every Muslim should make voluntary and disinterested donations. In the statist version introduced by Zia, zakat took the form of an automatic 2.5 per cent tax on all deposit accounts.[64]

Islamization was then extended to education. Islamic and Koranic studies became compulsory. In 1982, diplomas issued by Islamic seminaries became recognized as equivalent to master's degrees in Arabic and Muslim civilization [Islamayat]. Students from seminaries could be entitled to government bursaries partly financed from the zakat. In its struggle against illiteracy the Government sought support from the madrasahs and encouraged the establishment of 12,000 of these 'mosque schools'.[65]

The most dramatic effects of the Islamization policy however, were felt in the legal system. Zia attacked judicial power, demanding that judges must swear allegiance to him – a decision which led some to resign and others to remain silent. At the same time civil law was being used concurrently with martial law and – more to the point – tribunals were charged with seeing that sharia law was respected. From 1979, the tribunals of the country's four provinces were placed under the surveillance of other tribunals charged with flushing out laws which were contrary to Islam. These in turn were replaced in May 1980 by a Federal Shari'ah Court, which broke new ground a year later when it appointed ulemas as judges. From 1982, some ulemas also sat on the Shari'ah Appellate Bench of the Supreme Court. The entire system was completed in 1984 with the creation of 'Qazi courts', which ensured that sharia was followed at the local level. Here again, ulemas could sit as judges.

This judicial apparatus was charged with administering an Islamic penal code, introduced by regulations in 1979. These covered the punishments set out in the Koran and the Sunna – as for example, beatings and amputations – to punish the those who committed murder, adultery, perjury and blasphemy. Women convicted of adultery could henceforth find themselves liable to 100 strokes of the cane, or even to being stoned. Rapists on the other hand, were liable only to a prison sentence. In practice, a raped woman could even find herself accused of adultery.[66] Islamization of the legal code therefore aggravated inequality between the sexes – as witness the presidential decree of 1984 on 'the establishment of proof' [*Qanoon-i Shahadat*] under the terms of which the testimony of one man was considered equal to that of two women.[67]

The treatment of women by the regime, which also included the introduction of a particularly strict dress code for air hostesses and television announcers, evoked protests from the Women's Action Forum and from the All-Pakistani Women's Association – founded by Liaquat Ali Khan's widow. When their members marched on 12 February 1983, the police dispersed the demonstrators with tear-gas bombs. The women's agitation underlined how far the Islamization policy had fallen out of step with a country where women had, little by little, taken up responsible jobs in all walks of public life, including the courts, as witness the establishment of the Women Lawyers Association.

Privately some senior elements in the Pakistan army showed their scepticism about the Islamization policy.[68] The senior officers, most of whom had been trained overseas in a more or less cosmopolitan atmosphere, struggled to combine their modern identity with their Muslim faith, but were disturbed by the excesses of the Islamization policy, which was supported mainly by middle-ranking officers who – like Zia himself – came from the Punjabi middle classes.

Islamization was out of step with the culture of a country where Sufism was an old tradition, one that the ulemas had always stigmatised for its heterodoxy without lessening its popularity. Besides, for the Shi'a, who made up 20 per cent of the population, Zia's policy was frankly discriminatory. *Zakat* was never a Shi'a practice and only Sunni sat in Shari'ah Courts. The Shi'a reaction to Islamization was the setting up in 1979 of a new organization called the Tahrik Nifaz Fiqh-i Jafaria (TNFJ), the Movement for the Establishment of Shi'a Law. With the support of Iran, this body echoed the ideology of Ayatollah Khomeini during the 1980s, and reacted violently against any surfacing of overradical Sunni militancy. Far from effecting the Islamisation of Pakistan, Zia's policy tended to nourish sectarian conflicts which inevitably became more bitter in the 1990s.

The ultimate impossibility of democratization

By the beginning of the 1980s, the militant Shi'a and the feminists were no longer alone in taking to the streets. The opposition began to take the initiative little by little. In 1981 eleven parties came together to launch the Movement for the Restoration of Democracy (MRD). The Muslim League and the Jamaat-i Islami, always ready to collaborate with the authorities, did not participate in this alliance. Nor, indeed, did the Pashtun and Baluchi separatists. The latter were grateful to Zia for freeing 9,000 prisoners captured during the Bhutto period; as for the Pashtuns, Zia continued to coopt them into the army and anyway, they approved of his involvement in Afghanistan against the Soviet aggressor.

The MRD was especially popular in Sind, since the architect of the movement was the PPP, and Sind had always been the bastion of the party's campaigns. The peasants of Sukkur, Larkana, Jacobabad and Khaipur mobilized *en masse* for a return to democracy and in the name of Sindi nationalism: Bhutto, founder of the

PPP, first political leader of the ballot box, martyred by Zia, was their symbol. It took three divisions of soldiers to quell the disturbances. In the course of three weeks of repression alone, the governor of Sind recorded 189 deaths and nearly 2,000 prisoners.

This was at the time when Zia seemed to want to acquire at least the semblance of popular legitimacy. On 12 August 1983 he assured the country that there would be elections before March 1985, and in December 1984 he organized a referendum asking Pakistanis whether they approved of his policy of Islamization and his continued wish to transfer power to the representatives of the people – a transfer that had in fact never started, but one that Zia announced regularly. The MRD called for a boycott of the election, and the small numbers seen at the booths on 19 December 1984 led many observers to doubt the official results: turnout 62.15 per cent, yes votes 97.71 per cent. Zia quickly announced legislative elections, while stating that political parties were still proscribed. The MRD again called for a boycott, but few took any notice and the electors were relatively enthusiastic about this ballot.[69]

The National Assembly and the regional assemblies produced by the ballot box in February 1985 largely consisted of property owners, representatives of the business community, and men with sufficient means to participate in an election without the support of a political party. Zia took advantage of the first parliamentary session to have himself enthroned as President of Pakistan and to appoint Muhammad Khan Junejo Prime Minister. By choosing a man from Sind he hoped to nip in the bud that province's mobilizing behind the MRD. Martial law was eventually lifted on 30 December 1985, and the parties regained their right to exist. The Muslim League reconstituted under the aegis of Junejo, and become the party of government once more, but in a very different form. Above all Benazir Bhutto returned from exile in London in April 1986, and was arrested in August for joining a demonstration in support of free elections.

Zia never really intended to liberalize the regime. In any case, he had radically changed the 1973 Constitution by passing the 8th amendment which allowed the President to dismiss any government, the one in Islamabad as well as those in the provinces; to dissolve both national and provincial assemblies and to nominate the chief judges and the military leaders. This presidentialization of the fundamental law of the land could only halt the democratization process, a fact to which the forced dismissal of every Prime Minister during the 1990s bears witness. On 29 May 1988 Zia reminded everyone that he was the only captain of the ship of state when he dismissed Junejo and pronounced the dissolution of the Assembly. He justified his decision by citing the need to take Karachi under direct control since it had fallen victim to Muhajir demonstrations. This pretext would be used again and again during the years to come: authoritarian repression had reached its limit.

An air accident on 17 August 1988 relaunched the whole process. The crash killed Zia and, notably, the US ambassador. All sorts of rumours circulated about the possible causes of this air disaster. The Pakistani commission of inquiry concluded sabotage, but was unable to establish who might have been its authors; while the Americans stuck to the hypothesis of a mechanical failure.

The day after Zia died, General Mirza Aslam Beg, Chief of Army Staff, declared that the military were withdrawing from the business of politics. He decided to respect constitutional procedure and allowed the president of the Senate, Ghulam Ishaq Khan, to take over as interim president. He then confirmed that the elections Zia had envisaged for 16 November would indeed take place on that date. That ballot marked the return to a multiparty parliamentary democracy.

Democratization under influence

The Pakistani democratization of 1980 to 1990 has sometimes been seen as a good illustration of the third wave of democracy,[70] which, after leaving Europe in the 1970s, spread into Latin America and Asia.[71] This analysis has not, however, been borne out in Pakistan, where power has remained in non-elected hands: the army and the President.

The return of the Bhuttos, or of 'diarchy'?

In 1988 the PPP was the only organization led by a popular leader, Benazir Bhutto. Apart from her family heritage, this woman had an emotional capital based on the 'martyrdom' of her father, the mysterious assassination of one of her brothers, and the placing under house arrest of both her mother and herself. On this foundation she developed a political programme with populist overtones. Its two themes were the return to democracy and the cause of the poor, both of which had been at the heart of Z A Bhutto's discourse in the early 1970s.

The PPP's return to the front of the political stage gave birth to the formation of an opposition coalition, the Islami Jamhuri Ittehad (IJI – Islamic Democratic Alliance),[72]which brought together eight parties including Nawaz Sharif's Muslim League and Junejo's Muslim League. The military and the Inter-Services Intelligence had supported the formation of this alliance, which had to contain the PPP in order to continue some of Zia's policies. They did their best to set Zia up as a martyr – and not without some success, since the commemoration of the first anniversary of his death in the Faizal mosque in Islamabad attracted a million people. The IJI, meanwhile, rallied Islamic groups such as the JI with an Islamic rhetoric inherited from Zia.

Sure of her success, Benazir Bhutto withdrew from the MRD before the November 1988 elections. In fact, far from repeating its performances of the 1970s, the PPP won only 92 out of 207 seats, with 25.1 per cent of the votes cast. The principal province, the Punjab, completely eluded it. The IJI, which won just 45 seats, did best there, and also carried the majority in the regional elections held at the same time. The PPP was therefore forced to ally itself with the MQM, which had taken 13 seats in the towns of Sind, while Benazir Bhutto had, of course, retained the support of the countryside, where the Sindis of the old stock, who were hostile to the Muhajirs, lived. The heterogeneous nature of this coalition was not, however, the only cause of the malfunctioning of the government she formed in December 1988.

Benazir Bhutto naturally tried to abrogate the 8th Amendment to the Constitution which General Zia had taken great care to have voted in to strengthen the power of the president, and through him, the army. To do so she needed a two-thirds majority in the National Assembly, and this she could not achieve.

She therefore remained dependent upon President Ishaq Khan, through whom the army continued to exert a strong influence, notably in the conduct of external affairs. So Benazir Bhutto had to keep Zia's Foreign Minister, Yakub Ali Khan, in her government. As to the management of matters to do with Afghanistan and Kashmir, she was very much in the hands of the ISI. Benazir tried to resist it – protesting, for example, against its right to appoint the judges of provincial tribunals. She even tried to appeal against this decision before the Supreme Court before deciding not to do so after all.

The first free elections since the 1970s therefore reestablished, under a new form, the old 'colonial diarchy'.[73] In British times this described the mechanism put in place during the 1919 reforms: where a protoparliamentary system had been introduced in the provinces, the governors, taking their authority from the viceroy, had control over the ministers; the executive was simultaneously under both a head of government and a governor. So in 1988 Pakistan remained shackled to the vice-regal dimension of their British heritage: the prime minister was responsible to a democratically elected Assembly, but was also under the thumb of a president who himself had not submitted to the people's vote, and owed his authority to military support.

The political parties, which had only limited room for manoeuvre, did not use it – on the contrary, they bolstered the arguments of those who already doubted the benefits of democracy. The long-distance duel between Benazir Bhutto and Nawaz Sharif tended to discredit politicians as a whole. Having become head of the Punjabi government, Sharif used this regional base to carry on a more or less daily opposition to Benazir Bhutto. For the first time in Pakistan's history, the principal province, which usually attracted all the resentment of the minority regions, took the lead in the mobilization against Islamabad. Benazir had to expend most of her energy responding to Sharif's criticisms. Her government became bogged down – when it was not completely paralysed by obstructionism. The PPP itself had launched hostilities of this kind on 7 December 1988 by making all the deputies leave the Punjabi assembly in response to Sharif's plan for a corrective financial law.

If the politicians' behaviour exasperated the military and the President, the fate of Benazir's government was sealed by altogether more violent disturbances in Sind. On 2 December 1988, the PPP and the MQM had ratified a 'Charter of Peace, Love and Rights' envisaging a settlement between the urban and rural populations of Sind. The text foresaw in particular an increase in the employment quotas in favour of the Muhajirs, facilitating their access to education and 'repatriating' some 250,000 'Biharis' still living in refugee camps in Bangladesh. In exchange, the MQM renounced all separatist demands. The matter of the 'Biharis' rapidly became a bone of contention between the MQM and the government, since such an influx of immigrants was unacceptable to most of the 'old-stock' Sindis. So the PPP failed to keep its promise; as a result, the MQM allied itself with the IJI. The two parties drew up a draft 17-point agreement in which the return of the 'Biharis' occupied a prominent position. Thus reinforced, the opposition set down a censure motion which almost succeeded on 1 November 1989. These political realignments started an eruption of violence in Karachi and then Hyderabad, where the police opened fire on Muhajirs at Pucca Qila on 27 May 1990.[74]

This 'incident' gave President Ghulam Ishaq Khan a further pretext to dismiss Benazir Bhutto from her position as Prime Minister. In his view the government had shown itself unable to maintain 'law and order'. In fact, the President and the military had been waiting for an opportunity to get rid of Benazir for a long time.[75] In support of his decision to dismiss the Prime Minister and dissolve the National Assembly, Ishaq Khan also cited the downward slide into politics for its own sake, exemplified flagrantly by the collapse of the alliance with the MQM.

Nawaz Sharif in power: no change

Unlike the 1988 scenario, it was from a position of weakness that the PPP presented itself to the electorate on 24 October 1990. Benazir Bhutto had been a disappointment and could not hold on to all her allies (of which one was the MQM). The IJI seemed to provide an alternative. In Nawaz Sharif it had an enterprising leader who enjoyed the support of the military. Son of a Punjabi industrialist who had been deprived of some of his wealth by Z A Bhutto's nationalizations, Nawaz Sharif had run the family business before entering politics. He had been a minister under Zia, then led the government of the Punjab from 1988 to 1990; he had gradually made that province the heartland of his party, the Muslim League, the mainstay of the IJI, the coalition he now led. In 1990 this alliance won 92 of the 105 parliamentary seats in the Punjab, while the Pakistan Democratic Alliance – whose mainspring was still the PPP – relied on its Sindi bastion, where it won 24 seats out of 45. Its considerable loss of seats – the PDA won only half as many seats as the IJI – must however be contrasted with the small discrepancy in the number of votes, 36.65 per cent compared with 32.37 per cent – a distortion linked to the first-past-the-post system. With 92 seats out of the 198 at stake the IJI had an absolute majority, but not the two-thirds majority necessary for a change in the Constitution.

Appointed prime minister in December 1990, Nawaz Sharif set the country on the path of economic liberalism demanded by the business community he came from. In February 1991 he announced a relaxation of exchange controls and eight months later no fewer than 89 public corporations were in the throes of privatization. He relaunched the Islamization policy and had a 'Shari'ah Bill' passed in May 1991. This law, however, did not satisfy all the Islamic parties in the coalition, because it barely extended the powers of the shariat courts, and recognized the non-Sunni ' right to apply their version of Muslim Personal Law. This measure, intended to mollify the Shi'a, angered the Jamaat-i Islami, which withdrew from the coalition on 5 May 1992, after Nawaz Sharif had given his support to a United Nations proposal concerning the introduction of an interim consensus government in Afghanistan.[76]

Nawaz Sharif's strong suit was his populist agenda. He brought in several measures that were widely publicized, but did lead to real social improvements. For example, he fixed a minimum wage of 1,500 rupees in July 1992, and gave permission for 40,000 households to obtain improved loans for the purchase of taxis, buses or trucks under a 'Self-Employment Scheme', soon rebaptized the 'Yellow Taxi Scheme'.

In the meantime, Nawaz Sharif seemed to be increasingly at odds with decisions by the military or the president. With the latter he got into a fight over the appointment of a new army chief following the retirement of General Beg and the sudden death of General Asif Nawaz Janjua.[77] Seeking to elude the president's supervision without bringing up the question of the 8th Amendment, he proposed in July 1991 a 12th amendment authorizing the prime minister to take over control of the administration of a province. The IJI, however, would not follow him in this for fear of upsetting the president. From that moment, Ishaq Khan lost confidence in his prime minister, and that lack of confidence was exacerbated when Nawaz Sharif failed to indicate whether or not he supported Ishaq Khan's reelection.

Like Benazir Bhutto before him, Nawaz Sharif fell in the end over the Muhajir question. Once again, disturbances in Karachi gave the president and the army good grounds for taking it out of civilian rule. In May 1992, after another outbreak of rioting in Karachi and other towns in Sind – partly linked to the MQM's split into the MQM (Haqiqi) and the MQM (Altaf), the army launched Operation Clean-Up and acted with particular vigour in Karachi, where they discovered arms dumps and torture chambers for which they held the MQM responsible.[78] On 18 April 1993, the president dismissed the prime minister and dissolved the Assembly, but Nawaz Sharif – who the previous day had had the nerve during a television programme, to denounce 'conspiracy' on the part of Ishaq Khan – appealed to the Supreme Court against the president's decision. On 26 May the judges ruled in his favour, declaring the dismissal non-constitutional. Nawaz Sharif was restored to his post, then fought to make the High Court of Lahore reinstate the government of the Punjab, which had suffered a fate similar to his own. The judges followed the lead of the Supreme Court, thus confirming the judicial authorities' U-turn. The civil state's legal triumph, was short-lived however. The army corps commanders met urgently on 1 July to resolve the crisis – a sign that it was they who had the upper hand in political life. On 18 July the Chief of Army Staff produced a compromise solution whereby Ghulam Ishaq Khan and Nawaz Sharif were both called upon to resign.

The corruption of the democratic process

The 1993 elections brought the PPP to power, even though it won fewer votes than the Pakistan Muslim League (N) – 38.1 per cent compared with 39.7 per cent – just because of the inherent distortions of this balloting procedure. However, Benazir Bhutto with 86 seats out of 202 was a long way from a majority. So once again she had to look for allies among the independents – some factions from the Muslim League (such as the group led by Junejo) and the MQM once again. This was a customary weakness.

Nevertheless, her position as Prime Minister looked more secure when the PPP managed to elect one of its senior members, Farooq Leghari, to the post of president in November 1993. This success seemed to solve the problem of the 8th Amendment, and reinforce the parliamentary dimension of the regime. In fact Leghari, unlike his predecessors, resolved from the start to do whatever his Prime Minister wanted. In accordance with her wishes, for instance, he suspended the NFWP government, substituting one from the PPP.

Nonetheless, the 'transition to democracy' became less and less smooth. Parliament was truly marginalized: the prime minister, far from seeking favourable votes from the deputies, preferred to resort to presidential orders, of which there were already too many: 93 in 1994 but 133 in 1995.[79] The government resisted the temptation to corruption even less than it had in the past.[80] Asif Ali Zardari, the prime minister's husband was a symbol of the degradation. He was minister of investments, but he was better known as 'Mr Ten Per Cent' as a result of the commission this post enabled him to pocket.[81] Quite apart from corruption, the criminalization of the state was also evident in another spate of political assassinations, the most spectacular of which was that of the prime minister's brother, Murtaza Bhutto. On his return from exile in Syria on 4 November 1993, with the firm intention of entering politics to take advantage of his prestigious name, he set himself up as a rival to his sister. He had the support of his mother, which led Benazir to dismiss her from her position as PPP vice-president. Murtaza was very critical of Asif Ali Zardari, and some commentators went so far as to lay at the door of the prime minister's husband the murder of his brother-in-law in Karachi on 20 September 1996.

Corruption and criminalization in the political sphere seemed to intensify as the war in Afghanistan developed. Contraband in arms and opium often flourished under the protection of politicians in return for certain services from the traffickers. These same gangs would carry on their dirty work around the polling stations, for example, on election day to keep opponents at a distance. This drift into illegality was also connected with the growth of religious extremism. The electoral decline of the Islamic parties, which had been evident since democratization in 1988, went hand in hand with the rise in power of small groups of Sunni and Shi'a which emerged as a reaction to General Zia's Islamization. On the sunni side, the Tahrik-i Nifaz-i Shari'ah Muhammadi (TNSM), established in 1989, came to public attention for the first time on 11 May 1994, when they blocked the Malakand Pass in the NWFP, demanding replacement of the civil law by the sharia. The movement was vigorously repressed as it became clear that it was sheltering Afghan fighters in cooperation with the drug barons. The ensuing troubles led to some forty deaths, and they did not subside until November 1994, after the NWFP government had strengthened the judicial powers of the mullahs.

Conflicts between Sunni and Shi'a also took a more violent turn during the 1990s, especially in Jhang district, where they were spurred on by socioeconomic rivalries.[82] The rival groups were supported on the one side by Iran and on the other by Saudi Arabia which was carrying on a long-range war for Islamic leadership on Pakistani soil.[83] Meanwhile, the Iranian Cultural Centre was the object of an attack in January 1997, for which no one claimed responsibility. In this context of 'sectarian' mobilization the state thwarted a military coup whose instigators – two colonels and two other officers – planhed to declare Pakistan a 'Sunni state'. Although it was put down, this conspiracy showed how popular Islamic arguments were among some middle-ranking officers: a legacy of the Zia era.

In the end, Benazir lost power not through some military decision but following the president's intervention in a sequence of events that is now common knowledge. Benazir Bhutto's personalization of power and growing authoritarianism had been steadily alienating Leghari, who had at first taken kindly to her but was not immune to a certain jealousy of her power. In 1994 Benazir made it a point of honour that she herself should nominate eleven High Court judges including three women who did not yet have sufficient seniority and who – according to the Constitution – should have been nominated by the chief justice of the Punjabi tribunal. When this news reached the Supreme Court, on 20 March 1996, it declared the nominations illegal. Benazir carried on regardless, so lawyers in Karachi and Lahore boycotted these 'political judges'. On 21 September, Leghari came down on the side of the Supreme Court. Benazir gave in and suspended the nomination of the eleven judges, but her relationship with Leghari became strained.

Three incidents, which tarnished the prime minister's image, gave the president the necessary grounds to justify her dismissal. First there was the disclosure in the London *Independent* that she had just purchased a luxurious villa in Surrey; then there was the murder of her brother, Murtaza Bhutto, which some people laid at her door because of their known political rivalry; finally, there were her attempts to buy the votes of some deputies from the Punjab, in order to put in place a government that would be favourable to her. Leghari decided to dismiss the prime minister and dissolve the National Assembly on 5 November 1996. This time the Supreme Court ratified her dismissal.

Nawaz Sharif II, or parliamentary dictatorship

The February 1997 elections took place in a climate of tension. President Leghari set up a Committee for Defence and National Security (CDNS), over which he presided, and which included the Chiefs of Army Staff of the four armies. This committee, although officially it had only a consultative role, was soon perceived as an attempt on the part of the president and the military to fence in legally elected governments.

The low turnout at the polls, 35.92 per cent, was less a result of calls to boycott them issued by the Jamaat-i Islami and the JUP – both of which, no doubt wished to avoid a further electoral rout,[84] – than of the disillusion of the PPP voters and the people's weariness with a perpetually unstable democratic process and corrupt politicians.[85] The elections, however, did give a crushing majority to Nawaz Sharif's Pakistan Muslim League (N): 134 seats out of 204 (including 107 won in the Punjab) against 18 for the PPP, which also lost Sind due to an alliance between the PML (N) and the MQM. The prime minister was finally in a situation where he could amend the Constitution. On 1 April 1997 the two chambers passed the 13th Amendment.

This had the effect of overturning four articles of the 8th Amendment: Paragraph 58 (2) which allowed the president to dissolve the National Assembly, was annulled; Article 101 obliged the president henceforth to consult the prime minister before nominating governors; Paragraph 112 (2b), which gave governors the power to dissolve provincial assemblies was abolished; Paragraph 243 (9) (2) was modified so the president lost his discretionary power to appoint military leaders.

Numerous observers were of the opinion that these reforms marked the first true steps towards democracy in Pakistan.[86] Nawaz Sharif nipped any such illusion in the bud by establishing a true parliamentary dictatorship.[87] The PPP had been decimated, and its leaders found themselves ensnared in judicial squabbles.[88]Above all, Sharif used his authority systematically to undermine the opposition, in defiance of the separation of powers.[89]

The judiciary was the first victim in his sights as Nawaz Sharif sought to reduce the power of the Supreme Court by reducing its members from 17 to 12. On 30 September 1990, Chief Justice Sajjad Ali Shah referred the matter to President Leghari, asking him to nominate the five sidelined judges in accordance with Article 190 of the Constitution. Nawaz Sharif then had the National Assembly pass a motion with a view to making the president dismiss the chief justice. Leghari refused to agree to this, and on 31 October the prime minister accepted Sajjad Ali Shah's decision on the five judges. On 2 December however, he resigned, at the same moment as the President. Responsibility for this sequence of events lay with Jahangir Karamat, Chief of Army Staff since January 1995. In the first instance he had addressed a note to Sharif which led to his decision in October, but he then came round to the idea that the prime minister, properly elected, is thereby invested with a superior legitimacy, and must be given a clear field. Therein lies the secret of the double resignation.

Nawaz Sharif took advantage of this to entrench his authority by getting Rafiq Tarar, a friend of his father and a man close to the Tablighi Jamaat, made President of the Republic. The growing influence of the Sharifs had the effect of making the regime look like a family business. The prime minister's brother Shabhaz was running the Punjab, and his policies, like those of Islamabad, largely served the Punjabis' interests and business interests in general. Turning his back on the calls for austerity, which the IMF had stipulated as a condition for his latest loan, Finance Minister Sartaz Aziz in fact announced that from 28 March there would be a supply policy based on tax concessions to the employers.

The 15th Amendment, adopted only by the lower chamber on 9 October 1998, was submitted to Parliament by Nawaz Sharif that same year to give the government the power to implement the sharia, to levy the *zakat* and to 'order what is good and forbid what is bad'.

The press lost no opportunity to stigmatize the dereliction of a government in which they had placed their hopes for a complete restoration of the democratic process. The Jhang Group – publishers of the English-language daily, *The News* – was particularly critical. As a result of its audacity it suffered harassment by the fiscal authorities, and searches accompanied by threats. In spring 1999 Sharif hardened his tactics further following a BBC report about the corruption of Pakistan's politicians. The editor of the *Friday Times*, Naja, Sethi, was placed under provisional detention for 20 days. During the summer the government stamped hard on the Press Council, using the same'powers as the civil tribunals to punish newspapers considered out of line. The army alone, that most powerful of all counterpowers, would put an end to this parliamentary dictatorship.

Musharraf's Countercoup

General Jahangir Karamat was not absolutely and definitively resigned to the supremacy of Nawaz Sharif. Certainly he placed the army at the service of the civil power as a means of covering up the failings of a painfully incompetent administration. So the census was organized, seven years late, under the overall supervision of the military in March 1998. The management of the Water and Power Agency, which oversaw water and electricity distribution, was also entrusted to the army – 70,000 soldiers were detailed to ensure that recalcitrant citizens paid their bills.[90] In spring 1998, 1,400 army teams were deployed to uncover the 'phantom schools' which got grants from the state for doing nothing at all – they found that 4,000 out of 56,000 public schools fell into this category.[91]

The army however, reaped its reward. Military expenditure remained very high – 64 per cent of the total budget – despite a grave financial crisis and a declining growth rate (3.1 per cent) in 1997–8. The army was further authorized by the Pakistan Armed Forces Ordinance (1998) to instigate court martials authorized to try certain cases and to pass sentences in Sind, where the military had been complaining for a long time that the law had been too soft on Muhajir militants. The military in general took up Sharif's rallying cry for some kind of nuclear action, answered in 1998 by weapons tests, in response to Indian 'provocation'. However, there was little enthusiasm in the military for involvement in the maintenance of law and order, because this would make it look as though they supported Nawaz Sharif's incompetent management. Karamat resigned in October 1998 because he disagreed with the Prime Minister's policies.

Sharif then tried to complete his nepotistic – almost sultan-like – programme[92] by appointing another family friend, Lieutenant General Kwaja Ziaduddin, in Karamat's place, but the army had so many reservations about this that he abandoned the idea. His lot was then cast in favour of General Pervez Musharraf,[93] who was to prove altogether more interventionist than his predecessor.

The Aftermath of 'Kargil' and the 'Taliban connection'

The first signs of a rift between Sharif and the army appeared in the aftermath of the 'Kargil war', so named after the Indian Kashmiri town where violent fighting broke out in summer 1999. Some hundreds of soldiers and mujaheddin secretly infiltrated the area. The counter attack by the Indian troops sent to dislodge the 'infiltrators' from the summits where they had built solid bunkers, led to a combat, whose like had not been seen since the 1971 war (see Chapter 4 below). The Indian forces had their first success when Sharif was literally summoned to Washington on

4 July 1999, and instructed to withdraw his Pakistani troops and any other support they might be giving the mujaheddin. The prime minister complied – much to the displeasure of the military chiefs, who felt betrayed: the more so because the civilian government had not even taken the trouble to consult them before giving in to the American demands.[94]

Nawaz Sharif upset the military establishment once more in September 1999, when he reminded it that he had given his word before the United Nations General Assembly that he would sign the nuclear tests ban treaty. He had no intention of doing so unless India did so too, but this reminder reinforced the military impression that Sharif might yield to American demands as a tradeoff against the lifting of the sanctions which had weighed so heavily on the economy, already in crisis, since the tests in 1998.

US pressure on the subject of the relationship between Pakistan and the Taliban was a third bone of contention. Although the Americans had supported Islamist groups waging war in Afghanistan, since it was in US interests, they also considered them a threat once the USSR had collapsed. In 1997 Washington had put one of them, Harkat-ul Ansar – later renamed Harkat-ul Mujaheddin – on the list of terrorist groups. American vigilance was further intensified after the bombings of the US embassies in Kenya and Tanzania on 7 August 1998, whose presumed instigator Osama Bin Laden, was a Taliban protégé. Washington demanded that Islamabad should obtain his extradition from the authorities in Kabul and that, at the very least, Pakistan should stop supporting the Taliban. In October 1999 Sharif did in fact seem to distance himself from these Islamic groups when he attributed to the Afghan fundamentalists a new outbreak of sectarian conflict in the Punjab, and announced that there would be searches in the *madrasahs*, which he suspected were being used as arms stores. The Pakistani military feared that they might lose their privileged link with Kabul, a link they considered vital to the 'strategic depth' of their country.

Musharraf instigated his coup on 12 October 1999, in response to Sharif's decision to replace him as head of the army by Kwaja Ziauddin, whom he had already placed at the head of the Inter Services Intelligence. At that time Musharraf was returning home on a plane from Colombo, but had been expecting to lose his job, and had been preparing his counter-attack for some time, in collaboration with senior officers. These officers organized on his behalf a 'countercoup' – to use the term Musharraf himself would use later to emphasize that he was simply reacting to Sharif's decision. In less than two hours the President found himself under house arrest, while the airports and national television were under military control. The announcement of the coup did not provoke a single demonstration. Rather, there were sighs of relief all round – a sure sign that the Pakistanis seemed to expect nothing of a civilian government, nor, indeed, even politicians in general.

History repeats itself

The calm – even satisfaction – with which Pakistanis welcomed Musharraf's coup is reminiscent of the atmosphere in the country after Ayub Khan and by Zia's seizure of power.[95] History was to a great extent repeatiing itself. The Constitution was in a state of suspended animation, every assembly was suspended, and no government was functioning anywhere – neither in Islamabad nor elsewhere. The president however, was still in office, and martial law was not imposed, Musharraf having contented himself with the issue on 14 October to the public of an order declaring a state of emergency and appointing the new strong man 'head of executive'.

Just like his predecessors Musharraf's first move on 17 October 1999 was to justify his actions by citing the hijacking of democracy wrought by to the mismanagement of corrupt politicians, and the necessity of restoring order in the country. This led him to bring legal proceedings against dozens of politicians, pre-eminently Nawaz Sharif whose trial opened rapidly. The principal accusation against him – that he prevented the pilot bringing Musharraf from Colombo from landing in Pakistan – made him liable to the death penalty.

His rival, Benazir Bhutto, who had put herself forward as the herald of the return to democracy along the lines described above, happened to be out of reach having fled to London to escape prosecution in the matter of her home in Surrey.[96] The political parties were still in existence but without their leaders. The press maintained an air of freedom, since censorship had not been introduced,[97] but justice the legal system was made to toe the line. On 25 January 2000, six out of thirteen Supreme Court judges, including the chief justice, declined to take an oath of allegiance to the new regime. *De facto* they also resigned, as did nine from the provincial tribunals. Of the 102 judges who made up the Supreme Court and the provincial tribunals, 89 took the oath. On 12 May a reconstituted Supreme Court approved the coup as a 'Necessity of State', at the same time asking Musharraf to agree to elections within three years.

Musharraf proclaimed himself head of the executive, while retaining his position as head of the army. He also appointed a number of soldiers to responsible posts. The body charged with guiding government action, the National Security Council, included in its ranks the heads of both the airforce and the navy.[98] Three of the four governors were also generals. The army thereby regained most of the positions it had enjoyed under Zia.

Democracy in Check

The political trajectory of Pakistan gives the impression of an eternal return in a rhythmic succession of cycles of about ten years, in the course of which democratic phases and military governments alternate. This is for the most part mere optical illusion, since Pakistan has never really tasted democracy.[99] Those episodes termed democratic have systematically degenerated into a drift towards authoritarianism on the part of the person in power (as with Z A Bhutto and Nawaz Sharif) and/or turned out to be mere illusion like the democracy of the 1990s, when elected governments found that they could do nothing against the strength of the army. Under these circumstances, how can we talk about a 'transition to democracy'?[100]

Pakistan seems doomed to authoritarianism not by some sort of Islamic cultural malediction but, rather, as a result of a whole bundle of political factors: fear of India led its first leaders to give absolute priority on the one hand to nation-building, and on the other to the development of a powerful army. Obsession with security has meant centralization and concentration of power in the hands of officials and the military, all to the detriment of political parties, which, since they were already feeble, have never really had the chance to be a prime mover on the political scene, and even fell into disrepute throughout the 1950s. More decisive still has been the effect of demographic power relations between the different linguistic communities making the Punjabis – who, predominated in the army – afraid that the law of numbers would mean power for the Bengali majority had there been free elections. The Punjabis rejected the democratic logic all the more resolutely as the political culture they had acquired in the colonial period followed the viceregal model. Finally, the army's grip on the Pakistani state could not have been maintained without the blessing (and financial support) of the United States, which considered Pakistan a key element of its regional policy.

Most of these factors, which explain why Pakistani democracy was in check during the 1950s, have continued to exercise their influence through the succeeding decades. Certainly the ethnic problem was removed by the 1971 Partition, and no doubt this was what allowed democratization of the Bhutto years. Yet the Indian syndrome has only been reinforced by regular defeats on the battlefield. The party-political machine is still inadequate: most parties relying on the prestige of a single charismatic figure, or on a dynasty such as the Bhuttos, while deputies have always changed party affiliation opportunistically. The viceregal culture has been trivialized to become the reference point for the behaviour of the military and the civil service, as Nawaz Sharif's behaviour in his second term shows. Finally, the geopolitical configuration has led the United States to support the various guardians of Pakistan's fortunes, beginning with Zia between 1970 and 1980, as a response to the Russian invasion of Afghanistan. Democracy is rarely imposed from the outside in any case.

But what are the intrinsic resources of Pakistan so far as democracy is concerned? The liberalization phases have come to nothing, because Pakistan contains so few natural democrats and its civil society has been too feebly structured. The domination which rich landlords, the world of big business, and certainly the military continue to exercise over Pakistani society prevents the development of trade unions – who never recovered from the anticommunist policies of the 1950s – and precludes the development of a peasant movement comparable to the one which has existed in India since the Green Revolution. The property owners and the 'tribal chiefs' – sardar in Baluchistan or khan in the NWFP – accounted for 75 per cent of the deputies elected in 1988 and 62 per cent in 1993.[101] Class solidarities have emerged far less readily than the vertical organization of caste and tribe that prevails everywhere in the countryside. These traditional hierarchies, combined with the omnipresent Islamic climate, hold society in an atmosphere of conservatism where women are often the first victims. Change will eventually come in the urban middle class – not so much in the merchant community, where the mindset is by no means liberal, nor among the Muhajirs, who are still only too ready to adopt the violent practices of the MQM, but among an intelligentsia who have found in the NGO (Non-Governmental Organization) a promising form of organization, and whose English language press is quick to show its critical attitude. Nawaz Sharif's PML(N) was not mistaken when it targeted the NGOs.[102] The Islamists, too, continually criticize their external financial support in order to undermine their influence. A decisive battle for the conquest of social space is now being played out on this field.

PART II

PAKISTAN'S FOREIGN POLICY

4

PAKISTAN IN THE GAME OF THE GREAT POWERS

Pakistan, outcome of a Partition which was a long time sought for but in the end came suddenly, remains affected by its antagonistic relationship with India, which has led to four armed conflicts in which it never managed to gain the upper hand. This difficult relationship forms the basis of its foreign policy, and explains why largely defined. Pakistan's position in the international power game is seen in terms of its neighbour, and shifts with the changing personalities in power in the two countries, and with changing geopolitical configurations; nonetheless, it seeks to fulfil the first requirement of the Pakistani authorities: 'strengthening the security and preservation of the territorial integrity of Pakistan' against what is perceived as an Indian threat. In diplomatic language, this major concern is called 'the quest for peace and regional stability'.[1] Even if the country cannot always rely on solid alliances in its effort to do this, it is still important to have 'friends' – if possible, friends from whom it can buy arms. The third consideration for Pakistan's foreign policy is the religious dimension of its national identity, reaffirmed by the name given to its new capital in 1967: Islamabad. Pakistan proclaimed to the world its fraternal goodwill towards Islamic nations (although this brotherly attitude has at times been ambivalent and compromised). In its search for allies, the country has fallen prey to unfortunate encounters with Arab nationalism; while the Islamic card, which it played against Soviet communism, has not prevented it from pledging eternal friendship to China.

Pakistan was thought of as the promised land for Indian Muslims, but its founding ideology was never clearly defined. After the death of the Father of the Nation, Muhammad Ali Jinnah, in 1948, there was a pervasive climate of political instability which was not conducive to the consolidation of a founding doctrine. The importance attached to Kashmir in Pakistan's negotiations could not compensate for this weakness, even though – albeit at great risk – it was useful to Pakistan's national plan. There are two principal approaches to the problem of Kashmir. One sees it as a failure to complete Partition, and hence as the missing part of the nation; the other stresses the Kashmiris' right to self-government, maintains that India alone has been duplicitous on this question, and serves as a national rallying cry against a hostile neighbour. By intervening in Kashmir, Pakistan, since its very first year of existence, has therefore put incompleteness and exteriority at the heart of its national vision – and kept them there.

The consequences of this decision are incalculable – both for the country itself and for its foreign relations. Pakistan's main condition for friendship with a third country is its stance on Kashmir. But few countries – least of all the great powers – are willing to commit themselves clearly and definitively on this bone of contention.

Thus Pakistan's foreign policy revolves around three main entities: India, the great powers, and the Muslim world. But in the end, it has to cope with the exigencies of power relations between the great nations and fluctuations in the world order. This chapter, therefore, takes a chronological look at Pakistan's ambitions as they have been embroiled in the crucible of the past half-century, and how they have emerged.

A Nation Finding Its Feet: 1947–54

From the start, Pakistan was in a very complex situation, for two reasons. The first involves Indo-Pakistani relations and the geopolitics of the region. Although it decided to follow its own course, the new state was born of the greatest anticolonial movement of the twentieth century: India's challenge to the British Empire. But its founders also intended to free it from another a threat, that of 'Hindu India' – in their view promoted by the Congress Party, which would dominate an independent India. The Indian leaders, mindful of the fact that the Muslim League had taken no part in the Quit India Movement against the British in 1942, saw the clumsy Partition of 1947 as the Machiavellian outcome of power politics. All of a sudden London wanted to weaken its former Empire by dividing it, and stretching between the USSR and the India of a Nehru with socialist sympathies a buffer state that was unlikely to enjoy good relations with either of its great neighbours. This is probably a generalization which takes insufficient account of responsibilities during Partition. Until the end of the Cold War, however, Pakistan was a great asset to the Western powers' anticommunist policy – or, rather, anti-Soviet, after the 1971 *rapprochement* between China and the United States – albeit with a few setbacks.

A second cause for ambiguity was the new Pakistani state's relations with Islam and with the *umma*, the community of the faithful. Movements like the Jamaat-i Islami, loyal to the universalistic logic of Islam, were against Partition from the start. Nevertheless these groups eventually supported Pakistan, accepting *de facto* the argument put forward so often by Muhammad Iqbal, then by subsequent leaders of the country: as a state that willed itself into existence, Pakistan must be open to the development of an Islamic solidarity. Still to be resolved was the contradiction between a nationalist concept of the state and the universalizing ideal of Muslim civil society. At the very least, the call for a brotherhood of Muslim states offered a way out, albeit theoretical.

The more ambitious notion that Pakistan was merely one step towards the unity of all Islamic states obviously glossed over the very real religious differences and power struggles between Muslim nations. Nevertheless, it maintained the hope (or the illusion) that sheer numbers would mean that the new Pakistani state would play a key role. In 1930 Iqbal had affirmed that Indian Muslims would be a more important asset to Islam than all the other Muslim countries put together, and the fledgling Pakistan was a little too boastful about having a bigger population than any other Muslim state – the fifth-largest in the world. Such presumptuousness did not go down well with Muslim communities in the Middle East, who were proud of their thousand-year history; nor with Arab nationalist movements, which understood the Indian Congress Party's anticolonial struggle better than the secessionist arguments that had given birth to Pakistan.

The seal of Islam was also the young state's certificate of anticommunism: this atheistic ideology, perceived as a monstrous, proliferating Hydra, could not live alongside an Islamic polity which was at times willing to make common cause with Christianity against the 'Godless ones'. Behind their mask of Islamic identity, however, leaders of Pakistan weighed up the pros and cons, ready to play for both sides. Liaquat Ali Khan, Prime Minister from 1947 to 1951, had at first intended to visit the USSR, but in the end – like Nehru, the Indian Prime Minister – he opted for an official visit to the USA in 1950. It was also in order not to let India reap all the benefits of a *rapprochement* with Beijing that the Pakistan government decided to recognize the People's Republic of China in 1950 and did not send troops to Korea, while they understood – in principle – why America was fighting there. Already the shoots of the *Realpolitik* which was to characterize the love-hate relations between India and Pakistan and the great powers were emerging. Beijing had already shown great tolerance towards a Pakistan that would soon be called to form pro-Western alliances. China exerted – and still exerts – a certain pressure on India, a competitor on its southern flank.

First Links with the West: 1954–62

From the time of his visit to the USA in 1949, Nehru outlined his concept of non-alignment: India would not be the keystone of the anticommunism which Washington hoped to build in Asia with the help of a highly prestigious Indian leader. America's disappointment meant new possibilities for Pakistan. During his American tour, Liaquat Ali Khan took full advantage of this to build up a picture of an anticommunist Pakistan whose strategic position should be reinforced by arms deliveries. The Korean War, which broke out in June 1950, underlined India's lack of dependence on Washington; moreover, New Delhi refused to be party to the 1951 Treaty of San Francisco, which inaugurated a security pact that allowed American troops to establish bases in Japan. In both cases Pakistan took the opposing stance.

So the ground was already prepared when new administrations came to power in 1953. In the USSR, Stalin's death led to a more favourable policy towards India, which had hitherto been perceived as labouring under a bourgeois regime. That same year, John Foster Dulles became the American secretary of state, and started a vigorous joint security policy. His chosen strategy – confirmed by Vice-President Nixon after his visit to southern Asia – involved an alliance with Pakistan, with a view to hemming in communist Eurasia. When Muhammad Ali Bogra, former ambassador to Washington, became prime minister in 1953, he was convinced that his country's security depended upon the backing of a great power. The hour of the treaties had struck. In May 1954, Pakistan and the United States signed a mutual support and defence agreement which was not a military alliance, but marked the beginning of American arms sales to Pakistan, and an officer training project. In September Pakistan signed the Manila Pact, founding document of the Southeast Asia Treaty Organization (SEATO)[2] and, above all, confirmed its alliance with Washington. In 1955 Pakistan signed the Baghdad Pact – of more direct local relevance – which united Muslim countries (Iraq, Iran and Turkey) with the aim of frustrating Soviet intentions towards the Middle East and its warm seas; Great Britain was also a member, whereas the United States was not – although it was the moving spirit behind it. When Iraq left after the 1958 revolution, this became the Central Treaty Organization (CENTO). Unlike NATO – and contrary to Pakistan's wishes – neither SEATO nor CENTO had its own military command, and did not make provision for an immediate joint intervention in the event of an attack on one of its member states. These treaties gave Pakistan no protection against India. At the same time, the Pakistani leaders wanted to retain the optimum room for manoeuvre.

The Bandung Conference in 1955 offered an opportunity to do this. Strongly supported by India, this meeting, in effect, was China's first appearance on the Afro-Asiatic stage to the detriment of New Delhi, which subsequently took a different tack and played the nonalignment card, thereby alienating both Communist China and Pakistan, member of SEATO and CENTO. As the only pro-Western representative at Bandung, Pakistan took advantage of its position to enlighten China on the subject of its political approach, making it clear that Beijing was not the target of its alliances. Beijing played the game: in 1956 the prime ministers of China and Pakistan visited one another's countries.

That year's Suez Crisis revealed the other side of Pakistan's reluctance to alienate itself from Western countries. Although Pakistan approved of Nasser's nationalization of the Suez Canal, it wanted international control of shipping. Prime Minister H.S. Suhrawardy condemned the intervention of French and British troops, but he had every intention of staying with the Baghdad Pact, which did not have a good image in Arab countries. Two years later, the bloody revolution that overthrew the Iraqi royal family transformed the situation in the Middle East. Pakistan, sticking to its pro-Western policy, was delighted – unlike India – when American and British troops went into Lebanon and Jordan.

General – soon to be Marshal – Ayub Khan's *coup d'état* in October 1958 reinforced this pro-Western line. In 1959, Pakistan – with Turkey and Iran – signed a defence agreement with Washington which provided for possible American intervention in the event of an attack by 'international communism'. To Islamabad's great regret, this did not mean India, but at least the USA promised sustained economic and military aid to Pakistan. In 1960, the affair of the U-2 spy plane which took off from Peshawar and was brought down over Soviet territory showed that Pakistan could be helpful to US military intelligence. It continued to be so despite Nikita Khrushchev's threats.

Pakistan's Western option was also an answer to the improved relations between Moscow and New Delhi in the post-Stalin era; all it did, however, was reinforce them. The first aid programmes to underdeveloped countries – as they were soon to be called – were aimed at Pakistan's two neighbours, India and Afghanistan – the very Afghanistan which laid claim to the whole of Pashtunistan, and hence to part of Pakistan. Bulganin and Khrushchev's long official visit to India at the end of 1955 gave the Soviets and the Indians the chance to criticize Pakistan's imperialism and military policies; however, there was no permanent hostility between the USSR and Pakistan. Deputy Prime Minister Mikoyan's visit to Pakistan in 1956 led to a trade agreement, but not until 1961 did a major oil exploration project signal a stronger relationship. Nonetheless, chaotic bilateral relations remained the norm. The first Russian veto against reinforcements for UN forces in Kashmir in 1957 set the tone: each great power played its own game in South Asia.

China followed the same principle: Zhou En Lai visited both India and Pakistan in 1956, when Sino–Indian relations were at their best. China and Pakistan stated that there was 'no real conflict of interests' between them. Ayub Khan, however, had his doubts: he went so far as to suggest that his country and India should give some thought to the defence of the subcontinent. But Beijing was able to follow a middle path, even on the Kashmir question, calling for a bilateral agreement without committing itself – whereas in 1954 New Delhi had signed a treaty recognizing China's sovereignty over Tibet. So there was no payback for India.

All in all, the pro-Western policy it had followed since 1954 did not completely live up to Pakistan's expectations. It is true that the country obtained the American aid that was vital to its continued survival, but India, too, received attention from Washington. For many US decision-makers, India was the field where the game of Asia's future would be played out: it was vital that India won the race for growth against the Chinese communist system. When India was plunged into crisis in 1957, there was a sizeable growth in American aid – much greater than in Pakistan, for which India's swift defeat in its war against China in October 1962 was a wonderful surprise. This defeat, however, brought New Delhi immediate American support of a new kind: Washington agreed to military aid for India without tying it to an agreement on Kashmir, contrary to Pakistan's wishes. The sight of 'The strengthening of Pakistan's most determined foe by Pakistan's closest ally'[3] caused great bitterness in Pakistan.

Although Ayub Khan had long been in favour of the alliance with America, he realized that it was time to revise Pakistan's foreign policy. The outcome of this alliance had been criticized in Pakistan itself for years. The pro-Western tack pursued since 1954 had come to grief on three fronts: it offered no military protection against India; there was no prospect of any diplomatic pressure for a referendum on Kashmir; and it compromised pan-Islamic solidarity by making Pakistan look like an ally of imperialism against the upsurge of Arab nationalism – it was with Nehru and Tito that Nasser launched the nonaligned movement. In future Pakistan would take a more independent line, and make a virtue of necessity. Without burning their bridges with Washington, Ayub Khan's government decided to take care of its own special bilateral relations. The Sino–Soviet quarrel and the Sino–Indian conflict are excellent illustrations of this changed situation: China became a chosen partner of Pakistan.

China and the Dangers of Adventurism: 1962–72

Opening the diplomatic field: from Western alliance to multilateralism

Just before the brief war between China and India in October 1962, China and Pakistan had decided to set their border in Kashmir: Beijing, mindful of its deteriorating relations with New Delhi, wanted at the very least to be sure of its Himalayan flank. The negotiations – which began a week before the war with India, and were intensified by the result – were completed in 1963. The countries swapped territories and redrew their border   to the great discomfiture of India, which claimed the whole of Kashmir as its own. In 1964, during a visit to Pakistan, Zhou En Lai stopped sitting on the fence over this issue, which should, he said, be resolved 'in accordance with the wishes of the people of Kashmir' : although he did not say it in so many words, this meant adopting Pakistan's idea of a referendum. Soon afterwards China and Pakistan signed their first wide-ranging trade agreement; they then – with Sukarno's Indonesia – began to organize the second Afro-Asiatic conference to counter the conference of nonaligned nations mooted by India, Egypt and Yugoslavia.[4]

This improvement in Sino–Pakistani relations was not to America's taste – especially since Ayub Khan was also angling for a *rapprochement* with Moscow, which seized the opportunity provided by Pakistan's newly independent spirit just at the very moment when India was getting more Western support than ever. A trade agreement; a more ambivalent Soviet approach on Kashmir; Ayub Khan's visit to the USSR: all this constituted nothing less than a reversal of alliances. Pakistan was still a member of SEATO and CENTO – somewhat hollow alliances, if the truth must be told. Ayub Khan did not break with Washington, but used the room for manoeuvre provided by the rapidly changing configurations of the conflict between the United States and the communist powers. By dubbing the USSR 'revisionist' from 1960 onwards, China changed the shape of international relations. The Washington–Moscow–Beijing triangle, based on three intersecting oppositions, opened up a whole new perspective for Pakistani diplomacy. In 1962 Muhammad Ali Bogra, Foreign Minister at the time, had set the tone by declaring that there was no such thing as friends for ever or enemies for ever – only the national interest counted. In 1965, when relations between Pakistan and the USA were at their lowest ebb, Ayub Khan observed – with Washington in mind – that Pakistan wanted 'friends, not masters'.[5]

There was still a need to achieve autonomy in foreign affairs. In the ongoing game of chess between the great powers, India and Pakistan could not do this: they were mere pawns in the shifting conflicts between Washington, Moscow and Beijing. Washington had furthered its efforts against the USSR by giving Pakistan military aid; it did the same for India against China. The State Department's main objective was to drive a wedge between the USSR – under Khrushchev – and China. The close ties between India and the USSR, and the tension between China and India, furthered this project without jeopardizing the improved relations between Russia and Pakistan. As for the quarrel between India and Pakistan, it was convenient for all three countries because it meant that no major power would emerge in South Asia. In these circumstances, the leaders of Pakistan were to make two major errors of calculation: they overestimated their support from outside and underestimated their internal weakness. These errors led to the Indo–Pakistani wars of 1965 and 1971.

The 1965 and 1971 wars: the international context

The weakness of the Indian army revealed by its defeat by China in 1962, and the continuing troubles in Indian Kashmir – which was losing more of its autonomy as each year went by – pushed Ayub Khan to open hostilities in 1965: Nehru had died the year before, and an obvious strengthening of the Indian army since 1963 meant that he had to act quickly. 'Kashmiri brothers' crossed the cease-fire line that had divided the ancient kingdom since 1949 – a line which, the Pakistani authorities maintained, had already been breached several times by Indian troops. The Pakistani army went into action in Kashmir on 1 September 1965. International opinion, which tended to sympathize with the Indians' accusations of aggression, soon became concerned about New Delhi's counterattack: Indian troops marched on Lahore, thus crossing not only the cease-fire line but also the recognized border between the two countries. China's military diversion – an ultimatum which India respected by withdrawing its troops from the border between China and Sikkim – looked threatening, and the USA and the USSR told Beijing so. On 23 September the war ended at the express request of the UN Security Council.

The USA, adopting a position of neutrality, suspended their arms deliveries to both countries. The USSR used its good offices to organize the Tashkent Conference in January 1966. At this conference, India and Pakistan respectively relinquished their territorial gains.

The leaders of Pakistan learnt some lessons from this fruitless war. The UN had been silent on the status of Kashmir. The Americans had let them down. The USSR had taken the unexpected role of peacemaker, rather than siding with New Delhi. China was the only great power to condemn India out of hand, and thus risk extending the conflict. From that time on, Pakistan was even more firmly committed to multilateralism,[6] a variant of nonalignment. Although it remained in SEATO and CENTO – somewhat moribund organizations – and did not forget America's support in the 1950s, Pakistan intended to conduct a foreign policy that was open to the three key powers it considered vital. Its good relations with China did not stop official visits to Pakistan by Prime Minister Kosygin in 1968 and President Nixon in 1969 (President Liu Shao Qi had been there in 1966). But Pakistan turned a deaf ear to Soviet and American proposals that it should get together with India to form a 'joint Asian security system' – diplomatic language for a front against China.

Without achieving anything in Kashmir, the 1965 war weakened both Pakistan and Prime Minister Ayub Khan, who left office in 1969. His successor, General Yahya Khan, had to deal with growing resentment in eastern Pakistan, which was uncomfortable with a two-headed state dominated by Punjabis and Pashtuns, and very critical of the way the 1965 war had been conducted. Sheikh Mujibur

Rahman's Awami League won an outright majority at the 1970 elections; this should have put the Bengalis in power. But the western military–political elite which governed the country could not accept the League's manifesto, which envisaged maximum autonomy and its own defence capacity for East Pakistan. An uprising in East Pakistan and its bloody suppression by the Pakistan army gave India a unique opportunity for military intervention without antagonizing international opinion. Neither the arrival of the US aircraft carrier *Enterprise* in the Bay of Bengal – which sent shock waves through India – nor China's condemnation of India's action could save Pakistan from defeat. Contrary to Islamabad's expectations, the Indo–Pakistani war of 1971 did not lead to direct military intervention by the great powers, which readily accepted a *fait accompli*: the secession of Bangladesh.

The Washington–Moscow–Beijing triangle was also shifting in 1971, and once again Pakistan's destiny was subject as much to this variable geometry as to its own decisions. Two crucial developments led to a virtual transformation of the geopolitical context in South Asia. President Nixon, in reversing United States policy towards China before the Indo–Pakistani war, opened up to Pakistan a Washington–Islamabad–Beijing axis which, in effect, accelerated the postwar signature of a peace, friendship and cooperation treaty between the USSR and India, one clause of which made provision for possible joint defence in the event of attack. The deteriorating relations between the Soviet Union and China, after China decided to extend the nuclear power it had acquired in 1964, at least acted as a moderating influence. Moscow and Beijing watched each other carefully. Once again the risk of a wider Indo-Pakistani conflict receded, and India – which seemed to be preparing for significant action in Kashmir, even in eastern Pakistan – calmed down, and did not add to its neighbour's crushing defeat.[7]

When Yahya Khan left office, Zulfikar Ali Bhutto, foreign minister since 1963, took over the reins of government. Known for his fiercely anti-Indian line, he nevertheless made an immediate about-turn, and in 1972 he and Indira Gandhi signed the Simla Accord, which decreed that the line dividing Kashmir should be respected. India obviously had the upper hand in South Asia, so Bhutto intended to rethink Pakistan's foreign policy. He would continue his predecessors' policy of multilateralism *vis-à-vis* the great powers, but with a new objective: a leaner, fitter Pakistan. It was time to reaffirm the nation's Muslim identity in a world that was soon to be hit by the oil-price shock.

Islamic Parameters: Z A Bhutto and Zia ul-Haq, 1972–88

Pakistan, a state created for Indian Muslims, played on its Islamic identity in shaping one of the main poles of its foreign policy from two aspects. Against India, this process of self-identity would make Pakistan less of a southern Asian country and bring it closer to the historic Middle Eastern heartland of Islam. But in opting very quickly for an alliance with the West – seeing this as the country's best hope for survival – its leaders put Pakistan in a bad position at a time of anticolonial and anti-imperialist conflict.

Part sincere aspiration, part rhetoric, this reference to 'sister Muslim nations' soon came up against the geopolitical realities of the time. The Indian struggle for independence had won New Delhi a fund of sympathy from nations like Egypt and Indonesia – with Pakistan the most densely populated Muslim countries. For many Muslim nations, Pakistan's difficult position during the Suez Crisis reinforced the negative impression left by the Baghdad Pact, which was perceived as an imperial-ist manoeuvre against Arab nationalism rather than a bulwark against the Soviets. Even on Pakistan's borders, tensions with Afghanistan showed very quickly that Islam was not a miraculously strong cement. Kabul was unhappy when Pakistan joined the United Nations in 1949, and pursued the question of Pashtunistan until 1963, when Prime Minister Muhammad Daud left office. How could Pakistan argue for Islamic solidarity, or pledge itself to the 'Muslim cause', when its own internal tensions had led to the secession of Bangladesh?

Nevertheless, Pakistan continued its process of Muslim self-identity – not without bitterness, reversals and difficulties. There were some successes, even though it sometimes had to clothe its national interest in the robes of Muslim brotherhood: an agreement with Turkey and Iran, fellow members of the Baghdad Pact and CENTO and, in 1964, founder members of the Regional Development Cooperation Association mooted by Ayub Khan. Islamic solidarity was more in evidence during the wars with India in 1965 and 1971. Some key countries, includ-ing Saudi Arabia, provided Pakistan with arms. Since 1969, Pakistan has been able to play a significant role in the Islamic Conference Organization – 56 member states and four observer states.

Z A Bhutto's 'Islamic' diplomacy

When Zulfikar Ali Bhutto reached the commanding heights of power in 1972, his intention was to strengthen Pakistan's Islamic image on the world stage, because it served his prime purpose: to revitalize the nation after the traumatic secession of Bangladesh. He considered that the time for this was ripe – for several reasons. His pursuit of multilateralism as a substitute for a special relationship with the USA; his desire to strengthen Pakistan's links with socialist countries – especially China, but also the USSR, North Korea and East European countries – meant that he was not in the camp of either of the great armies of the Cold War. The rally to Islam was like a transcendent geopolitical theme which Pakistani nationalism could adopt without losing its identity. The oil-price shock of 1973, which gave new power to the Middle Eastern countries, seemed to confirm such a vision in terms of both geopolitical power games and – hardly less important – financial interests. Although Pakistan was not itself an oil-producing country, economic and military growth in the Middle East offered the prospect of plentiful work in the Gulf States, and hence foreign cur-rency; and opportunities for military cooperation – particularly in Saudi Arabia.

Bhutto began his new term of office by making long official visits to several Muslim countries (in the Middle East, North Africa, Sun-Saharan Africa). As a result of these contacts he organized the Islamic Conference's second Summit in Lahore in 1974; 35 states were represented, as was the PLO. So the humiliation of 1971 was eclipsed, to be replaced – as Bhutto had wished – by specific international entities like the Islamic Development Bank. Ties with Saudi Arabia grew stronger, symbolized by the great Faisal mosque in Islamabad. Even relations with Afghanistan improved.

As far as Bhutto was concerned, the fact that the oil-producing states of the Middle East were more powerful was no reason to abandon Pakistan's old dream of leading the Muslim world, even if this did ruffle a few feathers in his brother countries. After the Indian nuclear tests in 1974, Bhutto announced that Pakistan would soon have what he – somewhat ill-advisedly – did not hesitate to call an 'Islamic bomb' in an attempt to give an international gloss to the supreme weapon. This nuclear option was the perfect illustration of his new estrangement from the United States, which was opposed to any nuclear proliferation. Chinese participation in Pakistan's nuclear programme was denied by Beijing but proved by the CIA. But Pakistan's nuclear policy was not prompted only by rivalry with India. Nuclear weapons, of their very nature, have an effect on the international power game. Bhutto thought that the price he would pay for it would be renewed American sanctions, but when he was gaoled by Zia-ul-Haq, who overthrew him in 1977, he wondered whether the USA had engineered his fall from power. Historians have not yet answered this question.

Zia ul-Haq and Afghanistan:
Islamic Pakistan and the power game

As master of Pakistan, Zia intended to be strong on foreign policy. Friendship with Muslim countries – including Bangladesh under another putschist, General Ziaur Rahman, who came to power in 1975 – would continue, as would cooperation with China, which opened a direct route to Karakorum in 1978. There would be the same continuity – albeit negative – in relations with the USA, which were still deteriorating – the American Embassy in Islamabad was ransacked by demonstrators in 1979. Then came the Red Army's incursion into Afghanistan, which altered the whole picture. Naturally, President Jimmy Carter weighed up the possibility of a Soviet push towards the south – at the very moment when Iran, which had sent the Shah packing a few months earlier, was no longer under American protection. Would Pakistan prove another weak link on the southern flank, caught in a pincer movement between the Soviet troops in Afghanistan and Indira Gandhi, who was reluctant to condemn Moscow? It looked as if a new link between Washington and Islamabad was needed. Zia realized this, and raised the stakes in the great power game.

Zia, a skilful politician who could juggle several balls simultaneously, played his hand on five fronts at once. Holding aloft the banner of Islam, he called on the community of the faithful and on Muslim leaders to support the Afghan mujaheddin, victims of the first attack by a great power on an independent 'brother country'. The Afghan cause became as sacred as the national cause, but to no great effect. Nevertheless, Zia did not take the mujaheddin position as a model for Pakistan. Against mujaheddin advice, he also played the card of mediation with the USSR dealt to him by the UN. While he worked for a Soviet retreat, he did not burn his bridges with Moscow. His third front was Washington. While he solicited aid for the

Afghan mujaheddin at the request of the White House, Zia laid down conditions, claiming massive military aid out of all proportion to the needs of his Afghan policy. Carter refused, but when Ronald Reagan became President in 1980 he agreed wholeheartedly, approving the sale of 16 F-16As, a fleet of fighter-bombers that could be used against India.

The fourth front was China. Beijing, which derived a certain satisfaction from watching Pakistan play piggy in the middle of a struggle between the superpowers, also nurtured Islamabad, a piece on its anti-Indian chessboard. The 1986 cooperation treaty between China and Pakistan concerned the civil use of nuclear power, but all the diplomats knew that Zia was continuing Bhutto's nuclear weapons policy. Reagan closed his eyes to this, lifting sanctions on Islamabad in April 1979 under the terms of the Symington Amendment. The US Congress let it go: the Afghan stakes were too high.[8] By the time Soviet troops withdrew, it was too late: strategic experts considered Pakistan a 'threshold state' with a nuclear capacity that could very quickly be activated. Washington – abandoning without a second thought the Pakistan that had served its interests so well in Afghanistan – reimposed sanctions in 1990 under the Pressler Amendment. Although these sanctions blocked the sale of the last few F-16s, they made no impression on Pakistan's nuclear policy.

The last front was Afghanistan itself. Zia used his cards in the power game to his best advantage, and profited from the Afghan conflict to bolster his armed forces more effectively than ever. His Afghan policy was not dictated by Islamic fraternity alone. He saw that channelling arms towards the mujaheddin would give him a unique opportunity to ensure that he had a say in the choice of future leaders of a country that had been a difficult neighbour for so long, but one which, once an ally – even a protected one – would obtain for Pakistan the strategic depth it needed to confront India. By choosing to single out the most radical Islamic groups, and by entrusting the secret services of Inter Services Intelligence (ISI) with the job of carrying out the arms deliveries, infiltrating groups – even participating in the factional infighting that plunged Afghanistan into civil war when the Soviets left – Zia believed that he was furthering the interests of Pakistan. In actual fact he was sowing the seeds of future trouble. The expansion of the Pakistani armed forces, so cleverly pushed through the weak points of the power game, entailed two consequences of the Afghan war which weigh heavily on Pakistan today: the rise of a radical Islam in favour of *jihad*, and the ISI and the military's strong hold on Pakistan's foreign policy, and on the civil state.

Pakistan After the Cold War: A Difficult Adjustment

From Benazir Bhutto to Nawaz Sharif: an elusive foreign policy

Pakistan's eleven years of (theoretical) parliamentary government – between Zia's 'accidental' death in 1988 and the return to a military regime in 1999 – ended in failure. Nawaz Sharif's overthrow by his chief of army staff, General Musharraf, in 1999, and the paralysis of the two principal political players – the Pakistan People's Party

PPP and the Pakistan Muslim League (Nacraz) PML(N) – in the absence of their leaders,[9] give the 1990s, in retrospect, the bitter taste of a lost decade. The weakness of the democratic process, the savage infighting of a political class mired in the futile rivalry between the Pakistan People's Party (in power under Benazir Bhutto from 1988 to 1990, then from 1993 to 1996) and the Pakistan Muslim League (in power under Nawaz Sharif from 1990 to 1993, then from 1997 to 1999) naturally led to the collapse of Pakistan's foreign policy.

This was not so much because of the quality of the politicians or diplomats, more the result of a system that no one wanted and no one could reform. In the first place, this system gave the military the deciding vote in outlining regional policy in two sensitive areas – Afghanistan and Kashmir – and, as a result, a *de facto* power of veto on the country's strategic policy, and thus on Pakistan's position in the power game. It also gave the Islamic forces an increased recognition out of all proportion to their electoral strength.

Every leader of Pakistan since 1972 bears part of the responsibility for this. Zulfikar Ali Bhutto, with his Islamic rhetoric ('Islamic socialism', 'Islamic bomb' . . .) and Zia ul-Haq, a devout Muslim who went even further, deliberately encouraging the Islamic militants in the Afghan conflict, and cementing the alliance between the ISI and armed partisans of *jihad*. After them, neither Benazir Bhutto – despite her image as a modern woman educated, like her father, in the United States and England – nor Nawaz Sharif – a businessman assumed to be in tune with the spirit of the new international economy – threw off this heritage. Attempts to do so – such as the sacking in 1989 of ISI leader General Gul, directly implicated in furthering an Afghanistan policy that pandered to fundamentalist factions; or renewed talks between Benazir Bhutto and Rajiv Gandhi, or Nawaz Sharif and I K Gujral – were always sporadic, and had no lasting effect. Much more significant was the advent, in 1994, of the Taliban, trained in the madrasahs of Pakistan and a tool of the Pakistani military, let down by Gulbuddin Hekmatyar, leader of the Hizb-i Islami and their chosen man from the Afghan factions, who was unable to prevail in Kabul.

All in all, the Pakistan of the 1990s found it extremely difficult to cope with the new world economic and geographic order in the wake of the USSR's collapse. Since India had been so close to Moscow, it seemed inevitable that India would be affected. Independence for the Central Asian republics seemed to open them up to Pakistani influence – especially when these republics, closely followed by Azerbaijan and Afghanistan, joined the regional cooperation organization of which Turkey, Iran and Pakistan were already members.[10] The OEC – encompassing 7 million square kilometres and 300 million people, and huge energy resources – could have been a real substitute for the South Asian Association for Regional Cooperation (SAARC), founded in the same year but handicapped by the conflict between India and Pakistan. In order for this to happen, however, the OEC had to become an area of intense economic cooperation, and today it is a long way from achieving this.

Like Pakistan, Turkey and Iran had ambitions for Central Asia, and there were three major constraints on Pakistan's room for manoeuvre. The new republics – and their communist apparatchiks, converted to nationalism – favoured a national, institutionalized Islam rather than the Wahhabi fundamentalist networks so dear to

Pakistan and Saudi Arabia. Although Russia was on the decline, it had every intention of keeping strategic control of Central Asia: this was obvious both in Tajikistan and in their support for the Afghan anti-Taliban forces led by Rashid Dustom and Commander Massoud. The renewal and strengthening of the special relationship between Moscow and New Delhi was another example. In the end, the anti-Shi'a policy of the Taliban and their supporters in Pakistan inevitably damaged relations with Iran. The agreement between Turkmenistan, Iran and India on transporting gas from Turkmenistan via Afghanistan and Pakistan, rather than installing a direct pipeline, added a definite geo-economic dimension to tensions between India and Pakistan: the international aspects of India's energy supplies were out in the open.

The fact that Pakistan fought on the West's side in the Gulf War[11] was not enough to guarantee good relations with Washington, for four reasons. The USA, now free of the Soviet threat, promulgated a non-nuclear-proliferation policy under which India and Pakistan suffered some criticism, but stood their ground: neither country had signed the Treaty of Non-Proliferation in 1968, and neither subscribed to its indefinite continuation in 1995. Although Islamabad agreed in principle with the Comprehensive Test Ban Treaty (CTBT) in 1996, Pakistan had no intention of signing any agreement unless India did so too. India's nuclear tests in May 1998 was followed a fortnight later by similar tests in Pakistan, despite strong American pressure. Nawaz Sharif argued that the great powers had not offered enough guarantees in view of the deteriorating situation in the region.

Nuclearization, Islamic networks and great powers: Pakistan and the challenges of the new world order

If the overt nuclearization of India and Pakistan meant that Pakistan could be sure that deterrents were in place on both sides, it did not put both neighbours on an even keel, since it raised the problem of the role of China and North Korea in Pakistan's arms and missile development. From 1991 onwards, India's economic policy became more open to international markets and foreign investment. Not only the USA but also the European Union and some Southeast Asian countries began to look more favourably on the country, which the US Department of Commerce was soon calling 'a big emerging market'. On another level, the economic sanctions imposed on India and Pakistan after their nuclear tests were much more onerous for Pakistan than for India, even if Washington was ready to relax them a little, to prevent Pakistan from sinking even deeper into financial crisis. A third factor – increased international terrorism, embodied in the figure of Osama bin Laden – was bothering Washington, and this delicate issue brought India and the USA closer together. New Delhi accused Islamabad of giving protection and arms to Islamist groups fighting in Kashmir, some of whom came from training camps in Afghanistan. Fourthly, the army's role in Pakistani politics posed new problems in Washington. Beyond the global nonproliferation policy espoused by the White House, the overt nuclearization of India and Pakistan, deep in conflict over Kashmir, worried American experts, who feared that any war could turn nuclear.

In spring 1999, three months after the meeting in Lahore that had revived hopes of normalized relations, the Pakistan army began Operation Kargil in Kashmir, attracting more American criticism. In the face of this massive influx of Islamic forces bolstered by regular troops, entrenched on India's strategic heights, the great powers called for calm, and praised the restraint of New Delhi, which engaged its troops, but neither crossed the Line of Control nor opened other fronts. In the absence of the diplomatic support from Beijing for which he had hoped, Nawaz Sharif had to bite the bullet: on 4 July, in Washington, he called on the mujaheddin to retreat. Thus the Kargil crisis revealed an explosive triangle: armed Islamic groups–civilian power–military power. Sharif paid the price of yielding to American pressure, then trying to take control of the army: he was deprived of his power and his freedom by military *coup d'état* on 12 October 1999.

The army took action in Kargil partly in the hope of bringing the Kashmir question to international attention with a military crisis between two nuclear powers, since Pakistan diplomacy had obviously not convinced the great powers in matters of principle (respecting UN resolutions; right to self-government). Pakistan had misinterpreted international feeling, and underestimated the Indian capacity to react. The credibility of the state of Pakistan, and of its diplomats, had been undermined by the recognized fact that an army that claimed to have no part in these incursions was arming and using Islamic groups to its own ends.[12] The international community was not taken in, and turned to the new Indian market. Pakistan's military strategy failed as well: Washington's call to respect the security line gave it more official status, and put Pakistan squarely among the troublemakers. It is true that none of the major powers approved of the way New Delhi dealt with the Kashmir question. Many had tried – in vain – to help. But no country was able to impose a solution, or to force India to accept an international forum for negotiation. So Pakistan's strategy of keeping the question of Kashmir in the public eye worked, but without offering any prospect of a solution.

General Musharraf's arrival in power did not improve Pakistan's image, although some foreign administrations saw the *coup d'état* as the last chance to get Pakistan out of a crisis whose economic dimension was reflecting fundamental structural problems. The army was also seen as the last bastion against a collapse of the state which could benefit only the fundamentalists. And so the great powers – wishing, for these two reasons, to maintain contact with the new government, while asking it to restore representative democracy as quickly as possible – ignored India's calls to have its neighbour condemned as a terrorist state, since this would have forced Washington to burn its bridges with Islamabad – the worst of all worlds. They did, however, call for a return to civilian government, and expected Pakistan to take a clearer line on radical Islamists and the Taliban. Pervez Musharraf, eager to dispel any idea that Pakistan was in diplomatic isolation, made more visits to numerous Muslim countries, with a view to proving – in the face of Western and Commonwealth condemnation of his coup – that he wanted to maintain his special relationships with 'brother countries'. These, however, were not enough to save Pakistan's economy and improve its diplomatic status. China's friendship might not last for ever, and Moscow continued to favour India. In the power game, US attitudes were more vital to Islamabad than ever.

In this context, President Clinton's very different behaviour towards the two countries during his tour of South Asia in March 2000 (a five-day official visit to India; a few hours of talks in Pakistan) emphasized – had there been any need to do so – the dilemma in which Pakistan finds itself caught today. Ten years after the end of the Cold War, Islamabad, whether under civilian or military government, has still not changed its mind on matters of security. Pakistan is locked into a spiral of regional tensions, symbolized by the priority it gives to the Kashmir question in its difficult relations with India. The country's security is still defined preeminently in military terms, contrary to the minority view that Pakistan's real security depends on its capacity to develop, and to solve its domestic problems (imbalances between the provinces, Islamic forces, health and education, social inequality, power structure, economy). Were this to happen, it could not only reduce defence spending, but also facilitate the establishment of normal economic relations with India.

In a changing world, Pakistan seems increasingly to be a prisoner of its fraught geopolitical heritage, which jeopardizes any geo-economic advantages it could acquire in a newly growing Asia. Muhammad Ali Jinnah's dream has only partly come true: although it has lost Bangladesh, Pakistan is genuinely part of the international community, but it does not enjoy the status for which it might have hoped. This disappointing situation – which is readily acknowledged in Pakistan itself – cannot be explained only by the country's foreign policy, still less by lack of international understanding or by demonizing Islamic cabals. Certainly Pakistan should have responded to the fundamental challenges inherited from Partition, but its diplomacy and defence strategies did not manage to carve out a coherent path. Face to face with its Indian neighbour, and caught in the game of the great powers, Pakistani leaders made choices that could not be dissociated from national considerations and internal power structures.

As it embarks on the twenty-first century under a military regime whose room for manoeuvre is extremely uncertain, in view of the challenges facing the country, Pakistan needs reform. The international community cannot turn a blind eye: Pakistan is indeed classified as a 'pivotal state' – that is to say, one of those developing countries 'whose fates would significantly affect regional, even international stability'.[13] Its potential position within the company of nations will depend on its ability to be a positive link in the global chain rather than contributing to the strategic maelstrom in the Middle East, Central Asia, China and South Asia. In order to achieve this, Pakistan will need to play a cooler hand in the double game of Afghanistan and Kashmir and, finally, call on its richest resource, its people, putting the country at their service.

5

LIVING WITH INDIA

Relations between Pakistan and India

A bloodbath of a secession in the name of the Partition of the Indian Empire, four wars in fifty years, the intractable question of Kashmir, a climate of suspicion and continual accusation: the history of relations between Pakistan and India is a history of failure. The nuclearization of both countries – official since 1998 – cannot fail to have an effect on conflicts between them: the arms race, a drift into nuclear war or an intensification of low-intensity campaigns behind the dubious shield of deterrence. Quite apart from open conflicts, ongoing bilateral tension is a handicap to both countries, especially Pakistan, at a time when the logic of globalization calls for closer commercial relations.

Feeling increasingly misunderstood by an international community that is circumspect about Islam, confronted by India's growing power on the global scene, Pakistan's leaders – civilian, military or religious – are still, for the most part, driven by their traditional tendency to demonize their big Indian neighbour. This difficult relationship with India is endemic to the intellectual and political history of the birth of Pakistan, but it is also indicative of Pakistan's difficult relationship with itself. Born of a feeling of insecurity and an affirmation of a fundamental difference between Muslims and Hindus, Pakistan cannot free itself from the people it left behind. It lives in an atmosphere of tension caused by a relationship with its Indian neighbour, which it describes by turns as hegemonic, bellicose, threatening, underhand and stubborn – the Kashmir question encapsulates this disagreement on both the ideological and the geopolitical front. After the 1999 *coup d'état*, the new military civilian regime should have got down to the business of the economic, political and social reconstruction of the country. In order that priority could be given to domestic problems, they should have stabilized relations with India, but these relations weigh so heavily on the experience of 'being Pakistan' that no one could change them without rethinking the ideological foundations of the nation, its sociopolitical parameters, and the reference points of Pakistan's regional policy.

This chapter will attempt to shed light on this ideological – even psychological – aspect of relations with India, then go on to recall the events leading up to Partition and the bone of contention that is Kashmir, which led to the 1947–48 and 1965 wars; it will then consider the effects of Bangladesh's secession in 1971, and the subsequent Simla Accord, the start of a new phase for a smaller but more homogeneous Pakistan. The countries' images of one another did not change much, but the geopolitical context altered, leading in the 1980s and 1990s to the nuclear arms race and a new war over Kashmir – this time, thanks to Afghanistan, branded with the seal of Islamism on the march.

These strained circumstances are germane to a wider domestic crisis, and to a regional framework characterized by the emergence of a more ambitious India: factors which lead us to wonder about the nature of the dilemma challenging Pakistan more than ever. Must it build its future in a position of opposition to India? Would it be better to turn its back on its neighbour, and forge closer relations with its Muslim 'brother countries'? Or does the logic of geography force it – at the price of a painful revision of its policies – to work for a better future based on dialogue and cooperation? In other words, should Pakistan think of itself as opposing India, separated from India, or with India?

Living with India: The Ideology and Psychology of Difference

The story of relations between Pakistan and India is the story of a divorce that went wrong, giving rise to bitterness, resentment and suspicion. The discrepancies between India and Pakistan,[1] the bone of contention over Kashmir, the arguments in the early years, continual armed conflict, the loss of Bangladesh, have fuelled, as decade followed decade, a very different process from the one of which Jinnah dreamed – before 1947, he believed that Pakistan, once established, would be on good terms with India.

Since Independence, Pakistan has lived not only next-door to India but in opposition to India. Its relations with its neighbour are freighted with emotional overtones that are difficult to pinpoint, but decisive. In the history of the young Pakistan, the long centuries of relations between Hindus and Muslims in the subcontinent impinge constantly upon the short lifespan of two fifty-year-old states. The well-entrenched feeling of difference that was fundamental to Partition brings into play identities defined as essential, almost immanent, which are in fact political constructions (Islam, Hinduism, with an emphatically capital I and H).

In this respect, there is a huge difference between India and Pakistan. In India after Independence, the secularists carried the day over the Hindu nationalists of the Hindu Mahasabha and the Rashtriya Swayamsevak Sangh.[2] The 1950 Constitution, shaped by Nehru's vision, is imbued with secularism. In this multicultural nation, 'religious communities'[3] have equal state recognition, and the state itself is not defined in terms of any religion. This does not stop many Pakistanis from frequently classifying the Indians as Hindus, making the Congress Party a Hindu party (although it partly depended during its long years of hegemony on the votes of Indian Muslims) and Nehru, an agnostic, a Hindu leader.

These simplistic labels are not symptomatic merely of a generalization – even a lack of understanding – of the other; such a simplification of Indian pluralism is crucial to Pakistan's legitimation project. After the rise and subsequent accession to power in New Delhi (1998) of the Bharatiya Janata Party – the political branch of Hindu nationalism – Pakistani ideologues maintain that their analysis has been vindicated. Those who are quick to call India Hindustan, in order to emphasize its Hindu nature, see the majority party in the Indian coalition government lay claim to this quality (calling India by its old Sanskrit name, Bharat), having achieved their success by fostering renewed anti-Muslim violence. But these people prefer to forget that this Hindu nationalism was built up precisely to counter the dominant secularist model, that it denounced Gandhi as a lover of Islam – for this he paid the ultimate price, his life – and that it was resolutely opposed to Nehru and his followers.

In Pakistan, on the contrary, Muslim identity is considered to be the nation's foundation stone. Jinnah, who had no intention of founding an Islamic regime, died too soon to be able to inspire a constitution that set out the nature of the regime with the necessary clarity, and subsequent governments have not been able to achieve this task. As for relations with India, characterized as they are by a history of conflict, his successors have always given priority to the founding affirmation of difference over hopes for harmony.

Jinnah's famous 'theory of two nations' – a Hindu one and a Muslim one – in claiming Pakistan's right to exist in 1940 has become the essential reference point, making religious affiliation the basis of a host of divergences covering every domain of thought and culture. The historian K K Aziz puts it like this:

> Thus Hindu–Muslim conflict was not merely religious. It was the clash of two civilizations, of two peoples who had different languages, different literary roots, different ideas of education, different philosophical sources and different concepts of art . . . when this cultural variance was combined with diversity in social customs and modes of livelihood the emergence of a united Indian nationalism was doomed without redemption.[4]

Knowing whether or not this is a valid observation, when the history and contemporary reality of today's India bear witness to intricate interweavings between the two faiths both in the strictly religious sphere and in the sociocultural field, does not help us to understand the founding philosophy of Pakistan. This philosophy chose to deny everything the two countries had in common in order to emphasize everything that divided them, and thus to justify secession.

For the theory of difference is not the only factor here – there is also the denunciation of Hindu/Indian hegemony. Let me quote Aziz again: 'The Muslim community . . . felt that the majority community was imposing its views upon them, that this imposition of its will was leading to an oppression which became increasingly unbearable as years passed.'[5] For him, 'Pakistan is the child of this feeling of insecurity'[6] evident in Jinnah's speeches and Muslim League resolutions before 1947. Aziz concludes that 'the real roots of the idea of Muslim separatism should therefore be sought in the minds of men rather than in political factors'.[7]

If we cannot understand the history of relations between India and Pakistan without considering this psychological aspect, it would be naive to leave it at that. A number of vested interests are involved in this demonization of India, which shows us how Jinnah's democratic project took the path to failure, and helps to explain the army's decisive role. Nothing is more likely to strengthen the feeling of Muslim identity, or to reinforce nationalist sentiments, than fear of the other and the spectre of an Indian threat. In this context, the Kashmir question is extremely useful to the predominant Pakistani attitude, since it conjures up the prospect of a secessionist move by a Muslim population under India's control. The Kashmiri Muslims – a very small minority among the Muslims of the Indian Union, but a very large majority in their State of Jammu and Kashmir – are proof, as far as Islamabad is concerned, both of the impossibility of peaceful cohabitation under Hindu domination and of vigorous repression by the Indian state. The fact that more than a hundred and twenty million Muslims live in India and have no intention of leaving does not come into it.

Once more we are faced with an obvious paradox: Pakistan has no hesitation in sending its troops, preceded by armed groups which it claims not to support, into this threatening India: it did so in 1947, 1965 and 1999. All these military initiatives ended in failure, for two reasons. In the first place, the fear of Hindu hegemony changed once Pakistan became a state and, moreover, a strongly defended one. Another factor came into the picture, one that made the overwhelming preoccupation with defence spill over into attack: the image of India as a weak country. The Indo–Pakistani war of 1965 followed the defeat of Indian troops in the Sino–Indian conflict of 1962, and Zulfikar Ali Bhutto persuaded Marshal Ayub Khan to attack before the Indian army could re-form and regain strength. The 1999 incursions into the Indian heights of Kargil were launched when the Indian government had fallen, and was supposed to limit itself to ongoing business until the next elections. Nevertheless, this underestimation of Indian power was not a mere moment of weakness or an isolated misinterpretation. There was also the feeling that Indian troops were inherently inferior. The myth of the Muslim soldier's superiority over his Hindu counterpart had long been part of the mental landscape of Pakistan's senior officers. This presumption – partly the legacy of the colonial theory of 'martial races', of the memory of successful Muslim conquests in North India, and of the idea of Islam's innate superiority – exacted a high price from Pakistan's troops.[8]

In order to find a way out of this paradox, which arises partly from the image of a threatening and bellicose India and partly from Pakistani activism, one thing is necessary: to make India shoulder most of the responsibility for these conflicts – Pakistan (if we can believe this) merely responds to its neighbour's provocations. Sometimes Pakistan's rhetoric is right on target – when, for instance, it recalls the Congress Party's ambivalent line before Partition. India's double speak on Junagadh[9] and Kashmir, and its promise – which was never kept – to hold a referendum in Kashmir, also left indelible marks on the Pakistani psyche. But even if we take these things into account, they do not absolve Pakistan of responsibility for repeated use of armed groups (tribes in 1947 and 1965; Islamists in the 1990s), or for direct support of anti-Indian secessionist forces.

Anti-Indian feeling and a selective collective memory encourage an official history which is taught in schools, and this in turn is complemented and made current by the propaganda war conducted by the state's Pakistan TV channel and the vernacular press.[10] Textbooks in both Urdu and English portray the history of India and Pakistan as a one-way street without bends, a 'murdered history' which does not describe the *Realpolitik* that actually goes on, but perpetuates 'prescribed myths'.[11] The fact that Indian textbooks have not always succeeded in avoiding the same distortions can only intensify the image war that forms the two peoples' concepts of one another from an early age. All in all, the original ideological difference, magnified by fifty years of conflictual history and by a culture of nationalist mythologies, gives relations between Pakistan and India an undeniably psychological dimension which jeopardizes all calls for a normal relationship and frustrates any attempt to 'think differently' in both countries.

In such a context, words are of little use. It would take a spectacular change of heart to achieve success in negotiations which turn all too often into a dialogue of the deaf. Only statesmen or women capable of confronting popular opinion in their own country, and turning their back on sterile political games, could turn over a new leaf. What is more, such people would have to be in power in the two countries at the same time.

The Partition Syndrome: Conflictual Beginnings and the Demonization of India

As a result of the massacres that attended it – leaving nearly half a million dead in the Punjab alone in just a few months – the forceps birth of India and Pakistan became a tragedy. Yet again, some meaning had to be drawn from these killings to justify Partition. The official history of Pakistan sees in this originary bloodbath not a murderous aberration but proof that it was impossible for Hindus and Muslims to live together in a unified India.

In that huge bloodstained migration, minorities on each side cut off their roots: Muslims went west; Hindus and Sikhs went east. The most fervent supporters of Pakistan came from Indian provinces where Islam was a minority faith; a number of the new state's leaders (such as Zia ul-Haq, Nawaz Sharif and General Musharraf) were born in present-day India, or – like Muhammad Ali Jinnah, father of the nation – lived there for much of their life. Countless families – especially in the Pakistani elite – originated 'on the other side'. Building a nation and a state, forging a national history, could not erase everybody's sense of a shared past. It is never easy to be a refugee – a *mohajir* – even when you have chosen such a destiny.

Before the Kashmir crisis broke out, in September 1947, the fact that the Radcliffe Commission[12] allocated most of the Muslim district of Gurdaspur, in the Punjab, to India gave rise to vehement protest: in giving India this territory, against the very logic of Partition, the British gave it direct access to Kashmir, thus facilitating future union. Before broaching the question of Kashmir, we must remember the low-level conflicts cited by Pakistan to lay at India's door the responsibility for a relationship that was wrong from the outset.

Two technical matters relating to the sharing-out of resources after Partition poisoned relations between India and Pakistan from the very first months. The first was to do with the overall command – under the British General Auchinleck – put in place to supervise the transition and oversee the sharing-out of military resources. Its early demise in November 1947, under pressure from India, deprived Pakistan's army of its fair share of equipment and munitions. Pakistan's frustration was not only material and strategic: there was a strong feeling that the country had been misled by unfulfilled promises from the other party. The same Indian lack of goodwill characterized the sharing-out of financial resources: Gandhi had to threaten to go on hunger strike on 12 January 1948 before New Delhi agreed to release money that should by rights go to Pakistan. Eighteen days later the Mahatma was felled by a bullet from a Hindu extremist who could not forgive him for this 'shady deal'. So on two sovereign questions – finance and defence – Pakistan considered itself the victim of Indian hegemony from the beginning.

There was a third problematic resource to share out, and this was even more crucial: the waters of the Indus, which in the plains of Pakistan nurtured the world's largest irrigation area, but whose upper basin belonged to India. At the end of the arbitration tribunal's mandate – which came on 30 March 1948, with no agreement between the two countries – India blocked access to these waters, forcing Pakistan to sign an agreement. Nonetheless, in 1952 India accepted the good offices of the World Bank. Eight years later, the Treaty of the Indus Waters was signed. Pakistan still cites this today to emphasize – in the context of Kashmir – the necessity of involving a third party to unblock deadlocked bilateral negotiations.

These differences, whether they have been settled or not, have left their mark on Pakistan's psyche, and helped to build up an image of an India that will not accept that Partition is a *fait accompli*. Here, however, there are two distinct factors to consider. When the Indian leaders finally agreed to the establishment of Pakistan: the All India Congress Committee declared that it 'believed firmly that when the present passion will have abated, the problems of India will be seen in their proper perspective, the false two-nation doctrine being then discarded and rejected by all'.[13] This way of looking at things, which sees Partition as an aberration engineered by the machinations of Jinnah and the Muslim League, is that of the majority in India, where there is widespread rejection of the logic of Partition – a rejection, however, which should not necessarily entail an obstinate denial of the resulting reality: Pakistan. To an outside observer it is clear that India has recognized Pakistan's existence for some considerable time – and not merely in diplomatic terms. This argument, however, does not convince numerous Pakistanis who still feel not only unloved but positively threatened by their neighbour. The nub of the problem, certainly, is the fact that images of the other have moved out of the domain of analysis and into that of belief – everything India says, however contradictory, is used to bolster the popular conception of an India that wants – either directly or indirectly – to drive Pakistan off the face of the earth.

Several points are put forward to illustrate this argument; they are made in different ways, but they all tend in the same direction. The first point is the stance of the Hindu nationalists, who have traditionally invoked the geographic unity of the Indian landmass to further the concept of a united India, Akhand Bharat, rooted in history and mythology. The Indus – even the Hindu Kush – would constitute its natural western border. This is an extreme minority view, but a united India is always used in Pakistan to situate Indian ambitions in a millenarian, essentialist – and hence presumably intangible – framework. In 1999, however, the Indian Prime Minister, Atal Behari Vajpayee, heir to the school of thought that promoted the concept of Akhand Bharat, visited the Minar-i Pakistan in Lahore, where the famous Muslim League resolution was passed on 23 March 1940, a memorial to Pakistan's will to independence – a highly symbolic gesture. Three months later, the Pakistan army went into Indian Kashmir, igniting the Kargil war. India felt betrayed: Vajpayee's gesture of goodwill had achieved nothing.

Further arguments are put forward as proof of India's eternal bitterness: Bangladesh's secession in 1971, achieved with the help of the Indian army; hypotheses that Pakistan will break up under the pressure of domestic, ethnic or sectarian tension; or the bellicose arguments of powerful people in India such as those who are unwise enough to consider it a good thing to establish a link between the nuclear tests in 1998 and their impact on regional power relations. Unfortunately, mistrust feeds even on its opposite. Brotherly or pacifist overtures are also considered suspect or dubbed hypocritical. Behind the Indians' reminders of the former links between the two countries, many people in Pakistan claim to discern a threatening nostalgia for a united India. Anyone who puts forward the idea that at some time in the future there could be some kind of federation in South Asia is perceived as a conspirator in the same dastardly plot. This mindset in Pakistan attributes ulterior motives even to those Indian leaders who have been most in favour of establishing normal bilateral relations, such as I K Gujral, prime minister from 1996 to 1997.

The disputes enumerated above, however, were not in themselves enough to foster such a mindset. In this context the Kashmir question, which exploded in the very wake of Independence, is crucial, and still not settled to this day. After four armed conflicts, it remains the dispute that gives rise to the strongest expressions of anti-Indian feeling.

Kashmir and the First Wars: 1948 and 1965

In 1947, although Hari Singh, Maharajah of Kashmir, was tempted by the idea of independence, he had to choose – as did all the princes of the former Indian Empire – whether to unite his state with India or Pakistan. As sovereign Hindu ruler of a state with a Muslim majority, he came up against both public discontent and two rival parties: the Muslim Conference, which wanted to join Pakistan; and Sheikh Abdullah's National Conference, which was more secular and more open to the idea of joining India, as long as Kashmir would be guaranteed a considerable degree of autonomy. While the region of Poonch rose up against the maharajah and proclaimed itself 'Azad Kashmir' (free Kashmir), from 24 October 1947 tribal armies

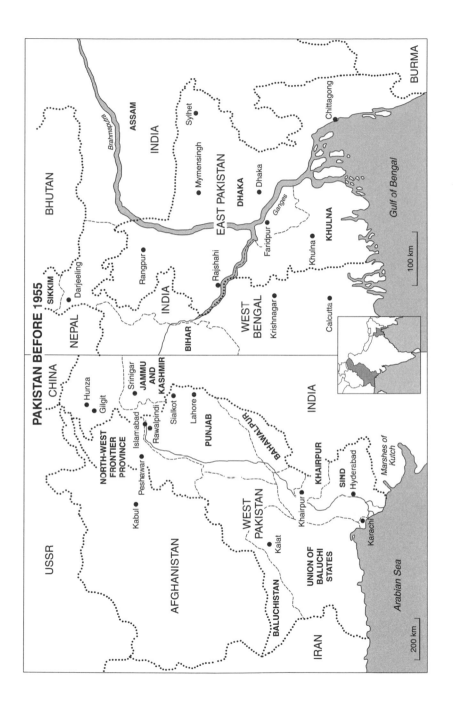

from the north of the kingdom marched on Srinagar. Hari Singh vacillated, and finally summoned India to the rescue. Nehru, the Indian Prime Minister, replied that he could act only if the maharajah signed an act of accession uniting his state to India; this he did on 26 October 1947. Most importantly, there was an understanding between Lord Mountbatten, governor general of India, and Nehru that this accession would be confirmed by referendum. The Indian army, swiftly deployed to Srinagar, blocked the tribal forces' advance. The Pakistan army went into Kashmir officially in May 1948.

The first war between the two neighbour states ended under UN auspices on 1 January 1949. In effect, the cease-fire line *de facto* runs between two Kashmirs. To the south stretches Jammu and Kashmir, now a member state of the Indian Union, which the Pakistanis call IOK: India Occupied Kashmir (100,000 square kilometres; 10 million inhabitants). To the east is Ladakh, mostly Buddhist in Leh but mostly Muslim in Kargil. To the south is Jammu – mainly Hindu, but with some predominantly Muslim areas. In the centre are areas with a very strong Muslim majority around the valley of Srinagar, heartland of *kashmiriyat*, a Kashmiri identity based on a Sunni Sufi Islam with a tolerant attitude towards the Brahman pandits in this region, which was noted for its contribution to Hinduism.[14]

To the northwest of the cease-fire line, in Poonch, Azad Kashmir (13,000 square kilometres; 3 million inhabitants) is a non-sovereign state. Its president, its government and its assembly are under the direct control of Islamabad. To the north of the line, the vast Northern Territories cover the former tribal lands of Gilgit and Baltistan (60,000 square kilometres; approximately a million inhabitants), with a significant Shi'a minority. This entire area, which India calls Pakistan Occupied Kashmir, does not enjoy the usual status of Pakistani provinces, for Pakistan defines the Northern Territories and Azad Kashmir, like Jammu and Kashmir, as 'disputed territories' to be subjected to a referendum.

So all the original planks of a debate that is still going on were in place. It involved several parameters at once: differing conceptions of the nation, strategic battle stakes, conflicting interpretations of historical facts, and points of law, each side accusing the other of blatant dishonesty. As far as Pakistan is concerned, Kashmir should by rights belong to it – is it not right next door, and are not most of its population Muslims? The maharajah's choice is contested in law: did he not leave Srinagar as a result of popular pressure, after the troops had massacred some of his Muslim subjects? Pakistan also invokes the precedent of Junagadh, united with India by force in September 1947 on the pretext that most of its population were Hindus. For Islamabad, Kashmir, 'a disputed territory', continues to exemplify 'the unfinished agenda' of a Partition aborted as a result of Indian machinations. For New Delhi, on the other hand, India is the victim of Pakistani subversion, because the tribal armies who infiltrated in 1947 were not Kashmiris but Pashtuns from Pakistan, sent at the instigation and with the organizational help of Pakistani officers. New Delhi had lodged a complaint about this to the UN Security Council on 1 January 1948.

The UN debated this matter for months, and passed several resolutions. The resolution of 13 August 1948 lays down four guiding principles: (1) withdrawal of the Pakistani troops; (2) withdrawal of the armed tribal groups; (3) interim government by civilian authorities under the control of a United Nations Commission for India and Pakistan, set up in 20 January and in place by July; (4) withdrawal of most of the Indian forces after the withdrawal of the Pakistani and tribal forces; India to maintain only 'minimal' forces in Kashmir until a final ruling was made. The resolution of 9 January 1949, after the cease-fire, laid down conditions for a referendum organized by an administrator appointed on 22 March, the American Admiral Nimitz. Since the UN Commission's official arbitration was ineffectual, the Australian Owen Dixon was appointed as UN representative. Although Dixon readily acknowledged that the interventions of the tribal and Pakistani troops violated international law, he also became convinced very early on that India had no wish either to withdraw its troops or to hold a referendum. At the end of his term of office, in August 1950, the only solution as far as he was concerned was to split Kashmir, on the understanding that the valley of Srinagar would itself be split . . . when its inhabitants had been duly consulted: a vicious circle in which Kashmir is still trapped fifty years later.

New Delhi averred that the maharajah's decision to join India was not legally contestable. Moreover, it expressed the will of the National Conference, Kashmir's most representative body, since Hari Singh had put Sheikh Abdullah in power. It was subsequently confirmed *de facto* by the specific 1957 constitution of Jammu and Kashmir, then by the Kashmiris' participation in several Indian elections which made the notion of a referendum obsolete (needless to say, Pakistan contested this argument). More fundamentally, India argued that it was a secular, multifaith nation, as its 1950 Constitution confirmed. And so the Muslim majority in Kashmir serve the conflicting arguments of two neighbours putting forward opposing points of view – exclusive and inclusive – of the nation. It is precisely on this fundamental question that India and Pakistan are divided.

Pakistan is quick to point out that its interest in Kashmir is not territorial but based purely on a wish to see the Kashmiris' right to self-government recognized. Nevertheless, the three faces of this former kingdom's strategic importance cannot be ignored. Kashmir, often called Pakistan's 'jugular vein', contains the upper basin of the Indus, which is vital to the country's irrigation system, and hence to its food supplies. India has never disputed the Indus Treaty signed in 1958, but could still used it to exert pressure.

The second element to consider is neighbouring China. As relations between China and Pakistan improved, the border adjustments agreed in 1963 – vigorously contested by India, which claimed the whole of the former kingdom of Kashmir – allowed Beijing to consolidate the strategic axis linking Tibet and Xinjiang (Sinkiang) along a sensitive boundary. The opening of the Karakorum road in 1978 improved links between Pakistan and Xinjiang, opened up the Northern Territories (Gilgit and Baltistan), and also linked Pakistan to Central Asia, avoiding the troubled north of Afghanistan. Once it had occupied the trans-Himalayan territory of Aksai Chin, at one time part of Ladakh, then swallowed up part of Ladakh as a result of the 1962 war, China controlled the trans-Karakorum fringes of Kashmir. Although it would not admit it, China is also an interested party in the dispute over Kashmir; it hopes –

and there is some basis for this hope – that the solution of its border dispute with India will one day give it absolute sovereignty over these territories.

A third issue: Kashmir is not only a cause of disagreement with New Delhi; it is the site *par excellence* of direct confrontation. For Pakistan it provides advance bases for tribal groups (in 1947 and 1965) or Islamists (today) infiltrating Indian Kashmir, and rear bases which can double up as training camps for Kashmiri militants from the Srinagar valley. Kashmir's continuing transitional status, and the presence of Kashmiris on both sides of the security line – something of a generalization in view of the ethnic diversity throughout the former princely state – offers incomparably more room for manoeuvre here than along the international border of south Kashmir, from the Punjab to the sea.

1965: a futile war

In a way, the 1965 war began in April in the Rann of Kutch, shared between Pakistani Sind and Indian Gujarat, where Pakistan got the upper hand in border skirmishes. In September there was renewed violence in Kashmir, where the situation had been deteriorating for months. Once Jammu and Kashmir joined it, India quickly reneged on its promise of a referendum, which would entail a withdrawal – which never materialized – of Pakistani forces from the north of Kashmir. The considerable autonomy granted to Kashmir, laid down in the Indian Constitution (Articles 306 and 370), was no longer respected after 1953, when Sheikh Abdullah was accused of playing the independence card, and imprisoned.

So began the Indian policy of political manipulation in Kashmir, by means of accommodating governments brought to power through dubious electoral practices, and often corrupted. In 1954, New Delhi arrogated legislative power in Kashmir, except in three inherently sovereign domains (defence, foreign affairs, communications). In 1957 the state Constitution announced that it would become fully part of the Indian Union. Early in 1965, Kashmir's status became even more in line with the normal status of other Indian states, and Sheikh Abdullah was arrested again. An increasingly powerful protest movement called for a war of liberation. In August, armed groups from Pakistani Azad Kashmir entered the fray in support of their 'compatriots'. The Indian army went into action on 16 August, crossing the cease-fire line. On 1 September, the Pakistani army, which New Delhi accused of organizing the armed groups' infiltration, went into action in its turn in Indian territory. On 6 September the nature of the war changed: Indian forces outside Kashmir crossed the international border and marched on Lahore, capital of the Pakistani Punjab, but did not push home their advantage. A cease-fire was declared on 23 September, under UN pressure.

In January 1966, with the Soviets as mediators, the Conference of Tashkent reached an agreement which nullified India's territorial gains without, however, specifying a procedure for an international settlement of the Kashmir question – to Pakistan's great regret. Yet again, a war between India and Pakistan gave vent to opposing views. New Delhi maintained that sending armed groups from Azad Kashmir – real Kashmiris or Pakistani soldiers – smacked of dirty tricks. Pakistan had launched Operation Gibraltar to take advantage of the situation: an India weakened by the 1962 war against China, Nehru's death in 1964, and the arrival in power of a successor who was not considered to be as strong as his predecessor: Lal Bahadur Shastri.

Pakistan, for its part, continued to put forward the same arguments: the Indians used oppression in Kashmir to put down an uprising by Kashmiris under their rule. What could be more natural for their brothers on the other side of the cease-fire line than coming to assist them? Anyway, how could it constitute infiltration, when Kashmir remained a disputed territory? The Pakistan army – if we take their word for it – acted only against the Indian invasion. There was only one obvious solution: consult the Kashmiri people – hold a referendum . . . This indecisive war, ended by an international conference that settled nothing, did not enhance the prestige of Ayub Khan, who was already beset by domestic problems. Three years later the marshal passed the baton to his chief of army staff, General Yahya Khan, whose leadership faced even more serious problems: the partition of Pakistan, this time soundly beaten by India, governed after 1966 by Nehru's daughter, Indira Gandhi.[15]

The Secession of Bangladesh and the Simla Conference: 1971–72

The Bangladesh war of secession had two major consequences for Pakistan and for relations between Pakistan and India.[16] For one thing, it was the end of a bipolar Pakistan – a western pole and an eastern pole. The Bengali linguistic identity prevailed over the religious unity that had established Pakistan in 1947, inevitably challenging the 'two-nation theory'. Pakistan put forward a different argument: the specific Muslim identity – as Burke, for example, maintains – was even more strongly asserted in that the Awami League rebels had struggled for their own country, Bangladesh, and not to join India. In so doing they had put into practice the theory behind the original resolution to form Pakistan, which envisaged two Muslim states at the two extremities of the subcontinent.[17]

More important still were the conclusions drawn from the Indian military intervention, which carried the day within three weeks.[18] The great and the good in Pakistan saw this action as symptomatic of a will to destroy it on the part of New Delhi, exacting revenge for the first Partition in 1947. This reading of the situation is not entirely mistaken, but it tends to underestimate the overwhelming responsibility of the administrative and military elite in western Pakistan for a massive alienation of eastern Pakistan. Moreover, it seeks to conceal the Pakistan army's bloody repression against the Bengali people. Strong international criticism allowed India to assume a right to intervene,[19] although New Delhi did not push home its advantage either in western Pakistan or in Kashmir. Although India knew that it was unrealistic to hope that it would regain Pakistan, it could look forward to crushing the Pakistan army in the west and occupying the whole of Kashmir. Fear of international condemnation, and the emergence of a new Sino–American approach, no doubt explain the moderate attitude of Indira Gandhi, for whom the break-up of Pakistan already constituted a major victory.

When Yahya Khan left office, Zulfikar Ali Bhutto, Foreign Minister in both preceding governments, took over the reins of power. He quickly opened negotiations with India to ensure the repatriation of more than 90,000 prisoners of war, and to spare some hundred officers being put on trial for war crimes. The first point was settled with Delhi's agreement in 1973; the second in 1974, when Pakistan recognized Bangladesh.

Meanwhile, Z A Bhutto and Indira Gandhi had signed the Simla Agreement on 3 July 1972. This constituted an important advance in relations between India and Pakistan. Nearly thirty years later it is still a landmark, echoed in the Clinton–Sharif agreement of July 1999, which ended the Kargil war.[20] But it contains several ambiguities. It affirms a mutual wish for a 'durable peace in the subcontinent' and the necessity of a 'friendly and harmonious relationship' between the two countries, which – under the terms of Article 1 (ii) – pledge themselves 'to settle their differences by peaceful means through bilateral negotiations or by any other peaceful means mutually agreed upon between them'. Article 4 (ii) specifies that the 1947 cease-fire line – now, after some minor adjustments, the Line of Control – 'shall be respected by both sides without prejudice to the recognized position of either side. Neither side shall seek to alter it unilaterally, irrespective of mutual differences and legal interpretations'.

At Simla Pakistan accepted its diminished status, but made no concessions on Kashmir. India considered it a victory in that the Accord made no reference to UN resolutions, nor to a referendum on the territory's future. Emphasizing the call to settle the problem by 'bilateral negotiations', New Delhi still considers today that at Simla, Pakistan gave up any notion of international involvement in this matter. Pakistan denies this: possible 'recourse to any other peaceful means' opens another door besides the bilateral negotiations so dear to India. There is a further ambiguity: is the Line of Control ratified *de facto*, and destined to become an official border which would confirm the division of Kashmir? The text does not go this far, since it forbids only unilateral alteration of the line. Indian diplomats contend that during last-minute talks on the night of 2–3 July 1972, Bhutto had promised Indira Gandhi in private that he would move towards a partition of Kashmir, but he did not include this in a text that would have had to be accepted by Pakistani authorities still smarting from the secession of Bangladesh. Like Bhutto himself,[21] Pakistani diplomats at Simla rejected this hypothesis of a secret clause. One even denounced this meeting – which he considered against the interests of Pakistan – as 'negotiation under duress', and thus of dubious legality.[22] However, Indian hawks – citing the 'proxy' war conducted in Kashmir by Pakistan since 1990, in violation of Article 4 (ii) of the Accord – still condemn the perceived weakness of Indira Gandhi, deceived by Z A Bhutto, and consider that Indian troops should have conquered the Pakistan-controlled north of Kashmir in 1971.

So the years 1971–72 were decisive. Paradoxically, memories of Bangladesh's war of independence set Pakistan against India, which was accused of drastically reducing it, rather than against the Bengali secessionists. Many also see the Indian army's open participation in the conflict as a precedent justifying further – more covert – intervention by Pakistan in Indian affairs, especially in the Punjab and

Kashmir. To India's wound in 1947, therefore, we can add Pakistan's wound in 1971.

As for the Simla Agreement, for India it remains a landmark that can only add to the sum total of bitterness, since Pakistan has not respected the commitment to 'non-interference in the internal affairs' in each other's (Article 1 [i]), nor the commitment to prevent 'the organization, assistance or encouragement of any acts detrimental to the maintenance of peaceful and harmonious relations' (1 [ii]). Article 2, which affirms that 'both governments will take all steps within their power to prevent hostile propaganda directed against each other', quickly became a dead letter. The Simla Agreement may have restored peace after the break-up of Pakistan, but it did not instil confidence. Since 1971 there has been no fully-fledged border war between India and Pakistan, although Kargil came very close to it in 1999. Islamabad has not stopped taking a hostile line towards India, based on a strategy that teeters between denunciation of the Indian threat, and covert or overt acts of confrontation. The 1970s and 1980s illustrate this logic of cold war or armed peace, affected since 1974 by the accelerating nuclear arms race.

The Nuclear Arms Race: 1972–98

On 16 October 1964, two years after its brief victorious war against India, China carried out its first nuclear tests. India, which had been involved in nuclear research since independence, redoubled its efforts and carried out a first test (pretending that it was a 'peaceful explosion') in 1974. This served only to confirm Bhutto's determination – announced in 1969 and reaffirmed in 1972 – that Pakistan would have nuclear weapons whatever the price.

Bhutto's decision – ratified by his successors – was based on the logic of all-round deterrence. In the face of the supremacy of India's conventional forces – confirmed in 1971 – only nuclear weapons could restore Pakistan's room for manoeuvre, not to mention its prestige in the Muslim world. Even though Pakistan boasts today that it built 'its' bomb as a result of the skill of its Atomic Energy Commission, established in 1956, the international community – not just Indian analysts – consider that its nuclear arms acquisition programme, which it kept secret for many years, enjoyed widespread support: financial support from Arab countries; technological support from China and various Western companies. The programme was kept secret because the United States would have taken a dim view of Pakistan's objective, and would not have believed in an entirely civilian nuclear programme. In 1977, the Symington Amendment gave the White House the option of suspending American aid to countries suspected of carrying out a nuclear arms programme. After some toing and froing, American sanctions were imposed in 1979: Washington did suspend aid, but soon renewed – and increased – it after the Soviet invasion of Afghanistan.

General Zia ul-Haq, instigator of the *coup d'état* that ousted Bhutto in 1977, made great play of Pakistan's new status as the chief channel for American support to the Afghan mujaheddin on the great chessboard of the Cold War. Zia derived two short-term benefits from this. First, President Reagan closed his eyes to Pakistan's nuclear programme, even though the Pressler Amendment, passed in 1985, requested him to check every year that Islamabad did not possess nuclear arms. Moreover, American military aid allowed him to send more combat aircraft, whose main target could only be India. For India, on the other hand, there could be no doubt: Pakistan had become a 'threshold state' with the capacity to build a nuclear bomb. General Zia himself admitted in March 1987 that his country possessed the necessary technology.

And so a second phase began, one which aimed to increase Pakistan's nuclear capacity, and above all to produce more and more powerful weapons, with Chinese and probably North Korean support. In 1989 the Hatf-I and Hatf-II ground-to-ground missiles (80-to-300-kilometre range) were tested. When the war in Afghanistan ended, in 1989, Washington resumed its policy of sanctions against Pakistan (1990). This was a hesitant policy, full of stops and starts and shilly-shallying on China's ability to achieve nuclear proliferation despite the net of international controls. America's change of mind, however, did not stop Islamabad in its tracks. Chinese M-11 missiles, or their components, delivered to Pakistan made headlines throughout the 1990s, which saw the testing of Hatf-III (600-kilometre range) and, in April 1998, of Gauri-I (1,500 kilometres), in response to the Indian Agni missile. The Indian nuclear tests on 11 and 13 May 1998 naturally prompted a reply from Pakistan, which carried out six tests on 28 and 30 May, despite American pressure. Following New Delhi's example, Islamabad had not signed the indefinite extension to the Non-Proliferation Treaty in 1995; nor ratify the Comprehensive Test Ban Treaty the following year.

The overt nuclearization of South Asia in 1998 therefore marks the failure of Pakistan's calls for disarmament, renewed since 1974. Ever since the first Indian tests, Islamabad had been arguing for a nuclear-free zone in South Asia. New Delhi had always said no, because as far as nuclear weapons were concerned, South Asia is not a region in itself but part of Asia: denuclearization of the region would make no sense unless China was involved. Going even further, New Delhi proposed a global disarmament according to a timetable accepted by all parties. No deal. The only regional advances in this domain were modest: in 1989, India and Pakistan agreed not to attack one another's nuclear installations. Obviously Islamabad did not pledge itself not to strike first, judging that such a decision, given its unequal position – in terms of both its conventional armaments and its nuclear capacity – would reduce its power of deterrence to nil. The draft Indian nuclear doctrine, put forward for discussion in August 1999, worried Pakistan, which was aware of the economic risks of an arms race by an India seeking to compete up to a point with China.

Has Pakistan's nuclear programme – secret from 1987, then open in 1998 – changed its strategic relations with India? On two occasions the tension between the two neighbours was so high that Washington stepped in to restore calm – India denies that the two countries came very close to war. In 1987, the big Indian military manoeuvres in Rajasthan known as 'Operation Brasstracks' were viewed in Islamabad as likely to lead to an attack on Pakistan's nuclear installations. In 1990 there was another crisis – this time over Kashmir, which once more became a hot – even burning – issue.[23]

Another War in Kashmir

The 1980s were difficult for India. Indira Gandhi was back in power in 1980, but after she declared a state of emergency that lasted from 1975 to 1977, and the subsequent defeat of the Congress Party, she no longer had the status she had enjoyed in 1971. Her mishandling of Punjabi regionalism only fuelled the movement, which turned secessionist; in the front line were Sikh extremists calling for the creation of an independent Khalistan. Islamabad was quick to support this movement, plunging Indian Punjab into a bloodbath of attacks and repression. Neither the occupation of the Golden Temple of Amritsar by the Indian army in June 1994 nor the assassination of Indira Gandhi four months later put an end to a conflict which continued until the early 1990s, when political life resumed. By providing the Sikh militants with bases and training camps, Zia ul-Haq, the Pakistan army and the secret services – Inter Services Intelligence (ISI) – embarked on another kind of conflict with India by backing the separatist movements rising in the border states. Pakistan engagement on behalf of the Sikh partisans of Khalistan could only, however, go so far. The border separating Indian Punjab from Pakistani Punjab is recognized internationally, and Pakistan has no rights over Indian Punjab.

The Kashmiri context is very different, because Islamabad disputes the legitimacy of the Indian presence there. In 1984, the Indian army's unexpected action on the Siachen glacier, near the Chinese border, caught Pakistan by surprise. Pakistan claimed that this was a violation of the Simla Agreement. New Delhi rejected this interpretation: the security line the two countries are pledged to respect ends at point NJ 9842. Siachen stands further than this. Then New Delhi pushed the virtual line towards the north, so that Siachen was theirs. Islamabad extended it due east, so that Siachen was theirs as well. Since 1984, mountain troops from both sides have been engaged in extreme weather conditions, in the world's highest battlefield: at an altitude of 6,000 metres.

In 1989, the situation in Indian Kashmir – especially at its heart, the valley of Srinagar – took a new turn. After the death of the charismatic Sheikh Abdullah in 1982, New Delhi's negligence and political machinations increased Kashmiri frustration, which was further exacerbated by local government corruption and blatant electoral fraud in 1987. The Jammu and Kashmir Liberation Front (JKLF), founded in 1977, embarked on a campaign of attack in July 1988; in 1989 they kidnapped the daughter of the new Indian Home Minister (a Kashmiri).

This violent outbreak of Kashmiri militancy, further reinforced by Indian repression, opened the way for a new intervention by Pakistan. The chaos in Kashmir was far more conducive to clandestine intervention than the Punjab, with its particularly Sikh character. Azad Kashmir under Pakistan's control would become an ideal support base for the fighters in the valley. Islamabad claimed to be giving the rebels only moral and diplomatic support, and began its international campaigns of denouncing the violations of human rights perpetrated by the Indian security forces – without much success, despite the very real violations documented by Indian and international NGOs. The fact was that no one believed that Pakistan was neutral in this matter. The Soviet defeat in Afghanistan pleased the ISI, which could now (mistakenly) dream of a second victory – this time over India. As for the collapse of the USSR, and the subsequent emergence of independent republics in Central Asia, these events bolstered Kashmiri hopes for freedom. After three futile wars, the revolt by young people in Kashmir meant that Islamabad could bring up the Kashmir question again – with renewed ardour.

Behind the democratic call for the right to self-government, reminders of Nehru's commitments and UN resolutions, Pakistan followed a policy of intervention in this territory. The independently minded, secular JKLF was not really in favour. The army and the ISI had other ambitions in Kashmir. Support for the JKLF dwindled after 1992 and was transferred to overtly Islamist Kashmiri groups such as the Hizbul Mujaheddin, which had Afghan connections and was known for its attacks against moderate Kashmiris. When Indian repression began to decimate the local rebels, from 1994 onwards, the Pakistan secret services sent in more mujaheddin from Azad Kashmir and Pakistan, even veterans of the war in Afghanistan, all trained for *jihad* in Pakistani or Afghan camps. More and more frequent artillery exchanges between official armies, along the Line of Control, covered the movements of infiltrator groups, the most notorious of which were the armed wings of Pakistani fundamentalist organizations, preeminently the Army of the Pure, Lashkar-i-Tayyiba, a satellite group of the Centre for Preaching, Markaz Dawa-al-Irshad, which had been in Kashmir since 1989, and the Movement of the Companions of the Prophet, Harkat-ul Ansar, in Kashmir since 1993 and rebaptized Harkat-ul Mujaheddin in 1998 (often being classified as a terrorist organization by the American administration). These Islamic guerrilla groups increased their attacks outside the valley of Srinagar, especially in mountainous areas of Jammu – even, through tiny satellite groups, in New Delhi.

Pakistan's policy in Kashmir is particularly complex, because it is the result of more or less fluid power relations between civilian government, the army and the ISI, and Islamic organizations. It must take into account on-the-spot developments, including the position of parties opposed to the presence of India, which came together in 1993 in an All-Party Hurriyat Conference (APHC), a cross-party freedom group, ill-assorted and without a charismatic leader. The APHC had to take a stand against the Indian strategy, and finally to take account of opinion in the international community, especially in the United States. The events of 1998–99 showed that American influence, strong as it might be, cannot always impose its will on Pakistan.

The significance of Kargil: 1999

Islamist fighters from Pakistani Kashmir usually infiltrate Indian Kashmir in the spring, when the snow melts from the mountain peaks along which the Line of Control runs. The movements observed in May 1999 were another matter: this was no infiltration but an occupation of territory which, while it is certainly uninhabited, is strategic, since it dominates the route from Kargil to Ladakh and Siachen. The action involved not only well-armed Islamist fighters but also Pakistani troops. The Indian counterattack was belated but massive, a virtual war, with the army and aircraft joining the battle so that the Pakistani army could not gain a foothold in the area.

What did Pakistan hope to gain from this? To alter the Line of Control *de facto* at an essential strategic point, or – at the very least – to use the ensuing crisis to bring the Kashmir question to international attention at last? To take advantage of the screen of nuclear deterrence in order to intensify low-level conflict? India's resolute stance, New Delhi's tactics of restraint – it chose to retake the Kargil heights without crossing either the Line of Control or the border – and American pressure on Nawaz Sharif caused Islamabad to abandon an operation that was in any case destined to fail. Nonetheless, the 'Kargil war' was a shock for India, which – after the constructive talks at Lahore – saw it as an act of treachery by Pakistan, especially since hopes had been raised by renewed dialogue over the past few months.

In October 1999, a putsch by General Musharraf, the strategic architect of Kargil, dealt another blow to relations between India and Pakistan and interrupted the deals on the future of Kashmir that were being brokered behind the scenes. After that India has tried to keep Pakistan in diplomatic isolation. It has deferred the SAARC meeting, and obtained a Commonwealth condemnation of Pakistan's military regime. Above all, it has strengthened its cooperation with the USA against terrorism, putting Pakistan in an awkward position. Obviously, General Musharraf has to tread a narrow path: he needs the Islamic groups if he is to exert pressure on India in Kashmir; these groups, however, jeopardize his country's stability and cause Washington to place Islamabad under surveillance. The military regime has called for an unconditional resumption of talks with India. New Delhi has refused to resume talks unless there is an end to Islamist infiltrations.

Peace, Diplomacy and Civil Society: From Hope to Failure

Kargil has shown that there can be an endless succession of military operations and diplomatic meetings, but 'peace' is nothing less than a prolonged cold war. There is nothing new about that, for behind the story of conflict related above we must examine a parallel history of dialogue between India and Pakistan – dialogue which has never succeeded in establishing normal relations between the two neighbours. This disappointing history, however, is very instructive in that it illustrates recent trends which, unfortunately, lead us to temper the optimism engendered by periods of comparative improvement.

Government diplomacy

After 1949, Nehru proposed a pact that the two countries would not go to war; this suggestion was repeated on countless occasions. Pakistan's answer was always the same: such a pact would be viable only if the major disputes between the two countries were settled. General Yahya Khan told Indira Gandhi this yet again when she suggested it to him in 1969. This fundamental disagreement has not precluded one-off agreements. In 1950, a pact between Nehru and Liaquat Ali Khan put an end to tensions affecting religious minorities in East Pakistan and eastern India. In 1958, an agreement between Nehru and Noon set the eastern borders of the two countries. Two years later, the Indus Waters Treaty, mentioned above, settled a dispute that was crucial to Pakistan. Even more progress could have been made. From 1946 onwards, Jinnah had envisaged a possible military alliance – even mutual protection – between India and Pakistan after Partition. This possibility was raised again by Muhammad Ali Bogra in 1953, Malik Farooz Khan Noon in 1957, Ayub Khan in 1959 (after China's invasion of Tibet) – but always with one condition: that the Kashmir question must be settled by mutual agreement.

On more than one occasion, optimism seemed to prevail. In 1953, Bogra and Nehru met twice in two months. They seemed to be reaching an agreement on solving the problem of Kashmir bilaterally, by referendum. These hopes came to nothing. India accused Pakistan of scuppering any agreement by joining the Western alliance in 1954. Pakistan – not without some justification – accused India of taking a harder line on Kashmir by imprisoning Sheikh Abdullah. Ten years later, between December 1962 and May 1963, the two Foreign Ministers, Z A Bhutto and Swaran Singh, met several times. India was thinking of making the Line of Control a recognized border, after a few adjustments. Ayub Khan was more inclined towards internationalizing the valley of Srinagar for five or ten years. There was certainly no agreement on the horizon, but the two parties showed a new flexibility. In May 1964 there was another hesitant move forward: India seemed willing to contemplate possible American or British mediation. Sheikh Abdullah had come out of prison in April. In Pakistan, he put forward the idea that India and Pakistan should share sovereignty in Kashmir, and announced that Ayub Khan and Nehru would meet on 26 May. Nehru's illness – he died on 27 May – put an end to these conciliatory overtures. Were they to be taken seriously, or were they a mere smokescreen? After 1962, Ayub Khan rejected the old idea of a possible alliance with India against China's increasing hegemonic ambition: after the war between India and China, Washington granted India military aid to the great displeasure of Pakistan, which grew close to China before coming up against India in 1965 and 1971.

Zia ul-Haq was a master of this two-sided policy, blowing hot and cold by turns. Even as he reinforced his military arsenal, taking advantage of the war in Afghanistan and American generosity, Zia made a surprise visit to New Delhi in 1982 to show that his intentions were good. That same year, a joint Indo–Pakistani commission was established. This, however, did not stop Pakistan from helping the Sikh rebels of Khalistan in their attempt at secession in 1983. These up-and-down relations, these contrasting attitudes, continued to be the norm. In 1985, India and Pakistan became members of the new South Asia Association for Regional Cooperation (SAARC), which seemed to promise a better future for the whole region. Its charter ruled that strictly bilateral problems were not to be raised there. This measure was totally unconvincing, and twelve years later Pakistan's President Leghari considered that the SAARC's lack of progress was due precisely to the fact that regional dynamics remained frustrated by disputes between his country and India, without SAARC offering a forum for mediation. In 1987, the increased tension caused by Operation Brasstracks tempered the optimism aroused by the launch of the SAARC. Zia ul-Haq's 'cricket diplomacy' was purely cosmetic. Ten years later, nothing had changed. Now the young Benazir Bhutto was prime minister, and at last Pakistan seemed to be taking steps towards democracy. In 1989 Rajiv Gandhi went to Islamabad: the first visit to Pakistan by an Indian prime minister since 1960. He and Benazir signed an agreement to the effect that the two countries would not attack one another's nuclear installations. A year later, after the 1990 crisis, the threat of nuclear war again hung over the region.

There was no fundamental change in the 1990s; talks between Nawaz Sharif and I K Gujral just managed to reinstate meetings between diplomats who, only too often, could discuss only the technicalities of hypothetical negotiations. Always the same question: where do we begin? With Kashmir, said Pakistan, since that is the 'core issue', and significant progress in this area will free up the whole mechanism of bilateral relations. With everything else, said India, who thought it would be better to start with less contentious problems: setting the border in Kutch at Sir Creek; economic cooperation; even the Siachen glacier.

The assumption of power by the Bharatiya Janata Party (BJP) in 1998, and nuclear tests by India – followed soon after by Pakistan – obviously cooled bilateral relations and worried the international community, which was afraid that the old conflict between India and Pakistan, exacerbated by the deterioration in Kashmir, would lead to disaster. In this context, the visit to Lahore by Indian Prime Minister A.B. Vajpayee, in February 1999 revived hopes considerably. True optimists thought that, after all, the Hindu nationalist party was perhaps the best bet for getting things moving again, despite its anti-Muslim extremists. The Lahore Declaration, signed by both Vajpayee and Nawaz Sharif, called yet again for a resumption of dialogue and for the peaceful resolution of disputes, while additional documents laid down the principle of nuclear restraint on both sides. At that very moment, however, the Pakistani military were preparing for their occupation of the Kargil heights.

Parallel diplomacy, civil society and economic interests

When diplomacy blows hot and cold, it is useful to have parallel channels that can maintain contact between the two countries. In the 1990s, unofficial meetings proliferated; they took two distinct but partly complementary forms. Parallel diplomacy – so-called 'second-tract diplomacy' – was built around people with close ties to those in power, especially former senior diplomats and former (and future) ministers. Their role was not so much to hold discreet negotiations as to think together. Their governments, which were kept fully informed, were not directly involved but could, for that very reason, put out feelers. The most famous network, the Neemrana Initiative, got down to work in 1991. Today it is in decline, but the continuing role of Niaz Naik, a crucial Pakistani prime mover, shows how important it is to maintain contact through experienced operators.

Further from the corridors of power, and often highly critical of them, are networks more deeply entrenched in civil society: academics and journalists, NGO workers, antinuclear activists. There are several such groups, but the most high-profile is the Pakistan-India People's Forum for Peace and Democracy, which puts out feelers in both countries and has organized annual public meetings in both Pakistan and India since 1995. There are also meetings of special-interest groups: parliamentarians or feminist groups, for example. In addition there are many people of good will of various persuasions, some more radical or anti-establishment than others. Nevertheless, they all have the same essential role, despite some sceptical murmurings that initiatives like this are simply preaching to the converted. They help to lessen nationalist tensions and reduce mutual demonization. They bear witness – as do certain articles in the Pakistani press (more in the Anglophone press than in the vernacular, it is true) – to the necessity of new thinking and having an eye to the future. The instigation of 'confidence-building measures', so dear to American the-oreticians of conflict resolution,[24] is most evident at government level, but the state must also allow civil society to play its part.

Love of peace and idealism are not the only factors. Economic interests also have a legitimate role. But in this domain, businesses and chambers of commerce rely heavily on fluctuations in the political climate and the contrasting analyses at the heart of the global economy. The logic of liberalization and the ridiculous weakness of bilateral trade – which, restricted by the two states, enriches only smugglers and third countries – mean that some industrialists in Pakistan want better economic rela-tions with India, while others fear Indian competition. At the same time, political, military or Islamist overstatements denounce those who give economic cooperation priority over the Kashmir question. Pakistan has certainly made some concessions under the auspices of the South Asia Preferential Trade Association, the commercial arm of the SAARC, but the proposed objective of a free exchange zone (SAFTA) including Pakistan seems highly improbable at the moment. As a member of the WTO, Pakistan should give its Indian neighbour 'most favoured nation' status: for the time being it refuses to do so. India, for its part, does not extend to Pakistan the 'Gujral doctrine' which advocates advantageous relations with its neighbours – Bangladesh and Sri Lanka, for example – without expecting anything in exchange. The real signs will be seen on other fronts – geopolitics of energy, for example – crucial to Indian supplies, and for Pakistan in terms of royalties. The construction of a gas pipeline from Turkmenistan to India via Pakistan would be highly significant.

A Question of Priorities

At a time when India is playing the game of economic reform, strengthening its diplomatic powers, publicizing its ambitions for the new century, Pakistan remains a prisoner of a history which prevents it from realizing its great potential. The ques-tion is easy to ask and difficult to answer: when will the leaders of Pakistan feel ready to rethink their regional policy and restore calm to their borders – above all in Kashmir – in order to give priority to domestic reform, without compromising the security that is every state's right? India is ready to recognize the security line as a *de jure* border, and seems to be committed to vague negotiations with the leaders of the Hurriyat Conference; nevertheless, its military apparatus is still very strong and New Delhi rejects the proposal of the Jammu and Kashmir Assembly to grant back the maximum autonomy for Jammu and Kashmir envisaged before 1953. Pakistan, in turn, refuses any attempt to make the *de facto* sharing-out of Kashmir official, and expects to be involved in any agreement between New Delhi and the people of Kashmir. The options in Kashmir are more precarious than ever. Islamabad continues to favour the activist line of slowly 'bleeding' India on its northern front, at the risk of increasing extreme Islamist militancy in Pakistan itself. The line of continued dialogue with New Delhi, bringing in Kashmiri delegates once relative calm is restored to Kashmir, seems, however, to be the most promising route. But if progress is to be made in this direction, perhaps we need a statesman capable of turning the page on fifty years of tension, frustration and suspicion.

For the moment, Pakistan is still mired in the trauma of a Partition which the country itself fervently desired. It has to live with India, and it must take on a positive – not merely reactive – identity, and accept the fact that its neighbour will have a more important role in the world of tomorrow. Although both countries have acquired nuclear weapons, any impression of symmetry between them is purely illusory. Pakistan may rightly reject the idea of an aggressive or surreptitiously hegemonic India. But both sides have to recognize the reality principle which acknowledges their unequal weight and the importance of peaceful coexistence, and which gives Pakistan and India the same rights and the same duties, in the interests – above all – of their people. True optimists might see something better than mere coexistence in the future: a fully-fledged normalization of bilateral relations. At the beginning of the twenty-first century, this still seems a long way away.

6

ISLAM AND FOREIGN POLICY
Central Asia and the Arab–Persian World

Pakistan is first and foremost an ideological concept: the Muslim state on the Indian subcontinent. It therefore has a duty to defend and represent all Muslims in the region, and its territorial limits are, when all is said and done, immaterial. The choice of Urdu as the national language is an excellent illustration of this ideological vision of identity: Urdu was the language spoken by Indian Muslims, but not by any of the ethnic groups which settled in present-day Pakistan (while 60 per cent of the population speak Punjabi). Naturally, Pakistan could have shaken off the conditions under which it came into existence, and become a 'banal' nation-state; but the conflict with India, and General Zia ul-Haq's choice when he took power in 1977, finally placed Muslim identity at the very heart of the concept of Pakistan, just as Maududi had wished.

Now this choice has important implications for foreign policy: it leads Pakistan not only to express its conflict with India in terms of *jihad*, but also to champion other jihads, like the one against the Soviet occupation in Afghanistan. It adds a permanent transnational dimension to domestic policy. The great religious parties and movements in Pakistan situate themselves explicitly within a transnational perspective: they were all founded before Partition in 1947 (Ahl-i Hadith, Jamiyyat-ul Ulama, Jamaat-i Islami, Tablighi Jamaat). Ethnic continuity also strengthens the link between Islamic solidarity and transnationalism: Pashtun or Pashtun ulemas, on either side of the Afghan border, are mainly – but not entirely – trained by the same religious organization, the Deobandi school, the most recent example being the Taliban.

This transnationalism is reinforced by sizeable waves of emigration – mostly to Britain, but also to the Persian Gulf: many Pakistanis are militant members of Islamic associations which identify closely with the *umma*, the Muslim community as a whole, and not only with the nation of Pakistan. The Rushdie affair, instigated in January 1989 by Pakistanis in Bradford, is a good illustration of the transnational dimension of emigration from Pakistan.

The spontaneous emigration to the Gulf States, moreover, was accompanied by 'service benefits' from the government of Pakistan, especially in the military sphere (pilots, technical workers, even entire corps such as the one commanded by General

Zia himself in Jordan in the early 1970s). Such activity, however, declined after 1990, because the Gulf States trained their own experts, and began to distrust the Pakistanis in their countries, suspecting them of being sympathetic towards Saddam Hussein during the Gulf War (and also because the Americans took over direct protection of Kuwait and Saudi Arabia). Finally, Pakistan played a key role in the establishment of the World Islamic Conference in 1969 (the second meeting took place in Lahore in 1974).

Pakistan's choice of identity prompts it to become involved with a regional Islamic body that is spread over a much wider area than the national space it was granted at Partition. But this expansionism is reinforced by an overriding strategic constraint: Pakistan is much weaker than India, and needs strategic depth against its powerful neighbour, whose tanks are less than a hundred kilometres from its cultural capital, Lahore. From the time of its birth as a nation, Pakistan's skill has lain in gaining two types of support: an Islamic solidarity – which calls simultaneously on conservative Arab states like Saudi Arabia and on more militant Muslim public opinion – and a set of alliances with the West, especially with the USA. The Afghan war (1979–89) was the acme of this policy; while during the next decade the Taliban's support for Osama bin Laden, marked the inherent contradiction between the two sets of alliances which have allowed Pakistan, despite its economic weakness, to hold its own against India and to play a major role in the region's politics.

The Weight of History

Pakistan's reaching out towards the Middle East and Central Asia can be explained in terms of the country's strategic constraints and self-image, but it also has more distant roots which may be seen less as primary causes than as a symbolic ensemble which allows us to locate the Pakistan of today in a wider historical context.

The first element here was the Ghaznevid (around AD 1000) and Ghorid (eleventh century) empires,[1] both centring on Afghanistan, which were the determining factors in the Islamization of North India. But the most important historical factor was the Mughal Empire, founded by Babur after the seizure of Delhi in 1527. The sixteenth century gave rise to a historical configuration that would be obscured by the arrival of the two great Western empires, British and Russian-Soviet. In 1501 Iran suffered a schism brought about by a Turkish-speaking dynasty, the Safavids; while Central Asia as we know it today fell under the yoke of another Turkish dynasty, the Uzbek Shaybanids, who drove a petty monarch (also Turkish-speaking), Babur, from his fiefdom in Ferghana. He took refuge in Kabul, which he used as a base for conquering North India and founding the Mughal Empire. All these empires were under Turkish hegemony, and their court and legislative language was Persian. The Mughal and Uzbek empires were Sunnite, and both expressed their rivalry with Iran in terms of the struggle against the Shi'a 'heresy'. Present-day Afghanistan is therefore a battlefield for three empires: a configuration that recurred after the collapse of the USSR and the emergence of an independent Uzbekistan. After its sixteenth-century schism, Iran cut off direct links between Central and South Asia and the Middle

East. A Persian-speaking Sunni religious culture then developed in these three areas, especially around the great *madrasahs* of North India, which enjoyed a revival in the second half of the nineteenth century as a reaction against English political domination. This Sunni militancy grew mainly as a reaction against the possibility of syncretism between Islam and Hinduism, illustrated by the emergence of the Sikh movement but also by the policies of Babur's grandson, Akbar. The 'Mughal myth' was brought back into the picture mainly by General Zia, during the Afghan war and when the new Central Asian republics gained their independence, at the very moment when the Iranian revolution (1979) was emphasizing more strongly than ever the profoundly Shi'a nature of Islam in Iran.

Present-day Pakistan's supranational dimension can also be situated within a long tradition of Muslim militancy in the Indian subcontinent, irrespective of the political regime. From the early nineteenth century onwards the subcontinent's religious men, on their return from prolonged visits to Mecca, revived this doctrinaire, militant, fundamentalist and rigorously Sunni Islam, which would become the hallmark of all Islamic resurgence in the region right up to our own time. They would be dubbed 'Wahhabi' both by British political agents and by Russian rulers of Central Asia, even though at that time Mecca was not controlled by Saudi Wahhabi.

None of these Islamic militants is struggling for the creation of a separate Muslim state; they all reiterate the doctrine of the return of Islam's political hegemony, but they accept their Mughal legacy; under the Mughal Empire the Muslims were in the minority, and lived in a predominantly 'infidel' environment: the idea of the 'Land of the Pure', Pakistan, was not on the agenda. They often accepted the reality of British domination, believing that re-Islamization must come before taking power. They defended their status of *millat*, in the sense of a religious community, within an empire which they did not question. They linked this defence to that of the entire Muslim world community, the *umma*.

So it came about that at the very moment when the Muslim countries of the Middle East left the Ottoman Empire to form nation-states, thanks to the First World War (Arab nationalism and Turkish Kemalism), it was the Indian Muslims who established a movement in support of the Ottoman caliph, who was threatened by Ataturk after 1920 (and done away with for ever in 1924): the Caliphate Movement.[2] Tens of thousands of Muslims decided to leave India, now a land of infidels, for Afghanistan, the Muslim world's last independent stronghold. It was also on the subcontinent that militant transnational movements emerged: the Tablighi Jamaat (1927), a purely religious movement which works for the return of an Islam separated from all specific cultural and national traditions; and the Jamaat-i Islami (1941), which promotes the establishment of an Islamic state – again, irrespective of nationality or specific territory. I should also mention the establishment of the great Deobandi *madrasah* near Delhi (1867), the first of an entire network of very active *madrasahs* and of a political party, the Jamiyyat-ul Ulama-i Hind, which became Jamiyyat-ul Ulama-i Islam after Partition.[3]

Pakistan as an Islamic State

We know that it was not militant Islamic movements that led to the creation of Pakistan. The country's founder, Muhammad Ali Jinnah, thought of Pakistan in terms of a nation based on a 'cultural community' rather than in terms of an 'Islamic state'. For the Muslim League, being a Muslim was not only a matter of religious practices; it was a culture, a way of life – 'Muslimness' was as important as ethnic origin (we find this stance again in the debate over the notion of the Bosnian Muslim). Jinnah made himself very clear: 'Hinduism and Islam are not religions in the strict sense of the word, but rather two different and distinct social categories.'[4]

The Muslim League, however, could not openly promote a lay vision of 'Islamness', because that would have meant yielding all strictly religious legitimacy to a party like the Jamaat, but also, no doubt, opening a Pandora's box: if 'Islamness' was merely an identity asserted against Hinduism, then once the Muslims were all together on the same territory, their basic identity would no longer be an Islam without an adversary but would fall into an ethnic or linguistic category (Pashtuns or Pashtuns; Baluchis, Sindis, etc.). Hence the promotion of a secular Pakistani nationalism proved impossible. There was no debate in Pakistan on the subject of 'Islamization against secularism', because those who were against deliberate Islamization were themselves obliged to go back to the spirit of Islam, as Ayub Khan's period in office (1958–69) shows: then it was the state which did its best to achieve an open-minded, modern Islam. The 1962 Constitution was the least Islamic Pakistan had seen, but the clause stipulating that there should be no contradiction between state laws and Islam was kept, even if the question was passed to a Council on Islamic Ideology controlled by the president. All the state could do was make an effort to control – even neutralize – Islamization; it could not counter it with a positive nationalist, unique, secular ideology of its own.

Little by little, the Islamic parties 'nationalized' themselves that is to say, interpreted this concept of Pakistan in their own terms, but gave it a supranational dimension. Under pressure from them, the Pakistan government Islamized the country's institutions. It was the 'secular' Ali Bhutto who reinstated, in the 1973 Constitution, the concept of Pakistan as a Muslim nation; it was he who declared that the Ahmadi were non-Islamic (something the religious leaders had been requesting for a long time), closed the casinos, prohibited alcohol, and appointed General Zia ul-Haq as chief of army staff. When General Zia embarked on a policy of Islamization after his *coup d'état* in 1977, his opponents could criticize him only for imposing an excessively narrow vision of Islam; they could not challenge the fundamental principle. He promoted Urdu – this time to the detriment of English. He introduced into Parliament the Shari'ah Bill, which stipulated that any court could pass judgement preclsely according to sharia law, taking no notice of state legislation.

There were two consequences of this Islamization: first, it took no account of ethnic origin, since everyone was a Muslim. But it also went beyond national sovereignty, since Islam transcends the logic of the state, and any non-Pakistani Muslim should be able to join such a community. General Zia's Pakistan might have had pro-Western leanings, but it also fostered a pan-Islamic activism which led it to support the Afghan mujaheddin, and also to allow into the country Islamic militants from all over the Middle East: extreme radicals who had been banished from their own countries.

This transnational dimension of Pakistan's identity is reinforced by the fact that Pakistan's borders are still somewhat indeterminate. For one thing, they do not correspond to any ethnic border; for another, along more than half their length they do not correspond to internationally recognized borders: the northern border with India is just a cease-fire line, and the 'Durand Line' which separates Pakistan from Afghanistan has never been recognized as an international border by any Afghan government. In addition, the presence along this border of 'tribal areas' where tribal custom overrides the law of Pakistan accentuates the vague nature of these territories. After 1997, Nawaz Sharif's government attempted to impose federal law over tribal custom, only to be confronted by opposition from tribal ulemas, who – on the basis that the Constitution of Pakistan provided for the institution of sharia law – took it on themselves to replace tribal custom with sharia law – still, of course, rejecting a federal law that was not 'shariarized' enough for their taste. Thus the invocation of the sharia confirmed the *de facto* deterritorialization of the concept of an Islamic state by depriving state authority of its legislative power, but also by reviving a very traditional ethos of territorial fragmentation: tribalism.

The influx of millions of Afghan refugees, the growth of smuggling on the border, extensive use of the Pakistani rupee in Afghan territory, Pakistan's open support of the Afghan Taliban – all this helped to make the border between Pakistan and Afghanistan even more vague, and led to the establishment of a new open space where the prevailing ethos is sometimes Pashtun custom, sometimes the sharia. The simple fact that no one in this essentially Pashtun space demands the creation of an independent Pashtunistan, or indeed union with Afghanistan, shows – more clearly than any affirmation of Pakistan's authority – that even the idea of the nation-state has given way to tribal and Islamic entities, which are more susceptible to Islamic revivalism, transformation of the tribal system (power passed from the tribal aristocracy of the *khan* and the *malik* to ulemas from modest, but still tribal, backgrounds), and . . . the development of the drugs trade.

Two historical events were to allow Pakistan to develop a policy of regional power based above all on Islamic supranationalism: the Afghan war and the fall of the USSR.

The Afghan War

After the Soviet invasion in December 1979, Pakistan adopted a coherent but dangerous policy based on both strategic and ideological considerations. In 1980 General Zia took the risk of supporting the Afghan resistance, despite warnings from Western countries (especially France). He soon received support from the Americans and the Saudis. General Zia's idea was to become an indispensable ally in Reagan's strategy of rolling-back the communists, and to use this alliance to achieve his own aims: virtually no punishment for developing an atomic bomb; support in a conflict with India; the establishment – over the long term – of a friendly regime – even a quasi-protectorate – in Afghanistan; and finally, an opening in Soviet Central Asia (apparently General Zia always believed that the USSR would collapse – or, in any case, that it would withdraw from Central Asia).[5] During the Afghan war, a whole body of militant Islamic literature in Russian was printed in Peshawar and sent secretly into Central Asia. So the war allowed Pakistan (and its military regime) once more to mobilize Islam, the only real foundation of its national legitimacy, to force its public opinion to accept this authoritarian policy. It was mainly English-speaking intellectuals who had reservations about it.[6]

In fact, the dispute between Afghanistan and Pakistan went back to the very establishment of Pakistan. Kabul was the only capital city not to vote for Pakistan's admission to the UN in 1947, on the pretext that the question of 'Pashtunistan' had not been settled: Kabul made no official claim to the North-West Frontier Province, with its Pashtun population – the main ethnic group in Afghanistan – but it demanded a referendum and negotiations on the drawing of the border. In 1955, when Afghanistan engineered an impressive *rapprochement* with the USSR (and India), while Pakistan joined the American camp, relations became strained and the two nations were on the brink of war in 1963, when Prince Daud (a 'Pashtunist') was King Zahir's prime minister in Afghanistan. When Daud fell from office in 1964, the situation became calmer; but when a *coup d'état* restored him to power in 1973, Pakistan gave refuge to Afghan Islamists who turned to armed opposition: trained by the Pakistani military, flanked by the Jamaat-i Islami party, they launched an unsuccessful uprising in 1975 and withdrew to Peshawar, where they lingered until the Soviet invasion in 1979 gave them another opportunity.

From this time on, there were two groups of Islamic opponents to the Kabul government in two different networks, both centred on Pakistan. The oldest was made up of traditional ulemas who, after Partition in 1947, refused to finish their studies in India, as had been the custom in Afghanistan up to that time (oddly enough, there had never been top-flight religious instruction networks in Afghanistan). They preferred *madrasahs* in Pakistan which had themselves sprung from the great Indian religious schools (the Deobandi, but also the Ahl-i Hadith) and which, for the same reasons (refusal to be part of an 'infidel' state), were independent of their parent schools in India. The whole Pashtun area experienced a particularly vigorous growth in the number of *madrasahs*, most affiliated to the Deobandi school, which taught in the various regional languages (Urdu, Pashto and Persian). The mullahs who trained at these schools went back to Afghanistan and opened branches of the parent school in Pakistan, sending their best students there. So a border network of *madrasahs* was built up – mainly, but not exclusively, Pashtun. The teaching was fundamentalist, but open to the traditional Muslim culture of the Indian subcontinent in its 'reformed' Shah Wali-ullah version.[7]

These networks, which were completely outside the control of any government, Afghan or Pakistani, grew stronger during the Soviet occupation, because the Afghan *madrasahs* – either destroyed or transformed into military bases – no longer provided high-level education. A sort of part-time training became the norm: the young *taleb* fought for a while, then went into a *madrasah* in Pakistan for training (and rest) before returning to the front. During the war, these networks belonged to conservative religious Afghan resistance parties: the Younous Khales tendency of the Hizb-i Islami, and above all Nabi Mohammedi's Harkat-i Inqilab Islami. Although they were recognized by the Pakistani authorities, Pakistan was not generous with military aid. On the other hand, they were heavily subsidized by the Gulf States, especially Saudi Arabia. This Saudi largesse also took the form of training grants, gradually introducing a much more 'Wahhabi' influence which was quite hostile towards local religious traditions, both learned and popular. This was the setting for the development of the movement which became known as the Taliban.

The second network covered Islamist movements, which recruited – in Afghanistan as elsewhere – among educated youth and the few professors of theology trained in Egypt under the influence of the Muslim Brothers.[8] These militants – who, unlike the traditionalist ulemas, were working for a real political revolution – found two sponsors in Pakistan: the Islamist Jamaat-i Islami Party, led by Maududi until his death in 1979; and the Pakistani army service known since the Afghan war as the ISI (Inter Services Intelligence). This double sponsorship (Islamist networks and secret services) would be a permanent feature of Pakistan's regional policy on all Islamic movements. But Pakistan was clever enough to allow most of the Afghan resistance movements to open offices on its territory, giving them monopoly control of refugees by allowing them to register only on condition that they belonged to a recognized organization [*tanzim*].

Pakistan's clever move was to channel international (mainly American) aid in the direction of parties it had selected itself, while giving the impression that it was supporting the entire Afghan resistance movement. The chosen party was Gulbuddin Hekmatyar's Hizb-i Islami. As so often, there was a double connection: ethnic as well as ideological. The Hizb-i Islami – like most senior members of the Jamaat (including Qazi Hussain Ahmad, its emir after 1987) and the ISI – was Pashtun. It also shared the same political ideology.

Pakistan also took advantage of the mobilization of international Islamic networks, particularly those under the influence of the Muslim Brothers. An office set up in Peshawar, the Mektal-ul Khadamat – run by Abdallah Azzam, a Palestinian Muslim Brother – was given money collected by a Saudi millionaire, Osama bin Laden. Volunteers from the Arab world came in their thousands, mainly members of opposition movements (Gamaat and Egyptian Islamic Jihad, whose spiritual leader was Sheikh Omar Abdurrahman; militants who went on to form the FIS, then the Algerian GIA, etc.). Both Saudi Arabia and the USA encouraged these 'Islamic brigades'. Thus Pakistan became the training and dispersal platform for all these volunteers, who either returned to their countries afterwards or stayed in Afghanistan. The Afghan war plugged Pakistan into Middle Eastern Islamic networks – especially Arab ones, under the influence of the Muslim Brothers – and thereby reinforced its international dimension.

Pakistan's Islamic activism was not limited to Afghanistan: taking advantage of the opening of the road between Gilgit and Kashgar, in Chinese Xinkiang, thousands of

Uigurs, on the pretext of a pilgrimage to Mecca, steamed into Jamaat guest-houses in Lahore and Karachi.

The withdrawal of Soviet troops in February 1988 marked the victory of Pakistan's grand strategy: to make the West endorse its vanguard role in Central Asia's Islamic movements. Needless to say, when the Saudis and the Americans encouraged a *jihad* against the Soviet invader they were also mindful of the need to contain Iran's Islamic revolution. The idea was to turn against the USSR and Iran the wave of Islamic radicalism that had been shaking the Muslim world since the end of the 1970s – party by accentuating the anticommunist aspect of the movement by popularizing the Afghan *jihad*; partly by playing on Sunni fundamentalism against Iranian Shiism.

This plan should have succeeded beyond their wildest dreams. But the withdrawal of the Soviet army two years later, followed by the collapse of the USSR (seriously weakened by the war in Afghanistan), opened new perspectives for Pakistan in the direction of ex-Soviet Central Asia, but also brought back into the *jihad* market thousands of Islamic volunteers who, free of their communist enemy, found a new adversary in the West – particularly the Americans after the Gulf War.

Dreams of Central Asia

After the collapse of the USSR, Pakistan had every intention of gathering the fruits of its policy. The aim was simple, but very ambitious: to acquire a strategic depth against India by installing a pro-Pakistan – that is to say, as far as Islamabad was concerned, fundamentalist and Pashtun – regime in Kabul, then to make every effort to establish, through Afghanistan, a corridor into ex-Soviet Central Asia which – among other things – could be used to secure gas supplies from Turkmenistan.

Islamabad did not expect that the governments formed immediately after independence would last, and thought that they would quickly be replaced by more 'Muslim' regimes. Unlike Iran, which was eager to see a continued Russian presence in Central Asia to counter American influence, the Pakistanis played the Islamic card from the outset, giving indirect support to doctrinaire movements, often on their own territory. Pakistan's strength – its economy was always its weak point – was to solicit foreign support and act by proxy, thus saving on men and money. It was the USA and the Saudis who financed most of the Afghan mujaheddin war effort, but it was the ISI which distributed the weapons and the money, giving preference to their favourites.

The Gulf War (1990–1), however, was a turning point: the radical Islamic movements became increasingly anti-West (particularly anti-American). Under pressure from Saudi Arabia, Pakistan finally abandoned Hizb-i Islami, which had failed in its attempt to retake Kabul from Massoud between 1992 and 1994 – not without destroying the town with bombing raids. So Pakistan found the Taliban card (1994): this change also showed how much Islamic fundamentalism had developed in Pakistan, where a 'modern' Islamist party like Jamaat-i Islami lost out to fundamentalist and traditionalist movements like Jamiyyat-ul Ulama Islam, focused on the *madrasah* networks which included the Afghan Taliban.[9]

During the 1990s, therefore, Pakistan pursued a very aggressive regional policy. First there was overt public support for the Taliban: after October 1994 General Babar, Pakistan's Interior Minister, took the American ambassador on a tour of the Taliban zones in the west of Afghanistan without even informing the legal Afghan government of the day (whose President was Borhanuddin Rabbani). The Pakistan army provided materiel and logistic help. *Madrasahs* in Pakistan recruited volunteers, who had no difficulty whatsoever crossing the border. ISI officers were on Afghan territory. Some were captured or killed by Commander Massoud's men. Relations between Massoud and Pakistan had always been cool, but they deteriorated sharply when the Taliban – on the advice of a Pakistani officer, Colonel Imad, consul in the town of Herat – took this small but strategic town in western Afghanistan which was held by Ismail Khan, an ally of Massoud ((September 1995). The Pakistani Embassy in Kabul was pillaged by Massoud's partisans. A year later, in September 1996, the Taliban took Kabul, and Massoud had to take refuge in his mountain fortress in the northwest. Pakistan recognized the Taliban regime, but only Saudi Arabia and the Arab Emirates followed suit. During the ensuing four years the Pakistanis made every effort to help the Taliban win a decisive victory in Afghanistan. In August 1998 they took the north (Mazar-i Sharif) and the centre (Bamyan), but never managed to bring down Massoud, whose guns were within easy reach of the capital.

This impasse continued in 2000, when the first cracks appeared in the Taliban's ranks. They were unable to maintain in action an army which was composed mainly of tribal recruits, and was therefore more dependent than ever on volunteers from Pakistan. The connection with Pakistan was simultaneously ideological (conservative Sunni fundamentalism), strategic (a protectorate in Afghanistan) and ethnic (the principal *madrasahs* for recruiting volunteers were in Pakistan-controlled zones – like the one at Akora Khattak, run by the Pakistani senator Sami ul-Haq, a member of Jamiyyat-ul Ulama-i Islam). Ismail Khan's spectacular escape from prison in Kandahar in April 2000, and the fact that he reached Iran, also illustrate an ethnic polarization and the increasing involvement of Iran, but in addition a decline in the Taliban's power. In fact, pan-Islamic ideology was not an adequate blanket for increasingly ethnic alliances.

Pakistan's Afghan policy was absolutely in line with its policy on Kashmir: first and foremost the use of international militias composed of Islamic volunteers; direct support for the mujaheddin; the same religious networks to train volunteers (who pass through training camps in Afghanistan); the same implacable denial that they are interfering. These are often the very organizations that are found in Kashmir helping the Taliban, such as Harkat ul-Ansar. So it was indeed a policy of aggression on all sides that Pakistan pursued.

In ex-Soviet Central Asia, Islamabad uses the same links as it uses in Afghanistan, but it keeps more in the background. The Pakistan government plays a very indirect role. In the early 1990s the networks involved were less political, but they still came from Pakistan: hundreds of members of Tablighi Jamaat, mainly from Lahore and Karachi, visited the mosques which were thriving everywhere. After 1993 they were expelled from Uzbekistan and Tajikistan, but Pakistan welcomed hundreds of Uzbek and Tajik militants fleeing repression. At the end of 1992, tens of thousands of Tajik refugees and fighters fled to Afghanistan, where they settled in three areas: Mazar-i Sharif (held by the Uzbek General Dustom), Taloqan (held by Massoud) and Kunduz (held by fundamentalists close to Pakistani circles, who joined the Taliban in 1996). The Pakistani Embassy in Dushanbe was closed for a while by the new Tajik government, which accused it of colluding with Islamists (the Iranian Embassy remained open). The Tajik opposition movement, led by Mullah Nouri, was regularly invited to important meetings of Islamist movements in Lahore.

A little later, after the Taliban's arrival on the Uzbek border (1998), it was the Uzbek Islamic opposition ('the Islamic Freedom Party' led by Taher Yoldashev and Joma Namangani) that was sponsored and trained by religious networks based in Pakistan.

Pakistani activism, however, soon reached its limits. First, ethnic and religious divides predominated everywhere over militant pan-Islamic solidarity. In non-Pashtun zones, the Taliban were seen as an occupying force. Islamists who were Tajik in terms of national identity and ethnic solidarity preferred Massoud to the Taliban, who took Kabul in 1996. More seriously, they began negotiations with the government in Dushanbe – through Russian and Iranian intermediaries under UN control – which led to an agreement on shared government, signed in June 1997. In October the Taliban hijacked a plane taking Mullah Nouri from Tehran to Dushanbe, and tried to force Mullah Nouri to renege on this agreement, to set up a regime in their zone, and to resume hostilities against all the impious governments of Central Asia. He refused, and they had to release him. So a Tajik bloc (Tajik Islamic Opposition; Massoud; the government in Dushanbe, led by Rahmanov) was established in opposition to both the Pashtun bloc (the Taliban, supported by Pakistan) and Uzbek hegemony (symbolized by the Republic of Uzbekistan). Thus the logic of ethnicity and nationality prevailed over Islamic solidarity.

Islamabad, however, had underestimated the importance of nationalism in Central Asia, and the new regimes' reservations about anything supranational.[10] Muslim activism in Pakistan bred a climate of suspicion that was exacerbated by the increasingly authoritarian nature of the existing regimes and their sense of a deepening Islamic radicalization, even if this was magnified to some extent by the rigours of the situation.

In 1998 there was a mini-crisis between Pakistan and Uzbekistan. After several officials had been murdered in the Ferghana valley (traditionally the cradle of Islamic fundamentalism), Tashkent, in a ministerial declaration by the Uzbek Foreign Minister in February 1998, violently denounced Pakistan's role in the training of radical Islamic Uzbeks around Lahore (naming the *madrasahs* where the militants were). An attempt in February 1999 to assassinate President Karimov – blamed on Islamists – led to repression against anything or anyone that might seem to be connected with Islamic militancy. In August 1999, a column of Uzbek Islamic militants, based in Tajikistan, crossed the southern part of Kirghizistan, probably with the intention of attacking Ferghana. They took a group of Japanese geologists hostage. Negotiations on their freedom took place in . . . Islamabad, emphasizing the close relations between Uzbek religious militants and religious circles in Pakistan. There was a climate of distrust between Pakistan and the Central Asian states. In May 2000 the Russians, who were staging a strong comeback in Central Asia, threatened to bomb training camps on Taliban-controlled Afghan territory, on the pretext that there were Chechen fighters there: heated discussions with Pakistan followed. Commander Khattab, an Arab Islamic militant who fought with the Chechens in the second Chechen wars (1999), had trained in Afghanistan with Osama bin Laden at the end of the Afghan war: these very real connections contributed to the idea that an 'Islamic International' was being organized from Afghan territory.

The only Central Asian state with which Pakistan enjoyed good relations was gas-rich Turkmenistan. With no ideological overtones whatsoever, these two countries wanted to build a pipeline linking the Daulatabad gas fields in Turkmenistan to Pakistan via the west of Afghanistan, with an ultimate eye on the Indian market. Unocal, an American company, made some preliminary moves but pulled out in August 1998, worried about the growing tension between India and Pakistan, the USA's media campaign against the Taliban's misogynous policies, and the fact that there was no prospect of a political solution in Afghanistan.

Relations with Iran also deteriorated markedly. The 1990s saw an unprecedented rise in conflicts and massacres between Shi'a and Sunni extremists in Pakistan. This intercommunal hatred spread to Afghanistan – the Taliban massacred Shi'a. More serious still was the fact that after Mazar-i Sharif was taken, in August 1998, radical Sunni (probably members of Pakistan's Sunni Sipah-i Sahaba Pakistan) killed the Iranian Embassy staff. Iran, which had been hoping to collaborate with Pakistan on the Afghan crisis, got nothing for its trouble: Tehran accepted on principle that there should be a pro-Pakistan Pashtun regime in Kabul, but wanted the Shi'a minority (the Hazaras) to have an important place in, and relative autonomy under, a coalition government. The fall of Hazarajat in August 1998 dashed these hopes. Afghanistan was not an overriding priority for Iran, but Tehran did hope for stability on its eastern flank so that it could concentrate on the Gulf, the Caspian Sea and the Middle East. Tehran therefore felt obliged to take an aggressive stance, but had to abandon any idea of a financially and economically costly military operation; thus Iran cooperated with Russia in a massive rearming of Commander Massoud, the last obstacle to total Taliban hegemony.

For the first time since the nineteenth century, Iran considered that Afghanistan consituted a real threat – especially Sunni fundamentalist movements directly supported by Islamabad. Quite apart from the Afghan question, the fact that Pakistan is now a nuclear power continues to worry Iran, despite its praise for this first 'Islamic bomb'. In fact, Iran has always been close to India, despite its façade of solidarity with Pakistan. Finally, the deteriorating situation on the shared border between Iran, Afghanistan and Pakistan has affected Iran badly: well-armed Baluchis smuggling drugs to the West, with the barely disguised collusion of Pakistan, are all too eager to engage in pitched battles against the Iranian forces of law and order. There is no trust left between Iran and Pakistan.

So Pakistan's extremely aggressive, ideological policy isolated it from all its neighbours. Nonetheless, before September 11 Pakistan did not come under the same Western pressure for its role in Afghanistan as it suffered for its intervention in Kashmir. The Americans, in particular, held back. They made no bones about putting pressure on Pakistan to withdraw its Islamic volunteers from Kashmir, because there it was a matter of strategic stakes. The USA wanted closer relations with India which, in Washington's view, should be used as a counterweight against a China that looks more menacing every day. At that stage Pakistan, which is close to China, had lost all strategic interest, and was seen as a troublemaker rather than an ally. But the Americans, who supported the Taliban until 1997, did not then have the same strategic interests in Afghanistan.

In fact, Washington's only – albeit overwhelming – problem was the presence in the Taliban camp of Islamic 'terrorists' like Osama bin Laden, but this was a policing problem, not a strategic one. Hitherto, the Americans thought they could get rid of Bin Laden by putting pressure on the Taliban. Washington wanted to separate the Bin Laden question from the situation within Afghanistan, and prior to September 11 refused to support Massoud against the Taliban as a means of either taming or defeating them. Washington's bet was that once the Taliban had won, they would have become intermediaries – difficult ones, no doubt, but responsible.

The situation was to change dramatically in the wake of the events of September 11. The Kashmir question has been stalled for years, and it is on the subject of Afghanistan that the Americans are seeking guarantees from the government in Pakistan. The crucial question remains whether the government in Islamabad is able to distance itself from the radical Islamic networks which have been instrumental in their policy in Kashmir, Afghanistan and Central Asia.

Conservative Sunni Radicalization

Since the end of the 1980s, we have witnessed the establishment of an internationalist Sunni sphere of influence around the Taliban and Pakistan. This is both religiously conservative (close to Saudi Wahhabism, even though the historic origins of this fundamentalism have no connection with the Wahhabi reform movement) and increasingly radical politically, putting its Saudi sponsors and the Americans at odds with each other. It combines 'salafism' (a determination to go back to Islam as it was at the time of the Prophet) and 'jihadism' (insistence that armed action should be taken against the enemies of Islam, at the expense of realistic political thought). This international connection is embodied in the Taliban's links with Osama bin Laden's extremist networks). However, there are similar militants in the northern Caucasus (the Jordanian Khattab, for example); they were also active in Bosnia until their organizations were broken up by the Bosnian government. This is not a highly centralized network under the shadowy leadership of Bin Laden, but an entire conglomeration of networks and people, most of whom met in Afghanistan at the end of the 1980s.

There are numerous diffuse radical groups in Pakistan. They have various origins, but they come together today in a fundamentalist, anti-American radicalization movement (the sharia, the whole sharia, and nothing but the sharia). They could be traditional movements like Jamiyyat-ul Ulama-i Islam, which represents religious men of the Deobandi school (founded in 1867), who have become radicalized over the last ten years; the Jamaat-i Islami, which is close to the Arab Muslim Brothers but has adopted an increasingly anti-American stance; or indeed more recent groups – very violent, and at first marginal – like Sipah-i Sahaba and Harkat-ul Ansar, which have linked up with movements formed specifically to fight in Kashmir, such as Harkat-ul Mujahiddin, Lashkar-i Tayyiba and the Al-Badar military unit. All these groups can now avail themselves of training and indoctrination centres (in Pakistan) and – prior to September 11 – military training bases (in Afghanistan). Thousands of volunteers from the entire Muslim world have passed through these camps (including the founders of the GIA and the FIS). They were the spearhead of the Taliban, and of the volunteers sent to Kashmir. These networks are often still marginal in the world's Muslim countries (except Egypt, Algeria, Yemen and Uzbekistan), but they played – and still play – an important role in Pakistan and Afghanistan, because they were organized and supported by more traditional clerical circles like the Taliban.

Two characteristic features of the radicalization of Islamist movements in Pakistan distinguish it from radicalization in the Middle East: unlike radicalization in the Middle East and North Africa (where the FIS, the Muslim Brothers, Refah, Hizbollah, and so on, make every effort to look more moderate, and so to get into politics), it affects the great traditionalist or Islamist movements; and it enjoys increasing support at the heart of the state apparatus.

Here, also, Pakistan is different from other Muslim countries where, after a state-encouraged phase of Islamization in the 1970s and 1980s, we find – in Turkey, Algeria, Egypt, Palestine and Jordan – growing confrontation between the state apparatus and the Islamists: purges of the army and the civil service, and a clampdown on religious education. In Pakistan, on the other hand, we have heard ex-Prime Minister Nawaz Sharif quote the Taliban, for example, during a debate on the Islamization of the law in September 1998; General Hamid Gul, former head of the ISI, has openly joined the Islamists in violently attacking the USA; there is no state control over the spreading network of religious schools; moreover, there is an obvious tendency towards Islamization among young army officers. This Islamization is – as we have seen – accompanied by an increasingly aggressive foreign policy. In short, Pakistan – which was always officially close to the USA – is now becoming the protector and promoter of a virulent Islamic radicalism, even if this is still peripheral (because it has made fewer inroads in the Middle East).

Now the essential feature of these radical movements is not so much their ideology as their activism: they advocate taking an active part in all the Muslim world's jihads. It is this 'jihadism' that is at the root of their internationalism, their indifference towards borders, and also their prestige in the eyes of young people who often seem to have lost both their sense of culture and their sense of direction. They support the Taliban in Afghanistan so that they can go on to attack Central Asia, particularly Uzbekistan; they are angry with India, Iran and Russia; they call for solidarity with the Chechens, the Uigurs of China, the Bosnians, the Moros in the Philippines, and so on. They obviously see the power of the USA as their chief enemy. In a word: they are internationalizing the internal political situation in Pakistan and Afghanistan.

The regional invocation of Islamism has allowed Pakistan to play a role that is out of all proportion to its real power – particularly its economic power. Until 1998, the country could play the Islamic card and the card of American support at separate tables, but the Osama bin Laden affair has ruined that game, all the more so after September 11.

Before September 11, General Musharraf sent out contradictory signals – sometimes talking about Kemalism in Pakistan; sometimes reaffirming his commitment to Islam. The disadvantage of a readjustment and a toning down of Islamic elements would be that it would bring ethnic connections to the fore. Significantly, the general declared during a press conference in May 2000 that it was in Pakistan's national interest to see the Taliban, 'who represent Pashtun ethnicity', in power in Afghanistan; this elicited a statement from the king of Afghanistan – a very rare occurrence.[11] At the time Pakistan did not have any other card to play, since prioritizing ethnic and purely national questions to the detriment of an – even mythical – Islamic solidarity would also have foregrounded the artificially multiethnic character of Pakistan itself. The Islamic dimension is an integral part of Pakistan's political mindset – even if, in the end, this could limit its relations with the countries of Central Asia.*

---

* For discussion of the impact of September 11 on these issues, see 'Epilogue: Musharraf and the Islamists: From Support to Opposition after September 11', pp. 259–280 below.

PART III

THE ECONOMY AND SOCIAL STRUCTURES

7

THE COUNTRY AND ITS PEOPLE

Pakistan is at the pivotal point between two worlds, the Iranian world and the Indian world. The Greeks and Romans were very perceptive when they imposed this divide on the banks of the Indus: to the west are countries and peoples who turn towards Iran, Afghanistan, even Central Asia; to the east, India and the monsoons.

To a traveller from Europe, the Baluchi plateaus and the valleys of the northeast belong – in terms of their landscape and their agriculture – to the Iranian–Afghan complex. Beyond the Indus, a fairly uniform countryside stretches from the Pakistani Punjab to the basin of the Jamuna and the Ganges.

The crucial role of these watercourses – the Indus and its tributaries, the five rivers of the Punjab (literally, in Persian, 'five waters' – is reminiscent of Mesopotamia. Paraphrasing Herodotus, we could call Pakistan 'a gift from the Indus'. Without irrigation, the greater part of the basin would be a desert. Thanks to irrigation, wheat is grown in winter, followed by cotton, rice, maize, a little sorghum and millet during the monsoon season. An annual crop of sugarcane is cultivated between Peshawar and Sind. Mangos, oranges, bananas and dates are also grown, especially in the south. From very early on, raising cattle and buffalo was a very important activity. In Sind, there is a striking contrast between the verdant countryside and the desert on the horizon where the banks of the Indus and the canals slope away. In the Punjab, the more extensive green area is also bordered by bare, arid land. After the threshold of Rawalpindi come the beautiful irrigated plains of Peshawar and Swat.

Mountains and plateaus form the greater part of the territory. Baluchistan alone covers 432,000 square kilometres out of a total of 775,000. Deserts of sand, gravel and stone, inhospitable chains of black, are punctuated by a few oases. The few inhabitants make their living mainly by raising sheep by transhumance. There are few towns; roads and railways are limited to a few main routes. Even in ancient times, Baluchistan was a secondary channel for communication, and we know how Alexander and his phalanxes suffered when they crossed it.

Towards the north there is higher country, rising to 3,500 metres in the Sulaiman Mountains to the south of Peshawar. To the northwest, the Hindu Kush rises towards the impressive crossroads of the Pamir (the *bam i dunya*, the roof of the world), the giant Himalayas and Karakorum,, including the great K2, the world's second-highest peak (8,620 metres). Along the Afghan border are crops which depend on the monsoons and the lighter winter rains, and irrigated valleys where

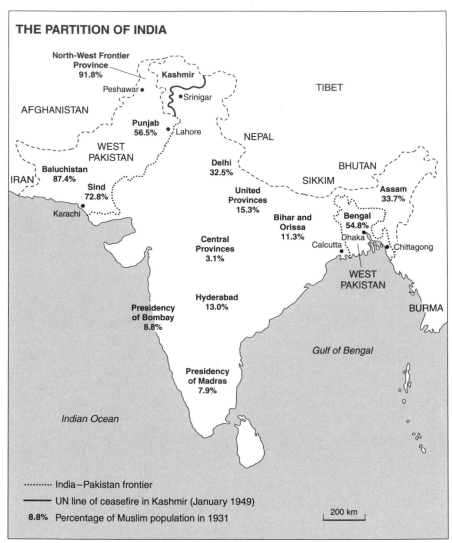

THE PARTITION OF INDIA

North-West Frontier Province 91.8%

Kashmir

Peshawar

Srinigar

TIBET

AFGHANISTAN

Punjab 56.5%

Lahore

NEPAL

WEST PAKISTAN

Delhi 32.5%

BHUTAN

Baluchistan 87.4%

SIKKIM

IRAN

Sind 72.8%

United Provinces 15.3%

Assam 33.7%

Karachi

Central Provinces 3.1%

Bihar and Orissa 11.3%

Bengal 54.8%

Dhaka

Calcutta

Chittagong

WEST PAKISTAN

Hyderabad 13.0%

BURMA

Presidency of Bombay 8.8%

Gulf of Bengal

Presidency of Madras 7.9%

Indian Ocean

·········· India–Pakistan frontier

———— UN line of ceasefire in Kashmir (January 1949)

8.8%   Percentage of Muslim population in 1931

200 km

Source: *The Cambridge Encyclopedia of India, Pakistan, Bangladesh, Sri Lanka*, Cambridge 1989.

wheat is followed by rice or maize during the same year. Higher up, towards 3,000 metres, only one harvest is possible.

Pakistan is well endowed from an agricultural point of view; much less so in terms of mineral resources: a little carbon, not much iron, copper in the west of Baluchistan. Oil production is sufficient for only a small part of the country's needs, and hitherto prospecting, notably in Sind, has yielded only mediocre results. On the other hand, the rich natural gas deposits in Baluchistan have been supplying energy since the late 1950s. Further deposits have recently been discovered in Sind. Finally, there are huge hydroelectricity potentials which have still not been fully exploited.

The British Legacy

The British took on a civilization which, in its more illustrious phases, had highly developed political, administrative and economic structures. That is why Britain wanted simultaneously to destroy, to conserve and to innovate. Although they put in place structures and an organization that were, by and large, identical throughout the Indian Empire – a division into provinces under direct administration, with 550 Princely States enjoying a certain degree of autonomy under a British resident – huge differences in the exercise of power and the measures taken to develop the country quickly became apparent.

The part of Bengal that would become East Pakistan in 1947 was neglected under the British: a dormant economy except for jute; a lack of infrastructure; an 'undergoverned' territory; a severe shortage of modern elites, especially among the Muslims. Although Bengal had been one of the most flourishing provinces in the subcontinent for at least two thousand years, it became – especially in the east – a vast repository of extreme poverty.

The Punjab, which had already benefited from the policies of Ranjit Singh,[1] was an astonishing contrast. This province, the eastern part of which would become part of Pakistan, received more attention, above all for strategic reasons – it was the main component of the 'great game' – from the British, who, throughout the nineteenth century, were afraid that the Cossacks would stream into the Indian Empire from Central Asia, which was still in the grip of the tsars, Senior civil servants and high-ranking military men watched over this province – from the Lawrence brothers to Sir Malcolm Darling in the first decades of the twentieth century, then Montgomery and Alfred Lyall. And once the ICS (Indian Civil Service) was opened to Indians, some of the most brilliant civil servants after Independence won their first spurs in the Punjab.

The formation of this solid enclave was facilitated by dividing the province into districts much smaller than those in Bengal or Bihar, making administration more efficient. Thus in 1872 C E Barnard, chief of a Bengali district, wrote to G R Elsmie, his colleague in the Punjab:

2

The first British people who visited Sind and the Punjab before the conquest had already realized the enormous – as yet underutilized – irrigation potential.

Developing the region could not fail to raise public revenue. There were also political motives: after the difficult conquest of the Punjab, it was considered prudent to send demobilized Sikh soldiers there to develop the agriculture.

Gradually, the British put in place the biggest network of irrigation canals in the world: at first in the Punjab, especially the western part; then in Sind, with the dyke to divert the waters of the Indus at Sakkar. Other projects benefited the Peshawar valley in the northwest. All in all, 37,000 kilometres of canals in the Punjab, 10,000 in Sind and a few thousand in the north irrigated 9.2 million hectares. The Punjab became the breadbasket of India thanks to the development of wheat cultivation, together with the cultivation of cotton and sugarcane. There was also tangible – albeit less spectacular – progress in Sind.

The development of irrigation was both quantitive and qualitative. Until that time it had mainly been a matter of flood irrigation: rivers were used when their waters were swollen, as in Ancient Egypt. The British dug new canals. The water was held in a barrage with sluicegates which sent water into the canals, ensuring a constant irrigation process that was more reliable and more productive. The first tubewells driven by a diesel engine arrived in the Punjab shortly before the Second World War; this complement to the canal waters developed rapidly after Independence.

This take-off of agriculture caused chain reactions, especially in the Punjab: the construction of roads and railways, the development of towns and markets, flour mills, cotton-spinning factories, a few sugar refineries, the beginning of a small, quasi-modern mechanical industry. In 1882 the prestigious Punjab University with its Government College, breeding-ground for new Muslim, Hindu and Sikh elites, was established in Lahore. The town became one of the most illustrious in the subcontinent thanks to its flourishing commerce and banks, often owned by Hindus and Sikhs.

This process of overall development – which we also see in Europe or in China at certain times – was due to an ideal combination of several factors: physical conditions that lent themselves to agriculture, as long as there was irrigation; and a superior political and administrative structure which, as we have seen, became Indianized after the 1930s. Note, for example, the care with which the British civil servants selected and encouraged the farmers in the eastern Punjab – mostly Sikhs – who settled in the canal colonies created from nothing to the east of Lahore. In other cases, to achieve good relations with the elites, the British favoured the big landowners in all regions.

In eastern districts (the future Indian Punjab) there were fewer canals, and the population grew relatively slowly (30 to 40 per cent between 1891 and 1941), but in new districts its growth was spectacular: the population of Lyallpur (now Faisalabad) went from 600,000 to 1.4 million in 1941; that of Montgomery (Sahiwal) from 417,000 to 1.3 million; that of Jhang from 402,000 to 882,000.

The people were a third, no less decisive factor. The province was home to castes of cultivators who quickly won the colonizers' admiration: farmers who stuck to their task, and were shrewd, eager for innovation. The highest caste was that of the Jats, who could be Hindus, Muslims or Sikhs. The Arains, who were exclusively Muslims, had a lower status. The traditional artisan castes – Sikhs, Hindus and Muslims –

began very quickly to set up workshops and small industries. In the towns, the Khatris (Hindus or Sikhs) stood out as the superior caste, usually in administration or business; they began the development of the tertiary sector, with a few Muslims. 'Even if a Khatri puts ashes on his head, he makes a profit out of it', says a Punjabi proverb.

Sind did not do nearly so well. Unlike the Punjab, there had been no Ranjit Singh to develop it. Its physical conditions were less favourable than those of the Punjab; sea water often infiltrated the south, and elsewhere there were briny sub-terranean waters; there was more extensive salt encroachment than in the Punjab. Moreover, the great works centred on the Sakkar barrage were not completed until 1932, when the world crisis – which also affected India – hindered the development of agriculture and the export of its products – the opposite of the situation in the Punjab in earlier decades. The British were less in evidence there, although there were some illustrious names: in the nineteenth century Sir Bartle Frere, and that incredible trainer of men John Jacob, artillery officer, then cavalry officer, finally a civil administrator who gave his name to Jacobad, where he is buried. There was another handicap: Sind was part of the Bombay Presidency until 1936, when it became an entirely separate province. Until that time, the region was partly neglected by the authorities in distant Bombay – even more so since, unlike the Punjab, it played only a minor role in the 'great game'.

The human setting was in a similar mould. The towns, which were not very important in 1941 – Karachi had only 400,000 inhabitants – were dominated by the Hindus and a handful of Parsees. As for the countryside, it was dominated by the great powerful landlords, the *wadera*, feudal lords who were not particularly interested in developing their estates – sometimes thousands of hectares – like the gentlemen farmers of the Punjab. Besides, there was no solid farming middle class, like the Jats and the Arains.

Then there were the mountainous areas. In Baluchistan – except in Quetta and certain districts under direct administration – the British limited themselves to strengthening the great tribal chiefs. The Bolan railway linked Quetta to the Indus plain, then went on as far as Zahidan, in Iran (for a long time there was only one train a week on this last section; today there are two).

In the northwest were the settled districts: first the North-West Frontier Province (NWFP), under direct administration, which had the advantage of irrigation in the Peshawar plain; then the Tribal Areas, a stretch of territory along the border with Afghanistan. This was the hideout for the disruptive Pashtun tribes previously chron-icled by Herodotus – an extremely tough society plagued by vendettas, where every dwelling was a little castle of clay. Political representatives lived in each zone, but acted only if there was serious tension. Until 1947, the Tribal Areas were on many occasions the theatre for military operations where the British deployed tens of thousands of men. The laws of the Indian Empire were not respected there. People and goods moved freely on both sides of the border. In short, no *imperium* had ever been accepted. All the invaders – from Alexander the Great to the Mughals, then the British – had suffered bloody disappointments; hence the wise decision by the British, followed by the Pakistanis, to keep their involvement in local affairs to a minimum.

Then, to the north, came the little Princely States: Swat, Dir and Chitral. Swat enjoyed a certain amount of development, thanks to an enlightened sovereign and progressive irrigation. The other two remained marginal, only lightly ruffled by the breezes of modernization. Stretching beyond were the territories which would be taken from the state of Jammu and Kashmir during the troubles at the time of Partition: Gilgit and Skardu, valleys with a great agricultural tradition thanks to their irrigation canals carved out along the sides of the giant mountains of the Himalayas and Karakorum. Hunza and Nagar, small principalities, continued to exist for several years after 1947.

So the British had direct administration over part of Baluchistan as well as Sind, the Punjab, and the NWFP. Alongside were Princely States which enjoyed considerable autonomy: Khairpur in Sind and Bahawalpur in the Punjab, merged with the two provinces after 1947. Swat, Dir and Chitral became part of the NWFP in the 1970s.

The Effects of Partition

Even before 1947, Pakistan was a mosaic. In the remote valleys of Baluchistan and the Tribal Areas, no one had ever seen a British person. Customs had not changed. At the opposite extreme, Lahore and the advanced areas of the Punjab were completing a first stage of modernization which was extending towards Sind. Building a modern nation, therefore, was difficult, especially since the Indus basin had come over belatedly to the Muslim League.

As we saw in Part I, Partition had some contradictory effects: the birth of a national consciousness and, at the same time, the emergence of new points of tension. Sikhs and Hindus left the countryside and, above all, the towns *en masse*; this greatly weakened the urban tertiary sector. Muslim peasants from India, especially the eastern Punjab, took over abandoned land in the Punjab. The same thing happened in the Punjab's towns, where the newcomers quickly became an integral part of the new state. But the situation was fraught from the outset in Sind, especially in Karachi, the country's capital until the 1960s. Muhajirs from the north of India spoke Urdu; those from Bombay and Gujarat spoke Urdu or Gujarati. They had few cultural ties with the Sindis. They were more entrepreneurial, and transformed themselves from civil servants or shopkeepers to industrialists. Karachi and Hyderabad, too, were dominated by Muhajirs; this sowed the seeds of a discord that would intensify as the years passed. Other conflicts emerged between the early leaders, who had come from India, and local dignitaries, who asserted themselves after Jinnah's death in 1948 and the assassination of Liaquat Ali Khan in 1951. There was another burdensome British legacy: the role of dignitaries: the *sardar* of Baluchistan, the big landowners of Sind and the Punjab, Pashtun leaders. None of these was the result of colonial power, but they had enjoyed its support. The gradual establishment of democratic institutions – elections, assemblies, provincial governments – which began at the end of the nineteenth century and culminated in the 1935 Government of India Act – strengthened rather than weakened the ruling classes. This phenomenon is still very much a part of life over fifty years after Partition.

As far as the economy was concerned, western Pakistan had been dealt a better hand than India. There was less demographic pressure on the space available. In 1951 there was no district, even in the Punjab, where the population density exceeded 250 inhabitants per square kilometre, whereas in the plain of the Ganges it was between 300 and 500. Another advantage was that three-quarters of cultivated land was irrigated, as opposed to less than 20 per cent in India. Road and rail infrastructure was comparable in Pakistan, but there was no major industry, whereas in India there were important industrial centres like Bombay, Calcutta, Ahmedabad and the Tata steelworks in Bihar. In addition, there were many more senior managers in India, and the Muslims paid a heavy price for the fact that their education system had fallen a long way behind during the nineteenth century.

As far as standard of living was concerned, western Pakistan did quite well. There were pockets of poverty – agricultural workers exploited by *wadera* in Sind; people eking out a precarious existence in the upper valleys of the Hindu Kush. Nevertheless, there was not the weighty rural proletariat typical of India, especially on the plains that stretched towards eastern Pakistan, the future Bangladesh. Because there was less demographic pressure, there were far fewer landless peasants and very small landowners in western Pakistan than in India.

The advanced level of development in the Punjab, especially in the canal colonies, compared to many other parts of the subcontinent, bears out the fact that a strong process of development does not involve only the rich. Around 1930, Jawaharlal Nehru brought up the problem of the huge differences in living standards between the dynamic Punjab and the central Ganges basin, where nothing much was happening. Greater population density in the second region was only part of the explanation for this discrepancy. In 1947, in political terms, India seemed to have the advantage; whereas in social and political terms western Pakistan was in a better position than India and – even more so – than eastern Pakistan, which was already one of the most difficult development areas in Asia.

Demographic Pressure: 1947–2000

How many mouths did Pakistan have to feed? How many strong right arms and brains could it count on? These crucial questions may be asked of all developing countries, but they have a particular meaning in a country where the rate of population growth has been – and still is – one of the highest in Asia, despite – for the most part – birth-control campaigns. This demographic pressure has grown over the years, and today it preys on an exhausted economy, leading to rising unemployment. The political tensions that have been at breaking point for the last ten years are partly linked to the growing number of young people without work. Even if censuses cannot be trusted because of faulty recording, the population has still grown very quickly.

From 1881 onwards, the British carried out a complete census in the Indian Empire every ten years. This custom, which has continued in India since Independence, was disrupted in Pakistan. Because of the secession of East Pakistan, there was no census in 1971. The 1991 census was postponed several times owing to inter- and intraprovincial disagreements. It was held in 1998, under army supervision. The results have provoked controversy, because preliminary inquiries by poll suggested 139 million and an annual population growth of 3 per cent – rates which have hardly fallen since the 1981 census. According to the 1998 census, the average annual growth rate between 1990 and 1997 was 2.6 per cent; 2.4 per cent in 1998. In *Dawn* for 21 February 2000, N B Naqvi wrote:

> Everyone knows that there are powerful interests opposed to the census. The Punjab government is afraid of losing seats in the National Assembly. In Baluchistan, the difficulty of counting Baluchis and Pashtuns because of the rivalry between them has made the census problematic. As for the Sindis, they are afraid that overprecise figures will jeopardize their representation at the provincial assembly.

Table 7.1 Population of Pakistan, 1951–98 censuses (millions)

	Punjab	Sind	NWFP	Baluchistan	Islamabad	FATA**	Total
1951	21.5	6.6	4.8	1.2	–	1.3	35.4
1961	26.0	8.5	5.9	1.6	–	1.7	43.7
1981	47.7	19.0	11.1	4.3	0.4	2.2	84.7
1998	72.6	29.0	17.5	6.5	0.8	3.1	129.5

* North West Frontier Province.
** Federal Administrated Tribal Areas.

Naqvi therefore suggests that there should be another census to give a clear picture of the population, and thus to facilitate better economic planning.

As for the average rate of urbanization, it rose from 17.8 per cent in 1951 to 32.5 per cent in 1998 – a more rapid process than that of India or Bangladesh. Nevertheless, there are significant variations between provinces: the Punjab 31.3 per cent; Sind 48.9 per cent; NWFP 16.9 per cent; Baluchistan 23.3 per cent; FATA 2.7 per cent.

According to the 1998 census, the death rate is 9.1 per cent and the birth rate 33 per cent, which looks like an underestimation. Infant mortality stands at 90 per cent. Finally, the ratio between the sexes has improved slightly, although there are still fewer women. This has been a typical feature throughout the entire subcontinent ever since the first British censuses: 108 men for every 100 women in 1998; 110 in 1981.

The age profile shows that 43 per cent of the population are under 15, a little over 53 per cent are between 16 and 64, and a little more than 3 per cent are over 65.

Birth control

Although most Asian countries embarked on a birth-control campaign in the 1950s or 1960s, the elites who ran western Pakistan, then the whole of Pakistan, did not do much. This attitude is all the more disappointing given that soon after he took power in 1958, General (subsequently Marshal and President) Ayub Khan made family planning one of his top priorities. The authorities in East Pakistan, then of

Bangladesh, were the only ones who took note of this and promoted family planning; this partly explains the new state's lower birth rate.

In western Pakistan, the ruling elite's inertia and hostility in religious circles prevailed. On several visits to villages in Pakistan, when I questioned the peasants in Urdu, I got the same answer: 'It is against the will of Allah.' Even the great dignitaries of Sind were no more concerned about this question than their poor farmers. In East Pakistan, on the other hand, intelligent propaganda has shown the mullahs that, contrary to their prejudices, family planning is not against Islamic principles. One of Islam's most eminent theologians, Imam Ghazali, declared as early as the eleventh century that coitus interruptus [azl] was permitted if a woman's beauty was endangered by too many pregnancies, or if the family could not feed all its children. Other theologians at many other times have echoed his words. For many years, several of them have accepted the idea of abortion up to and including the third month.[3]

As in other parts of Asia, birth control has been adopted readily by the upper classes, where couples often stop at two children, especially if one is a boy. The urban middle classes have also taken to the idea, albeit to a lesser extent. It was in the 1980s, and later during the return to democracy (1988), that the authorities made particular efforts to support two hundred private family planning organizations. In 1999, 21 per cent of couples practised birth control, as opposed to 14 per cent in 1990, reducing the average number of children per couple to 5.6, as against 6.5 in 1981.[4]

Emigration

As well as its strong population growth, Pakistan has another distinctive feature: the scale of its emigration.

Emigrants to the United Kingdom, who began to leave soon after Independence, include a wide range of people from professionals to unqualified manual workers. In the USA, the Pakistani community is made up mainly of professional and executive workers: several thousand doctors, businessmen, engineers;[5] like their counterparts in the UK, these families have settled permanently. The influx of Pakistanis into the Middle East was caused by the boom which followed the oil-price shocks of 1973 and 1979. After reaching a peak of 3 million, their number has fallen as a result of a slowdown in the local economies. Most of these migrants are people with few or no qualifications, on temporary contracts. For some time, emigration – particularly to the Middle East – has served as a (relative) safety valve on demographic pressure. In the 1980s, about 10 per cent of the economically active population worked abroad. The money they sent to their families at home, especially in the case of workers in the Persian Gulf, was a sizeable contribution to the budget of numerous poor households.

The brain drain, a common phenomenon in many developing countries, is particularly marked in Pakistan. It is not unrelated to political instability and the inefficient functioning of institutions.

The largest contingents of unqualified manual workers come from mountainous areas in the north and northwest, poor districts of the northern Punjab, and Baluchistan. There are few Sindis. As for upper-class migrants, they come from every community and every region.

Table 7.2 Estimated number of Pakistanis abroad (1998)

United Kingdom:	750,000
United States, Canada:	about 1 million
Middle East:	2.5 million
Europe and Southeast Asia:	50,000–100,000

Source: S.J. Burki, *Dawn*, 29 August, 5 September 1999.

Internal migration

While the repercussions of cross-border migration have been only economic, migration within the country has had both economic and political effects. The attraction of towns, a universal phenomenon, is particuarly strong in poorer areas. People who cannot go abroad leave the valleys of the Hindu Kush or the plateaus of the Punjab for the towns. Thus Karachi has become the most important Pashtun town, while it has also attracted a strong contingent of Baluchis and Punjabis. For decades, Sindis have made up little more than 20 per cent of the population of the metropolis.

The particularly acute lack of modern elites in Baluchistan attracted many civil servants and tradesmen from the Punjab. During the Afghan war, waves of refugees, especially Pashtuns (Afghan Pashtuns), arrived; of the 3.7 million who came in 1990, about 1.5 million remain. In the NWFP they did not cause too many problems, since they belong to the same ethnic group. In Baluchistan, on the other hand, they strengthened local Pashtun communities, arousing the hostility of the Baluchis. Sind, for its part, witnessed an influx of Baluchis and Punjabis who were given newly cultivated land.

All these migratory movements which followed the colossal 1947 intermingling with refugees from India have created points of tension. The different communities do not mix much, except the upper classes. Muslims who converted years ago have kept the traditional caste system, forbidding out-of-caste marriages, called *zat* in Pakistan. For the Pashtuns, it is the law of the tribe that is important. Even marriages between Sunni and Shi'a are rare, except among well-off families. So national cohesion is jeopardized by the lack of a melting-pot effect.

The working population and jobs

In 1998, the number of economically active people was put at 38.6 million (67 per cent in rural areas and 33 per cent in the towns) – that is, 28.7 per cent of the total population.

The rate of economic activity in agriculture seems low in comparison with a country like India (about 55 per cent) or Bangladesh (more than 60 per cent). It is even a little lower than that of China, despite China's strong economic growth since 1980. The number of economically active people relative to the total population is also quite low; this is the result of a very marked population growth.

The unemployment rate is inevitably very approximate, and we must remember that there is substantial underemployment. Nonetheless, there is no doubt whatsoever that the number of Pakistanis without work is growing as a result of both a fall in the emigration rate and an economic slowdown; this has contributed to renewed intercommunal tension and violence since the 1980s.

The *Economic Survey* (1998–99) finds that 'despite a net growth in GNP over a long period, social indicators are low', and that they are lower than those of several other Asian countries, except in the case of life expectancy. Even India scores higher in these various domains, despite slower growth – except for the decade 1990–2000.

The rise in living standards is very uncertain, especially in country areas. Most studies of the 'poverty line' are based on calculations taken from opinion-poll inquiries, which are often of dubious value. There are very few field studies based on observations gleaned from peasants or local administrations. We could make the same observation in the context of the play of sociopolitical forces at village or sub-district level. Despite the gaps in the available knowledge, we can advance the hypothesis that poverty is still less acute in Pakistan than it is in India. Data on total or *per capita* GNP is flimsy, but useful for basic comparisons.

Table 7.3 Working population

Sectors	1951	1998
Agriculture	65.3%	45.1%
Industry	9.5%	11.2%
Services, construction, various	25.2%	43.7%

Table 7.4 Standard of living, education and health (1998 census)

Literacy	45%
Life expectancy	63 years
Fertility	5
Access to drinking water	48%
Number of people per doctor	1,600

Table 7.5 Per capita GNP, 1997 (dollars)

	Exchange rate parity	Buying power parity
Pakistan	500	1,580
India	370	1,660
Bangladesh	360	1,090
Indonesia	1,110	3,390
China	860	3,070

Source: World Bank Atlas, 1999.

Primary and secondary education are inadequate from both a quantitive and a qualitative point of view; this is true of all Asian countries. According to a World Bank report, about half of the children in Pakistan were in primary education in 1994; this figure had risen a little by 1999. As for the standard of the universities, it has fallen. The University of the Punjab, a brilliant star at the dawn of Independence, has lost its lustre, torn to shreds by dissension, the pernicious influence of the religious parties, and the mediocrity of many teachers. The University of Karachi has gone down too. The twenty-three universities established since 1947 are not much better. There are 640,000 male students and 350,000 female students. Certainly there are a few very good institutions and a few excellent business schools, but the children of Pakistan's intelligentsia – unlike their Indian counterparts – prefer to study in the USA or the UK. Despite everything – despite the colossal brain drain, too – Pakistan, like India, is relatively well endowed with senior managers. Multinationals in both countries do not employ many expatriates, unlike their branches in China or Indonesia.

For many years now the newspapers have been full of articles about the terrible state of the school and university system. Three thousand primary schools in Sind and five thousand in the Punjab existed only on paper in 1998. As for the universities, Zia ul-Islam noted that a few years ago, anyone with an MSc or a diploma from a medical faculty was automatically admitted to study for a doctorate in Britain, whereas nowadays 'no one recognizes our university degrees'. Another article complained of numerous irregularities: cheating in examinations with the collusion of important people.[6]

Many newspaper articles also criticize the inadequacies of the health system. Health provision – a total of 872 hospitals, 4,555 dispensaries, 6,155 basic health units and 852 maternity clinics, covering the towns much better than the country (1998–99 figures) – leaves a lot to be desired. According to a Federal Bureau of Statistics report,[7] of the 6,155 basic health units, 53 per cent have no doctor and 70 per cent have no female staff, even though in some traditional milieux a woman may not be examined by a man.

For several years, numerous Pakistanis have been demanding greater efforts to improve education and health. In 1993 a Social Action Programme was launched, with the support of the World Bank and the Asian Development Bank. It aims to extend primary education and to improve primary health care, especially through vaccination campaigns, improving access to drinking water, and encouraging birth control. Despite these efforts, education and health spending remains at around 2.2 and 0.79 per cent of GNP respectively.

Whatever the impact of the birth-control policy, we can envisage a fall in the birth rate simply by virtue of the modernization of society, especially in towns. For a while, however, any such fall will be cancelled out by the numerous children born to the young people who make up such a significant proportion of the population. As for another spurt of emigration, this looks unlikely, even if Pakistanis have been going to work in eastern Asia for some years. So Pakistan will continue for a long time to experience a population growth which it should have started to control earlier.

8

ECONOMIC DEVELOPMENT

In 1947, there were several development options. Unlike the Congress Party – which, prompted by Nehru, had by 1938 established a National Planning Committee to oversee future planning – the Muslim League did not pay much attention to the economy. This was partly because the creation of Pakistan was not definite until the last moment and partly because all their energies were devoted to ensuring the partition of the empire. There were further differences between the two neighbours: India, under Nehru's leadership, was strongly influenced by the socialist tendencies of the London Fabian Society. However, the Qaid-i Azam, the rich merchants from Bombay, and the comfortably off urban classes had little or no use for socializing ideology. For every conceivable reason, prosperous landowners, whose political influence was decisive, were not particularly attracted by the agrarian reforms advocated by the left wing of the Congress Party.

Moreover, thanks to Mahatma Gandhi, the Party leaders had been forced to face the realities of life in the whole of India, including rural areas; this explains the emphasis on rural development in India's first five-year plan. The Muslim League and its leaders became interested in the rural world only at the eleventh hour, just before Partition, in order to rally the villages to their cause.

1947–90

Immediately after Partition, the leaders of Pakistan did not opt for a straightforward liberal economy. They inherited a system based on strong administration and a firm state apparatus, deeply affected by the war economy of 1939–45. They were also influenced by the widespread theory – with no Marxist overtones – that the state should intervene in cases where the private sector could not or would not act. In effect, the first five-year plan was never more than a dead letter: it did not start until 1955, owing to the problems of establishing the new state and the political instability which followed the assassination of Prime Minister Liaquat Ali Khan in 1951.

Western Pakistan had the best hand where agriculture was concerned, but virtually no modern industry. The idea was to remedy this by measures aimed at encouraging prosperous merchants – mainly from Bombay and Gujarat – to become industrialists. Most of these efforts were concentrated on the textile industry, because

Pakistan acquired vast cotton-growing areas, while nearly all the spinning and weaving factories were in India. Other industries – cement, agrobiology, mechanical, chemical fertilizers – would come later. Small semi-artisanal industries which had grown up in the Punjab in colonial times developed rapidly, and some even went into the export market. In contrast to these positive trends, agriculture stagnated – so much so that the western Punjab, formerly the breadbasket of the Indian Empire, had a shortage of wheat. In the year 1953–54 Pakistan imported a million tonnes of wheat, prompting a deputy in the Punjab Assembly to remark that his constituents were 'forced to eat grass'!

All this changed in 1958, after General Ayub Khan's coup. A practical man who had no time for politicians and their intrigues, he surrounded himself with competent civil servants, young economists trained in the USA, and brilliant advisers, mainly American graduates from Harvard. He concentrated on economic development, and the second five-year plan (1960–65) was successfully implemented. Western Pakistan exploited its assets better, while eastern Pakistan came out of semi-stagnation thanks to government grants. People still talk about the 'Pakistani miracle'. South Koreans went to Karachi to learn and be inspired. Today, the pupil has overtaken the master, as a Pakistani ambassador ironically observed recently.

The pragmatism of the early 1960s was accompanied by substantial foreign aid (the USA, the World Bank). This aid – which, in general, was used appropriately – financed 40 per cent of the second plan and 34 per cent of the third (1965–70), but this 'golden age' proved short-lived. The war with India in 1965; the resurgence of internal unrest; burgeoning corruption; the waning influence of Marshal Ayub Khan, who suffered failing health and surrounded himself with sycophants; an unstable economy – all this provoked the fall of the regime in 1969.

Pakistan then went through another phase of instability: the military government of General Yahya Khan; then, in 1970, general elections which exacerbated the tensions between the two halves of the country. From the beginning of 1971, the secession of East Pakistan looked more or less inevitable. After ineffectual and cruel repression from March to December 1971, the Pakistan army surrendered at Dhaka after Indian troops had come in to support the partisans of independence. The economy was weakened by a conflict which caused the withholding of some foreign aid and a rise in the defence budget, not to mention the costs and losses arising from the war itself. Nevertheless, the secession appeared to be to Pakistan's long-term advantage, because public investment in the eastern province had been going up and up, finally exceeding investment in western Pakistan in 1965–70. In addition, profits from jute exports were falling owing to the growth of exports from the east.

A new era began for Pakistan with Zulfikar Ali Bhutto's arrival in power. This brilliant, charismatic leader could have been Pakistan's Nehru, but he had no respect for democracy and perpetrated every kind of abuse of power and dubious manoeuvre, including physically eliminating his opponents. He was hanged in April 1979. During his term of office, internal unrest increased and Baluchistan was subjected to repression. Economic prospects looked equally bleak. Jettisoning Ayub Khan's pragmatism, Bhutto implemented a populist policy which hindered growth without bringing any attendant social benefits: he nationalized several industries, most of the banks and insurance companies, and cotton and rice exports. The state proved incapable of managing and developing all the enterprises which were brought into the public sector. Production slowed; losses accumulated. What was left of the private sector, including the vitally important textile industry, made slow progress. Since there were successive waves of nationalization between 1971 and 1976, there was little private-sector investment, because no one wanted to innovate for fear of being nationalized. Small businesses, on the other hand, continued to flourish.

As for agriculture, there was not much agrarian reform. And as if heaven wanted to punish men on earth, weather conditions destroyed crops on several occasions, making the weaknesses of the planning regime even more apparent. Inflation quickly swallowed up the workers' pay rises. The oil price rise of 1973 raised the cost of petrol imports. Finally, it became obvious that socialism could be as corrupt as capitalism.

There was, however, a positive aspect to this depressing overall picture. The Prime Minister's impassioned speeches in both town and country, in which he excoriated the prosperous landowners – although he was one himself – and the 'twenty-two families'[47] who had dominated whole swathes of private industry before the nationalizations, did not improve the lot of the general population. On the other hand, these fine phrases did make ordinary people aware of their rights. In Sind, farmers dared to confront their landlords; in the factories, workers were less likely to tolerate exploitation. In 1978, a senior civil servant in the railway department told how railwaymen had come to his office to complain – quite legitimately – about their working conditions: 'Before Bhutto, such a scenario was inconceivable.'

In 1977, the curtain fell yet again. After rigged elections, there were demonstrations and troubles throughout the country. In July, General Zia ul-Haq took power; he would remain in office for eleven years. He and his entourage were inclined to be pragmatic, and the unsatisfactory economic situation reinforced this. It was the end of 'Islamic socialism'. There was some denationalization; the country became more open to foreign private investment, and foreign trade was encouraged. This development was not peculiar to Pakistan. From the end of the 1970s, the words 'opening', 'liberalization' and 'lowering Customs barriers' were heard from India to China, by way of Southeast Asia. Ruling elites began to question their development policies, and to take account of the inadequacies of the paths they had been following – the path of Nehru, and especially of Indira Gandhi. These reassessments, which began in their own countries, were subsequently influenced by the liberal policies of Margaret Thatcher and President Ronald Reagan.

Two external factors helped to improve prospects for development. As a result of the Soviet invasion of Afghanistan at the end of December 1979, Pakistan again received generous economic aid – mainly from the USA, the World Bank, and Japan. The second factor was linked to the boom in the Middle East, where – as we have seen – Pakistanis flocked in order to find work. In 1982–83, official cash remittances reached a peak of 2.9 thousand million dollars, of which 2.4 thousand million came from workers in the Middle East (1.4 thousand million from Saudi Arabia alone). Between 1980 and 1985, these remittances made up 9.3 per cent of GDP per year.

Once more there was progress on the agricultural front. Little by little, Pakistan stopped importing wheat and became an important exporter of rice. Cotton production also rose, and this stimulated textile exports. Large industry took on a new lease of life and diversified, although textiles still played a disproportionate role. Although – as for many developing countries – they are approximate, GDP data confirm these trends.

Table 8.1 GDP growth

1950–1960	+ 3.00% per annum
1960–1970	+ 6.77% per annum
1970–1980	+ 4.84% per annum
1980–1990	+ 6.24% per annum

Financial year: July–June

Source: Economic Survey, 1998–1999.

These very respectable figures are markedly better than those for India, where average annual growth between 1950 and 1980 was 3.5 per cent, as against 5.5 per cent for 1980–90. Obviously, had the population not grown so rapidly, the people would have benefited more from the effects of economic expansion. We must also take note of the low rate of savings and investments, even if they are underestimated. Between 1960 and 1990, savings represented 13 to 14 per cent of GNP. Internal investments did not vary much, fluctuating around 16 to 17 per cent of GNP, with just over half coming from private sources. Foreign aid also comes into this picture.

Deficiencies in the taxation system, wastage and corruption are also evident in the form of scanty public revenue, a constant feature since the 1950s which would become critical after 1990. Vasim Jafarey, an honest and experienced former governor of the Central Bank, was observing in 1980 that there was no lack of money in Pakistan, but the public coffers were empty. Total public revenue, from taxation and other sources, was between 16 and 18 per cent of GDP between 1970 and 1990.

After 1980, alarm bells sounded from the Finance Ministry and the World Bank, where experts deemed that the taxation system should be strengthened and reformed in order to reduce domestic debt: between 1980 and 1990 the fiscal deficit stood at 7 per cent of GDP a year – unsustainable over the long term. President Zia might have been the leader of an authoritarian regime, but he did not dare bring in the necessary reforms because of pressure from vested interests and other lobbies – big landowners and important businessmen. In addition, national defence was more expensive than it was in other Asian countries, because of the wars and the generally tense relations between Pakistan and its Indian neighbour. This was a constant brake on the economy, and its influence became more pernicious as time went by. Between 1970 and 1990, military expenditure reached 5.5 to 7.2 per cent of GNP per year, against 6 to 8 per cent allocated to development.

The countryside

As ever, water is the key to agricultural development. Several major projects, some of which had started before 1947, enlarged the area of cultivation by building diversion dykes on the Indus and its tributaries, and new irrigation canals. There was the Kotri barrage[2] on the lower Indus, the development of the Thal desert, the sluicegates at Gudu, Taunsa and Chasma, also on the Indus, which brought new land under cultivation between 1950 and 1990.

In 1960, under the aegis of the World Bank, India and Pakistan reached an agreement that settled the disputed legacy of the Partition of the Indian Empire, which cut the Punjab's canal system in two. India kept the three rivers in the East. From the Indus and the two rivers in the West, the Jhelum and the Chenab, new canals were to irrigate the zones deprived of water by India. Pakistan built the great Tarbela barrage,[3] an impressive dyke on the Indus where the mountains end, and the barrage of Mangla, near Islamabad. Both supplied electricity and irrigation. Around these major projects, diesel or electricity tubewells proliferated, to make up for any inadequacies in the canal supplies.

Problems that had been apparent since the beginning of the century assumed alarming proportions: waterlogging and salinity. In former times, the groundwater level fluctuated in a dynamic equilibrium, rising and falling according to the seasons. Canals that were not lined with cement lost large amounts of water to infiltration. Where there was insufficient natural subterranean drainage, and no canal, the groundwater level rose, leading to an excess of water which rotted the roots of the plants. When the rising groundwater came up against salty strata it brought the salt up to the surface, making the ground inhospitable to any cultivation. In the lower Sind, there was a further risk of salination from the sea at high tide.

In 1960, with the help of the Americans, the irrigation authorities began to search for answers to these problems. The best solution was to increase the number of tubewells; these lowered groundwater and increased the potential for irrigation. All the same, where the subterranean water was briny, as it often was in Sind, horizontal drains had to be dug. The land that had been salinated had to be washed out to eliminate the salt. These costly and complex projects have still by no means got rid of the problem. In 1990, waterlogging affected 0.5 million hectares before the monsoon and 2.3 million after it; and a quarter of the canalized area was affected to some extent by salinity.

It was between 1965 and 1970 that the Green Revolution emerged in Asia on the initiative of the Ford and Rockefeller Foundations, with aid from America and the World Bank. The 'Open Sesame' of this process was water. The Indus basin, where three-quarters of the land was irrigated, was an ideal location, all the more so in view of the fact that the usual yields of wheat and hulled rice went from 1,000 or 1,300 kilograms per hectare to 2,000 – even with an imperfect irrigation system and not enough chemical fertilizer.

Better irrigation prompted the farmers to replace sorghum and millet, cultivated during the monsoon, with rice, which was more lucrative. Cotton yields went up thanks to new varieties, chemical fertilizer, and pesticides (cotton is especially vulnerable to parasites). Cattle-raising and tree-growing also developed, supplementing the revenue derived from agriculture, which was still the most important source.

Key points of the Green Revolution

1. New seeds (wheat, rice, maize, sorghum, millet) react better genetically to chemical fertilizer than the old ones. Short-stemmed varieties (which avoid the problem of too much water) often ripen early, allowing for two crops a year.
2. These new varieties, with the introduction of chemical fertilizer, need more water than traditional varieties without chemical fertilizer.
3. The new, genetically homogeneous, varieties are more vulnerable to parasites; hence the importance of antiparasite treatments.
4. These varieties of wheat and rice gradually decline in quality and have to be replaced every four or five years; hence there is a continuing process of research and an increasing number of new seeds. Hybrid varieties (maize, millet, rice) have to be renewed every year.
5. Use of the tractor is not a crucial issue.
6. Any one variety is not necessarily suitable for all physical conditions.

It is not surprising that the Punjabis, with their rich agricultural heritage, were the first to embrace the Green Revolution. More spectacular still was the development of Sind. In 1967, agriculture was in a pitiful state, and even the great *wadera* (major landowners) did not bother with it much. Our inquiries in 1985–86 and 1993 indicated that things had changed radically: yields of wheat and rice had caught up with those in the Punjab, or were not far short; cotton was making great strides; there were superb cattle-raising ranches. In a word, the *wadera* had become dynamic.

The Green Revolution has had social consequences. For many years there was widespread socialist-populist propaganda to the effect that 'the rich get richer while the poor get poorer'. In fact – albeit within varying timeframes – all the landowners, whether they have extensive, medium-sized or small landholdings, have followed the Revolution, so that – thanks to more abundant harvests and a low level of mechanization – the income of agricultural workers has risen. There are more jobs in transport, small shops, building . . . Labourers use tractors more, so it is easier to get two harvests a year out of the same piece of land. The sickle is still used for harvesting, but wheat-threshing is partly mechanized. This global development process has led to a better life for the poorest people in Sind and the Punjab, the NWFP and Baluchistan, but there is still gross exploitation, especially in Sind.

There is still pluvial cultivation [*barani*] in the North Punjab plateaus (Potwar) and some zones of the NWFP. Here, progress is slower, because lack of water means there can be no true Green Revolution. There is limited irrigation potential. If there are plenty of showers in winter, with the help of a little chemical fertilizer a peasant can harvest between 1,200 and 1,500 kilograms of wheat per hectare. If there are not, yields fall to 500–700 kilograms per hectare at the most. As for maize, that depends on the monsoon, which is unpredictable but more copious than on the plains. As in colonial times, emigration and the army are still safety valves: they allow families to send sons out in the world to help make ends meet.

There has been enormous progress, but this is being jeopardized by demographic pressure and by serious deficiencies which became more and more apparent during the last decade of the century: the bad state of the irrigation systems, a decline in agronomic research, incorrect use of several chemical fertilizers . . . Despite much greater wheat yields, imports rose from 300,000 tonnes in 1980–81 to 2 million tonnes in 1989–90.

Table 8.2 Agricultural statistics (July–June)

	1949–1950	1989–1990
Net cultivated area	11.4	15.0 million hectares
Gross cultivated area•	12.5	19.8 million hectares
Gross irrigated area	9.3	15.7 million tonnes
Use of chemical fertilizers	negligible	1.9 million tonnes
		(nitrates, phosphates, potassium)
Main cereal crops:		
Wheat	3.9	14.3 millions of tonnes
Rice	0.8	3.2 millions of tonnes
Total cereals and foodgrains••	6.8	
Ginned cotton	0.2	20.1 millions of tonnes
Sugarcane	7.8	1.6 millions of tonnes
Livestock:		
Buffalo	5.8	14.7 millions of tonnes
Cattle	9.2	17.6 millions of tonnes
Milk production•••	7.8	14.5 millions of tonnes
Beef and mutton	0.55	1.37 millions of tonnes
Poultry	0.01	0.22 millions of tonnes

* Two annual harvests from the same piece of land
** Wheat, rice, maize, sorghum, millet and legumes.
*** The first milk and meat figures are for 1971–72.
Source: Economic Survey, 1990–1991.

Agricultural organization

China before 1949, India, Bangladesh and Java were so densely populated that land redistribution was not easy to contemplate, and big estates of tens or hundreds of hectares were very rare. In Pakistan, on the other hand, such redistribution could be envisaged, because there were vast estates of more than a hundred hectares. But since 1947, the landlords' influence in local councils and assemblies, at both provincial and national level, has persisted throughout all the various regimes: civilian or military, authoritarian or democratic. Despite the move to democracy after 1988, despite the huge advances made by the urban middle classes, the business community and the liberal professions, out of the 207 seats in the National Assembly the major landowners occupied 156 after the 1988 elections, 106 in 1990, 129 in 1993 and 126 in 1997. The overrepresentation of the prosperous agrarian strata clearly precludes any thoroughgoing agrarian reform.

Things have certainly moved on. Thanks to the Green Revolution, many farmers with a little land (2 to 5 hectares) have been able to raise their yields and their income. The landless agricultural workers are less oppressed. Nevertheless, there will be no tangible decline in the major landlords' influence for some time to come. Several important people in Sind and the Punjab now consider themselves entrepreneurs, but the feudal structures are still in place.[4] Since democratization in 1988, the press has revealed some things which have been going on for years, but were never common knowledge. For example, the 'great and the good' in Sind had their own 'private prison' where agricultural workers in their employ who fell into debt were reduced to bonded labour, and sometimes chained up at night.[5] Elsewhere, in the Punjab, employees of the village brickyard were subjected to forced labour.[6] Although some major landowners did not win seats in elections, others still influenced the electorate.

Table 8.3 Agrarian profile

	Number of holdings distribution in %	*Cultivated area*
below 0.5 ha	13	1
0.5–1 ha	14	3
1–2 ha	20	9
2–5 ha	34	31
5–10 ha	12	23
10–60 ha	7	27
over 60 ha	below 1%	7

Source: Census of Agriculture, 1990.

President Ayub Khan's agrarian reforms (he imposed a ceiling of 200 hectares of irrigated land) and those of Prime Minister Bhutto (60 hectares) were not particularly effectual, because the landowners got together and shared out their estates artificially within their own families.

The 20,000 landowners in the last category of Table 8.3 owned on average 100 hectares of cultivated land. Of these landowners, 5,000 owned more than 100–200 hectares. There was another special feature: out of 5.07 million farmers, 3.5 million were landowning farmers, 600,000 were both smallholders and agricultural workers, and 954,000 were simply agricultural workers. This last category was especially prevalent in Sind. In other cases, since the Green Revolution, a number of landowners had taken back the task of farming their own land, depriving their workers of employment. Those with very small holdings sold their plots and went to work in the towns.

The relation between people and land was still better than it was in India and Bangladesh, despite strong demographic pressure. Since three-quarters of cultivated land was also irrigated land, at least a third of which produced two harvests a year (wheat–rice, wheat–maize, wheat–cotton), even those who owned only half a hectare to a hectare were able to – or had the opportunity to – make a basic living. Those who owned more than a hectare were less likely to be poor, and with 2 hectares or more a family did not do too badly, especially if there was a son or two working outside in business, transport, small industry or the army.

Industry

The introduction of modern industry followed a pattern similar to the one that began in the second half of the nineteenth century in the India of the time: initially very localized, dominated by a few small communities, then spreading further and further in spatial and social terms.

The starting signal was given in the 1950s. Taking advantage of government incentives, merchants – mostly from Bombay and Gujarat – became industrialists and launched the textile industry – mainly in Karachi, the capital city at that time. These small minorities – we could call them castes – were Khoja and Bohra Shi'a and Memon Sunni , all descended from former Hindu merchant castes. The Chinioti, whose name derives from the little town of Chiniot, were Punjabis, traditionally leather specialists. In around 1965, about ten families controlled 50 per cent of modern industry, and in the 1960s in general, it was generally believed that major industry was in the hands of twenty-two all-powerful families.

Gradually, other Pakistanis went into major industry – including the father of ex-Prime Minister Nawaz Sharif, from Amritsar in the Indian Punjab, who established a big iron-and-steel works at Lahore. The towns of the Punjab were industrialized, just as Pashtun entrepreneurs were making their mark in Peshawar. Ginning factories, new mills and weaving companies grew up as a result of cotton cultivation. The clothing industry began in the 1970s. Sugar refineries were established as the cultivation of sugarcane took off. There were several firms making chemical fertilizers using gas from Baluchistan; there were also cement works, engineering companies, machine-tool makers, manufacturers of vehicles, tractors and bicycles, often in partnership with Western or Japanese industry.

Despite the lack of iron ore and coking carbon, the authorities succumbed to the temptations of heavy industry. In 1970 a steelworks was established in Karachi with the aid of the Soviet Union. This project swallowed up a lot of capital which could, no doubt, have been better used in other branches of industry. Public-sector involvement increased strongly during Bhutto's regime; this led to the difficulties enumerated above.

Small industry gradually broadened its scope: diesel engines, threshing machines, agricultural tools, sports goods, small surgical instruments, leather goods, clothes, carpets . . . By 1999, this sector accounted for 80 per cent of industrial manpower and 30 per cent of exports. Small enterprises, which were not affected much by the socialist policies of the 1970s, were not well supported by the banks, but resourcefulness and family connections compensated for this with some success. Their contribution made up about 5 per cent of GDP. This system had its flaws, starting with the use of child labour – in the manufacture of carpets and sports goods, for example – which is condemned regularly by international organizations and numerous Western countries. Private bodies in Pakistan campaign bravely against abuses which the government is trying to curb. Some progress has been made, but we must realize that such matters are very complicated, and require a judicial and policing system that can reach beyond the larger towns. Above all they require health and safety inspectors and a police force that is not in league with small businessmen and other influential local people.

As far as infrastructure is concerned, until about 1980 roads and electrification projects were not much in evidence in rural areas; this hindered the development of agriculture, commerce, and small industries. In due course the situation improved. Despite some progress, main through roads were reaching saturation point between 1980 and 1990. As for electricity, after a phase of rapid expansion in urban areas, such efforts ceased to keep up with the overall rhythm of development: an inadequate power supply, frequent and lengthy power cuts, badly maintained lines, and lack of new investment were the norm during the 1980s. Power stations were run mainly on natural gas from Baluchistan and imported oil, as were the big barrages. Nuclear power played a very small part.

Finally, the banking system – which was very weak at first, because it had been emasculated when the mainly Hindu managers left – grew stronger. Several private banks have emerged in the main towns. Before the spate of nationalizations, the state had already opened banks which were intended to support industrialization.

Table 8.4 Industrial production*

	Cotton thread	Cotton fabric	Chemical fertilizers (active ingredients)	Cement	Sugar	Steel
1949	8.4	37.4	nil	0.4	0.017	negligible
1990	912	294.8	1.5	7.5	1.86	0.8

* In millions of tonnes, except for textiles; cotton thread in millions of kg; fabric in millions of square metres.

Source: Economic Survey, 1990–1991.

Other industries, which had started from virtually nothing in 1947, achieved these results in 1989–90: bicycles, 530,000; sewing machines, 107,000; vehicle tyres. 915,000; paper, 33,000.

Production of crude oil, which was negligible in 1947, reached 3.1 million tonnes in 1989–90, while imports rose to 4.1 million tonnes of crude oil and 4.5 million tonnes of refined oil. Power-station capacity rose from 1,862 megawatts in 1971–72 to 7,777 megawatts in 1989–90.

The rail network grew by only 200 kilometres between 1960–61 and 1990–91, when it covered 8,775 kilometres. During these same years, road construction grew appreciably: from 66,236 to 171,000 kilometres, half of these being hard roads, mostly asphalted.

External economic relations and foreign aid

Between 1950 and 1990, Pakistan – unlike the East Asian tigers, but rather like India – did not manage to promote its exports with the necessary force. The numerous customs barriers, both tariff and non-tariff, started to be reduced between 1980 and 1983, but the balance of trade remained negative throughout this entire period.

For many years, the authorities have been worried about the prominence of cotton textile and raw cotton exports (60 per cent of total exports). Leather comes next, followed by rice and synthetic textiles. In 1947, nearly all exports were of raw materials: raw cotton, skins, wool, rice for western Pakistan, jute for eastern Pakistan. Gradually this situation changed: the proportion of raw materials in exports fell to 33 per cent in 1970 and to 20 per cent in 1990. During this time, the proportion of manufactured products rose from 44 to 56 per cent, while semi-manufactured goods remained stable (24 per cent). In 1990–91, the principal export markets were the USA (10.8 per cent), Germany (8.9 per cent), Japan (8.3 per cent), the UK (7.3 per cent) and Hong Kong (6 per cent). Among Pakistan's main imports were equipment goods (52 per cent in 1970–71; 33 per cent in 1989–90), consumer goods (11 and 19 per cent) and industrial raw materials (40 per cent). As for the main suppliers, they were Japan (13 per cent), the USA (11.8 per cent), Germany (7.3 per cent) and Saudi Arabia (6.2 per cent).

Table 8.5 Balance of trade (millions of dollars)

	1980–1981	1990–1991
Exports	2,799	5,902
Imports	5,563	8,385

Source: Economic Survey, 1997–1998.

Foreign aid increased markedly between 1960 and 1965, then reduced because American aid (except food aid) was suspended during the conflict between India and Pakistan in 1965, and again in 1971. The level of foreign aid was kept down under the Bhutto regime, but there was a strong rise between 1980 and 1990. Then the USA again suspended economic and military aid, because it suspected that Islamabad was in the process of acquiring nuclear weapons. Other external sources of finance (the World Bank and the IMF, the Asiatic Bank, Japan, Germany, for example), however, still gave generously. In 1989–90, external aid funded 25 per cent of investments: 80 per cent came from international institutions, Western countries and Japan, the remainder from Middle Eastern countries and China.

The Finance Ministry raised the alarm as early as 1991: in ten years the level of aid had doubled, as had debt servicing which, combined with domestic debt, threatened Pakistan with an impossible dilemma. Of the 2.2 thousand million dollars worth of aid given in 1989–90, 1.2 thousand million went in debt servicing, leaving a net transfer of 970 million. With an optimism that would be rudely shattered, ministry experts put forward a solution to this problem: achieving 10 thousand million dollars worth of exports in 1993 (the actual level was 6.8 thousand million).

As well as credits – generally on favourable terms – Pakistan received grants – especially from Japan, the USA and Arab countries – worth between 500 and 650 million dollars a year between 1985 and 1990. As for private foreign investment, this reached an average of 66 million dollars a year between 1978 and 1985, and 166 million between 1985 and 1990. This was quite a respectable total compared to that of India, as a result of a less restrictive policy. Nonetheless, these amounts were too small to have much of a beneficial effect on the balance of payments.

Between 1950 and 1990, the economy showed signs of remarkable vitality on several occasions. Quite apart from these fluctuations, the economic landscape had changed considerably, thanks to the development of major industry and the strength of the small business sector, particularly in the Punjab. If we take Asia as a whole, Pakistan's industrial sector came after those of China, India and South Korea – which had started out at a higher level with the first five-year plans – and belonged to a middle-ranking cluster of countries including Indonesia, Thailand and the Philippines. It was ahead of that of countries like Bangladesh. There was a noticeable modernization process in the countryside with the advent of the tractor, new seeds, chemical fertilizers. Equally important was the improving infrastructure: roads and power supplies. The development of the service sector (banks, commerce) spread from Karachi and Lahore to a growing number of medium-sized towns in Sind, in the Punjab, in the NWFP. Very few regions were left out of this overall economic development process – mainly in Baluchistan and the FATA.

Any assessment of the years 1980–90, when there was relatively strong growth, must, however, be qualified, because financial abnormalities gradually took root, or increased, in both agriculture and industry. Around 1990, red warning lights were flashing everywhere on the economic dashboard.

Economic Deadlock

The last decade of the twentieth century opened with a fanfare: the launch of a reform programme which – as in India six months later – went much further than the 'small steps' taken in the 1980s. Liberalization, opening up, deregulation, privatization – these were the goals announced by Nawaz Sharif after his election victory in autumn 1990. There were grounds for hoping that Pakistan would make better use of its advantages, and be able to resolve the problems that were beginning to undermine the economy.

Public-sector companies were privatized, and bureaucratic shackles on the private sector were loosened. Measures were taken to attract foreign investment. Certain subsidies (for pesticides and fertilizers) were abolished or reduced. But after an encouraging start, the process seized up. Frequent changes of government, domestic problems, pressure from lobbies which blocked tax reforms, corruption, and all kinds of other misuses of power held up development.

Nine years later, in a speech on 15 December 1999, General Musharraf gave a sobering account of the economy. A whole series of blockages had made their mark. Some of these arose from domestic economic and political factors; others were linked to the international situation. The underlying difficulties outlined above assumed unprecedented dimensions between 1990 and 2000. Never, since 1947, had the economic future looked so bleak. Nevertheless, Pakistan still had some human and material assets. Would the country be capable of making better use of them?

The political burden

In a world that is becoming more open to foreign investment and trade, it stands to reason that the hostile relations between Pakistan and India – whichever party might be to blame – are not compatible with strong economic expansion. Nuclear tests by the two neighbours in 1998 led to stiffer penalties for Pakistan, even if some of the sanctions were gradually lifted, because its economy was much more vulnerable than that of India. The mini-war in Kargil in spring 1999 did not improve Pakistan's image; nor did the hijacking, in December 1999, of an Indian Airlines plane by Islamic militants demanding freedom for mujaheddin prisoners in Indian Kashmir. In 2000, relations between the two countries were at their lowest ebb, full of mutual bitterness and mistrust.

Pakistan's international status looks increasingly precarious. After the Russian withdrawal from Afghanistan in 1989, relations between Washington and Islamabad became strained; military and economic aid stopped in 1990. During a brief visit to Islamabad in March 2000, President Clinton made his position quite clear in a rather chilly atmosphere. In his speech, which was broadcast on radio and television, he emphasized Pakistan's increasing isolation, and the need to combat international terrorism, to cease violence in Kashmir and to get back to democracy without delay. His exhortations did not seem to make much impact over the next few months. Relations with China had cooled; relations with Iran were difficult. In both cases the major reason was Islamabad's support for the Taliban in Kabul. Iran was very hostile to this, and China was worried that an upsurge of fundamentalism in the region would encourage the Muslim Vigurs in Xinjiang (Sinkiang).

Since the beginning of the Afghan wars there has been an explosion of *madrasahs* in Pakistan – there are now 5,900 with 500,000 pupils, thanks to funding from Saudi Arabia, direct or indirect CIA support until 1989, and the encouragement of the Zia government. In many *madrasahs*, religious instruction is followed by training in the use of kalashnikovs, rocket launchers and explosives. At the same time there has been a proliferation of extremist movements, with military training camps for Pakistanis and foreigners. Here the holy war in Kashmir and 'anywhere else' in the world is fomented – including war against the USA. This worries China, Western countries, India (naturally), the Central Asian republics and Russia. The Americans are putting pressure on the Taliban to hand over Osama bin Laden, the Saudi millionaire accused of international terrorism, who is very popular with Pakistani militants.

This proliferation of extremist movements also has its effects within the country;

people are afraid that the state and society will be 'Talibanized'. As for young Pakistanis who go to fight in Kashmir or Afghanistan, they do not serve as a calming influence on their return.

Naturally, problems inside the country have had economic repercussions. Since the late 1980s, Karachi, home of 35 per cent of major industry, has been racked by violence: murders, politically motivated criminal gangs, struggles between groups of Muhajirs and Pashtuns, trouble between Sindis and other communities. Some industrialists have transferred their factories to the Punjab, where there are fewer disturbances; others are sitting tight, waiting for things to settle down. As for foreign investors, they are in no hurry to set up in Karachi. Bloody clashes between Sunni and Shi'a in several big towns and in rural areas (Jhang in the Punjab, Parachinar in the FATA, Gilgit in the North) aggravate the situation.

The trade in heroin from Afghanistan and Pakistan's Tribal Areas is a further complication. Heroin production, which rose during the war against the Soviets, shot up under the Taliban. Another consequence of the Afghan wars is arms trafficking, because arms consignments from the USA, Arab countries and China have not crossed the border. Breaches of common law, extortion by every kind of gang, clashes between Pashtun tribes, and rural violence in Sind and the Punjab complete this picture. Is it any wonder that Pakistan's industrialists are reluctant to invest? Is it surprising that foreign firms and foreign financial backers – of commercial investment or public development aid – hang back?

Since its creation, Pakistan has been trying to achieve a satisfactory balance between central government and the provinces – a task made all the harder by Punjab and Punjabi influence over politics and the army. This question is still not settled. For example, Pakistan urgently needs to increase its water resources. For thirty years, a planned barrage on the Indus at Kalabagh has been blocked by squabbles between the Punjab, which is in favour, and Sind and the NWFP, which are against.

Finally, public services are crumbling rapidly. The ranks of good, honest and competent public servants – and there have been many – have been depleted by political and bureaucratic manipulation: arbitrary sackings under Ayub Khan or Zulfikar Ali Bhutto; biased recruiting with no regard for qualifications by Bhutto senior and his daughter, and by Nawaz Sharif. One senior civil servant has regretted the fact that it is 'very difficult to find honest, experienced senior managers'. This problem is accentuated by the fact that some civil servants prefer to remain in their province and take advantage of a not particularly savoury situation.[7]

Democracy and development

Despite the margin for error, GNP figures are more or less accurate indicators. Between 1990 and 1995, GNP grew on average by 4.6 per cent a year, falling to 3.5 per cent between 1995 and 1999 and recovering to about 4 per cent in 1999–2000. During the Zia years (1977–88) there was an average annual growth rate of 6.24 per cent – almost as good as during Ayub Khan's term of office in the 1960s.

It would be simplistic to conclude from this that democracy and development are incompatible. The governments of Benazir Bhutto and Nawaz had inherited the distortions that emerged under General Zia – or before, if we remember the low tax revenue and the relatively low level of savings. Nevertheless, the seeds of political trouble were sown during the Zia era. The two leaders, each in their own way, made mistakes and handled matters badly, but such things do not have much to do with democracy. As for the fall in cash remittances from workers in the Gulf, that, of course, is not directly linked with politics. It is not democracy itself which is the main reason for the economic deadlock, but the way it works. Pakistan – like Bangladesh in a different context – is proof that democracy is not the magic remedy which many development strategists consider it to be. Between 1950 and 1970, they were playing a completely different tune: 'Underdeveloped countries are not ready for democracy; what they need is a benevolent dictatorship.' This judgement looks as reductive as the one put forward today – on the one hand we have the economic and social success of South Korea and Taiwan long before they became democracies in the late 1980s; on the other we have the many failing dictatorships in Africa and the Middle East.

Financial difficulties

The deep-rooted defects in the financial system have finally led to a disastrous situation where the combination of domestic and foreign debt constitutes a double trap. Some of the sanctions imposed after the 1998 nuclear tests have been lifted; this has restored foreign aid and facilitated negotiations with the World Bank, leading Western countries, Japan, and various international commercial banks. In this way Pakistan has secured a rescheduling of 2.9 thousand million dollars (public and commercial credits). These measures are welcome, but they have only afforded some breathing space. Negotiations with the IMF with a view to new debt rescheduling arrangements have proved difficult.

After the nuclear tests, the government froze sums held in foreign currency in the country by the Pakistanis, obliging them to be paid in rupees to make up for the shortfall in foreign currency resulting from the sanctions. This measure, which would be revoked by General Musharraf's government, undermined savers' confidence and jeopardized subsequent money transfers.

Table 8.6 Debt

	1990–1991	*1999–2000*
Domestic debt	448	1,622 billion rupees*
Foreign debt	15.5	38 billion dollars (March 2000)

* 1999: 1 dollar = 51 rupees; 2000: 1 dollar = 54 rupees.

Foreign debt includes six thousand million dollars' worth of short-term commercial credits. The cost of servicing both debts accounts for 65 per cent of state revenue as against 48.6 per cent in 1994–95, while tax receipts fell from 17.2 per cent of GDP in 1993–94 to 16.2 per cent for 1997–2000. In view of this general stagnation, it is not surprising that rates of saving and investment, which were already low, fell further. Between 1960 and 1990 the rate of saving averaged 13–14 per cent of GDP; the rate of investment 16–17 per cent. In 1998–99 they were estimated to be 12 and 14.8 per cent respectively. There was one positive factor: inflation, which had risen sharply, fell from 8 per cent in 1997–98 to 6 per cent the following year, then to 3 per cent at the end of 1999. Thanks to foreign aid, foreign currency reserves emerged from their nadir of 400 million dollars in June 1998 to reach 1.5 thousand million dollars in April 2000, although this level cannot be relied upon.

Other exterior sources of capital also dried up. Foreign currency remittances from workers outside the country, which had already been dropping for many years, continued to fall. Between 1980 and 1985 they stood at an annual rate of 9.3 per cent of GDP; this fell to 3 per cent for 1990–96. This fall accelerated after 1998–99: 1,060 million dollars compared with 1,490 million for 1997–98. It fell again the following year.

Disagreements between Nawaz Sharif's government and foreign electricity companies which had begun to build power stations also had a negative effect on future private foreign investment (see below).

Moreover, some foreign companies, banks and factories shut up shop and left Karachi. Others played a waiting game: putting their expansion plans on hold, or cancelling them. Nevertheless, as we shall see, some multinationals continued to do good business.

For all these reasons, foreign private investment, which had been encouraged by the reforms of 1990, fell back. After a flood of 3.4 thousand million dollars between 1992 and 1997 – which was excellent – things wound down. Portfolio investments collapsed: between 1997–98 and 1998–99, 9 million dollars compared with 204; direct private investment went down from 436 million to 296 – a trend which intensified in 1999–2000.

A Supreme Court ruling at the end of 1999 forbidding the charging of interest on loans, since this is against the laws of Islam, did not make domestic or international financial agreements any easier. Hopes – aroused by the 1990 reforms – that development could be fuelled by exports, have not been fulfilled. The financial crisis in East Asia has certainly did not helped matters, but the prime movers go deeper, and originate within the country itself. Between 1995 and 1998, exports went up on average by only 2.1 per cent a year, and imports fell.

A rise in exports in 1999–2000, owing to strong performances by cotton and rice, did not make up for the rise in the price of imports, which rose in the wake of oil prices – by about a thousand million dollars.

A marked influx of contraband goods from Afghanistan (from cars to refrigerators, televisions and other semi-durable consumer goods) harmed local economies. For the Taliban this, like heroin, was a way of getting hold of foreign currency. These goods come mostly by plane from Dubai via Kabul. Losses of public revenue rose to as much as a thousand million dollars a year. International sanctions imposed on the Kabul government in late 1999 put an end to air trafficking from Dubai, but other channels opened up – for instance, ground routes via Turkmenistan and Iran.

Table 8.7 Foreign trade (millions of dollars)

	Exports	Imports
1997–1998	8.6	10.1
1998–1999	7.7	9.3
1999–2000	8.4	10.5

An economy of wastage

Pakistan, like China and India, suffers from what is called an economy of wastage, which goes much further than corruption alone. It is a matter of mismanaged allocation of public funds due to political and administrative weakness, to overt or covert grants which owe more to political opportunism than to a concern for social justice, squandering money, lack of essential public investment, not enough spent on infrastructure. Then there is loss of revenue: tax fraud, smuggling, non-collection of taxes. Finally there is corruption, in all its various forms.

Rough estimates from local sources can provide some ballpark figures. Even if we bear in mind that these amounts overlap to some extent, they reveal sizeable losses.

Table 8.8 An economy of wastage

Smuggling:	3–5 billion dollars per annum
Tax evasion:	2 billion dollars per annum
Bad bank debts*:	4 billion dollars (cumulative; 1999)
Unpaid electricity bills:	nearly 2 billion (cumulative; 1999)
Theft of electricity from KESC**:	35% of production (1998***)
Losses to the state due to corruption:	2.5–5 billion dollars

* Arrears rose from 80 billion rupees in 1993 to 220 billion rupees in 1999. The list of defaulters includes prominent figures from the administrations of Benazir Bhutto and Nawaz Sharif, and numerous other politicans.
** Karachi Electricity Supply Corporation.
*** About 450,000 illegal connections; 46,000 rigged meters.

The black economy represented 50 per cent of GDP in 1998 as against 20 per cent in 1973. This does not include income from drugs. The size of this economy explains – and we will come back to it – why the economic situation is not as bad as official statistics seem to indicate. Obviously, if this situation were rectified it would free up huge capital sums which, if they were used better, would set the economy on a more solid footing.

A new lease of life for agriculture?

Big irrigation projects, the growth in the number of tubewells and the Green Revolution held the promise of agricultural progress; nevertheless, the alarm bells began to sound long before Nawaz Sharif's reforms in late 1990. These reforms made little impact on the rural world – this also happened in other Asian countries, including China and India.

The same applied to international cooperation, which had been so active at the beginning of the Green Revolution. State agricultural aid to developing countries fell after 1980. According to John Mellor, 'In American aid programmes, the number of specialists has fallen by 81 per cent over the last decades. The attitude of European donor countries has followed this pattern.'

Since ancient times, irrigation has been of paramount importance in Pakistan. At the present time it is the greatest obstacle to agricultural progress. The canal system has been deteriorating for decades owing to lack of maintenance and investment – not to mention the declining quality of the irrigation authorities, and the spread of corruption and other abuses. Barely more than 35 to 40 per cent of the water in the canals reaches the plants, and this deficit is only partially compensated for by tube-wells. Systems which are dependent on electricity still experience power cuts due to faulty supplies.

Bringing the system up to scratch would be a herculean task: there are 61,000 kilometres of canals, 88,000 outflows, numerous diversion barrages in a state of disrepair and 1.6 million kilometres of watercourses. As far as watercourses are concerned, there was progress in the 1980s: the restoration of these small, partly cement-lined canals, which reduced water loss, in return for a modest investment to which the farmers themselves contributed. Since 1990, however, there have been fewer such initiatives. In 1995, a World Bank report noted that the irrigation system was at 'breaking point'. Two years later, Manzur Ejaz elaborated: 'The system has deteriorated to such a point that it will be impossible to restore it in a few months. This is why it does not seem realistic to count on a rapid recovery for agriculture.'[8]

As for the Kalabagh barrage project, it is still deadlocked. Nonetheless, it is more of a priority in view of the fact that the Tarbela barrage upstream is less effective because it is silted up – this problem has haunted these major constructions for many years. Even if an agreement is reached, where will the necessary 12 thousand million dollars come from?

Waterlogging and salinity are also problems for the future. Both seem to be on the rise, despite drainage works.[9] Salinity can reduce harvests by 25 per cent – up to 40 or 60 per cent in the worst-affected parts of Sind. Again there must be a two-pronged attack: better maintenance of pumps and drains, and new projects.

Basic research also leaves a lot to be desired. In early 2000, Kauser Abdulla Malik, President of the Agricultural Research Council, noted that the rich seams of research opened up between 1960 and 1970 had run dry. Funds were inadequate, and overall budgets allow for four or five civil servants for every researcher.[10] The development and popularizing of new seeds also suffered from a lack of public funding. Finally, the system of credit from banks or cooperatives had been inadequate and inefficient for many years. Lack of liquidity, nonrepayment of loans, and abuses of the system by big landowners made it less effective.

In addition, there were technical problems. Until 1991, thanks to research and popularization programmes (the propagation of new techniques), cotton production had done very well, especially in the Punjab. Since that time, Pakistan has been dogged by bad luck: the dangerous leafcurl virus struck in 1992, and the usual pesticides had no effect on it.

Before the Green Revolution, farmers grew wheat from November to April [*rabi*] and during the monsoon [*kharif*] sorghum, millet, even maize, part of this crop for animal feed. Other farmers grew mainly cotton, sown in May and harvested in two or three stages until December or early January. Yet others concentrated on rice during the monsoon and contented themselves with growing secondary crops between November and April. Today, a number of farmers grow wheat after cotton, but they cannot sow their wheat in November, the ideal month, because the cotton harvest is still going on; this holds up the sowing and leads to lower yields. It would be better to create new varieties of wheat with a shorter growth cycle. Rice tends to replace the traditional monsoon crops because it is more profitable; this, too, delays – albeit for a shorter time – the sowing of wheat.

In the last decade of the twentieth century, the weather turned nasty; after 1987, while India enjoyed moderate monsoons, Pakistan had to face up to a series of natural catastrophes. On several occasions it was abnormally excessive rains battering Sind and the Punjab; they ruined the cotton, which is vulnerable to both drought and too much water, and very much at the mercy of the parasites which multiply if there is heavy rain. Over the last few years, too, scanty winter showers have also held up the harvesting of wheat which was already insufficiently irrigated, especially that of wheat which is completely dependent on rain.

In 1991–92, cotton production reached its peak: 2.2 million tonnes. Its decline was matched after 1995 by a modest growth in wheat production, while the growth in rice production was more sustained. Sugarcane production grew even more rapidly until its steep fall in 1999–2000. Between 1980 and 1984, wheat imports fell to 350,000 a year. After 1988–89 they fluctuated between 2 and 2.5 million tonnes, reaching a peak of 4.1 million in 1997–98, then falling back to 2.5 million in 1998–99. Rice exports rose from 1.2 million tonnes in 1990–91 to 1.8 or 2 million tonnes in recent years.

In 1999–2000, things began to look brighter. Rice and cotton had favourable monsoons in 1999, and wheat production continued to grow, to the point where Pakistan became an exporter. Favourable government measures, a bigger growing area, timely winter rains and better fertilizer distribution go some way towards explaining this success.

Other sectors of the rural economy have shown greater dynamism over a decade or so. Cattle-raising by big and middling landowners – even, in some areas, by smallholders – is developing rapidly. By 1992 or 1993 there were already magnificent ranches in Sind and the Punjab where, in well-maintained stables, lived rows of cows crossbred from both local and foreign breeds (Holstein, Frisonne, Jersey) whose milk production was better than that of pure local breeds. The raising of male and female buffalo, cows and bullocks flourished: 35.5 million animals in 1990–91; 43.6 million in 1998–99. The growing use of tractors made it possible to raise fewer bullocks and more cows and she-buffalo.

In recent years, better country roads have made it easier to collect and transport

Table 8.9 Agricultural statistics (millions of hectares)

	Cultivated surface (net)	(gross)	Irrigated surface (gross)		
1989–1990	15.0	19.8	15.7		
1999–2000	16.7	22.9	18.0		

Agricultural year	Wheat	Rice	Cotton (ginned)	Sugarcane	Total cereals and vegetables
1989–1990	14.3	3.2	1.5	35.5	19.9
1995–1996	16.9	3.9	1.8	45.2	23.5
1997–1998	18.8	4.3	1.6	53.1	24.9
1998–1999	18.1	4.7	1.5	55.2	25.3
1999–2000	21.0	5.1	1.9	46.3	26.8

Source: Economic Survey, 1998–1999.

milk, even if there is still some way to go. Nestlé, for example, collects milk from 2,000 villages for it two centres – at Sheikhupura, near Lahore, and Kabirwala, near Multan. The company buys 170 million litres (the figure for 1999) direct from the farmers, for which it pays cash, thus avoiding the middleman and benefiting producers. Turnover went from 800 million rupees in 1992 to 5.5 thousand million rupees in 1998 – a tripling in real terms, allowing for the rupee's fall in value.

Fruit and vegetable growing are making progress, as is flower growing; here, a small farmer can make a big profit on less than half a hectare of well-irrigated land. Here and there little ponds destined for fish farming have sprung up; these, too, are profitable.

Table 8.10 Growth of production (thousands of tonnes)

	Milk	Meat (beef and mutton)	Poultry	Eggs	Skins
1971–1972	7,800	554	14	583 millions	21
1991–1992	16,280	1,500	169	4,490	40
1999–2000	25,560	1,635	322	8,463	45

Source: Economic Survey, 1998–1999.

To be sure, the figures in Table 8.10 are approximate, especially the number of eggs (!). Nevertheless, they are interesting because they are indicative of trends. The number of goats and sheep rose more slowly: 47 and 24 million respectively in 1999–2000. Fruits such as oranges, mangos, apples and apricots are also grown in large numbers, and many are exported: 42 million dollars' worth in 1990; 71 million in 1999.

As for tools, rustic locally made threshing machines and new forms of transport have made their mark. In the Punjab in 1992 there was a striking proliferation of barrows with tyres pulled by a donkey. Until that time, donkeys had been used mainly with packsaddles. The new method was cheaper than an oxcart or a horse-drawn cart, even if it carried lighter loads. Who knows who came up with this bright idea? Six years later, in the Indian state of Uttar Pradesh, six hundred kilometres from Pakistan, the same carts were in use.

The diversification of the agricultural sector and of cattle-raising has an important social dimension, because it creates more jobs in both upstream and downstream areas: more intensive work on the land, packaging, transport, and the use of several products for industrial purposes. It is quite an experience to see little boxes of tomatoes piled up by the roadside ready for the lorries in the NWFP, the potato seeds which go by lorry from Gilgit to the Punjab, or the milk-collectors who, with half a dozen cans tied to their little motorbikes, go between the villages and the milk-processing plants.

These trends, which are common to several Asian countries, have by no means realized their full potential. They do not need too much help from the state – just research, road maintenance and reliable power supplies. The small plots of irrigated land they need are coming on stream, and can be watered by sprinklers or drips installed by the farmers themselves. The advantage of these new methods is that they use less water. A typical example is the apple orchards in the northern and northwestern valleys, and in Baluchistan. Production rose from 130,000 tonnes in 1980 to 580,000 tonnes in 1998; 100,000 tonnes were exported to the Middle East, but even this was not enough to satisfy the demand. Raising production levels and quality could double exports and bring in a further 80 million dollars.

An overview of agriculture betwen 1990 and 2000 revcals some positive aspects which could become more prominent. We must also take note of the resourcefulness of these farmers, especially those who have a son or two helping the family by working in town. At first sight, then, the situation in the countryside does not look too bad. If you talk to the farmers, however, you get a flood of complaints: abuses of the system, corruption, poor-quality fertilizer, sugarcane that withers away because a power cut has stopped the tubewell and so on. Other farmers complain about the government's pricing policy for agricultural produce.

The problems that plague the rural economy are not going to cause a serious collapse of production. Recoveries like the one in 1999–2000 are still possible. Nevertheless, enormous public investment is called for, especially for projects involving water. It is not clear where this is going to come from.

The industrial sector

There has been a perceptible slowdown: the industrial production indicator went from 100 in 1980–81 to 202 in 1990–91, but was only 270 in 1998–99. Large industry was the worst affected: a 2.5 per cent annual growth rate between 1995 and 2000 compared with 8 per cent between 1980 and 1990. Small industries account for 30 per cent of exports and 5 per cent of GDP, and absorb 80 per cent of industrial manpower. The Punjab is still ahead, but several small enterprises have been established in the northwest and in Sind. The small industrial sector has also been affected by the downturn, with a 5 per cent annual growth rate compared with 8 per cent between 1990 and 1995.

Despite longstanding efforts at diversification, the cotton industry's share has not shrunk much: 27 per cent of industrial production, 60 per cent of exports (including raw cotton) and 38 per cent of large-industry employment.

These global figures mask differences within each branch. In 1990 there were already completely refurbished textile factories in Karachi. New mechanical engineering and car firms sprang up. But a thousand firms were classified as 'ailing companies' – badly managed and on the verge of bankruptcy, although some of them had the benefit of bank loans on favourable terms. General Musharraf's government is trying to find 400 million dollars in aid to revive some of them. Because of the economic climate, many factories – including Karachi's steelworks – are operating at 50 to 70 per cent capacity.

Table 8.11 Industrial production

	Cotton fabric (millions of square metres)	Cotton thread (millions of kg)	Cement (millions of tonnes)	Nitrate fertilizer (millions of tonnes)
1990–1991	293	1,040	7.76	2.05
1997–1998	340	1,530	9.36	3.30
1998–1999	384	1,540	9.60	3.40

Source: Economic Survey, 1998–1999; 1999–2000.

Non-nitrogenous fertilizers are not growing much. The same goes for many consumer goods: bicycles, sewing machines, tyres. At the Karachi steelworks, production of cast iron for steel fluctuates around the million tonnes mark. The vehicle industry – jeeps, cars, lorries, tractors – is having a difficult time. Then there is the privatization programme. Between 1991 and 1992, 70 companies were taken out of the public sector, followed by 40 more before 1998; these included companies in the car, cement, fertilizer and food industries, and five banks. Further privatization of gas, oil and big electricity companies is being discussed or under way. Even if it seems to lead to irregularities which are not to the state's advantage, the reduction of the public sector cannot fail to benefit the economy as a whole. The fall-off in foreign aid and private investment has also had a negative effect on Pakistan's industrialists. Although industrial production rose slightly in 1999–2000, there is no prospect of a real recovery.

The energy sector

As we have seen, the discrepancy between supply of and demand for electricity became critical in 1990, with a 15 per cent shortfall in supplies, reaching 33 per cent in peak hours. In order to remedy this situation, in 1993 Benazir Bhutto's government set up a Task Force on Energy. At that time, India was in the same situation, and is still, as a result of indecision and bureaucratic foot-dragging which are hardly likely to tempt investors. Pakistan began by finding out what other countries like Chile, Argentina, Thailand and the Philippines were doing. The country needed an extra 3,000 megawatts as quickly as possible.

Thanks to an arrangement that was extremely favourable to foreign partners, the Independent Power Projects (IPP) were started: private power stations produced electricity which was bought by the WAPDA (Water & Power Development Authority) or the KESC (Karachi Electricity Supply Corporation). As a result of complex agreements, government borrowing from international banks, foreign private investment and the participation of the World Bank, sixteen new power stations were started. Once they were completed, they would provide 4,650 megawatts at a cost of about 5 million dollars. The first few began to function.

This apparent success is misleading, for political as well as economic reasons. After its return to power in February 1997, Nawaz Sharif's government accused Benazir Bhutto of receiving generous 'under-the-table' payments, and the IPP of corruption, and demanded that the contracts should be renegotiated. An editorial in the daily *Dawn* on 25 September 1999 spoke of 'a witch-hunt which harasses foreign investors and undermines the country's image abroad'.

Table 8.12 Power stations

	Hydroelectric	Thermic	Nuclear	Total (mw)
1990–1991	2,890	5,741	137	8,768
1993–1994	4,726	6,456	137	11,319
1997–1998	4,825	10,655	137	15,617
1998–1999	4,825	10,763	137	15,725
1999–2000	–	–	–	16,764

Sources: Economic Survey, 1998–1999; 1999–2000.

The government supplied no proof, so the question remains open. On the economic front, the situation is clearer. Since 1991 the two electricity companies have become less efficient. Partly because supplies are being stolen, 45 per cent of production is lost, and the sum total of unpaid electricity bills amounted to 2 thousand million dollars at the end of 1999. It is not surprising that the companies are on the verge of bankruptcy, and that they are unable to afford electricity at the price agreed with the IPP. The IPP agreed to reduce the price, but the whole dispute was still rumbling on in October 2000.

Although it is difficult to disentangle all the threads of this intrigue, certain facts are clear. Today, Pakistan, which at one time did not have enough electricity, now has a surplus. At the same time, the parlous state of the older networks leads to frequent breakdowns and power cuts. There is one consolation, and it is an important one: if an economic upturn does materialize, it will not be frustrated by lack of electricity.

What about other power sources? The search for oil deposits is not making much progress: annual production remains at about 3.26 million tonnes. In 1998–99, crude oil imports stood at 4.7 million tonnes, and imports of oil products at 11 million tonnes.

Pakistan is well endowed with natural gas; new deposits have recently been found in Baluchistan and Sind, taking production from 14 thousand million cubic metres to 20 (1990–98). For many years there has been a project to install gas and, possibly, oil pipelines from Turkmenistan across Afghanistan, or from Iran. The first idea was frustrated by the ongoing civil war in Afghanistan; the second is still under discussion. Hydroelectricity is also a promising option: huge barrages on the Indus (Tarbela downstream, Kalabagh upstream), and small power stations in the upper northern valleys.

Transport

The rail network is still 8,775 kilometres long. The service is heavily criticized because it is badly maintained and has not been modernized; today, roads account for 90 per cent of the movement of people and goods.

The road network comprises 139,000 kilometres of main roads and 110,000 kilometres of secondary roads. The 7,144 kilometres of trunk roads take 63 per cent of road traffic; 3,000 kilometres of them are in a poor state. According to a World Bank study, it would take 450 million dollars to keep the trunk roads and local roads in a decent state of repair. A magnificent toll motorway has been opened between Lahore and Islamabad via Sargodha. There are other major construction projects all along the Indus, including a direct route between Peshawar and Karachi.

Table 8.13 Methods of transport

	cars, jeeps	lorries, buses	motorcycles, tricycles	other vehicles*
1991	765,000	196,265	1,430,000	507,000
1998	1,167,635	251,000	2,130,000	714,000
1999	1,206,000	382,000	2,220,000	732,000

* tractors, horse-boxes, etc.

Source: Economic Survey, 1999–2000.

The overall number of motor vehicles is rising rapidly, placing a heavy burden on the main roads. Table 8.13 shows how important the black economy is: the number of motor vehicles has gone up by 64 per cent in eight years – that is, by almost 8 per cent a year: this is much higher than the official growth rate of GDP.

General Musharraf: a first assessment

General Musharraf's coup was popular at first, but ten months later there was general gloom and disappointment. Pakistan has become even more isolated internationally, and many enlightened citizens consider that domestic problems should take precedence over Kashmir. Military and religious organizations have not been brought into line. As for public order, it remains precarious.

It is taking a long time to clean up public finances, so negotiations with the IMF and the World Bank on foreign debt and new credits are delicate. Attempts to raise taxes and reduce smuggling attracted strong opposition – from small shopkeepers to Pashtun tribes who threatened to resort to arms if their profitable 'business' with Afghanistan was jeopardized. Despite some success with better tax collection and the fight against corruption, the financial situation is still shaky.

We are a long way from the situation that prevailed after General Ayub Khan's coup in 1958. As soon as he came to power, he tackled the economy with a series of sensible and vigorous measures. No doubt he had an easier time than General Musharraf, because smuggling, corruption and religious parties were much less in evidence than they are today, and the Kashmir question was less burning than it has been for the last ten years. We must admit that the future is uncertain.

Plus points

Despite all these doubts, there are positive factors in Pakistan which should stop the country from falling apart. First, a resolute government that inspires confidence could claw back some – if not all – of the millions of dollars that are wasted every year; this would allow it to tackle the problems of the agricultural sector, fight against environmental degradation, and boost industry with a well-run credit system. Industry could forge ahead, because at the moment its capacity is underutilized. Moreover, expansion would not be hindered by lack of electricity, as it is in India. There would be more money for education and health. A rise in the consumption of meat, fruit and milk, increased trade, and other signs like sales of domestic appliances, whether they were smuggled in or not, confirm that large amounts of cash are 'spread about' throughout the country – the prosperous middle classes are not the only ones with money. We must also consider something that eludes statistical and economic analysis: sheer human resourcefulness, which makes up for gaps and weaknesses in the system.

The contempt for politicians of every hue that is voiced everywhere, from the depths of the countryside to the best districts of Karachi or Islamabad, should not lead us to forget the more wholesome aspects of society: farmers with a few hectares, craftsmen and small industrialists, business leaders who are consolidating their position, eminent intellectuals, the many Muslims who are religious but not bigoted, sickened by the fundamentalists' hypocrisy and intolerance. The new middle classes, both urban and rural, bear witness to profound changes whose political implications are still not clear.

Despite an accelerating brain drain since 1999, there is no shortage of young people with a good education, often obtained abroad; and not all of them are motivated only by the desire to make money. Many multinationals, for instance, employ very few expatriates; they have no difficulty in finding very competent executives in Pakistan. In this respect, Pakistan, like India, has a big advantage over countries like Indonesia or China, where the average cost of an expatriate and his family can be as much as 250,000 dollars a year. In 1997, Nestlé employed 10 expatriates in Pakistan compared to 102 in China, where its turnover was only four times greater than its turnover in Pakistan (the population of China is nearly ten times bigger than the population of Pakistan).

Although some multinationals are now reluctant to go to Pakistan, others are confident of a bright future. Nestlé is counting on increasing its milk collection by 10 or 20 per cent a year, and dominates the growing market for bottled mineral water. Novartis, which is heavily involved in pesticides and pharmeuticals, continues to do business, and sees no reason to leave.

Ordinary people, who had no voice for many years, plumped for democratization between 1988 and 1999. Nongovernmental organizations, brave and honest men and women, roundly condemn abuses of the system, from the exploitation of children to the treatment of women, and speak out against political scandal. These same people constitute a counterweight to the surge of fundamentalism, to which they are totally opposed. Finally, there are politicians and senior civil servants who are known to be honest and experienced. Some of them serve in General Musharraf's Cabinet.

Afterword (July 2000)

Since 1999 there has been some improvement in the economy. Substantial external aid came in following September 11, providing Pakistan with some debt relief. Foreign exchange reserves have reached a fairly comfortable level, partly due to higher remittances. The fight against corruption has made some progress. Yet the fiscal deficit remains serious. Private investments fell in the past few years from 16% to 14% of GDP, partly due to the law and order situation, partly due to political uncertainty. Exports have remained at the same level in 2001/02 as in the previous year, i.e. $9.2 billion. As for public funds available for development, they remain well below the requirement for economic and social tasks. When we add the consequences of a severe drought, there is no wonder why the growth rate in 2001/02 is somewhere between 3% and 3.5% of GDP.

9

BETWEEN CASTE
AND TRIBE

When you take the Khyber Pass out of Afghanistan and discover the 'world of the plains' – the great valleys that open out on to the immense valley of the Indus – you wonder whether the human universe you are about to encounter, which wants to be freed from Hindu influence, is not still, in some way, part of the old hierarchical traditions described by Louis Dumont.[1] In Afghanistan itself – contrary to the custom in Iran and Central Asia – people call one another *sahib*, as if the culture of 'rank', familiar to us through the work of Rudyard Kipling, had permeated the fiercely Muslim, warlike and egalitarian culture codified in the *Pakhtunwali*. Does not this title acquire deeper and deeper undertones as you go east and south?

Were there castes during the Indus civilization? This is a legitimate question inasmuch as we often find a distribution of socioeconomic functions between several groups, all of which claim a common ancestry and practise endogamy, in societies where one privileged group sets up its own relations of interdependence with those it dominates. Archaeological evidence[2] suggests that the founders of the Indus civilization, having acquired more wealth, technical ability and power than those from more ancient cultures, made good use of their skill and their ability to work in order to dominate other groups.

As Sir Denzil Ibbertson has observed,[3] it would be rash to concentrate on the creation of hierarchical and functional relations between the subcontinent's groups according to a Hindu – and, more specifically, Brahman – view of a social order linked to a cosmic order. In fact, a group's identification with its lineage, as well as its recognized or acquired role, is the result of practical necessity: wealth production; the prevention of conflict. This identification – be it secular[4] or, on the contrary, sanctified by religion – is proof against political and religious upheaval.

The Indus basin acquired its population by a process of sedimentation. In other words, it was formed by successive layers of invaders who overcame formerly dominant populations. Throughout the past millennium, Muslim conquerors have imbued present-day Pakistan with their personality, imposing themselves on – or simply juxtaposing themselves to – societies organized along lines sanctioned for many years by Hindu traditions, lines which go back to pre-Aryan times.

At the end of this long maturation process, how is society organized in Pakistan? More speciifically, what are the regional differences which must exist in such a varied and densely populated country?

The Common Feature: The Importance of Blood Ties (*BIRADARI* and QAUM)

The overriding importance of blood ties (real or mythical) seems to be common to all population groups in Pakistan. This primary solidarity and pride in identity which, together, allow an individual to claim his place in the social structure are expressed in the word *biradari* or *biraderi*. This word, which defines a concept similar to phratry, comes from the Persian word *biradar*, meaning 'brother'.[5] In broad terms, the *biradari* is the community of descendants from an ancestor who is still present in the elders' memory; hence it brings together about four generations: grandparents, parents, brothers, uncles, and cousins of both sexes, and female partners. The fact that this concept is expressed in a Persian word leads us to believe that it acquired greater importance at the time when, under Persian conquerors, vast communities were rearranged and scattered, while the simple extended family became the privileged site of human relationships.

The *biradari* unites against adversity and adversaries. However, it is subject to internal rivalry, generally between two of its branches. It is strongly cohesive in an unstable or hostile environment – that is to say, when interethnic, sectarian or tribal quarrels mean that it has to be on a sort of war footing. But while social relations are governed by tradition, and there is relative security and prosperity, rivalries rage at the heart of a single *biradari*. They can be quite extensive, and attempts by certain members to set themselves up as privileged heirs of the family tradition sometimes give rise to implacable jealousy that can degenerate into violence.

The notion of the extended family is at the heart of all the ethnic groups in Pakistan. Naturally, there are different words for it. The Pashtuns, for example, speak of *tarbur*, 'cousins', a word that sometimes has the sense of enemy, as if to show how fatal rivalries that strike at the heart of a group which includes collaterals. In other regions of the Punjab they use *khandan*, 'family', to denote this same social group, while they use *biradari* for a much wider group of blood relatives.[6]

The *qaum* is a group descended from one ancestor – often eponymous, usually distant, and of some status. As with most of the languages spoken in Pakistan, this word is of Arab origin. It is equivalent to the Latin *natio*: people who are linked by birth. In its wider sense, *qaum* encompasses all those who are united by some kind of common destiny – this could be a nation in the modern sense, an ethnic group based on a linguistic community, a network of related tribes, a single tribe or even one part of a tribe. Nevertheless, in many regions such parts are given specific names, such as the Punjabi *zat*, which also means 'caste' (as we have seen, a caste is often simply a tribe or an ethnic group with a certain status or function).

Every Pakistani is proud of his or her *qaum*. They identify with it even if it has suffered reverses of fortune. They marry within it, and always hope that their *qaum* will keep or recover a status that is worthy of its founding fathers, thanks to the diligence,

effort and intelligence of its members. In earlier times it was common practice for
the grandees of the same *qaum* in a given region to meet regularly to discuss questions of common interest. This does not happen so often these days, except in the
case of certain business *qaum* like the Memon.

The Millennial Substratum

Over the course of hundreds of years, blood communities organized themselves in
such a way as to keep the minimal level of peace that was indispensable to their
cooperation and, thereby, to their prosperity. To that end, they formed pacts or
enshrined their mutual relationships in statutes. In general, wherever an authentic
and solid tribal group came across groups that were less close-knit and less committed to defending their characteristics as a group, there was homogenization by
means of progressive assimilation.[7]

So, when these opposing groups were very homogeneous, relations between
groups linked by even nominal kinship, who were incapable of considering each
other as strangers, followed, after their own fashion, the *biradari* logic of social structure. In other words, when members of the same vast community were not fighting
a threat from the outside, they experienced internal conflicts – mainly over land, but
sometimes over influence or prestige. These struggles normally took place between
tribes or parts of tribes. This tribal culture in the midst of a homogeneous ethnic
group was prevalent in the west and north of the country.

Things were very different when heterogeneity prevailed, and was so pronounced
that any unity made up of several groups, even religious ones, seemed impossible.
When the conquering group was so small that their assimilation into one of the erst-
while dominant communities would have deprived them of all their ascendancy, they
formed an aristocratic or tutelary group superimposed on or juxtaposed to the pre-
existing one. This enabled them to bring out the differences and inequalities that
affected the people, and thus to strengthen their dominant role. Heterogeneity
became a stabilizing factor insofar as every clearly identified *qaum* – and even, in the
Punjab, every *zat* – had its function within society. Moreover, social ranks within
communities led to a certain collective social mobility – in a downward or upward
direction (this was usually a slow, surreptitious process).

Among the various conquering peoples, the Rajputs made a big impact on the
social landscape, creating a social order whose remnants are still present today in the
plains, the most densely populated area. The Rajputs – whom some have linked to
the fifth-century Hephtalite conquerors, while others say that they go back much further in time – contributed to the creation of a stable social order which they
controlled with the Brahmans. The Rajput system – with its rules of chivalry and eti-
quette, its hierarchy of groups in strict 'castes' – played a major part in shaping the
social mindset of the Indus civilization. Their name means 'sons of the king', and
they set themselves up as members of the 'old nobility' – *kshatriya* in Sanskrit.
Although their legitimacy was confirmed by the Brahmans, it owed more to arms
than to religion. They had no hesitation in treating the Muslim conquerors as equals
as soon as they had to deal with them; when they were islamized, they kept their

status and most of their ancestral customs. In short, for the most part they took on the role of nobles and made it a dominant one, leaving the Brahmans to carry out priestly duties.

Under Rajput suzerainty, other communities – albeit almost their social equals – had a domainal function. The Jats were landowner-farmers with estates of various sizes. On occasion the Jats and the Rajputs fought for preeminence; the Jats secured and maintained it at the time when, and in regions where, Sikhism was triumphant (the late eighteenth and early nineteenth centuries, from Amritsar to Peshawar and Bannu). Together with other, smaller, wealthy and warlike communities who also spoke Indian languages – like the Gakkhar in the western Punjab – the Jats and Rajputs vied with aristocratic groups from the west, who spoke Iranian languages: the Baluchis and the Pashtuns (or Pashtuns).

Although there was some initial resistance, they brought their hierarchical social vision to areas where heterogeneity was the rule. Thus there are still communities who are allotted specific activities and, no doubt, the further back in time they were subjugated, the lower their social rank. Even today, they are divided into categories which correspond to a greater or lesser extent to the great stratification system of the Hindu social vision: landless peasants, market gardeners, craftsmen, dustmen and gravediggers – each of these categories including multiple subdivisions (especially where craftsmen are concerned).

Can we call such an organization a caste system? Partly, inasmuch as these communities are to some extent prisoners of their place in society, even if a modicum of limited mobility is possible. Nevertheless, the endogamy they practise does seem to be linked to origin, not rank. Thus communities from different stock do not marry, even if they are on the same hierarchical level. These differences, however, are not ritual differences; they are not concerned with categories like 'pure' and 'impure', as in Hinduism – only with social hierarchy. Moreover, modern perceptions, influenced by Western cultures, tend to merge the notion of caste to that of tribe, as the use of the word *qaum* shows.

In general, everyone takes a pride in his ancestors and has reason to believe that some of them, at a given moment, were eminent – even extremely important. Even today there are communities which consider themselves Rajput, even though they are confined to fairly menial jobs in their villages.[8] No one is surprised by this, because in such a compartmentalized, hierarchical world, any group can, in one way or another, believe that it is descended from fallen princes. If we simply observe the hieratic pose of roadsweepers, for example, we can easily imagine that they are descended from the people who brought the Indus civilization to its peak. This was how the society in which the Rajput princes were able to follow their vocation as leaders for many years was organized. Today, this social space corresponds to the densely populated regions of the Punjab and Sind.

Nonetheless, this is not the major part of Pakistan. Vast stretches in the west and northwest are part of a tribal (or other) regime where social functions are carried out not by rigid groups but indiscriminately by any member of the clan, following a random logic (in former times there was a system of taking turns, organized by councils of elders). So one's rank is fortuitous, and its fluidity is not hindered by tradition –

quite the opposite. This tribal world played an important part in building the dominant edifice of the Indus valley throughout the last millennium as it became islamized. At the same time, Islam introduced its own hereditary elites: the descendants of the Prophet, or Sayyid; those of his family, the Qureshi; those of the first Arab conquerors of Sind and the Punjab in the eighth century, the Abbasi, and other 'Arabs'; finally, descendants of saints and holy hermits, the *pirzada*. There are also some remainders from epics of Iranian and Turkish conquests. All in all, Pakistani society is characterized by structures which owe a great deal to the tribe but also to the caste, and to the religious influence of Islam.

These structures, however, have changed over the last two centuries – first as a result of an ancient evolutionary process which gradually speeded up in the days of the British Empire; later as a consequence of the brutal shock of Partition. In order to respond to the demands of royal or imperial power, the function of the nobleman or leader gradually merged with the exploitation of land, because it was natural to consolidate the military aristocracy by directing it towards agriculture. The British, for their part, favoured the emergence of big latifundia, because this meant that they could exercise a form of indirect administration through the medium of rich noblemen – notably for taxation purposes. From that time on, the *jagirdar* and the *lambardar*, general farmers, and – in a tribal context – the *khan* and the *sardar* could overtake the *zamindar* (landowner-farmers) in terms of income generated by their purely agricultural activities. Simultaneously, a kind of hierarchy of autonomous principalities emerged, vassals of the British Empire. Shortly before Partition, the British entrusted a few big landowners with the cultivation of cash crops (cotton, rice, sugarcane).

Later, there was a rigorous religious – but not social – process of standardization. All in all, landholdings and other means of production remained in the hands of people of the same social rank. The trend towards developing vast, modern, competitive agricultural holdings, already present in colonial times, became stronger. So, during the 1960s, Pakistan became one of the world's major cotton producers without experiencing major social change; this did not exactly promote social mobility. If there were 'nouveaux riches' in the rural world, there were very few 'parvenus'. For the most part, the status quo prevailed.

Nonetheless, Partition brought into the country Muslim elites from the east, who would take over responsible jobs and be leaders of the commercial, industrial and banking worlds. They were mainly city people who sometimes acquired some landholdings in order to take their place in society, and put down roots.

This picture of social relations includes complex networks of solidarity between genuine tribes, between semi-castes and between city-dwellers brought to the country by Partition. It does not take account of religious solidarities, which were mainly characteristic of minority groups – Shi'a, Zhikri, Ahmadi, Christians, Parsees, Hindus and Sikhs – nor the links between members of the same Sufi brotherhoods. Finally, there were very strong ethnic and linguistic solidarities. Apart from the major languages (Punjabi, Sindi, Urdu, Pashto, Baluchi), there were some ancient and venerable ones like those spoken in the upper valleys, and some highly respected ones like Saraiki, which is close to Punjabi and has a poetic literary tradition.

The social fabric, however, is the most obvious – and maybe the most determining – factor. The best way of looking at it is to take it from west to east, following the trajectory of invasions and conquering elites over the centuries. In this way we can situate the origins of large and important communities as they journeyed eastwards, joining elites like the Rajput–Jat as they went.

The World of the Tribes

The genuine tribes have various origins, but are mainly Baluchis or Pashtuns. Most often they are the result of the fragmentation of older tribes whose name lives on in their memory.

In general, these tribes identify with an eponymous ancestor, who has bequeathed his name to his direct descendants through the line of the eldest son. Some – but very few – tribes are named after the ancient tribe from which all their kin are descended. This 'witness' tribe does not necessarily have a leading role. Tribes and their subgroups often bear the name of the eponymous ancestor, followed by an ending – a simple *i*, or *ani*, *zai* or *khel* (the last two are more specifically Pashtun). The extended family is the tribes' basic social unit. It is not always called a *biradari*, and seems to be less plagued by internal conflict than more heterogeneous circles.

In the Indus basin – and sometimes even in the Ganges basin and in the Deccan – the tribes have provided dynasties which had power over lands of very different dimensions, from a small principality to an empire. Most of these dynasties no longer speak their ancestral languages, and have even lost all ties with their original ethnic group.

The Baluchis

The Baluchis, who came from Iran – more precisely, from the region of Kerman – at the beginning of the fifteenth century, after a journey about which there are many legends, spread pastoral and agricultural communities from the oases, who had been under Persian influence for years, through all the coastal and mountain regions from the Makran to the Sulaiman Mountains, by way of Afghanistan. They have imposed a linguistic – even an ethnic – unity throughout the territory where they have settled, including the previous occupants within their own tribal system. Only one community who speak a Dravidian language but are Muslims, the Brahuis, have preserved their own character. They were probably brought into the Baluchi system in about 1490, to stop them in their conquering tracks and respect their pact with Delhi, but they are integrated in real terms, since they have produced a dynasty, the *khans* of Kalat, who arbitrate in tribal disputes, ensure the Baluchis' cohesion, and act as their representatives in neighbouring communities or states.

The Baluchi tribes made many incursions into Sind and the Punjab, where they formed dominant communities, even princely dynasties. They were subdivided into big groups, each group named after one of the four great ancestors – Rind, Hot, Lashar or Jato (the last name is a woman's name). This form of membership is useful mainly as a reference point in the study of tribal history; it was of little consequence in the life of the tribes, whose affinities were dictated purely by self-interest. According to the principle that the eponymous ancestor's name was passed down through a single male line, smaller tribes have the name Rind or Jatoi; this is considered completely normal.

The tribe – *tuman*[9] in Baluchi – is led by a chief, the *tumandar* – the suffix *dar* implies both responsibility and ownership. So the world of the Baluchis is a world of chiefs, with all the rivalries, disputes over succession and forms of power that this implies.

The *tuman* are subdivided into *para*, and these in turn form *phalli*, or clans. Tribal political problems often arise at the level of the *para*, for the simple reason that the *tumandar* tends to favour his own *para*, while the others are inclined to disagree. This emphasizes the important role that an outsider like the Brahui *khan* of Kalat can play in settling conflicts. The name of the tribes – and especially of the *para* – is none other than that of an ancestor, followed by *ani*.

The westernmost part of Baluchi country, the Makran, is a mosaic of different clans: some have broken away from tribes which remained on the Iranian side; others, who came from the east, were attracted by the transit possibilities afforded by the double border (Iran and Afghanistan) and the ports of Gwadar and Pasni. Of this group on the road to integration, the Rind and Bil near the border, and the Ghishki around Turbat, seem to enjoy a kind of good-natured supremacy.

Further east, we come to the world of the Brahui, where the family of the *khan* of Kalat are traditionally dominant. This family had its hour of glory in the eighteenth century when its head, Nassir Khan, managed to raise an army, representing all the Baluchi tribes, which contributed to the conquering march of Ahmad Shah Abdali (later Durrani), the last emperor, who came down from the mountains of present-day Afghanistan (after several others, including Alexander the Great). The authority exercised over the tribes by the *khan* of Kalat has been through periods of eclipse and renaissance. It is now simply a kind of moral leadership and a capacity for benevolence which are no equal for the importance that has gradually been acquired by Pakistan's central and provincial government. In order to strengthen their power, the *khan* of Kalat welcomed into their ranks several Hazaras from central Afghanistan, who are now well settled in urban areas, notably in Quetta.

In the eastern mountains, the social landscape is full of contrasts. This is an area where rival tribes which have made their mark on Pakistan's history and society occupy adjoining territories. Going from north to south – that is, from the Pashtun territory around Quetta to the Arabian Sea – the *tuman* concerned are: the Qasrani, Bozdar, Sori, Lund, Khosa, Khetran, Leghari, Tibbi Lund, Gurshani, Drishak, Marri, Raissani, Bugti, Mazari and Bizenjo.[10] Their chiefs have the non-Baluchi title *sardar* or *nawab*, and exercise real political authority. Power stakes – or mere prestige – can lead to endless conflict.

Rivalries between these tribes sometimes take the form of successive armed retaliations and vendettas. But at the heart of each tribe, quarrels between *para* are even more compelling, and unite families which support the various factions. Thus, for the Marri, *sardar* Kheirbakhsh belongs to the Ghazani clan; he must oppose the hostility of the Bijarani, who question both his authority and his policies and, it is said, have government support. For each faction, the idea is to gain the support of the two other clans, the Loharani and the Mazarani. For the Bugti – according to the same logic – *nawab* Akbar must grapple with periodic revolts by the Kalpar clan.

It is beyond the Derajat, a piedmont region that stretches along the right bank of the Indus and includes Dera Ghazi Khan and Dera Ismail Khan, that we begin to come across minority but dominant Baluchi tribes, which have been both superimposed on the oldest inhabitants and set alongside Pashtun groups. These tribes were established at the end of their migration around the areas [*derra*] founded in about 1480 by Baluchi warlords, whose names they took. Some went as far as the Salt Range in the north, to Muzaffargarh and Multan in the west (with some Rind travelling to Lahore); others settled in the south, going as far as Shikarpur (with some Leghari travelling to Hyderabad, and some Khosa reaching Bahawalpur). This migration was facilitated by an alliance between the great Baluchi military leader Mir Chakar and Emperor Houmayoun in 1555.

Nevertheless, these are still minority tribes. According to an Indian Empire census at the end of the nineteenth century, they account for only 13 per cent of the population of Dera Ismail Khan, 9 per cent at Dera Ghazi Khan, 15 per cent at Muzaffargarh and 19 per cent at Multan. Numerous Baluchi communities no longer speak their native language; they speak Punjabi or Sindi dialect. They were superimposed on the Jat community, and seem to have absorbed some elements of their culture. For the most part they are farmers, but in the semi-desert regions they are still camel-drivers and caravaneers.

Among these tribes are several which also live in and around the Sulaiman Mountains, notably the Leghari. We also find – going from north to south – the Mihrani, Djiskani, Korai, Gopang and Sanghia, and tribes which have kept the names of their great 'founding fathers': Hot, Jatoi, Rind, Lachari. Finally – but in smaller numbers – the Chandia, Nutkani, Goshra and Mirani, to name but a few.

The importance of the Baluchi tribes is obvious when we look at the family names of Pakistani politicians from almost every province – names are often the names of tribes: Jatoi, Khosa, Leghari, Mazari, Mirani. Certain princely families also originate from these tribes – for example, the rajahs of Dera Ghazi Khan, who were Leghari.

This situation tends to temper the grievances of Baluchi leaders who claim that their community has been subjected to 'Punjabi colonialism'. In effect, several of these so-called 'colonizers' are none other than Baluchis who, having carved out fiefdoms in the neighbouring province, have to a greater or lesser extent 'gone native', and have finally 'come home'.

In any case, the solution of continuity between the Baluchi world and the Rajput–Jat world is by no means a violent one.

The Pashtuns

The advent of the Pashtuns is shrouded in legend, and provides much food for thought. Given that Herodotus mentions names of ethnic groups or tribes that are very close to those used in the same places today, it is tempting to conclude that they have been in the region for a very long time. Their settlement process, however, was patchy: some of their communities, called Kutchi or Powinda, are nomadic societies which still practise a widespread transhumance – between the Central Asian plains and the Indus basin, across the Hindu Kush.[11]

The Pashtuns (the word probably comes from the adjective *pakhtana*) are also called Afghans – some of them consider that this is the only way they should be referred to. This is an ambivalent concept, because 'Afghan' refers both to members of an ethnic group and to members of a multiethnic nation, Afghanistan. More than one inhabitant of Pakistan's North-West Frontier Province has no hesitation in calling himself 'Afghan', to the amazement of his foreign questioner, who wonders – sometimes with some justification – if this is some kind of pun which emphasizes the 'artificiality' of the Durand Line (which is, nevertheless, a hundred and ten years old).

In fact, Pashtuns and Pashtuns along various parts of this border have similar social characteristics, and speak the same language, Pashto,[12] which, however, does vary, because it has been influenced by Persian on the one side and Urdu on the other.

The Pashtun tribe, or *qaum*, is a less homogeneous social unit than its Baluchi counterpart. The closer you get to the Indus, the more the Pashtuns accept members of the artisanal community as *hamsaya* (see Note 8). This useful labour force forms an integral part of the tribe, but for several generations its members have been kept in a dependent position which means they cannot own land or marry out of their own community.

Even further east, the Pashtuns are segregated from other, larger groups who have the generic – vaguely pejorative – title of Hindkis or Jats. In fact, although the Pashtuns do not follow the caste system, they, like the Baluchis, cannot bring themselves to assimilate too many foreign elements. In places where they form only a dominant and leading minority, they try to occupy a rank equivalent to that of the Rajputs, and to make the Jats work for them.

Tribal life is governed by a complex power mechanism and by a way life that is set down in a precise tradition, the *Pakhhtunwali*. The body at the heart of the tribe, with supreme authority over communal life and the settling of disputes, is the deliberative council, or *jirgah*. Management and external relations are entrusted to a chief, the *khan*, who often comes from a group whose special function is to lead; this, in principle, guarantees his legitimacy and impartiality. Collective life is mainly organized at the level of the tribal fraction, who live in the same valley or, at the very least, in a homogeneous demarcated territory. There, the representative of the community is the *malik*, assisted and vouched for by a local *jirgah*.[13]

The tribes and tribal fractions take the names of their eponymous ancestors, followed by endings: *i, zai, khel* or – rarely – *ani* (as in Baluchi) or *tchi* (as in Turkish). The leading tribes or fractions are called *khankhel*, and their members are traditionally respected.

The *khan*'s functions seem to have developed in colonial times, as principalities were established or great estates grew up in a wave of land privatization. So the title *khan* was assumed by sovereigns, autonomous nobles, feudal lords and important landowners, and became hereditary. The Mongol and British empires largely relied on *khan* of Pashtun stock to administer their territories. In the Pashtun context there seems to be some kind of power game between *khan* and *malik*, settled with varying degrees of skill by the *jirgah* and government authorities.

In Afghanistan, as in Pakistan, the Pashtun world split – especially after the eighteenth century – into two big groups, each formed of related or simply allied tribes: the Ghilzai and the Durrani. The Ghilzai were famous for the short-lived dynasty founded by Mir Wais in Kandahar in the early eighteenth century; the Durrani for the dynasty founded fifty years later in the same town (after the Afshar years) by Ahmad Shah Abdali, later called Durrani – a dynasty which, after many vicissitudes, consolidated the present-day Afghan border.

Although this relatively recent split was only one among many others, its implications for the Pashtun mindset over the years are undeniable. Thus, according to some traditions, the Ghilzai were Mahmud of Ghazni's chief supporters in his conquests, which took him as far as Delhi and beyond – they took their name from a Turkish word which the sultan applied to them. Related groups are the Sarwani (or Sarbani), and the Lodi, who founded two dynasties which occupied the throne at Delhi between 1450 and 1555: one which bears their name, and the Suri. Moreover, most of the Kutchi (or Powinda) tribes have connections with the Ghilzai.

As for the Durrani (formerly Abdali), their legends say that they are descended both from a tribe of Israel and from the Companions of the Prophet. They consider that they are the only people who are worthy of the name Afghans, and they are related to Shahab ud-Din of Ghor, who established the first sultanate in Delhi at the dawn of the thirteenth century.

The Durrani are not the only ones who have ancestors from outside the Pashto-speaking world. Indeed, there are several tribes in this position, and they all consider themselves to be part of one or other of the two great groups. There are the Kakar, who are said to have Kuchan ancestry; and the Waziri, who are reputedly Rajputs. The Karlanri – who, with their numerous ramifications, could almost be considered a tribal group in their own right – are of Turkish origin, and their ancestors were brought to the region by Tamburlaine.

These historical backgrounds – some recent and authenticated, others the stuff of hypothesis or legend – show how constant the west–east migration was in the middle Indus valley. Most of these population movements began in the tenth century, with the Ghaznevids. They gathered momentum from the end of the twelfth century with the arrival of Shahab ud-Din of Ghor; then – after the Mongol and Timorid agonies of the thirteenth and fourteenth centuries – the Lodi and Sur dynasties, in their turn, encouraged Pashtun expansion. The Great Mughals who came after them had no intention of losing the advantages thus afforded to the consolidation of their empire. It was the same – even more so – under Ahmad Shah Durrani in about 1750. From then on, throughout Pakistan's territory – especially in the big Punjabi towns – we find representatives of an oligarchy of Pashtun origin, who no longer speak Pashto but cherish – in a world passionately interested in genealogy – the memory of their ancestors.

These movements played a decisive role in the distribution of Pashtun communities. Around Quetta, the migratory waves of Pashtuns and Baluchis became settled – all the more so in view of the fact that both reached their highest point at the same time: in the fifteenth and sixteenth centuries. There is also a process of osmosis in this region: a given tribe can gradually come closer to its neighbouring ethnic group, and eventually become a permanent part of it. So the Khetran, who are generally recognized to be Baluchis, may be of Pashtun origin; and among the Pashtuns there are completely integrated tribes who are nevertheless called 'Baluchis'. Opposite the Khetran, the Qasrani, and other Baluchi tribes from the northeast of their ethnic territory are Pashtun tribes from the southwest of theirs: the Tarine, close cousins of the Durrani; the Atchekzai from the same group, and – more important in numerical terms – the Kakar. There do not seem to have been big population displacements in this region, but only about a hundred kilometres to the northeast you find yourself in the tracks of the great invasions.

If we look at Pashtun settlement from south to north, we see that the major routes which enabled them to spread to the Indus basin were not uniformly open to them, and that the Khyber Pass was not the most important path.

The Gomal Valley and the Zhob Pass, which both come out at Dera Ismail Khan, seem to have been the preferred routes for numerous tribes – especially the Ghilzai, many of whom subsequently formed part of ruling elites throughout the subcontinent. So did the Lodi (subdivided into the Prangi and the Suri), who, as we have seen, put two dynasties on the throne in Delhi. The Sarwani and the Niazi, who settled in neighbouring regions, became important feudal lords in Muslim kingdoms and empires. The Niazi became governors of Lahore, and – in alliance with the Ghakkar – challenged the authority of the Suri sultans.

To this prestigious number we can add the Sulaimankheil, Lohani, Marwat and Tator – important in numerical terms. Less prevalent in Pakistan, but famous for their members' deeds, especially in Afghanistan, are the Hotaki, Kharroti, Kosar, Nurkhel and Malekhel. Apart from these twelve or so tribes from the Ghilzai group, there are two from the opposing group: the Shirani and the Ushtarani. The first group were made famous by one of their outstandingly active and ambitious groups, the Babar. The second are said to be descended from the Prophet and were instrumental in promoting the Babar, their longstanding allies.

Further north, in the regions of Kohat and Bannu – at the opening of the Kurram, another important migration route – are Pashtuns who belong to the Karlanri group. They may be less tribally diverse, but their historical role – and hence their rise at the very heart of Pakistani society – are noteworthy. They are the Mangal, the Bannutchi, the Daur, the Orakzai, the Turi, the Jaji and, above all, the Khattak.

The Khattak, urged on by the waves of successive migratory movements typical of the Pashtuns, went north and came to the right bank of the Kabul, where the Emperor Akbar entrusted their chief, Akor, with the task of guarding the route between Attock and Peshawar. From their capital, Akora, they dominated – and still dominate – a goodly portion of the Kabul basin, in Pakistani territory. One branch, the Bangikhel, seceded and withdrew to Bannu, showing how fatal internal dissension can be for any victorious tribe.

Finally, and even further north – around the Khyber Pass, and therefore in the vast region that surrounds Peshawar – are well-entrenched mountain tribes which settled many years ago, like the Afridi and the Shinwari.

As for the neighbouring plains, they are inhabited by Pashtuns from the Durrani group, chiefly the Yussufzai, old adversaries of the Khattak for dominion over the hills, plateaus and valleys around Peshawar, and, still further north, the Ghoriakhel, origin of the famous Mohmand, a tribe which lives in territory through which runs the border between Pakistan and Afghanistan. From all these tribes come great families like the Durrani, the Khattak, the Babar, the Niazi and other *khan*.

In the High Northern Mountains

The influence on Pakistani society of the many and varied ethnic groups in the mountains has not been particularly significant, but it cannot be ignored, since these groups live close to the lines of communication which connect Pakistan with Afghanistan, Tajikistan, China and India. These people have always been fascinating to researchers and tourists because of their unusual and ancient culture, and the beauty and grandeur of their surroundings.

On the whole, their social structures emphasize the strength of blood ties, which more or less correspond to kinship within the village. Their communal life is ruled by fairly strict rules of honour and arbitration by authorities – either religious bodies or deliberative councils.

If we look west, we find the Kalash, who have preserved their ancient polytheistic religion, and their neighbours, the Koh. Then there are the Kohistani, whose reputation as rough – even savage – people seems to be exaggerated; the Hunza, Shi'a of both persuasions, who receive aid from their coreligionists (notably the Aga Khan Foundation);and the Balti, also Shi'a, who live at the foot of the Karakorum. Further south, the Kashmiris and Tanaoli live in the central pre-Himalayan mountains to the north of the Punjab. We are all aware of the Kashmiris' political importance. The integrity and diversity of this archipelago of cultural and linguistic social entities, all of which want to be independent and free of destabilizing influences, are nevertheless under threat as a result of the economic and political importance of Pashtun and Jat–Rajput communities.

The Punjab and Sind: Predominantly Rajput and Jat

The Punjab and Sind still bear the hallmarks of the former Rajput–Jat supremacy. Over the course of history relations between them were hierarchical, but today they share supremacy.

After decolonization, Partition and the establishment of an Islamic republic, the nobleman was out of a job. Henceforth, the *qaum* whose members had the best chance of achieving respect and wealth would be that of the landlords, the *zamindar*. The Mongol and British empires encouraged a limited number of latifundia, but there are many people with smaller landholdings who could be called farmers. They may be landowners, 'mixed' farmers (those who work on other people's land as well as their own), or just ordinary farmers. All these people – who enjoy high status but are not necessarily rich – think that cereal production is their best bet; market gardening is considered less prestigious. On the other hand, raising animals, especially cattle, is regarded with favour.

Relations between members of the same *qaum* or *zat* in the villages were traditionally based on a system of solidarities – if not sanctified, then at least established by dint of long usage.[14]

Here, the *biradari* play a major role; members mark their unity in the face of other extended families in various ways. The most spectacular is the Vartan Bhanji, which bears some similarity to the Amerindian potlatch described by Marcel Mauss. Whenever there is a major family event (a birth, a circumcision, a wedding, a funeral), members of the *biradari* give presents – in principle, more valuable than those given by the recipients on similar occasions. This establishes relations of indebtedness which the *biradari* is supposed to cement. Someone who wants to break the ties of family solidarity gives a present of exactly the same value as the one he received last time; this immediately causes trouble. Nevertheless, since everyone is not equally wealthy, richer people give poorer people generous presents, but do not expect equally valuable ones in return; in this case the debt is one of gratitude – thus one can appear to be a 'benefactor member' of the *biradari*. This principle of indebtedness between equals, but also between strong and weak, is – in economic terms – a driving force of social life in the Punjab and Sind. Once a *biradari* is not threatened by challenges from another *biradari* in the race for supremacy in the village or the district, internal disagreements and rivalry can have free rein. These are usually between *patti*, or branches of the same *biradari* (the role of the *patti* was strengthened under the British, who used them as a kind of taxation base). In some urban areas the word is used to describe a district.

Relations between landowners and farmers are governed by two systems of sharing out the harvest, called *thakka* and *hissa*. The first is a kind of contract which allows the farmer to choose what to plant, but he has to pay for the materials. The second divides costs and profits equally between landowner and farmer, but there are variations linked to the provision of water for irrigation (according to which this is provided by the landowner, the farmer, or a third party).

Other economic actors in the village are the agricultural workers or craftsmen who are paid in kind, according to a system of functional interdependence, called *seypi*, which lays down reciprocal obligations. These people come from different communities (*qaum* or *zat*) to the farmers, known by the generic name *kammi*. In the *seypi* system, the *kammi* is dependent on the *zamindar*'s *biradari*, which provides him with the necessities of life in return for his work. He works on its behalf – if necessary, against the interests of his own *biradari*. At elections, for example, he votes as 'his' *zamindar* tells him to. In other words, this system maintains the subordination to the landowner of people from many artisan *qaum* or *zat*.

There are many of these *qaum* or *zat*, and they correspond to very precise fields of activity which, in turn, are classified according to a certain scale of worthiness. Modern economic conditions have brought changes which have sometimes put these classifications to the test, but for the most part they are still intact. Craftsmen, for example, have moved to the villages with considerable savings behind them; there they manage to get hold of and cultivate some irrigated land, but their change in fortunes does not mean that they immediately acquire a higher status. They remain as they were, and although they own land, they are not recognized as *zamindar* – they are still compelled to fulfil their obligations under *seypi*.[15] They therefore have a tendency to behave as much like rich *zamindar* as possible – that is to say, they live like Rajputs so that their children and grandchildren – and, if possible, their own *patti* or *biradari* – will, in the long run, attain a higher status. This means that their wives must observe purdah, and that they have to give generously at a Vartan Bhanji. In fact, this social mobility strategy means that a considerable portion of their assets goes on prestige spending rather than on productive investment that would benefit the village. Despite all this, they would not think of disowning their *qaum*; they would merely like it to have a better public image.[16] This process is reminiscent of the Sanskritization of the Hindu world, and proves that there are many similarities between the Rajput–Jat model and the caste system.

Another classic case is that of Christians, many of whom are from *zat* with a particularly menial image. In the villages they have managed to reach the rank of *kammi* – a lowly rank, but one which is part of the *seypi* system. Some, through education and professional training organized by their diocese, make a career in town, then manage to buy some land. In countless villages, social climbing like this is considered too outrageous to be allowed. People say that repeated abuses of the 'law of blasphemy' are committed for the specific purpose of punishing them. If this is really so, true 'blasphemy' would affect not Islam but, rather, an old Hindu residue which no one dares acknowledge.

The Rajputs

At one time the Rajput community was concentrated in present-day Indian Rajasthan; from there it spread – mainly north and northwest, hence following the course of the Indus and its tributaries.

The Rajputs are divided into two big groups: one is said to be 'solar'; the other 'lunar'. These distinctions are connected to the founding myths of their emergence as an ethnic group: one group descended from Ram, the other from Krishna.

Some great Sindi families, like the Bhuttos and those with the title 'Jam', share these origins, as do those descended from the Kalhora dynasty, which ruled over this region. In this province, as in the Punjab, there are also islamized descendants of the great Chauhan and Tunwar groups which founded dynasties in Delhi at the end of the first millennium.

Much more numerous, but highly localized in the Punjab, are the Bhatti and the Punwar, who for many years dominated the inner valley of the Sutlej up to the Rajasthan desert – like the Noon, the famous Bhatti clan of Multan. Further north, all along the Sutlej, we find the Wattoo, Jaja, Khishi and Dhidi. In the Chenab area are the Hiraj and the Sial. Some of these ancient tribes are (like the Pashtuns) simply individual clans from older communities. The Wattoo, for example, probably originated from a Bhatti clan.

In the Jhelum region we find the Rajha, Gondal, Mekan and Tiwana. In the mountain regions, starting with the Salt Range, we begin with the illustrious name of Janjua; then there are the Dhund, Kahut and Mair. Near the Jammu border are the Manhas, Chibh, Jhakar, Salahria and, further west, the Rajbhansi.

Towards the west, to the north of the Salt Range and further north still, despite a Bhatti hegemony which at one time made itself felt as far as Kashmir, come clans which belong to the big Rathore community, of which – in some opinions – the Janjua are merely a branch. We also find the Dhund, Kahut, Jodra and Gheba.

Other warriors

Although they have not merged with them, several communities are traditionally allied with the Rajputs and occupy the same rank. In the high northern hills and the Hazara, there are the Thaka. Finally, and above all, in the Potohar are the Ghakkar, who founded an independent – even conquering – principality between Rawalpindi and Wah. Despite their alliance with the Niazi, they eventually had to submit to the royal power of the Suri in 1470. You can still see their fortified castles and palaces not far from Islamabad. They had close links with the Karral of Hazara.

The Awan deserve close attention, because of their historical importance and, above all, because they settled in the west, right up to the edge of Baluchi and Pashtun territory. Legend has it that their origins go back to Imam Ali and his second wife, Hanafiya. Historians describe them as valiant warriors and farmers who imposed their supremacy on the Janjua in part of the Salt Range, and established large colonies all along the Indus to Sind, and a densely populated centre not far from Lahore. They are related to the Khattar, who are to be found mainly in the plains between Attock and Rawalpindi; the British described them as fierce and unscrupulous. Historians believe that they have links with the peoples who arrived at the time of the Kuchan conquest in the early centuries AD.

Another important community is that of the Meo, who gave their name to Mewat. These quasi-Rajputs, who made their home near Delhi, converted to Islam; after Partition, large numbers of them took refuge in the Pakistani Punjab.

As for the Dogar, or Dogra, they settled north of Lahore right up to Sialkot, and claim to be of Rajput origin.

In the southern Punjab and northeastern Sind, a princely community with mysterious origins played an important role: the Daudpotra, the founding family of the reigning dynasty in Bahawalpur. They came from the Sindi Kalhora dynasty, but also acknowledge an Arab ancestor, Abbas, who was supposedly the Prophet's uncle.

In terms of numbers, apart from the Rajput community, the largest pastoral and agricultural community are the Gujjar. A longstanding legend links them with the Kuchan invaders. Most of them seem to live in Gujarat, around Bombay. They also live in other places with their name: Gujranwala in the central Punjab, and Gujarat further north. The distance that separates these population enclaves gives an idea of the sheer extent of their migrations. We find them from India to Afghanistan, by way of Sind and the Punjab. They consider themselves people of high status, but their station in life varies from one place to another. In Afghan Nuristan, for example, they work as shepherds on the mountain pastures. Their community is divided into several subgroups.

Communities of Arab origin

There are communities which have no connection with those which established local domains and became major landowners before the arrival of Islam, but consider that they are at least of equal social rank because their origins have an undeniable prestige conferred by this religion. This is true of the Sayyid, Qureshi, Ansari, Muhajir, Sheikhs and Arabs. These communities do not practise endogamy; they marry into communities of 'honourable' rank.

The Sayyid are supposedly descended from the children of Ali and Fatima – hence from the Prophet himself. They form oligarchies, which in general received considerable wealth from the successive Muslim dynasties in the region. They have a particular kind of influence inasmuch as their forebears include holy men who brought peace and moral authority to whole swathes of territory such as the Kagan Valley to the north of Hazara. The Guilani or Jilani (the different spellings correspond to different regional pronunciations) are descended from the founder of the Qadiriyya, and are Sayyid on two counts: among their ancestors are the children of Hassan as well as those of Hussain. We find them among the Pashtuns, the Punjabis and the Sindis.

Two other large Sayyid groups are the Zaidi, who are descended from Hussain's grandson (the last imam, in the opinion of a few Shi'a minority groups), and the Bukhari, who identify with a family descended from Hussain which formerly lived in Bukhara. Some of the Sayyid are Shi'a – notably those around Jhang and Sargodha, where they have extensive landholdings. All in all, the Pashtun Sayyid, not subjected to any spiritual dogma, are more inclined to work in the tertiary sector, while the others are more inclined to work the land.

The Qureshi are thought to be from the Prophet's tribe. In Multan they are sometimes called Sheikh Qureshi. Some of them are particularly well respected because they are descended from Baha ul-Haqq, a holy man whose mausoleum is in the town. Among the other Qureshii, the Siddiqi are descended from Caliph Abu Bakr and the Farooqi from Caliph Omar.

As in nearly all other Muslim countries, in Pakistan we find the Ansari, descendants from the Prophet's companions in Medina. There are also a number of Muhajir,[17] whose ancestors were men from Mecca who followed the Prophet to Medina.

The Sheikhs are, in principle, descended from Arab tribal chiefs. In reality, it seems that this title of respect was assumed by converts who wanted to conceal their local origins.

Finally, the Arabs say that they are from the tribes which, after 711, helped to found Muslim emirates in Sind and at Multan. In fact, it is probable that many families who identify with this community are actually descended from Arab merchants who came later and settled in the important trading centres of Bombay and Peshawar.

Groups of Turkish and military origin

As well as Pashtun tribes, warlords from the west came with members of their own ethnic groups, who put down roots in their empire, especially in the Indus valley.

Thus in various parts of the region there were communities which should by rights have played a leading role, but were in fact relatively ineffectual. They are all of Turkish origin. Some bear the name Mughal, because they came with Babur. They tend to become part of Rajput or Jat *zat*. Others have the name Turk, and are descended from senior imperial functionaries who came from Central Asia in the seventeenth century. Yet others, the Qizibach and the Afshar, came with Nadir Shah in the eighteenth century. This last community of Iranized Turks still speak Persian.

The Jats: landowning farmers

There are more Jats than Rajputs, and they are spread out over virtually the whole of Sind and the Punjab; they are a fundamental feature of Pakistan's social landscape, because these great experts in arable farming have been able to keep their land over time, through all the waves of migration and political vicissitudes. For centuries they have been owner-farmers, raising a few animals as a sideline.

By clinging tenaciously to their social rank, in some places they have eclipsed the Rajputs, who have 'been brought down a peg or two' by economic problems or political reversals. As a result, there is a lot of assimilation between Rajputs and Jats, and several communities could be put into either category. What with landlords becoming farmers, and farmers aspiring to be or succeeding in becoming landlords, the threads are not easy to disentangle.

The Jats are particularly in evidence in Sind, where they form the majority of the population. Further north, along the right bank of the Indus, they have relied on the Awan to keep going and maintain their landowner status in the face of Baluchi and Pashtun invaders. Their status in the Derajat, however, has been reduced by warriors from the west. Their related communities, which are like tribes, naturally claim an illustrious ancestry. I cannot name them all, nor provide an exact list of their territories, because they have moved constantly as a result of a century of economic change in the region.

The Tahim live in the western Punjab and the north of Sind. They claim descent from one of the Prophet's companions in Medina, and also seem to be related to the Bhuttos.

The Langah, who dominated Multan shortly after the Timurid invasion and fulfilled a princely function, have settled along the lower reaches of the Chenab and the Indus, and are concentrated around Multan and Muzaffargarh. The Tchhina are further north, along the Chenab; we do not know if they are the same people as the Tchima of Sialkot and Gujranwala, a very large community.

The Sumro can also call themselves Rajputs; they founded a reigning dynasty in Multan. For many years, however, they have predominantly been farmers. They live mainly between Leiah and Dera Ismail Khan, along the Indus to the west of Jhang.

The Nol, Bhanga, Harral and Marral live between Jhang and Sialkot. They seem to have lived there for a very long time – as have the Langrial, who for many years have worked as nomadic shepherds in the steppes to the east of Multan.

In the plains, and on the high plateaus governed by the Sikhs in the early nineteenth century, there are many Jat communities. Their members are divided in varying proportions between Sikhism and Islam. As a result, some (the Virck, between Lahore and Gujranwala) are present in large numbers in Pakistan; others (the Bal and Pannun) less so.

In the Himalayan piedmont, the Jats have resisted Sikh proselytism. They are Hindus (who left in 1947) and Muslims. From east to west, we find the Tarar, who claim to be of Rajput origin; the Varaich, the Chatta, the Sarai, who are related to a Sindi princely dynasty, and the Hinjra.

This picture of the world of the Jats emphasizes – should such emphasis be needed – how far they have spread, and how closely they are linked with other landowning communities. All these great landowing and elite groups have made their mark on the politics and government of the country. Once again, family names are revealing. The current president of the republic is a Tarar. The names Chatta, Sumro, Khakar, Wattoo, Guilani, Farooqi, Sheikh and Qureshi – to mention just a few – are very familiar to any follower of political events in Pakistan. This reveals the aristicratic nature of Punjabi and Sindi society, emphasized by the more modest status of less 'moneyed' communities whose names are not often in evidence in the corridors of power, and are rarely used as patronyms. Despite the social mobility brought about by modernization, there is still a strict relationship between social status and position in life.

Low-status farmers

In Rajput–Jat regions, certain agricultural activities, because of the nature of the work they entail, are considered impure and left to specific communities.

In essence, this applies to gardening and market gardening. Many of the growers for whom these are statutory occupations raise various crops, including cereals. By dint of their tried and tested working methods and their disciplined approach, their standard of living often belies their social status. Such communities – mindful of their longstanding presence in the region, and their links with ancient dynasties – strive to climb the social ladder. These gardeners, who go by the Hindi-Urdu name *mali* or the Persian name *baghban*, prosper on the outskirts of towns, where there is plenty of animal fertilizer of all kinds, and a high demand for horticultural products (flowers, fruit, vegetables).

The biggest gardening community in Pakistan are the Arains, who probably came from Sind and the Multan region, and spread rapidly upstream along the principal tributaries of the Indus. They are very industrious and take great pride in their work; in some places they have managed to form agricultural working groups. Some of them have discovered that they have Rajput origins; others say that they belong to farming communities which were displaced as a result of extensive Muslim conquests. Now that they have become rich, they are increasingly proud of their origins, which they trace back to Arab ancestors.[18]

These people are related to the Kamboh, who, before Partition, were concentrated to the east of the Sutlej but also much in evidence around Lahore, where they concentrated on and excelled in cereal-growing. After 1947, all those who had embraced Islam went to Pakistan. The Kamboh are proud to be able to include among their ancestors a general by the name of Shahbaz Khan, who performed great deeds under Emperor Akbar.

Merchants and shopkeepers

Established tradesmen belong to endogamous communities who observe the restrictions imposed by the rules of their profession. For example, they leave transport, animal-selling, market and travelling salesmanship to others.

In colonial times, the merchants in regions that are now part of Pakistan were Hindus who also had a crucial role as moneylenders. Before 1947, the geographical distribution of their related groups was fairly clear. Since Partition, migrations which have replaced Hindus with Muslims have complicated the picture.

The Banya, who are predominantly retailers of various descriptions, comprise the 8 per cent of Muslims in their community, and a few Hindus who stayed on. In the NWFP and Baluchistan, they are called Kirar. The Bohra are a community of some importance in Pakistan, because many spread throughout the whole country, especially Sind, from their heartland in the Bombay region. They are Isma'ili Shi'a who do not recognize the authority of the Aga Khan but that of a 'great master' descended from the Prophet – hence a Sayyid – whose spiritual teachings and instructions on how to conduct themselves socially and economically they follow scrupulously. Historians have traced their conversion back to the thirteenth century, but they claim an Egyptian ancestry linked to the Fatimid Empire. Wise and careful people with a reputation for being very strict in all their dealings, they are not only tradesmen, but businessmen in a wider sense.

Their chief and most fearsome competitors are the Khoja and the Piracha (or Paracha). The Khoja – who are also longstanding Shi'a Muslims – are divided into Twelvers and Isma'ilian disciples of the Aga Khan. In Pakistan, the Khoja were originally Khattri and Arora (Hindu merchant castes) who became Shi'a Muslims. The name Khoja, which comes from a Persian word meaning 'master of one's art', has for several years been given to any tradesman in the subcontinent who becomes a Muslim. These Khoja were joined shortly before Partition – but above all after it – by Khoja from Bombay who had the reputation of being good businessmen. There are sizeable groups of Khoja in Karachi, Lahore, Jhang and in the Derajat.

As for the Piracha, they, too, are Khattri who converted to Islam very early, but they are mainly Sunni . They claim to be the oldest-established tradesmen in the region. Some of them are travelling salesmen, while others are successful in international trade, even in industry. So they are socially diverse, but their community is bound together by endogamy and by pride in its ancient origins. Some claim royal forebears, and add the title Rajah to their name. One of their most important centres is at Mukhad, near Rawalpindi. There are many in the Salt Range and from Attock to Peshawar, but also in the Indus basin.

Transport workers and pedlars

There are communities which have traditionally worked for many years in transport or as minor travelling salesmen. They have suffered from competition from the rail network, from farmers who take their own produce to market, and from bigger tradesmen (Bohra, Khoja and Piracha) who are willing to play the part of forwarding agents. Nevertheless, they seem to keep going, notably by becoming lorry drivers or mechanics; in this field, however, certain Afghan Pashtun tribes, mainly Kutchis, are equally – even more – in evidence.

These communities of transport workers, who comprise enough Muslims to remain solidly entrenched in Pakistan, seem to be Banjara and Kabana. The Banjara – under the direction of their leaders, the *naik* – are particularly well organized.

There are also groups who specialize in the distribution of fruit and vegetables, and their name simply denotes their activity: *kunjra* in the languages of the subcontinent, and *sabziforouch* in Persian. Then there are the *tamboli*, who are meant to sell only betel nuts but in fact hawk all kinds of light merchandise.

Technicians

In addition to people who hold important assets like land, goods, wealth, and means of transport temporarily or permanently, in accordance with tradition, there are others whose place in society results from their skill and know-how, handed down and improved over the course of generations – that is to say, their 'art' in the old sense, or their 'technical competence' in today's terms. There is a certain hierarchy to these communities – some trades are considered more worthy of respect than others. It is easiest to list them in terms of this hierarchy – or, at least, attempt to do so.

The barbers, or Nai, take the generic name of their profession, but they are subdivided into various clans with Rajput names – those of their former patrons, or of ancestors who fell on hard times and were forced to take up a trade. Most of the barber clans fall into one of two categories: the Turkia, who arrived with the Ghaznevid conquerors; and the Gangrel, converted Hindus. Apart from the activities entailed by their station in life, barbers also perform minor surgical operations (notably circumcisions). They also help to broker arranged marriages between families, and help to organize wedding ceremonies.

The Bhat and Dum-Mirasi are genealogists-rhapsodists who maintain the historical memories of many related communities of every social rank by means of highly rhythmical songs with musical accompaniment. They perform at every kind of family and communal celebration. They call themselves Chunhar or Kanet – names which seem to imply a Rajput connection. A related group are the Naqqal, storytellers and travelling actors, who go from village to village in the service of rich landowners.

All these activities involving music, song and narrative must not be confused with those which, while they employ similar arts, ultimately have a religious purpose.

These are the province of brotherhoods, and above all of the famous Qawwal, singers of mystic songs, who form a separate and respected group, even though they come from a modest social background.

Singing boatmen, dancers, and animal-handlers, on the contrary, are more or less excluded from the social edifice, because the amusements they provide are considered inferior. As for trades which have some practical use, these seem to be classified according to the double criterion of degree of difficulty and the 'nobility' of the materials they use. At the very bottom of the ladder are trades which are considered downright impure.

It is tempting to list the communities which pursue these activities in descending hierarchical order, but this order – which has no religious overtones in Pakistan – is not absolutely strict.

In the first place, we could mention people who use physical or chemical methods to produce particularly important substances. The Nungar and Shoragar are skilled at gathering saltpetre, or soda from a plant which grows in arid aones. The Agari produce salt by evaporating briny water in a kind of pan [*agar*].

The Sunar (or Zargar), goldsmiths and pawnbrokers constitute an endogamous community that is subdivided into clans. They are ranked a little lower than shopkeepers and are assisted by the Nyaria, smelters of precious metals, who are skilled at gathering up, sorting and recycling the goldsmith's 'scraps'.

The Tarkhan seem to include several groups of building workers, such as the Raj, stonemasons and builders, and the Barhai, who are carpenters.

The Lohar – or smith – community are very much a part of life in both villages and towns, but they are looked down on because of the dark, dull metal with which they work. The Siqligar, or armourers, belong to the same community but have a better image. In any case, metallurgists are becoming more important as they acquire the skills of the modern craftsman.

Fishermen and boatmen live in separate groups, and their commercial relations with the villagers do not normally involve money. They are called Mallah, or Mohanna. You find them on the great rivers in Sind and the Punjab. Much has been written about the picturesque nature of their daily life.

River fishermen are members of the Jhinwar community. Sometimes they catch quail or waterfowl, and they are tied directly into village life under the *seypi* system. They also work in the fields, and as woodcutters, basket makers, water-carriers and cooks, as occasion demands. Their wives often fulfil the role of midwife. Members of this community have various names: Men, Machhi, Machhara, Sammi.

Professional cooks belong to the same community and, under the name Bhatyara, stick to their speciality. They work in towns, near markets, and wherever there are plenty of clients, often providing a mobile catering service. They should be distinguished from the Khansama, who work as cooks in big houses and often enjoy better living conditions, although they have lower status.

Weavers, called Julaha or Paoli, are not a very coherent community, because by origin they can be former landowners who now work in the textile trade or, on the other hand, people of menial status who have chosen to be weavers in the hope of climbing the social ladder. This combination might explain why members of this profession are proverbially thin-skinned and unusually proud. Nevertheless, the development of the textile industry in Pakistan has completely transformed their lives: most of them are now tailors in urban areas, or skilled factory workers. They also work as supervisors in the carpet industry (where most of the work is done by poor people of humble status).

In many villages, where the *seypi* system still exists, textile workers still make sheets and bedcovers. Weavers and tailors in general claim to be descended from prestigious communities: the Janjua, the Khokar, the Bhatti.

The Dhobi are a complex community of laundry workers and dyers who work mainly in the towns or on great estates.

The Chamar and Mochi are shoemakers and saddlers – that is to say, they work with leather but do not process it. There are several communities, but their names, which are reminiscent of Jat names, tell us nothing about their history. They seem to have ancient and distinct origins, because they constitute a recognizable phenotype. Over and beyond their professional duties, they work in the fields and in building in various capacities. Their work is part of the *seypi* system.

Tanners and leather-dyers – the Khatik and Tchamrang – are considered inferior to shoemakers. In fact their community is thought to belong to that of the dustmen and cleaners. Their status – but not their income – has risen as a result of the development of the leather and leathercraft industry in Pakistan.

The Chuhra are consigned by tradition to 'unclean' jobs – paradoxically, that means jobs that ensure cleanliness. They make brooms, rubbish baskets and cereal baskets. They clean public areas, clear out places reserved for human waste, and gather cow dung to make round bricks which, when dried, are used as fuel. They also wash corpses and perform various tasks connected with funerals. In short, they do 'impure' work in terms of a traditional schema inspired by Hinduism. The name Chuhra is no longer used. They are sometimes called *mehtar*, 'sweeper', a name which describes their profession; most often, however, they are given the simple title *kammi*, or artisan. There are several names for this community, according to the places where they settled. In Sind and the Indus basin, they are called Kutana. Elsewhere they are called Musalli or Dindar – names which reflect their conversion to Islam – and Massih if they are Christians. So they are referred to in euphemistic terms. It is believed that they have been in the country for a very long time, but it is difficult to reconstruct the history of their community because until recently they have welcomed into their ranks members of wandering groups who wish to become part of village society.

Wanderers

To a greater or lesser extent, wandering communities are exempt from the principles which rule urban or village life. They observe few dietary, religious or, quite simply, traditional taboos. They are willing to hunt wild boar, porcupine, lizards – even crocodiles if they can find any; they are even prepared to eat carrion. According to rules which vary from one group to the next, their wives prostitute themselves; finally, there are groups which are prepared to steal, or even to launch armed attacks.

These communities can be parasitical to varying degrees, and therefore vary in terms of their potential for integration into settled societies. Some of them are skilled infrastructure workers, or practise traditional medicine. Others are simply entertainers: musicians, dancers, wild-animal handlers. Since they are the least attached to any specific area but the most internally cohesive of any group, they travel continually – just like those (possibly related) communities which left the sub-continent at the beginning of our Middle Ages to go west, a movement which is still going on. They include the Od, who are also called Beldar; the Changar, who are travelling artisans; and the Nats, highly organized musicians and boatmen who are notorious for their plundering expeditions.

In the Towns

The tribal systems and the – related but separate – systems of superposition and jux-taposition of endogamous communities seem, on the basis of the evidence, to be linked to the acquisition and handing down of territories or land. In the Rajput–Jat tradition, the keystone of the social edifice seems to be ownership of cultivable land. At first sight, therefore, these systems seem to be part of the rural world, and we may well wonder how urban life – where tradition seems to play a less obvious part – is organized. We may think of Pakistan as a rural country, but it has huge urban centres like Karachi, Lahore, Peshawar and Rawalpindi, and large towns – beginning with the capital, Islamabad – which are mainly in the Indus basin and indicate their – often very ancient – founding principle by names ending in *abad*, *pur* or *pura*.

In fact, the social organization of the countryside gives us an idea of what its urban counterpart is like. Thus communities from several ethnic groups, or certain bodies with tribal origins, contribute to urban life: those which specialize in building, craft and artisanal work, and trade. It is natural, for example, for the Sabziforoush to run vegetable markets, the Lohar to do metal and mechanical work, and the Sunar to be jewellers. As throughout the East, the community or corporate nature of these activities is emphasized by the fact that members of a given profession live in their own district, notably in the bazaars. Only the general shops are mixed, although there are still roads reserved for Kirar or Banya. Naturally, these city-dwellers gradually lose their village or tribal allegiances as the economy becomes strictly monetary. Finally, the towns are places where all the country's ethnic and tribal groups live together, without losing their distinctive identities.

On what system of wealth creation or distribution is this urban economy based? Certainly the state and its various agents are major employers and clients. The big landowners, too, have urban residences where they spend part of the year so that they can supervise their affairs and be close to the centre of power. They therefore contribute to the urban economy. The interregional – even international – trade which often led to the development of these towns also makes its own contribution: income from it is used to buy durable goods and to finance public works. The private sector, however, does not make much of a decisive or constructive contribution, except to invest in the industrial, commercial or service sector. So the dominant figure in the urban landscape is, in effect, the major investor.

Curiously enough, business leaders in Pakistan are usually from that country, except for Muhajirs who came from Uttar Pradesh at the time of Partition. These natives, however, come from a community which left the Indus basin some centuries ago to come together and make their fortune in three main regions of the subcontinent: Gujarat, Maharashtra and Bengal. In the second half of the eighteenth century, and to consolidate the stability created by the British, these communities spread widely throughout the subcontinent, even the Empire – including London. Rather like the Pashtun tribes, some of them played a polarizing role by including within their sphere of influence numerous associates and subcontractors. Each of them observes the strict rules of endogamy, emphasizing yet again the primordial importance of family relationships.

The great 'pole communities'

It is customary to distinguish four endogenous 'pole communities' which are extremely coherent internally: the Memon, the Chinioti, the Khoja and the Bohra. Two other less closely integrated but quite distinct groups are also very influential investors: on the one hand, the mohajirs of Karachi; on the other, families from a Jat, Rajput, Baluchi or Pashtun landowning background.

The Memon were originally Lohana Hindus from Tatta, near Sind. They were converted to Islam by a Sufi member of the Qadiriyya in the fifteenth century. This holy man, known as Sayyid Yussuf Sindhi, called the new converts '*mumin*', or people of faith – this name was subsequently slightly distorted and became Memon. It is said that in order to escape the harassment – even vindictiveness – of their former coreligionists, these people emigrated *en masse* to Saurashtra, and especially to Gujarat. After the eighteenth century, many of them made money in the import–export business, then in processing. The Memon rose fairly rapidly up the ranks of the great investors of the British Empire, opening industrial concerns and branches in Bengal, Burma and Hong Kong.

Their major business leaders also founded dynasties which played a crucial in the spectacular take-off of Pakistan's banking and industrial sectors. Well-known names include Habib, Adamjee, Dawood, Bawany, Rangoon-wala, Haroon, Djaffer and Younous. These are mostly first names; there is only one more recent surname, Rangoon-wala. This shows that the Memon identify exclusively with their own community, whose name certain families still bear. Their communal ties are strongly institutionalized; several bodies – like the All India Memon Foundation and the United Memon Jamaat of Pakistan – are like caste councils with a well-defined economic role. These bodies preside over every aspect of marriage unions, including issues of patrimony. Since Partition, they have played an instrumental role in the creation of a modern economy in Pakistan. They were badly affected by the secession of Bangladesh, and by Z A Bhutto's subsequent nationalizations of key industrial sectors. As a result, they diverted their investments to more hospitable countries. Nevertheless, they still play an important part in the Pakistani economy although they have diversified and reduced the scale of their activities. They are particularly prevalent in Karachi.

The Chinioti are Sheikhs from the medium-sized town of Chiniot, on the Chenab, halfway between Sargodha and Faisalabad. For some of them, Sheikh is also their family name. We should not confuse them with the Sayyid and Qazi who, by tradition, dominate the town. The Chinioti community have modest origins. They emigrated to present-day India, especially to Calcutta, in the nineteenth century, and specialized in the leather and skin trade. At the beginning of the twentieth century, some of them made profitable investments in the agro-alimentary, textile and rubber industries, then transformed their industries to the Indus basin, especially to Multan. At the time of Partition, the Sheikh family, heads of the Colony group, and the Monoo family were very prominent investors in the textile industry in the Punjab; these groups subdivided by taking the first names of the various heirs. So the Kaiser group took its name from Qaiser (Caesar) Sheikh. Another very important family, the Saigol, is connected – albeit tangentially – to the Chinioti group. They are Sheikhs who came originally from Chakwal, but it seems that some of their ancestors lived in Chiniot in the sixteenth century. The Chiniot's efforts at endogamy have not precluded marriages between the Saigol and the Monoo. In general, their factories and head offices are in big towns in the Punjab, such as Lahore.

The Chinioti's firms were by no means badly affected by Z A Bhutto's nationalization programme, because they were not in strategic sectors and were not so big as to raise fears of monopoly. So the Chinioti filled the gap left by the Memon, and expanded their activities considerably between 1970 and 1980. Crescent and Nishat became holding companies. Later, the close relations they had been able to establish with Mian Nawaz Sharif when he was head of the Ettefaq group, leader of the Punjab's provincial government, and finally served two terms as prime minister made them even more important economic actors. They benefited particularly from a privatization programme that was begun with great determination in 1992 and vigorously renewed in 1997.

General Musharraf's regime regards the Chinioti with suspicion because of their blatant collusion with recent governments, above all the preceding one. No doubt the Memon now have an opportunity to take their revenge, especially since Karachi, where most of their business and holdings are, has experienced a downturn and a chronic lack of productive investment. The main Chinioti groups are Crescent, Nishat, United, Saphire, Sargodha, Colony, Sunshine, J S K Chenab, Ruby, and Khurshed. Their great business leaders – some of whom are women – are called Fazal-Ibrahim, Arshad, Fatima, Nagina, Jahanghuir Elahi, Ayesha, Monoo, and Mian Habibullah; Yusuf and Naseem Saigol are related to them.

The Khoja – who, as we know, are all Shi'a – are divided into Twelvers and Isma'ilians. The first group, who do not seem to have amassed great amounts of wealth, are nevertheless skilled businessmen who have been able to take over some of the activities of the Twelver diaspora – often of Iranian origin – in the big coastal towns of the Gulf and the Indian Ocean. The second group are much more prominent: some of them, such as the Hashwani brothers, have built up a considerable fortune in direct investments, but also by taking a share in – or even control over – the hotel, oil exploration, and cotton trades. The Khoja are part of the very close community of the Aga Khan's followers, who are known to be spread over several countries.

All the Bohra are Isma'ilians. It is known that they do not recognize the Aga Khan's authority but that of a Sayyid. Although they are not among the country's forty-five biggest investors, some of them are highly respected members of the business community. They are businessmen of varying importance who know how to make their guiding principles, their solidarity and their presence work for them on all five continents.

Major individual investors

There are some business leaders who have no ties with any specific organic group. They may seem to be isolated individuals, but in fact they do fall into identifiable social categories and are prepared, where necessary, to defend their common interests.

The Muhajirs, who come from Uttar Pradesh and speak Urdu, have settled in the two great southern towns, Karachi and Hyderabad. They came to Pakistan after Partition, bringing with them their professional skills and some capital. They have set up numerous businesses – mainly small or medium-sized, but some on a national scale, taking advantage of potential demand in sectors abandoned by the big businesses communities. They have become increasingly important economically, especially in Karachi – to the point where their obvious success threatened to make them a dominant community, since they were very much in evidence both in industry and in every trade that is required for the development of a great urban centre, and equally prevalent in the liberal professions and, above all, in administrative circles. Discriminatory measures against them prompted them to unite under the auspices of a well-known political party, the MQM, whose bursts of violence and separatist tendencies have brought undeserved opprobrium down on this enterprising, energetic group of citizens. They seem to have attracted the hostility of communities with strong family ties without having been able to form such a community themselves. They are now inclined to criticize Pakistani society for its archaic nature – symbolized, in their opinion, by the influence of 'feudal groups'.

There are several Pashtun families whose wealth has enabled them to launch a wide range of business activities. Two groups deserve particular attention: the heirs of Habibullah Khattak, and the Seifullah family of Bannu. The first group, who own numerous foreign companies and subsidiaries, appeared at first to fall within the Memon sphere of influence. Like the Memon, they were badly affected by the nationalization programme. The second group, which has done very well over the last decade, is linked to the Memon Younos group.

The Sharif family, who were originally from Kashmir, are a special case. Extremely close, but with no family ties to any other business community, they set up the first large foundries in Pakistan, and built up the highly diversified Ettefaq group. We know that Nawaz Sharif combined his career as a business leader with a political career culminating in two terms as prime minister. The Ettefaq group is known to have formed alliances with businessmen from the Chinioti community.

The Zoroastrians, or Parsees, are a close but not strictly endogamous community. Like their coreligionists in Bombay, the Parsees of Karachi are enterprising businessmen who inspire confidence. From their ranks came the founders of the thriving Avari hotel and services group.

Finally – and naturally – we must consider the part played by descendants of Rajput and Jat families in the formation of financial and industrial elites. Most of these families invested in sectors allied to agricultural production, and considerably increased the fortune they had acquired through the great monocultures. These families have also become involved in politics, and several of their members have been given government posts. Like the Seifullah and Sharif familites, they have helped to maintain a close link between the business world and the corridors of power – all the more so by forming alliances with great Memon or Chinioti families. These great business leaders and men of politics from a landowning background include Jam Mashooq Ali, Manzoor Watto, Khalid Ahmed Kharral, Nawaz Khokar, Chaudry Shujaat Hussein, and several members of the Noon, Jatoi and Sumro families.

Outlines of a pyramid

Can we say – with Mahboob ul-Haq, a respected economist and former finance minister – that twenty-two families manipulate Pakistan's economy in their own commercial interests? If certain British analysts are to be believed, are there not more like forty-five such families? Must we go even further, and put the number at two hundred – even two thousand, if we include owners of latifundia? In any event, it is clear that there do not seem to be many actual or potential investors for a country with a population of 140 million.

In both town and country, the overall structure is remarkably like that of a pyramid. In every sphere of production and exchange, the Pakistanis seem to find it difficult to attain a balanced relationship between the multitude of small businesspeople and the few families or communities who have the most decisive capacity to invest, via those who have access to modest or average wealth. Contrary to Z A Bhutto's hopes, this trend was accelerated by the nationalization of the big banks. In fact, most loans went to entrepreneurs, businessmen and landowners who were going to be successful anyway, and were willing to provide political support. The resulting distortions are even more harmful than the creation of monopolies: economic immunity – any industrial, commercial or agricultural concern which supports the state or the party in power benefits from 'handouts' in the form of low interest payments or tax breaks. In other words, the *seypi* system has taken on national dimensions: the holding and exchange of wealth favour not so much its creation as the weaving of enhanced networks of solidarity.

The majority of economic actors are in a situation of dependency or indebtedness. There are the same relations between the small trader, the carrier and the wholesaler as there are between the wholesaler and the bank, the bank and the government, but above all friends and patrons, who are themselves in an unequal relationship with those who are richer and more powerful than themselves.

This situation also exists in the country, where poor smallholders, patrons and exploiters of the *kammi*, needed the help of latifundia owners and the government.

In short, the country has got into debt because – among other reasons – most of its people were in debt – even deeply in debt, as the system of child labour shows.

Are the Communities Changing?

It seems that in Pakistan there is one salient feature: the strength of communities linked by blood ties, and their struggle to the death to defend and, if possible, improve their social rank. This seems to apply as much to the Baluchis and Pashtuns as to the Rajput–Jats; as much in the towns as in the countryside. The greatest inequalities in the countryside are those of land distribution, especially in the Punjab and in Sind; the sheer numbers of small farmers have not brought about any progress – on the contrary: they constitute a powerful brake on a social mobility which might threaten their traditional privileges. Who can blame these farmers for wanting to protect the prestige of their 'community' – that is to say, their family line?

This is where an ambiguity arises. The word 'community' is used as the occasion demands to describe something that is not – or is no longer – an ethnic group, a tribe, or even a caste, but a related group not linked to any particular territory. Modern language also takes account of completely different kinds of community – those of a village or a district, for example, where solidarity is a matter of necessity. So Pakistani society seems to be torn between two kinds of communitarian solidarity: that of the *qaum* (that of blood) and that of communal life (of the soil). There is nothing surprising about this; the same applies in many other countries. In Pakistan, however, the situation is particularly painful because it is so unbalanced.

When we take into account the fact that reciprocal relations between landowners and politicians, disputes between *biradari*, and dependencies linked to the *seypi* system mean that, in a given constituency, elections are often decided in advance, we realize that real politics in Pakistan is in fact 'parallel' and 'informal', as is much of its economy. We must recognize, however, that such traditional – even 'unequal' – relationships help to ensure the survival of many groups of people in times of economic stagnation and serious underemployment. The hierarchical structure can therefore look like a 'structure of poverty'.

So – can economic actors 'get anything out of ' all this? If they are to fly in the face of the logic of rivalry, and the resulting chains of indebtedness and waste, they must choose between local ties and blood ties, and give priority to whichever serve their most compelling interests – that is, their social interests. The present government has pledged to work towards encouraging such a choice. This is an immense task, fraught with one enormous danger: resorting to clear but illusory simplifications. In fact, in Pakistan the system of social hierarchies is in the realms of the implied and the unspoken, and of practices that are beyond any attempt at precise definition. At the present time, a campaign like the one instigated by Dr Ambedkar[19] in India, a country where the castes are willing to speak their names, is inconceivable.

There are, however, some changes under way not only in the towns, where inter-mingling is undermining the cohesion of consanguinous communities, but also in the countryside.

In the towns, ancestral pride is giving way to the need for some modicum of eco-nomic success, while credit and social institutions – and interpersonal relations – are taking over from a system of handouts based on personal solidarity, which perpetu-ates dependency. Here there are stirrings of class consciousness – or, at the very least, an awareness that wealth is not fairly distributed. The trade unions are marred by artificiality in that they, like politicians, are influenced by clientelism. The position of leader is not an easy one for someone who is not from a background that encourages taking the initiative, speaking in public, and gaining access to knowledge. Gradually, however, there are growing hopes that collective initiative is more likely than recourse to clientelist expediency to achieve a decent standard of living.

In the countryside, class sentiment is probably more closely linked to a weakening of blood ties and hierarchical structures. We can see this from Muhammad Azam Chaudhary's reports from a village in the Punjab.[20] He notes that his interviewees now tend to have only a rough idea of their *got*, which in other places is called their *qaum*, and that ties between villages belonging to the same *zat* (sometimes called a *biradari*) are rare. Hazy descriptions of the various social ranks within a blood com-munity show that they no longer have the relevance they had in the past. The dominant factor now seems to be the local tie – that of the *pind* or village commu-nity – rather than the continuation of hereditary ranks. This is obvious when we note the growth of the deciding body called the *panchayat*, or council of elders; it is confirmed by the fact that social prestige is beginning to depend more on personal integrity and wisdom than on the extent of one's landholdings. If the tendency towards emphasizing local interests rather than considerations of birth continues, then there will be further scrutiny of the relations between poor villagers and rich landowners, who will have to understand that their own self-interest compels them to behave like 'good princes' if they are to maintain their status.

Finally, there is some interaction between town and country insofar as the farm-ers – connected by necessity with markets in the towns, and gradually becoming educated – are being imbued with urban culture; while collective movements, which began in the towns but are now active in the country, are revealing blatant inequal-ities and extravagant practices. Finally, the most deprived sections of the population, who are from a rural background, and poor people in the countryside could find common cause as members of the same proletariat. In today's Pakistan, however, ties to blood communities are still too strong to allow us to talk about the 'labouring masses', except in the most conventional rhetorical sense.

The focal meeting-point between town and country is elsewhere: in a factor that reveals the limits of the old caste system. The 'rejects' of an economy which, in becoming monetary, causes many individuals to go bankrupt will not, as in the past, join wandering parasitical communities but will be concentrated on the outskirts of the towns, as elsewhere in the Third World. In the districts euphemistically called *kachhi abadi* ('houses made of unbaked bricks' – other countries call them shanty-towns) congregate social outcasts whose sole aim is survival, and who are less concerned with social ties than with basic human existence. These people disrupt social and economic relations; they lower the price of labour and have a dampening effect on urban planning and the development of social services, even as they show how great is the need for them. They have no stable allegiances, but could constitute a powerful force which could easily be won over by a clever government. This could be a major social player waiting on the sidelines. Two urban groups in Pakistan have broken free of the ties of consanguinity: the Muhajirs, who came from India and now constitute a middle class; and the underclass in the *kachhi abadi*. Were these two forces to unite, this could be the beginning of a renewed and accelerated breaking down of the system of tribal or 'communitarian' elites.

The road to change is still very long, despite the current government's stated policy of empowering the impoverished. This would involve loosening the ties of clientelism that are an important part of life for so many people in Pakistan, and strengthening solidarities based on relations other than the traditional ones of birth; it therefore entails not only institutional reform, but a genuine change of attitude.

PART IV

A PLURAL CULTURE?

10

THE DIVERSITY OF ISLAM

One of the principal characteristics of Islam in Pakistan is its extraordinary sectarian and ideological diversity. As elsewhere in the world, the main demarcation line is between Sunni and Shi'a. Shi'a in Pakistan are divided in turn between Twelvers and Isma'ilians; Isma'ilians themselves fall into two distinct groups: Nizari and Bohra. There is a third, separate group: the Ahmadiyya.

The Sunni have their own internal divisions, which relate more to ideological developments: there are the modernists, the traditionalists and the fundamentalists; they all came into existence in the nineteenth century as a reaction against the presence of the British, and are a continuing influence in the Indian subcontinent, especially in Pakistan.

This religious diversity was relatively peaceful (except for the anti-Ahmadi movement) during the first few years in the life of the young nation of Pakistan. Since the 1980s, however, it has led to conflicts characterized by an unprecedented violence.

The Sunni

The majority of Pakistanis (between 75 and 80 per cent, according to which statistics you consult) say that they are Sunni . As elsewhere in the Muslim world, they consider themselves the upholders of Islamic orthodoxy, and differ fundamentally from the Shi'a in that they recognize the legitimacy of the first four caliphs who came after the Prophet Mohammed. The overwhelming majority of Pakistan's Sunni Muslims belong to the Hanaphite school of religious law [*mazhab*].

There are several diverse Sunni tendencies in Pakistan which can be traced back to the collapse of the Mughal Empire and the gradual domination of the British, which began in the eighteenth century. Each tendency reacted to this in a different way.

Traditionalists

The Deobandi. – The biggest Sunni school for ulemas (doctors of the law) is the Deobandi school. It takes its name from the town of Deoband in India, to the north of Delhi, where their biggest *madrasah* was founded in 1867 by Muhammad Qasim Nanautawi (1833–77) and Rashid Ahmad Gangohi (1829–1905). In reaction against the colonial presence – although they took their inspiration from British education methods – the ulemas of Deoband dropped English and 'Western' sciences from the education curriculum, and promoted instead the study of the Koran, the Hadith, and Islamic law and science. They followed the tradition of certain Sufi orders and emphasized individual spiritual discipline acquired through instruction from a spiritual master, but they strongly opposed the worship of saints – like the Wahhabi, by whom they were influenced.[1]

Believing that Islam was a universal religion, the Deobandi advocated a notion of a composite nationalism according to which Hindus and Muslims constituted one nation. Indian Muslims therefore had a duty to join the Hindus in the struggle against the British. After 1919 they came together in the Jamiyyat-ul Ulama-i Hind, and opposed the Movement for Pakistan. The Muslim League of Muhammad Ali Jinnah (1876–1948) attracted only a dissident minority group; its leader, Shabbir Ahmad Usmani (who died in 1949), founded the Jamiyyat-ul Ulama-i Islam (JUI) in 1945. Today this organization represents the Deobandi in Pakistan, but since the 1980s it has been divided into several factions (there seem to be at least eleven[2]), some of which are extremely militant. Some 50 per cent of the ulemas belong to the Deobandi school.[3]

By tradition, the Deobandi are influential in Sind (with both the Sindis themselves and the Muhajirs, Muslims who emigrated to Pakistan after Partition). A number of eminent Deobandi leaders chose to make their headquarters in this province. Sind's Dar ul-Ulum Ashrafabad – a seminary established at Ashrafabad in 1949, and considered the Deobandi school in Pakistan – has produced many of the country's most prominent learned men. The Deobandi are also influential among the Pashtuns of the NWFP and Baluchistan, owing to the historic links between the town of Deoband in India and the Afghan capital, Kabul. Since the 1980s, the Deobandi have been trying to extend their sphere of influence to the Punjab, where they have established *madrasahs*. Whereas in India, before Partition, they drew their membership from comfortably off urban circles, in Pakistan the Deobandi attract people – especially students – from more traditional social strata, most particularly from rural and tribal communities.[4] They demand that sharia law should be applied both in personal law and in the country's wider legal system.

The Ahl-i Hadith. – The other group which shares the Wahhabi legacy is that of the Ahl-i Hadith (people of the Tradition), founded in 1864; their emblematic figure was Nazir Hussain (1805–1902). The Ahl-i Hadith are more radical than the Deobandi and reject the teachings of the Hanaphite school, acknowledging only the Koran and the Sunna as authoritative sources of Islamic law. There are fewer of them – because of their small proportion of ulemas (20 per cent) and few disciples – and they are found mainly in the northern Punjab and in Karachi. Their membership base is very much as it was in India in the nineteenth century: predominantly the urban merchant class.

The Barelwi or Ahl-i Sunnat wa Jamaat. – The Barelwi movement, in contrast, is the embodiment of popular Sufi traditions in the Indian subcontinent. Unreformed in this sense (unlike the movements described above), it takes its name from Bareilly in present-day Uttar Pradesh, the birthplace of its founder, Ahmad Riza Khan (1856–1921).

There are several features typical of the Barelwi: the great importance they attach to the Prophet Muhammad (an object of genuine veneration to them); the role of saints and spiritual teachers as their intercessors before Allah; and the celebration of popular festivals (especially *mîlâd*, which commemorates the Prophet's birth). They also embody popular religion as experienced by the masses. All this notwithstanding, they are scrupulously orthodox and consider themselves true Sunni – hence the other name they use, 'Ahl-i Sunnat wa Jamaat' (the Sunni party). They are the Deobandi's main rivals in Pakistan, and the Deobandi condemn both their worship of saints and the quasi-divine status they confer on the Prophet.

Unlike the Deobandi, the Barelwi were unequivocal supporters of the Movement for Pakistan. After Partition, in 1948, they formed their own representative association in Pakistan, the Jamiyyat-ul Ulama-i Pakistan (JUP). They are dominant in the Punjab and in regions of Sind where the worship of saints is particularly popular – especially in rural areas; but since 1947 their influence has also made itself felt among newly urbanized and relatively deprived sectors of the population. Like the Deobandi and the Ahl-i Hadith, Barelwi ulemas fight for sharia law to be applied throughout the country.

The modernists

In addition to these traditionalist groups, another important tendency came into the picture in the nineteenth century in reaction to the British presence: the modernists. They refused to submit to the ulemas' authority, and made an effort to consign Islam to the private sphere. They looked on the English as guarantors of their rights against the Hindu majority, and accepted their presence. Their leader, Sayyid Ahmad Khan (1817–98), who did not see any incompatibility between Islamic law and the study of English and the sciences, took it on himself to form a Muslim elite on the Western model. In 1875 he established the Mohammedan Anglo-Oriental College at Aligarh, in present-day Uttar Pradesh (in 1920 it became the Aligarh Muslim University). This university produced generations of Westernized intellectuals. The other important modernist leader, and follower of Sir Sayyid, was the poet and philosopher Muhammad Iqbal (1876?-1938). He was critical of the *taqlîd*, the passive acceptance of the answers provided by schools of religious law, and favoured a reconstructed religious thought based on the third source of law after the Koran and the *sunna*: the *ijmâ'* – consensus. According to Iqbal, the *ijmâ*, which is traditionally controlled by the ulemas, should be handed over to a representative assembly, as it was in Turkey.[5]

The thought of Sir Sayyid and Iqbal inspired young urban educated Muslims like Muhammad Ali Jinnah, who, subscribing to Iqbal's theory of two nations, used the notion that Islam was in danger in order to mobilize the Muslim masses to demand the formation of Pakistan; nevertheless, he believed that Pakistan should be a secular state where religion was relegated to the private sphere. Many groups in Pakistan subscribed to his notion of modernism, notably parties which have emerged as a result of the break-up of the Muslim League: the modern Pakistan Muslim League (PML) and the Bhutto family's Pakistan's People's Party (PPP).

The neofundamentalists

The Tablighi Jamaat. – The Tablighi Jamaat ('the preaching party') was founded in 1927 by a religious scholar influenced by the Deobandi school, Muhammad Ilyas (1885–1944), at the height of the Hindu–Muslim rivalries. In the north of British India, the first half of the twentieth century was a time of competitive proselytizing in an effort to gain or win back converts. Ilyas became a missionary, starting in Rajasthan villages, where local Islamic practices were strongly influenced by Hinduism. His self-imposed task was to encourage Muslims to 'purify' their religious practices, and to create a totally Islamic environment.

So the principal objective of this basically pietist movement is re-Islamization. The life of a believer is based on six principles: the profession of faith; canonical prayers; the knowledge and remembrance of Allah; mutual respect; sincerity of intention; and proselytism.

The Tablighi Jamaat flourished under the leadership of Ilyas's son, Muhammad Yusuf (1917–65), who refused to leave for Pakistan in 1947 and kept the headquarters of his organization in Delhi. There is, however, a branch in Raiwind, near Lahore. In Pakistan, as elsewhere in the subcontinent and in other regions where it has spread (the Tablighi Jamaat and the Ahmadi are the most transnational organizations in South Asia), it has a remarkable capacity to mobilize: its annual assembly in Pakistan attracts nearly two million people and is believed to be the second-largest Muslim gathering after the pilgrimage to Mecca.

As the followers of the Tablighi Jama'at are supposed to concentrate on deepening their faith, they are not permitted to engage in religious controversy or discuss politics within the movement. This apolitical stance – which has always been the official line – is now being questioned by several scholars: Marc Gaborieau, for instance, holds that its ability to mobilize millions of people worldwide, as a result of its strategy of active proselytism, could conceal a political agenda and/or foster political ambitions in the longer term.[6]

In Pakistan, the Tablighi Jamaat is particularly influential among the Pashtuns, the Muhajirs and the Punjabis. It draws its members essentially from the petty bourgeoisie (tradesmen, junior civil servants, etc.) and from some wealthier social circles (liberal professions, businessmen, etc.).

The Jamaat-i Islami. – The Jamaat-i Islami ('Islamic party'), founded in 1941 by Abul Ala Maududi (1903–79), is the fundamentalist party *par excellence* in the sense that it advocates a return to Islamic doctrine in its original form. Its ideology is in line with that of the major international fundamentalist movements, especially the Muslim Brotherhood.[7]

Maududi held that Islam should govern every aspect of life. He was virulently critical of the traditional ulemas, maintaining that they limited themselves to a passive reading of the sacred texts, rather than exercising their faculties of reasoning. He agreed with them on the question of Islam's legislative tradition (the supremacy of the Law – that is to say, the sharia – imposed by Allah, sole lawgiver and sole sovereign lord), but his system of thought gave them no institutional status, and deprived them of their traditional prerogatives. Maududi also disagreed with the ulemas on the question of mysticism and popular religious devotion; he wanted to retain only the juridical and political aspects of Islamic thought. He proposed that the Islamic state should be based on sharia law as the defining law of the country, which should apply to every aspect of the legal system (constitutional, civil, criminal); the state should be led by morally and religiously upright men who modelled themselves on the first Companions of the Prophet. Thus he established the Jamaat-i Islami in 1941. Although Maududi rejected all Western ideology, he drew inspiration from both fascist and communist parties, as we can see from the extremely centralized structure of his organization. He did not have much consideration for mysticism, but he did admire Sufism as an organizational model: the pivotal role of the spiritual master [*pir*] corresponded very closely with his own concept of the role of the *amîr* (leader) in the Jamaat-i Islami.

According to the Maududian ideal, the disciplined elite who constitute his organization must work for the creation of an Islamic state which would gradually take over social and political affairs. The main difference between the Jamaat-i Islami and the Tablighi Jamaat, therefore, lies in the fact that the former is aiming for an Islamic revolution via control of the state apparatus (Islamization 'from above'), whereas the latter considers that Islamization on an individual level is a necessary precondition for the building of an Islamic state (Islamization 'from below').

Maududi was against the Movement for Pakistan at the outset, arguing that the Muslim League's nationalism was, in principle, contrary to Islam. He believed that nationalism was a threat to the cohesion of the Muslim community, and would have a divisive effect on the *umma* which would hinder the spread of Islam's universal message. He also believed that the movement for the creation of Pakistan was led by people who rejected any notion of a religious state, and favoured the establishment of a liberal democracy along Western lines. Nevertheless, Maududi came to Pakistan after Partition;[8] thereafter he adapted himself, in both thought and action, to the evolution of Pakistani politics.

The Jamaat-i Islami is strong in the Punjab, in Sind (especially in Karachi) and in the NWFP, where most of its *madrasahs* are situated (mainly concentrated near the Afghan border); its membership base, which is similar to that of the Ahl-i Hadith, is predominantly middle-class, mostly the urban petty bourgeoisie who have had a modern education.

The Jamaat-i Islami played a crucial role in the Islamization of the Pakistani state, especially under Zia ul-Haq (1979–88), but it is too doctrinaire and elitist to attract real popular support. It usually fares poorly at elections, but it is still capable of mobilizing in the streets and the universities, where its student branch (Islami Jamiat-i Tulaba) always seems to be ready to resort to violence.

The Shi'a

Twelver Shi'a

Shi'a (literally 'partisan') doctrine is based on its specific concept of the imam and the imamate: the legitimate political leader of the community must be a descendant of the Prophet, whereas for the Sunni , the imam or caliph can come from a less restricted background. The Shi'a believe that after the Prophet's death, leadership of the community should have gone to his cousin and son-in-law, Ali. Hence, they do not recognize the three caliphs who came before Ali as legitimate. Moreover, according to their doctrine the imam's position as religious and political leader of Islam has a superhuman – even miraculous – dimension.

The biggest Shi'a group are the Twelvers[9] [ithnâ'asharîyya], so called because they recognize the line of the twelfth imam, whereas the Isma'ilis, also known as Seveners, believe that the seventh imam is also the final.

In terms of ritual, there are no major differences between Shiism and Sunnism, except that as well as the pilgrimage to Mecca [hajj], also visit Ali's tomb at Najaf and the tomb of Shi'a Hussain (Ali's son, and the third imam) at Kerbala [ziyârâ] in Iraq. The month of muharram, which commemorates Hussain's martyrdom at Kerbala, is of capital importance; it is the most widely celebrated Shi'a festival.

More fundamentally, because of the events that marked the birth of this sect, the Shi'a extol martyrdom and persecution. The death of Hussain, one of the founding moments of Shiism, imbues this sect with strong emotional overtones, and its devotees with an intense feeling of guilt that is absent from Sunnism. Hussain's martyrdom is also the catalyst for a strong sense of religious identity, especially when the Shi'a are in the minority. From time to time, when their community is under threat, they are forced to resort to taqîya – that is, dissembling their faith; at such times they usually adopt Sunni rituals.

It is estimated that Twelver and Sevener Shi'a make up between 15 and 25 per cent of the population of Pakistan. They are to be found mainly in Sind (Karachi), the Punjab, and the Northern Territories (Gilgit and Baltistan).

Nizari Isma'ili Shi'a, or Khoja[10]

Isma'ilism – also called Sevener Shiism – originated in a question of succession: that of Imam Jafar al-Sadiq (who died in 765). As well as according primordial importance to the imamate (the imam is endowed with an inherited charisma), Isma'ili doctrine oppose to the exoteric aspect of the religion [zâhir] an esoteric reality [bâtin]. The zâhir represents the apparent and generally accepted meaning of revealed texts which set out rites and precepts; the bâtin corresponds to the hidden, transcendent and immutable truths which the disciple must seek beyond texts, rites and precepts. These truths are interpreted by the imam, who is master of the Scriptures and therefore very important. In terms of ritual, the symbolic meaning of the rites is often more important than their performance.

Isma'ili missionaries from Fatimid Egypt settled in Sind in the tenth century, winning numerous Hindus over to their faith.[11] Further schisms caused by disputes over the succession followed, and in the second half of the fifteenth century two distinct groups emerged: the Muhammad Shah, whose line of imams came to an end about two centuries ago; and the Qasim Shahi, from whom modern Aga Khans are descended.

Aga Khan I's installation in Bombay marked the beginning of the modern period for Nizari Isma'ilism. After nearly seven centuries in Persia, the headquarters of the Nizari imamate were transferred to Bombay in 1848.

The second Aga Khan, who took office in 1881, laid the basis for a modernization of the Nizari community which would culminate in the long reign of Sultan Muhammad Shah, Aga Khan III ((1885–1957). He introduced socioeconomic reforms aimed at making the Nizari a modern, educated and wealthy community. He abolished the system of *parda*,[12] encouraging women to get an education and practise a profession. As for politics, he helped to form the Muslim League in 1906, and gave large sums of money to the Movement for Pakistan. The founder of Pakistan, Jinnah, was himself a Khoja.

The Khoja of Pakistan have settled mainly in urban areas of Sind (especially in Karachi, which has taken over from Bombay as their biggest population centre) and in mountain regions of the Northern Territories. Although there are only about half a million of them, they are influential, especially in trade and industry, and very much involved in the country's development. Most Nizari in the North make their living as farmers.

Mustali Isma'ili Shi'a, or Bohra

The Mustali Isma'ilians broke away from the Nizari in 1094. In 1130 there was a further division in their ranks between the Tayyibi and the Hafizi.[13] The former would become the 'Bohra'.

The Tayyibi, who lived in Yemen in the early days, have preserved several Fatimid Isma'ili traditions. They consider the exoteric [*zâhir*] and esoteric [*bâtin*] dimensions of religion equally important, but they have introduced some innovations which have given this branch of Isma'ilism its distinctive character (cosmological doctrine; the system of the ten intellects, etc.).

The first *dâ'î* – or[14] Isma'ilian 'propagandist', Abdallah, arrived in India in 1067. Hindus who converted were called 'Bohra'.[15] The arrival of Jalal, the twenty-fifth spiritual leader, or *dâ'î mutlaq* ('supreme propagandist'), marked the end of the sect's Yemeni phase and the beginning of its leaders' establishment in India. When the twenty-sixth *dâ'î mutlaq*, Daud (1567–91), died, a quarrel over succession split the Bohra yet again. Daud Burhanuddin (1591–1612) was enthroned as *dâ'î* in India; the Yemeni Bohra were informed of this. Four years later, however, Sulayman, grandson of the twenty-fourth *dâ'î* and Daud's 'vice-*dâ'î*', claimed the succession for himself and went back to India to secure his rights. The great majority of the Bohra – and some Tayyibi Isma'ilians in Yemen – recognized Daud Burhanuddin as the twenty-seventh *dâ'î mutlaq* and were thenceforth known as Daudi. A minority – mostly Yemenis, with a few Indian Bohra – accepted Sulayman as their spiritual leader, and were thenceforth called Sulaymani.

The Daudi Bohras' religious practices are very similar to those of other Muslims, especially the Shi'a. They observe the five pillars of Islam, and have added two more: submission to the 'hidden imam' [*walâya*] and a strict obligation to be pure [*tahâra*] which means that they have to wear special garments when they pray.[16]

The Daudi are organized along the lines of the model developed during the

Yemeni phase of Tayyibi Isma'ilism. The *dâ'î mutlaq*, sole representative of the hidden imam, has all the prerogatives entailed by his position. He has absolute authority over his community, and rules autocratically. The recalcitrant are excommunicated – they are not only excluded from any religious premises, either mosque or sanctuary, but also forbidden to organize ceremonies like weddings or burials; they are also subjected to a total social and professional boycott.

Unlike the Nizari, who emigrated to Pakistan in their thousands, four-fifths of the Bohra remained in India; their headquarters are still in Surat, in Gujarat. There are only about 33,000 Bohra in Pakistan today, 25,000 of them in Karachi alone. They are mainly tradesmen, and they are still under the authority of the *dâ'î mutlaq*.

The Sulaymani Bohra are very different from the Daudi – they are said to be one of the most progressive South Asian Muslim groups. Their spiritual leader lives in Saudi Arabia, near the border with Yemen; the sect's headquarters for the entire subcontinent are in the Indian town of Baroda. There are a few thousand in Pakistan; like the Daudi, they are concentrated in Karachi.

The Ahmadiyya

There is a third sectarian current in South Asian Islam: the Ahmadi movement, founded in the Punjab in 1889 by the eponymous Mirza Ghulam Ahmad (1838–1908) mainly as a reaction against the Arya Samaj Hindu revival movement and Christian missionaries. Prophetology lies at the heart of Ahmadi doctrine, and is also the major cause of hostility from anti-Ahmadi Muslims. Ghulam Ahmad believed that he was endowed with the spiritual qualities of a prophet, and therefore considered himself to be one. This claim went against a sura in the Koran (33, 40) which declares that Muhammad was the 'seal of the prophets' [*khâtam al-anbiyâ'*].

The second distinguishing feature of Ahmadi doctrine is its belief in the 'human' death of Jesus, and his burial in Kashmir. This allowed Ghulam Ahmadi to argue with Christian missionaries who maintained that their religion was superior to Islam by emphasizing that – according to both Christian and Muslim belief – Jesus' death on the cross was only apparent, and that he still lives as an ontological principle. The Prophet Mohammed, on the other hand, died and was buried like other mortals. Ghulam Ahmad sought to propagate the notion that Jesus escaped crucifixion and went to India, where he died a natural death in Srinagar, Kashmir, at the age of a hundred and twenty.

Finally, Ghulam Ahmad pronounced a new theory of the *jihad* – his third point of difference from other Muslims. He saw it as a purely defensive war, or a war waged with the pen; this was his response to attacks from Christian missionaries who accused Islam of being a warlike religion.

If Ahmadiyya religious thought differs somewhat from orthodox Islamic thought, there is nothing particularly new as far as religious practice is concerned – this still draws its inspiration from Hanaphite rites.

In 1914, when Ghulam Ahmad's successor – a man called Nuruddin – died, the sect divided into two groups, the Qadiani and the Lahori. The Qadiani (so named after Qadian, Ghulam Ahmad's birthplace) perpetuate the doctrine of their spiritual guide as he preached it, and see him as a prophet [*nabî*[17]], condemning as *kâfir* (unbelievers) those – including fellow Muslims – who do not subscribe to this view. The Lahori[18] revere Ghulam Ahmad as a *mujaddid* (reformer), and are opposed to a break with the rest of the Muslim community. Nevertheless, as we shall see, they are no more immune than the Qadiani to attacks from Muslim 'orthodoxy' in Pakistan.

Since the Ahmadi movement began in the Punjab, the Ahmadiyya became citizens of Pakistan after Partition. Qadian became part of the Indian Union, and the (majority) Qadiani branch moved its headquarters to Rabwah, in the middle of the Pakistani Punjab. The Ahmadiyya (Qadiani and Lahori) make up 0.12 per cent of the population; they are one of the most educated groups in Pakistan, and have by tradition held senior posts in government, the army, and industry.

Sufism

Sufism[19] is the mystic, esoteric face of Islam. It complements the sharia, or external law, and reveals the inner meaning of Reality (Allah). It was first brought to the subcontinent by individual saints, then, after the thirteenth century, by whole congregations. Its many brotherhoods – which also illustrate the diversity of Islam in Pakistan – include the Chistiyya (from Afghanistan), the Suhrawardiyya (from the Near East), the Qadiriyya (which came from Iraq in the fifteenth century) and the Naqshabandiyya (brought from Central Asia by the Mughals in the sixteenth century).

In Pakistan – especially in Sind and the Punjab – Sufism, a vehicle for the expression of popular religiosity, usually takes the form of the worship of saints, who are said to have the power to intercede with God. Sanctuaries [*dargâh*] managed by descendants of the *pir* (spiritual master) – there are many all over the country – contain the tombs of saints, and are pilgrimage sites [*ziyârâ*]. Some are said to contain relics (hairs belonging to the Prophet, for example); this adds to their prestige. True centres of worship, they are visited by the faithful (Muslims as well as Hindus; Sunni and Shi'a alike), who come to receive the saint's blessing. Visitors make propitiatory gifts of food (*tabarruk*, the equivalent of *prasâd* in Hindu temples), brought to the sanctuary as offerings or tokens of gratitude. These *dargâh* ceremonies are reminiscent of popular Hinduism, just as the relationship between the *pir* (spiritual master) and the *murid* (disciple) recalls the relationship between the guru and his *chelâ* (the Hindu equivalent of disciple). The anniversary of the saints' death ['*urs*] is the crowning moment of life at the *dargâh*; it draws big crowds – sometimes several hundred thousand people. One of the most regularly visited mausoleums in Pakistan is that of Data Ganj Bakhsh, the patron saint of Lahore.[20]

The influence of the *pir*, whose position is always inherited by a family member (preferably a son), is due to the belief that they inherit the *baraka*, the religious charisma passed on by a saint to his descendants. Since they tend to receive many donations from the pious as if they were personal gifts, many of them are immensely rich and own vast estates. As a result of their religious and social duties (weddings, services, etc.), they have strong links with their disciples in close clientelist networks.

This is why the *dargâh* are a political force to be reckoned with: they represent an essential component of Pakistan's political life.

Intergroup and Group–State Relations

Thus Islam in Pakistan covers a myriad of groups and subgroups, and is fraught with divisions which can lead to conflict. Truly enough, the Sunni do not present a united front, but the divisions between the different subgroups are above all doctrinal; these differences have led to rivalries (notably between the Deobandi and the Barelwi), but not necessarily violent confrontations. Moreover, the Sunni movements, over and beyond their ideological allegiances, share a common appropriation – or an attempt at appropriation – of Islam by virtue of which they claim to be the only true Muslims; some of them – either together or separately – put pressure – sometimes violent pressure – on the state to purify Pakistani society by eliminating other sects. Hence there is a complex triangular dynamic which sets the state and Sunni groups against non-Sunni groups and/or non-Muslims (such as the Christians, who are victimized both by the state and by Islamic groups). In this context, the relationship between the first two groups seems to be unassailable: it conditions the destiny reserved for the third group – a destiny which, in the Pakistan of today, increasingly takes the form of exclusion.

The Anti-Ahmadi movements[21] of 1953 and 1974

The anti-Ahmadi movements of the 1950s were a prelude to contemporary sectarian conflicts. They were started by the Ahrar[22] (not by the Jamaat-i Islami, as is often believed, even if they played their part[23], who wanted the Ahmadiyya to be declared a non-Muslim minority. This move certainly did not succeed – not only did the state refuse to give in to this pressure, but several Islamic leaders (including Maududi) were imprisoned, and the Constituent Assembly of the day took advantage of the disturbances to exclude the religious leaders from the drafting of the Constitution. Nevertheless, it showed how hostile Pakistan's Sunni groups were towards sectarian and religious minorities – a relentless hostility which was to increase over the following decades. Some of the most prominent Shi'a leaders, however, also took part in this move against the Ahmadiyya, sometimes in league with the very Sunni leaders who were to become the most vehement anti-Shi'a.[24]

The Ahmadi question, which was pushed into the background when a military regimes were in power, resurfaced during Zulfikar Ali Bhutto's period in office (1971–77). In 1973 there were violent anti-Ahmadi riots accompanied by rumours, propagated by Islamic parties, to the effect that Bhutto was not only a bad Muslim, but also enjoyed the financial and organizational support of the Ahmadi community. This combination of riots and rumours forced him to declare them a non-Muslim minority by constitutional amendment in 1974. Their leader, Hazrat Mirza Tahir Ahmad, fled to London; from where he continues to lead his community.

The Zia years: Islamization and sectarianism in Pakistan

Zia ul-Haq (notably under the influence of the Jamaat-i Islami, to which he was close) took his own measures against the Ahmadiyya in 1984: he added an article to the penal code which forbade them to call themselves Muslims, to preach their faith, to use Islamic terminology, or to practise Muslim rites.

Since the introduction of these discriminatory laws, the Ahmadiyya have regularly been subjected to persecution in Pakistan – as much by the state and Islamic groups as by society in general, which takes a dim view of their financial clout and their excellent organization. The anti-Ahmadi laws sometimes serve as a pretext for resolving personal disputes. Today, individual attacks and riots against the Ahmadiyya are still going on; as a result, some of them have gone into exile.

The main effect of Zia's Islamization policy, however, was to create a chasm between Sunni and Shi'a.[25] Of course there had been differences between these two main sects throughout the entire history of Islam, but they were mainly doctrinal. In the subcontinent at the beginning of the twentieth century, a dispute that went beyond mere religious differences set Sunni against Shi'a: hitherto, the communities had lived together relatively peacefully, but in Lucknow, which was known to have a large Shi'a population, there were increasingly violent confrontations between supporters from both sides. This violence sprang from socioeconomic as well as political causes: its roots lay in the decline and impoverishment of the Shi'a aristocracy, while some Sunni groups were fairly prosperous. It was accentuated by the fact that the British imposed a legal aspect on the rift between the two sects (by arbitrating disputes, authorizing or forbidding religious commemorations, controlling processions, etc.), thereby politicizing the conflict.[26]

In Pakistan, it seems to have been Zia's Islamization policy which played the role of catalyst in this conflict. Following a narrow Sunni interpretation of Islamic law, he tried to make the payment of *zakât* (canonical alms) obligatory for Shi'a, thus going against the Shi'a tradition according to which such payments are voluntary. In 1979–80, the Shi'a expressed their opposition to this measure with a campaign of violence, even defying the martial law which prohibited demonstrations. In the end Zia gave in, much to the chagrin of the army and Sunni Islamists. The military did not approve of the Shi'a' show of force – they had dared to defy martial law, and hence their authority. The Shi'a' activism was also a strategic problem for the army, because it was supported by Tehran at a time when Pakistan was very worried about Khomeini's international ambitions: Iran was obviously trying to spread its internal revolution to other countries? As a matter of fact, Iran did play an important part in politicizing the Shi'a of Pakistan.

As for the Sunni Islamists, they considered that Zia's capitulation constituted a blow against Islamization – all the more so as some Sunni were pretending to be Shi'a in order to avoid paying the new compulsory tax. The Sunni Islamists began to think of the Shi'a as a major obstacle on the road to the Islamic state of which they dreamed. As a result, Zia's government, in an attempt both to contain Shi'a violence and to limit Iran's influence in Pakistan, made an effort to strengthen Sunni institutions – notably by choosing to set up new Sunni *madrasahs*.

This spectacular proliferation of *madrasahs* – the other major effect of Zia's Islamization policy – has become a fundamental characteristic of Islam in Pakistan. These Koranic schools have a major impact not only on the conflict between Sunni and Shi'a in Pakistan but also on relations between the various Islamic movements and the state. Before Zia came to power, there had been few religious schools [*díní madárís*] – only 137 when the country was created – and their influence was negligible. From 1979 onwards, Zia implemented a reform programme which would allow the *madrasahs* to be an officially recognized part of Pakistan's education system, just like secular schools, on condition that they included 'modern' subjects (English, social sciences, arithmetic, etc.) in their curricula. The General used the proceeds of the *zakât* to finance existing *madrasahs* and set up new ones. He hoped that this policy would enable him not only to strengthen Sunni institutions and make the ulemas accept his leadership, thereby stamping his regime with the seal of Islamic legitimacy, but also to exercise some control over these schools, and hence to temper the zeal of clergy, teachers and students alike. Now, these schools were affiliated to the main Islamic currents in Pakistan (Deobandi, Barelwi, Twelver Shi'a, the Jamaat-i Islami and the Ahl-i Hadith, in order of numerical importance[27]). This strategy was at least temporarily effective, because – with the exception of the Shi'a – Islamic movements in general supported Zia's regime in the early days (as a result, they were later discredited in the eyes of the Pakistani people).

The combined policy of financing through the *zakât* and official recognition of their qualifications led to an explosion in the number of *madrasahs*: in 1974 they accounted for 18 per cent of all educational establishments in Pakistan; by 1983 this proportion had risen to 40.3 per cent. In 1999 the total number of *madrasah*, of all sectarian persuasions combined, was put at 7,000.[28] Thus hundreds of thousands of young people have been educated in these schools, but the government never attempted to implement a policy that would have enabled them to find jobs; this sowed the seeds for future problems.

The Deobandi and the Shi'a were the two schools of thought whose number of affiliated *madrasahs* grew most rapidly. It was the Deobandi *madrasahs*, some of which also provided military training, that were the breeding-ground for talk and literature about sectarian violence. The main Sunni party involved in the anti-Shi'a campaigns – the Sunni Sipah-i Sahaba Pakistan (SSP, the Pakistani Army of the Companions of the Prophet), founded in 1985 – was originally a branch of the Deobandi party, the JUI, from which it soon broke away but with which it still maintains relations. Its Shi'a equivalent is the Tahrik-i Jafaria Pakistan (TJP, Pakistani Shi'a Movement), founded in 1979.[29]

Not only did the *madrasahs* receive state funding, they were also financed by foreign powers – the Shi'a schools by Iran; the Sunni schools by Iraq and Saudi Arabia, two countries which are very anxious to make sure that Pakistan remains a predominantly Sunni nation. The war in Afghanistan made matters worse, because a power struggle was also being waged there between Saudi Arabia and Iran. Moreover, the Pakistani state used the *madrasahs* to bolster Sunnism in strategically important places like the NWFP, because from there they would be able to start a *jihad* in Afghanistan.

The 1990s: an explosion of sectarian violence

As a result of the Islamization policy and the intensifying rivalries between foreign powers on Pakistani (and Afghan) soil during the 1980s, the sectarian conflict between Sunni and Shi'a assumed tragic proportions during the following decade, leaving several hundred dead and thousands wounded. This violence, which has become ubiquitous in some parts of Pakistan, explodes with particular force during *muharram* processions which commemorate the tragedy of Kerbala. Sunni and Shi'a pursue their respective traditions of *maddhe sahâba* and *tabarrû*: the first takes the form of a recitation glorifying the first three caliphs recognized by Sunnis; the second that of attacks against them. The month of Ramadan can also be violent: religious fervour reaches a peak at this time of year, so it is easy for sectarian organizations to manipulate their militants into committing acts of terrorism against members of the rival sect.

The scale of this violence has continued to grow during the 1990s. Support from the Gulf states has radicalized Sunni groups; everyone is trying to raise the stakes by violent means, physical as well as verbal, in order to obtain the biggest share of the funds. As for the war in Afghanistan, not only has it transformed militant organizations into paramilitary organizations won over to the 'kalashnikov culture' and influenced by Taliban militancy, it has also fostered the emergence of criminal networks living off the drugs trade and smuggling. Now these traffickers have established links with sectarian militants: the former see sectarian violence as a cover for their criminal activities; the latter obtain money and training that helped them to continue their terrorist acts. The participation of the Mafia and other criminal organizations probably explains this escalating violence – such groups have fewer scruples about killing people while they are praying in mosques or at cemeteries (in January 1998, for example, 25 Shi'a attending a funeral were murdered at the cemetery in Mominpura, Lahore, setting off a cycle of violent episodes which left 150 dead in various parts of the country).[30]

The state finds it very difficult to control these sectarian organizations, since they claim to be acting in the name of Islam. Since sectarianism itself is considered to be an 'Islamic' problem, these organizations have enjoyed the tacit support of Pakistan's leading political parties, both secular (the PPP, the PML) and religious. Religious parties have used their influence to stop sectarian militants being arrested, in the hope that this tactic will gain them the support of pro-Islamist voters. The police are too incompetent and corrupt to be able – or even willing – to stem the tide of violence between Sunni and Shi'a. As for the army and the secret services, they are suspected of taking advantage of the trouble caused by sectarian conflict to put pressure on governments during democratic interludes. Finally, the sectarian movements still have the support of the Taliban and 'jihadist'[31] organizations like the Harkat-ul Ansar (HUA), now the Harkat-ul Mujahiddin (HUM) – a 'subsidiary' of the SSP, which is waging a guerrilla war in Kashmir.[32]

The *madrasahs*, an element of society which the government promoted with a view to being able to control it better, also presents it with a problem. Those which it finances itself are still in a dependent position, and few of these propound extremist ideas. But the others – especially those that are funded from abroad – are another matter. Several times since 1995 the government has tried to prevent foreign financing of *madrasahs* that preach sectarianism, but to no avail – they simply falsify the source of their funding, presenting it as income from gifts or all kinds of business activities (such as publishing). Moreover, militant teachings do not necessarily appear in their textbooks: they are often disseminated orally, which makes it more difficult to control them. Young people usually start attending these schools at a very early age, so they are easily indoctrinated into believing that they are the only genuine Muslims. They often find it impossible to get a job; hence they have no alternative but to struggle for a 'true' Islamic society from which other sects would be excluded.[33]

There is another reason why the government is finding its struggle against sectarian organizations difficult: the biggest parties, such as the SSP, seek to recruit members mainly from those who are excluded from society, the victims of the breakdown of traditional communities; however, the bulk of their support comes from certain middle-class circles, especially those which are vying for power with big Shi'a landowners. One of the SSP's objectives is precisely to fight the big rural magnates, many of whom – in the Punjab, the principal sectarian battleground – are not only Shi'a, but Sufis as well:[34] since the SSP has strong ideological links with the Deobandi, it is also trying to fight against the influence of the *pir*.

The roots of the conflict between Sunni and Shi'a also lie in urbanization and the changing social status of certain sectors of the middle class: they have either become poorer or suddenly become spectacularly rich, like the workers who have returned from the Persian Gulf; in fact the emergence of sectarian organizations coincided with the return of large numbers of these workers in the mid-1980s. In general these people are from deprived rural backgrounds, but they have seen their income rise by 600 to 800 per cent, and when they came home they settled in the urban areas. Thus the rise of the sectarian organizations has satisfied the need of whole categories of people (migrants, but non-migrants as well) for an urban religious identity, and has also provided an alienated middle class with a sense of status.[35]

So Islam in Pakistan has a very peculiar complexion. It may be the official ideology that unites the country, but it is nevertheless extremely diverse, at a crossroads between the Arab–Iranian and Indian worlds. For the most part, ordinary people express their religious sentiments through Sufism, which in this corner of the world means the worship of saints. Today, however, the composite nature of Islam in Pakistan is in jeopardy more than ever. There are many deep-seated causes of sectarian conflict: quite apart from mere doctrinal differences, there are economic, social and political factors to consider. But above all, such conflict is a symptom of an ideological confusion which means that both the state and the Islamist parties feel a need constantly to reiterate the fact that Pakistan is a Muslim country, and to define the 'true' Muslim in ever narrower terms.

11

ISLAM AND POLITICS

Many Westerners were shocked when General Zia ul-Haq, soon after he took power in 1977, brought in flagrantly 'Islamic' punishments like public floggings, and compared Pakistan to Saudi Arabia, where Islamic law controls every aspect of life. Nevertheless, Islamist disciples of Abul-Ala Maududi, who served in Zia's first government, soon joined the opposition on the grounds that this Islamization of the law was a mere 'cosmetic' façade, and that there was still a long way to go before Pakistan could really be called an 'Islamic state'. Whom are we to believe?

If we are to understand the extent of Islam's influence over political life in Pakistan, we must go back to the events that surrounded the country's foundation. The decrees issued in the late 1970s were themselves the result of what happened during Pakistan's first ten years of life – especially the long constitutional debate, begun in 1948, which finally produced the 1956 Constitution. This first text – which was the result of hard-won compromise, and for the most part is still valid – imposed limits on Islam's role within the state.

The Significance of Islam at the Time of Partition

Pakistan, which was created in 1947 to unite regions of the Indian subcontinent where the Muslims were in the majority, could not dodge the question of religion's role in politics: Islam had figured prominently in the process which led to Partition. First, the demand for such a state was based on two premises which were spelled out in the 1940 Lahore Resolution, which put forward the Muslim League's ideological agenda: inasmuch as Islam embodied a civilization which was diametrically opposed to and incompatible with Hinduism, the Muslims of the subcontinent constituted a separate nation; as a small minority (24 per cent of the population of British India) they would not be able to protect their rights in elected institutions in the event that colonial domination was supplanted by a united India. For its advocates, the creation of Pakistan was essential for the protection of the religious identity of the subcontinent's Muslims. In addition, in the campaign for the 1945–46 elections the Muslim League consistently used religious arguments: they employed men of religion (genuine or spurious) for propaganda purposes: ulemas (doctors of religious Law) and, above all, *pir* (Sufi masters), who were especially influential in the countryside; the League was therefore in their debt. This call to religion explains the Muslim voters' massive support for the League's programme – even in regions where the Muslims were in the minority, which were destined to remain part of India.

Partition left hundreds of thousands dead (they are considered martyrs [*shahîd*]) and millions of refugees, known as Muhajirs [*muhajir*], after the first Muslims who followed the Prophet into exile at Medina and established the first 'Islamic state' in 622. In the early years Pakistan found it difficult to forget these religious associations, the tremendously powerful emotions they had aroused and the suffering and sacrifice to which they had given rise.

Finally, there was the sheer weight of an increasingly overwhelming Muslim majority. Massacres and population movements on both sides of the border at the time of Partition had constituted a thorough ethnic 'cleansing' [*safa'i*] (a phrase already in use at that time), since high-caste Sikhs and Hindus had fled from both halves of Pakistan. Only 3 per cent of the population in the west were non-Muslims in 1971: apart from a few high-caste tradesmen who stayed in Sind, Baluchistan and the NFWP, and a few well-educated Parsee (Zoroastrian) businessmen, they were mainly Untouchables who were still Hindus or had become Christians. Only in eastern Pakistan (which became Bangladesh in 1971) was there still a significant minority (25 per cent) of Hindus, mainly low-caste: with conflicts and riots, the number of non-Muslims continued to decrease – today, Hindus and a few Christians make up only about 10 per cent of the population of Bangladesh.

Once the eastern part of the country had seceded, minorities – now only 3 per cent of the total population – became demographically negligible. Nevertheless, two groups were ideologically significant – albeit in a negative sense – because they were the indispensable scapegoats of those who wanted a scrupulously pure Islamic state: the Christians (about 1.5 per cent of the population) and the tiny heterodox Ahmadiyya or Ahmadi sect (well below 0.5 per cent), which originated in a breakaway Sunni group at the end of the nineteenth century, led by Mirza Ghulam Ahmad (who died in 1908). This visionary, who regarded himself as a modern-day prophet, surrounded himself with a strong community of educated and influential believers who were deeply committed to missionary activity on a worldwide scale. From the start the Ahmadiyya clashed with orthodox Sunni theologians who considered belief in any prophet after Muhammad to be a form of apostasy punishable by death; in 1974 the Parliament of Pakistan would pronounce them non-Muslims.[1] In 1947, however, non-Muslims could make their voices heard in the constitutional debate, because they made up about 15 per cent of the total population, and held 15 of the 68 seats in the Constituent Assembly as a result of the system of separate electorates.

Even this Muslim majority, however, is – as we have seen – by no means homogeneous, even though it had to present a united front against the Hindus at the time of Partition. If we are to understand the first riots of the 1950s, and above all the sectarian conflicts which broke out in the 1980s, we must remember that the great majority of Pakistan's Muslims – 75 per cent or more (there are no reliable statistics) – are Sunni, or orthodox, Muslims; they follow the Hanafi school of religious law – the predominant school in the Indian subcontinent – which entails a plethora of spiritual concepts and political options. The Sunni will always be politically dominant, and will lead debates on the Islamic constitution.

Alongside them is a significant Shi'a minority – estimated at between 15 and 25 per cent – whose wealth gives them influence. As we have seen, the Shi'a are divided into two main subsects. On one side are the Twelvers, who – as in Iran – await the return of the twelfth imam; they own estates around Jhang, in the Punjab, and in Sind – Zulfikar Ali Bhutto (1928–79) belonged to this group. On the other are the Isma'ilis, distant heirs of the Fatimid caliphate of Cairo, who recognize only seven imams; they are the great traders of India's western coast, from Hindu merchant castes, and have themselves been divided from the outset into two rival sects: the Khoja, led by the Aga Khan – including Muhammad Ali Jinnah, the founder of Pakistan – and the Bohra, whose leader, the Sayyedna, is in Bombay. Some of these Isma'ilis, who moved from Bombay to Karachi with Jinnah at the time of Partition, were members of the twenty-two great families who dominated Pakistan's economy until Bhutto took power in 1971. Each sect retains its own family laws on marriage, divorce and inheritance, as codified by the British under the title Anglo-Muslim law. The other very tiny sect is the Ahmadiyya, which – as we have just seen – was pronounced a non-Muslim minority in 1974.

It was Jinnah, a member of the Isma'ilian Shi'a minority, who took the initiative in the constitutional debate. He was both governor general of the new dominion of Pakistan and president of the Constituent Assembly; his assistant was his Prime Minister, Liaquat Ali Khan (1895–1951), *ex officio* president of the Muslim League. Like their Indian counterparts, these men had to prepare and gain acceptance for a constitution as quickly as possible, in order to establish the country's political institutions and define the role which would be played by religion. Would Pakistan be simply a country with an overwhelming Muslim majority, but no special constitutional niche for Islam? In other words, was Pakistan moving towards a 'secular' constitution, like the one that would be promulgated in India in 1950, under whose terms religion – at least in principle – is a personal matter, and all religions are recognized to have equal status? Or, on the contrary, should Islam and the Muslim majority be accorded special favour by making Pakistan a religious state, thereby conducting a constitutional 'experiment' (this, too, is a term used at that time) comparable – in its own way – to the one Israel was conducting at the time (to make a now-classic comparison)?

Jinnah – who had not hesitated to exploit Islam's vote-winning potential – now tried to calm things down, and to confine religion to the private sphere. At the first meeting of the Constituent Assembly, on 11 August 1947, he said: 'In the course of time Hindus would cease to be Hindus and Muslims would cease to be Muslims, not in the religious sense, because this is the personal faith of each individual, but in the political sense as citizens of the state.'[2]

This flew in the face of modernist politicians and men of religion, who could not do without some kind of Islamic legitimation. Jinnah soon became aware of their significance. Ignoring his initial declaration, which was subsequently censored, he promised on 25 January 1948 that the law of the country would be based on Islamic religious law, the *sharia*. Four days later, galvanized by fundamentalists, 'enraged Amazons' – according to the newspapers, they were in fact veiled women –

demonstrated in front ot the Punjab's Legislative Assembly, demanding that when farmland was handed on, women should be entitled to the portion laid down under Muslim law (about half of what the man got); under the customary law approved by the British, they had been deprived of their share.[3] Their apparently progressive cause was well chosen, but in fact this demonstration had been fomented by the men of religion.

So was Islam on the way to becoming the official religion in 1948? Was Pakistan destined to become an Islamic state? These terms had not yet been defined in constitutional form, and nothing had really been decided. Before we examine the ins and outs of the constitutional debate, and its outcome, we must understand the various protagonists' points of view.

Protagonists in the Constitutional Debate

We can divide the protagonists into three unequal camps: as well as a secularizing elite, which tried with varying degrees of success to play a mediating role in the debate, the main protagonists fell into two other camps – the modernists and the men of religion. They in turn had conflicting points of view which divided them further: secularizers and modernists followed a Western model; men of religion opposed this with a – supposedly – traditional model.

The secularizing elite

Jinnah's first option, a secular state, was favoured by two groups of people. First there were the non-Muslims – essentially the Hindus of East Bengal – who consistently fought for their secular option during the constitutional debates, but had no real chance of affecting the final decision. In the same camp – but with far more influence – was a secularizing Muslim elite from the three major state institutions: first, the administrators who took over from the Indian Civil Service; they included Ghulam Muhammad and Iskander Mirza, who succeeded Jinnah as governors general and tried to promote the idea of a secular constitution after the troubles in 1953. Then there was the army, which was champing at the bit throughout the constitutional debate – apart from the isolated example of the Rawalpindi conspiracy in 1951. Not until 1958 did Ayub Khan, who had worked closely with Ghulam Muhammad and Iskander Mirza, cross the Rubicon with the first military coup, and soon started to use religion for his own ends by switching to the modernist camp. Third, there were secularizers in the ranks of senior lawyers; it was these people who put forward the secular point of view most succinctly in judgements and writings such as those of A K Brohi, and above all Judge Muhammad Munir after the anti-Ahmadiyya riots of 1953.[4] For public servants, technical competence and the responsibility for maintaining the continuity and effectiveness of the state were sufficient guarantees of legitimacy; they had only to draw attention to the somewhat dubious religious pretensions of the modernist politicians, and espoused a declaration by Iskander Mirza, Interior Minister when the Constituent Assembly was dismissed in 1954, to the effect that 'religion and politics could and must be kept separate'.[5]

The modernists

The modernists, united around the Muslim League, believed that Islam was an indispensable ingredient of their political legitimacy. They were, however, reluctant to abandon their own political culture – that of a Western-style democracy on the British model, where laws are made by elected assemblies. They simply wanted to impart an Islamic legitimacy to their own institutions.

To this end they drew on an important authority: the poet, philosopher and politician Muhammad Iqbal, who was himself part of the early-twentieth-century Arab modernist tradition. Iqbal linked medieval political institutions to those of the modern world by means of the Arab concept of *ijma'*: 'consensus'. Traditionally, the consensus of the community – which is believed to be the third source of the law after the Koran and the *Sunna* (the Tradition of the Prophet) – allows Islam to be adapted to historical circumstances; however, the definition of consensus is a matter for the ulemas. For the modernists, with Iqbal at their head, the definition of consensus should be a matter for a much wider elite which should interpret public opinion. From there they moved on – imperceptibly – to the idea – hinted at by Iqbal and sanctioned by thinkers such as Fazlur Rahman (1919–88) – that directly elected assemblies could be the forum where consensus could emerge. Finally, it was explicitly acknowledged that the modern interpretation of Islamic Law, which would be the law of the country, would be the task of elected Muslim members of these assemblies; they would explain the consensus of the community and give it the force of law, without feeling that they were bound by the letter of medieval Muslim law. In this way Pakistan would become a Muslim state, and the assemblies, which would hold legislative power, would have Islamic legitimacy.

This clever hypothesis, however, came up against both theoretical and practical difficulties. The elected Muslims would find a consensus that was valid for them as believers. What about elected non-Muslims in a country where – since East Pakistan was still part of it – they made up more than 15 per cent of the population? This question was raised by modernist theoreticians of the time such as Khalifa Abdul Hakim, who had an official position, and the lawyer Kemal Faruki. They concluded that in an Islamic state, non-Muslims cannot take part in defining a consensus, and hence in making laws which would be binding on Muslims. They must have a separate role, preferably with separate electorates; those they elect would be second-rate members – even second-class citizens, as the men of religion would want them to be. This was the first formulation of the – subsequently recurrent – problem of the status of non-Muslims in an Islamic state: a problem which neither the modernists nor the fundamentalists could avoid, because it has to do with the very nature of this type of 'ideological state' (to use the kind of language that was much in vogue at the time).

The men of religion

The men of religion identified with political models that belonged to the past. They wanted to reform – even replace – Western-style institutions on the basis of medieval precedents. They had their disagreements, but they agreed on at least three points. First, they affirmed the supremacy of the Law revealed by God, which it was their sole mission to interpret – as opposed to the modernists, who had lawmaking aspirations; so the men of religion found common cause in the edifice of medieval law. Second, they believed that religious communities should be kept separate, and that they fell into a natural hierarchical order: in a Muslim state, non-Muslims could not enjoy the same prerogatives as Muslims. Finally, they were suspicious of Western democracy and the multiparty system. These three points of agreement constituted the point of departure for the differing approaches of the traditionalists and the fundamentalists.

The first approach was that of the ulemas, with their traditional religious knowledge – especially religious law, which they studied in books written in Arabic. The ulemas lived according to the medieval model: the *sharia*, the Law revealed by God and interpreted by the ulemas, should apply to every aspect of social life. Muslim sovereigns applied it through the intermediary of the ulemas – all teachers and judges were in fact ulemas. The ulemas did not have any novel ideas about how Pakistan should be governed. They wanted the modern state to be like a medieval caliphate, and their first priority was to make the government recognize their elevated status and restore them to their previous position.

The most dynamic among them, who belonged to the Deobandi school, had been recruited before Partition to campaign for Pakistan.[6] Jinnah had taken them from the Indian Association of Ulemas (the Jamiyyat-ul Ulama-i Hind, JUH), which fought alongside the Congress Party for an undivided India. Their leader, Shabbir Ahmad Usmani (who died in 1949), had formed an organization in Calcutta in 1945 in order to state the claim for Pakistan, the Association of Ulemas of Islam (Jamiyyat-ul Ulama-i Islam, JUI), which moved to Karachi after Partition and was immediately granted official recognition: Usmani became a member of the Constituent Assembly. He sought the assistance of two important people who played a part in the constitutional debate, Mufti Muhammad Shafi and his disciple Ihtishamul Haqq Thanavi, and also relied on the good offices of two great Indian authorities: Sulaiman Nadwi, who settled in Karachi, and Muhammad Hamidullah, who worked as a researcher at the CNRS in Paris. Another group, affiliated to the rival Barelwi school,[7] the Association of the Ulemas of Pakistan (Jamiyyat-ul Ulama-i Pakistan, JUP), was set up by Abdul Hamid Badauni in Karachi in 1948, but it played a minor role. These ulemas' associations, which became political parties in 1956, were a unique feature of Pakistan's political culture, which encouraged religious parties.

The fundamentalists, however, who had more definite ideas and strategies, snatched the initiative from the ulemas. Two personalities came to the fore. One was Muhammad Asad, born Leopold Weiss (1900–92), an Austrian convert who worked for the Punjabi government, devised a draft constitution, and became an intellectual model for the Egyptian Islamist Sayyid Qutb (1906–65). The fundamentalists' true guiding spirit, however, was the dynamic Abul-Ala Maududi (1903–79). Although he was schooled in the traditional disciplines of the ulemas – contrary to the popular hagiography, which says that he was self-taught – he wanted to re-erect the entire edifice of Islamic thought in a way that would adapt it to the modern world. He began with the supremacy of God and the transcendence of the revealed Law. An Islamic state should be completely orientated towards putting this Law into practice. To this end, it needed an authoritarian government led by the most worthy Muslims; there was no need for political parties, since the 'ideology' – this is the word he uses – which is Islam is indivisible; the Consultative Assembly around the head of state, and the head of state himself, should be elected on merit alone, with no partisan electoral campaign. If such an Islam – which should influence every aspcect of Muslim life – were put in place by state authority, all citizens would have to be good Muslims, and there would be no further problems. Maududi started to formulate this model of the Islamic state[8] in 1939. His 'Islamic revolution', however, would be a slow process, because upright leaders would have to be trained to take over from politicians who served corrupt regimes.

Even in this maximalist concept (I hesitate to call it utopian) there was still room for compromise and strategic skill. In 1942, Maududi – mindful of the possible creation of Pakistan – had set up his own religious and political organization in India, the Jamaat-i Islami (JI), thus surrounding himself with a small, close-knit group of disciples. He was against the Muslim League and its plans for Pakistan, because he did not consider that modernist politicians had the requisite Islamic qualities. He was, however, capable of adapting to new circumstances: in 1947 he went to Pakistan with his supporters and set up his headquarters in Lahore; here he held court with both modernist politicians and ulemas, and became the 'catalyst' for debate on the Islamic state.[9]

To this list we must also add a last and less important debating partner, the Ahrar party (the 'free' Muslims), a kind of armed militia set up in 1931 to defend the Muslims against attack from Hindu paramilitaries. This small party was obsessed with two ideas: it wanted some form of Islamic socialism; and it wanted the Ahmadiyya excluded from the Muslim community. Originally allied with the Congress Party, and won over to Pakistan only in 1949, the Ahrar would be in the news when they began the anti-Ahmadi movement.

Towards a First Compromise: The 1956 Constitution

India had voted in its Constitution in 1950, but to the Pakistanis' great shame, their constitutional debate went on for eight years: from 1948 until 1956. The complexity of the subject was not the main reason for the delay. Pakistan's governments had to deal with a number of urgent matters: the unresolvable dispute over Kashmir; the no less thorny problem of the institutional balance between the two halves of the country, which would find a tragic solution in the secession of Bangladesh; economic crises and the lack of foreign currency; poor harvests – not to mention the political instability caused by the institutional vacuum. The debate itself was tortuous. Until his death in September 1948, Jinnah – followed by his Prime Minister, Liaquat Ali Khan – tried to reorganize and strengthen the Muslim League in order to push through a modernist constitution; Liaquat Ali Khan paved the way for this on 12 March 1949, when a majority of Muslim members of the Constituent Assembly – opposed by the Hindu deputies – passed an Objectives Resolution which would feature at the head of all Pakistan's constitutions: a compromise according to which Western democratic elements would be preserved, while the Islamic nature of the state would be guaranteed. After the assassination of Liaquat Ali Khan in 1951, however, and the political troubles that followed, the Muslim League was in a weaker position: for more than a year, the constitutional initiative had been with its religious opponents.

The ulemas had made great efforts to set themselves up as religious experts: in 1948 Usmani had drawn up a detailed plan for a Ministry of Religion and Justice, and decided whom to put in the various posts. But they had no constitutional doctrine, and they had let their fundamentalist opponent Abul-Ala Maududi, who was much better at this kind of thing, act first.

In January and February 1948, Maududi, who held court with both modernists and traditionalists, had delivered two lectures at Lahore's College of Law, in which he revealed his plans for making Pakistan an Islamic state. He was ready to go over the ulemas' heads and strike a deal with Westernized politicians: if they agreed to a gradual introduction of the *sharia* into existing institutions, Parliament could discuss interpretation of the Divine Law. If this process was followed, he said optimistically, Pakistan could become an Islamic state within ten years! Inspired by Maududi, the ulemas raised the stakes during 1948, forcing the government to pass the famous Declaration of Objectives, which guaranteed the Islamic character of the future Constitution, in 1949.

A commission made up of ulemas, the Board of Talimat-i Islamia, was then given the task of informing members of the Constituent Assembly about the 'Islamic teachings' which would be enshrined in the Constitution. In 1950 it presented a somewhat medieval picture in which the head of state would hold office for life: he should be a male Muslim, a kind of caliph who would use Islam as an 'ideological' (this was the very word they used) cement to unite a country where non-Muslims would be sidelined. Finally, this head of state would be chosen by the ulemas themselves, not by an elected Assembly; with the aid of a council of ulemas, he would have the power to define and interpret Islamic law, and would be responsible for dispensing justice.

Such a programme, which deprived the democratically elected modernist politicians of all legislative power, and negated all the validity of the consensus they were supposed to represent, could not, of course, be enshrined in the Constitution. The unequal treatment of non-Muslims would damage Pakistan's image in India and the West. After an interim report on the constitutional debate, therefore, Liaquat Ali Khan buried the ulemas' recommendations for the time being. Then, during 1952, an idea came to light which subsequently became very popular: remove Parliament's ultimate legislative authority, and give the courts – especially the Supreme Court – the job of deciding whether or not a given law conformed to the demands of Islam. Muhammad Asad had devised this notion in 1948; Maududi took it over and promoted it in 1952, getting the ulemas to accept it. It was not enshrined in the early constitutions, but it was implemented under Zia ul-Haq's regime.

Then, for political reasons, the debate became public. The ulemas made a mistake. Pulled in the wake of the Ahrar, with the clandestine encouragement of Mian

Mumtaz Daultana, head of the provincial government of the Punjab, and supported by the most radical fringe of the JI, which enlisted Maududi against his will, they launched an anti-Ahmadi campaign, demanding that the Constitution should pronounce the Ahmadiyya non-Muslims. In early 1953, this campaign led to murderous riots in Lahore, which gave the secular government an excuse to be ruthless. Maududi – who had eventually jumped on the bandwagon – was arrested and condemned to death (he was subsequently pardoned). This was when Judge Munir wrote his famous report. Immediately afterwards, Muhammad Ali Bogra's government sketched out a secular Interim Constitution – this was never made public, for it collapsed in the face of opposition from both the modernists and the men of religion. The secularizing elite's final effort, in October 1954, was dissolution of the Constituent Assembly by the governor general, Ghulam Muhammad, who wanted both to resolve an internal political crises and to reduce the pressure from the men of religion. The secularizing project, however, could not succeed: the politicians needed Islamic legitimacy.

The debate went on for another two years with another Constituent Assembly, without much in the way of new advances. It finally produced the 1956 Constitution, which represented the final balancing act between the modernists and the men of religion. The latter had their way on various points: Pakistan was proclaimed an 'Islamic republic'; the President had to be a Muslim; at the head of the Constitution was the 'Declaration of Objectives' which affirmed the sovereignty of Allah and guaranteed Muslims the right to live according to the Law of Islam; it also included 'Principles of Policy' which stipulated that links with other Muslim countries should be established, and that the necessary measures for the religious instruction of Muslims, together with the promotion of their religious institutions and the standards of Islamic morality, should be taken. The head of state must set up a teaching and research organization to 'help rebuild an Islamic society', and a Consultative Commission on Islamic Ideology which would have the duty of ensuring that the laws passed by Parliament were in conformity with the Koran and the Tradition (Sunna) handed down by the Prophet: members of this Commission would be chosen by the government.

These Islamic clauses fell well short of the men of religion's minimum demands: the word *sharia* was carefully avoided; the Commission charged with ensuring that laws were in conformity with the Koran and the Tradition had only a consultative role; and the ulemas were in the minority on it. It was not the theologians but the state which would have the last word. This compromise definitely favoured the modernists, who had made only token concessions to the religious groups.

Since these groups (that is to say, the JUI, the JUP and the JI) had not been able to achieve a special place in the state apparatus, they changed themselves into political parties so that they could promote their ideas in public. This decision went against their declared principle according to which there should be no parties in an Islamic state, where political truth was indivisible. These religious parties, which are a unique feature of Pakistan's political landscape, may be minority parties (their best performance was 15.5 per cent of the vote in the first general election in 1970), but they have an incalculable influence because of their continuing strategy of outbidding: they always support the conservatives and give their demands religious overtones, so that their opponents have to do the same. Ayub Khan might have known how to escape this trap, but Bhutto – as we shall see – fell right into it. Finally, the most powerful of these religious parties – powerful not in terms of number of votes but in terms of enterprise and nuisance-causing capacity – is the JI: it has a coherent political doctrine, and if it needs back-up it can call on the terrible Students' Association (Islami Jamiat-i Tulaba, IJT), which is only too willing to resort to violence, imposing a reign of terror in campuses and often in the streets.

How the Compromise Changed

Would the 1956 compromise remain throughout all the changing regimes, or would it be fundamentally altered by subsequent constitutions: Ayub Khan's in 1962, and the one drawn up by Bhutto in 1973 – which, thanks to subsequent amendments, is still in force? In fact, these constitutional changes led the country in various different directions.

Ayub Khan's modernism

General Ayub Khan, who took power with the first military *coup d'état* in 1958, had modernist inclinations. He had worked closely with the secularizing elite during the constitutional debate, and he was prepared to grant the men of religion only the minimal concessions to guarantee Islamic legitimacy. He had other concerns: anxious to govern effectively, and to encourage development, he sought to depoliticize society and impose an authoritative regime of guided democracy, on the lines of the military dictatorships that were much in vogue at the time in the Third World (Egypt, Nepal, Indonesia . . .). Quite apart from its other effects, this banished the question of the Islamization of the state from the scene. Ayub Khan took advantage of this situation to renege on the concessions made to the men of religion in 1956.

His first – highly symbolic – attempt failed. He tried to adapt the 1962 Constitution – which increased the authority of the head of state by establishing a presidential regime, and depoliticized society by implementing a pyramidal voting system – to suit himself by proposing to remove the adjective 'Islamic' from the country's official name, describing it as the 'Republic of Pakistan' rather than the 'Islamic Republic of Pakistan'. This caused uproar among the men of religion, and the General had to retreat and restore the adjective 'Islamic' by a 1963 amendment. He therefore had to subscribe – at least with token gestures – to the Islamic nature of the state: from that moment on, Islam was the indispensable ingredient of political legitimacy. This was the final nail in the coffin of Pakistan as a secularizing state.

Nevertheless, Ayub Khan refused to give in. He kept his sights fixed on modernism, come hell or high water – notably with the proclamation in 1961, after six years of hard bargaining with the men of religion, of the Muslim Family Law Ordinance, which restricted polygamy and protected women's rights. Under Ayub Khan, therefore, changes in the compromise tended to take a modernizing direction.

Bhutto opens the floodgates of fundamentalism

Ayub Khan's fall from power in 1969, and the troubles attendant upon the secession of Bangladesh, led to a repoliticization of the country, and raised fresh legitimation problems. Zulfikar Ali Bhutto, who came to power in 1971, devised a new constitution in 1973; its distinctive feature was the reestablishment of a parliamentary regime. At that time, the Islamic clauses were not altered much: the Consultative Commission on Islamic Ideology became a Consultative Council on Islamic Ideology, but there was no significant change in its composition: its members were still appointed by the government, and the ulemas were still in the minority. The real changes in the compromise under Bhutto were of another kind, or came later.

Where ideology was concerned, Ayub Khan's paternalism was replaced by 'socialism', which in fact meant populism, for Bhutto owed his power to the way in which he had exploited the legitimate grievances of the working classes. But he did not stop at profane language: he flagrantly and deliberately used religion to whip up the crowds, as Liaquat Ali Khan had done for a while before he was killed. An impassioned public speaker, Bhutto praised the merits of 'Islamic socialism', which was quickly rebaptized 'Mohammedan equality' [*musawat-i Muhammadî*]. Ending Pakistan's isolation, he gave himself international legitimacy in the name of Islam by playing a dominant role in the Islamic Conference Organization, the Muslim countries' federal body, summoning it to a meeting in Pakistan. The outbidding tactics of the religious parties, which criticized his nationalization policy on behalf of the wealthy, gradually drew him on to the terrain of laws and the Constitution; paradoxically, it led him to change the compromise not in a modernizing direction, as Ayub Khan had done, but in the direction of fundamentalism. This was done in two stages. First, he yielded to the men of religion's demands by pronouncing the Ahmadiyya non-Muslims, whereas preceding conservative governments had pushed this demand firmly into the background after the 1953 riots. This concession, fraught with danger for the future, was agreed in 1974 by a socialist Parliament which was completely under Bhutto's thumb. By thus drawing a line of demarcation between Muslims and non-Muslims, Bhutto gave full approval to the division between full citizens, the Muslims, and the non-Muslims, whose constitutional status was thereby lowered to that of second-class citizens. They were debarred from high state office and had to hold separate elections; and although they were free to practise their religion, they could not proselytize, whereas Muslims were encouraged to do so. Thus Bhutto opened the floodgates for the persecution which would increasingly be the lot not only of the Ahmadiyya but also of the Christians (and, incidentally, the Hindus, even the animists), as we shall see below.

The second stage marked the end of Bhutto's regime. Cornered by a right-wing coalition which he – mistakenly – believed would defeat him in the 1977 elections, he proclaimed that the law of the country was now *sharia* law. This term – hitherto carefully avoided in official texts – is imprecise; it, too, is fraught with danger, because it covers every domain that is codified in medieval Islamic law. Was Bhutto going to give the men of religion everything they wanted? Had his regime survived, it would soon have found itself in a legislative, political and constitutional impasse. So Bhutto, in taking a direction that was diametrically opposed to that of Ayub Khan, set the compromise on a path that was no longer modernist, but led straight into the clutches of the men of religion.

Zia ul-Haq puts fundamentalism into practice

Paradoxically, General Zia ul-Haq, who is usually held uniquely responsible for the Islamization of Pakistan's legal system, restored matters by setting limits on the Islamization of the country. As a conservative and JI sympathizer, he must have harboured fundamentalist convictions, but his behaviour was by no means fanatical; in fact it was coolly reasonable. Taking advantage of Bhutto's concessions, he made a great show of declaring that he was in favour of the Islamization of state institutions, producing a programme that was very much like that of the JI. The JI, falling straight into the trap, provided ministers who served in Zia's first government. It quickly realized that this had been a mistake, and joined the opposition.

If we examine the decrees promulgated at this time closely, we see that they actually place very strict limits on the application of the *sharia*, confining it to a few prominent domains of criminal law. First there is the meting out of Islamic punishments: stoning or whipping for adultery; amputation for theft; whipping for the use of intoxicants; prison or the death penalty for blasphemy. As for criminal proceedings, only the rules of evidence were changed: the worth of a woman's evidence was reduced by half, so that it took two female witnesses to equate to one man. Another decree introduced two canonical religious taxes, which were added to existing state taxes and would be used to finance religious institutions: compulsory alms [*zakât*] and land tax [*ushr*]. Finally, there was an innovation that would have far-reaching consequences for the rampant Islamization of the legal system: the establishment of special shariat benches in provincial courts and the Supreme Court which would repeal laws that were contrary to Islam (this initiative was reminiscent of Maududi's suggestion, described above). These decrees were only partially enforced: thieves did not have their hands amputated, and there were no stonings; in general, the only such punishment used was whipping; nevertheless, some people were condemned to death for blasphemy.

All in all, these decrees covered only a small – albeit very public – part of the legal system. Anglo-Indian law was still in force, and ordinary courts continued to sit; the power of the shariat benches, attached to provincial courts to ensure that laws were in conformity with the *sharia*, was limited to certain aspects of the law, mainly criminal law. Outside their remit were family law (where the *sharia* had an elective status, as a result – strangely enough – of Ayub Khan's modernist ordinances in 1961), tax and financial legislation, and most procedural codes.

In effect, Zia had established a dual system dominated by Anglo-Indian-type modernist law, where Islamic law was relegated to a minor – albeit symbolic and spectacular – role. The problem of the intellectual and juridical coherence of this juxtaposition has not yet been solved.

After Zia: No Change, or Back to Fundamentalism?

Would there be no further concessions to the men of religion after General Zia's death in 1988, and the restoration of democracy? This seemed likely, and those who voted for Benazir Bhutto certainly hoped so. In fact, if we look at the two prime ministers who alternated between 1988 and 1999 – Benazir Bhutto (1988–90; 1993–6) and Nawaz Sharif (1990–3; 1997–9), we cannot be so sure. Over the course of those ten years, Islamic legislation made great strides, and there was an unprecedented increase in intercommunal violence. But does this mean that the fortifications against the encroachments of the men of religion had fallen into disrepair?

Five time bombs

The advance of religious legislation can partly be explained by the lingering effects of Zulfikar Ali Bhutto and Zia ul-Haq's Islamization policy. They started a process that went on after they had gone: some of the institutions they had set up, like the Islamic courts or the funding of religious education, continued to have (often undesired) effects. Finally, and above all, in a system where minority religious parties won concessions through a process of tactical outbidding that came close to moral blackmail, governments could not renege on their predecessors' concessions for fear of being considered bad Muslims. In such circumstances, the previous regime's decisions still functioned like time bombs, strengthening Islam's hold on institutions and society in general.

The first time bomb was the Islamization of the legal system, which did not stop when General Zia died. Where criminal law was concerned, the 1990 Qissas and Diyat Ordinance organized and regulated, on the basis of medieval models, recourse to private vengeance for murder and personal injury. A Shari'ah Act – which Zia had not managed to push through – was voted in in 1991: it was couched in very vague terms, but it strengthened the hold of medieval models on the interpretation and application of the law. The most egregious measure, however, was surely the 1991 amendment to the 1986 law on blasphemy: hitherto, the penalty for blasphemy had been death or imprisonment. The Shari'ah Federal Court, deeming imprisonment an inadequate penalty, demanded that blasphemy should always carry the death penalty; the victims of this amendment, which was implemented in 1991, were mainly members of religious minorities – notably Christians – some of whom were executed on the basis of false accusations brought by Muslims.

This brings us to the second time bomb: the discriminatory measures against non-Muslims. Since the historic vote to exclude the Ahmadiyya under Bhutto in 1974, and above all since the restoration of democracy after Zia's death, Muslim activists have used this discriminatory legislation as an excuse to harass non-Muslims; they have spread false rumours of sacrilege (burning the Koran, for example), accused them of blasphemy (which, let us remember, has carried the death penalty since 1991), and burned down churches and houses belonging to Christians; there have been forcible attempts at converting the Hindus of Sind and the Kalash animists around Chitral, in the northeast, along the Afghan border.

It is not only non-Muslims who have suffered the consequences of Islamic laws. Two groups of Muslims are also affected: women, and minority sects. The third perverse effect of Islamization has been to revive a medieval ruling according to which not only non-Muslims but women, too, are inferior to male Muslims. So, in Pakistan's new application of criminal law, as we have seen, the testimony of two female Muslims (or two male non-Muslims) is equivalent to the testimony of one male Muslim; by the same token, in cases of private vengeance, injuries inflicted on a woman are compensated at half the rate of injuries inflicted on a man. Finally, and above all, the application of the ordinance on adultery – which, in theory, should punish men and women equally – imposes a heavier penalty on women: consenting (even raped) women are condemned to a whipping, while guilty men are acquitted for lack of proof; it is by no means unusual for families to resort to false accusations of adultery so that they can get rid of daughters or daughters-in-law whom they consider to be a burden on them.

The fourth time bomb is sectarian conflict. Zia had given a special place to the Sunni version of Islam, especially where the collection of compulsory alms was concerned. This prompted the Shi'a to become religiously and politically active; in answer, the Sunni became more radical and created militias. Over the last decade, armed conflict between Shi'a and Sunni militias left hundreds dead. The discriminatory institutionalization of religion has brought in its wake a politicization and radicalization of sectarian divides, which from now on will be a basic ingredient of politics in Pakistan.[10]

The fifth and final time bomb is unemployment among students of religion. By its massive funding of traditional education in the *madrasahs*, the government has thrown on to the employment market thousands of young people who have acquired a traditional religious knowledge which will not help them to find a suitable job. This is a huge army of disaffected people who can readily be brainwashed for political ends; they are by no means harmless, since some *madrasahs* – notably among those which are affiliated to the Deobandi school – are only too willing to spread the doctrine of holy war (*jihad*) openly, even to provide paramilitary training. Their former pupils fought in Afghanistan and Kashmir; the Taliban, who now control Afghanistan – Afghans for the most part, but some of them of Pakistani origin – also come from *madrasahs* in Pakistan. It is quite feasible that something very similar could happen in Pakistan itself.

Limiting religious encroachment

Is there no end to the insidious advance of religious legislation? It seems that there is. Despite increasing pressure from the men of religion, Pakistan's constitution and legal system are still based on a compromise between modernist institutions and religious appendages which, although they are significant, are nevertheless limited in effect. During Nawaz Sharif's second term in office there was another attempt – skilfully frustrated by political obstructionism – to promulgate a second Shari'ah Bill to succeed the one passed during his first term. The fact is, however, that periodic references to the supremacy of the *sharia* have not led to a widening of its application, because there are enough guardrails to prevent this application from straying outside the limited domains to which it is restricted. Since Zia's time, Pakistan's legal system has been a dual system where Western-type Anglo-Indian law is still the norm.

Moreover, despite the religious parties' fervent rhetoric and ability to mobilize in the streets, they seem to have lost some of their self-confidence, because they have not done very well in elections over the past ten years. The JI did not put forward a single candidate at the last general election in 1997, and the JUI did very badly (1.6 per cent of the votes – that is, 2 seats out of 204). Will these political parties retreat to the political fringe? Or will they reenter the political fray when General Musharraf's military regime is over? For the moment – despite the residues of past decisions over the previous twenty years – the compromise between the state and the men of religion is still very much as it was. The guardrails – for which Zia is chiefly responsible; we tend not to give him the credit he deserves – are still in place. Islam's role in Pakistan's institutions and politics may attract a lot of public attention, but it is still limited: the state still has the last word, and has been adept at setting up a system of checks and balances to maintain its sovereignty.

12

LANGUAGES AND EDUCATION

In Pakistan, the language question involves numerous paradoxes and reflects many social and political tensions. This is a multilingual state whose official language is English, the tongue of its former colonizers, and whose native language, Urdu, is the mother tongue only of the Muhajirs, who make up a mere 6 per cent of the population. During its brief history,[1] Pakistan has seen the growth of many ethnic movements based on linguistic claims. One of these movements, the Bengali movement of 1948–52, developed into a genuine ethnonationalism which played a crucial role in the 1971 Partition. At about the same time – in January 1971 and July 1972 – there were Muhajir–Sindi riots, which reached such a pitch that the Muhajirs subsequently established nationalist organizations (see Chapter 1 above). Other ethnic groups – the Pashtuns and the Baluchis, for example – chose language as their identifying feature. Nevertheless, we should not look at the language question solely from an ethnic point of view. It is an integral part of class relations, because it also involves government, education, business, the media – in short, every domain of national and social life. Both political and social stakes are involved.

Multilingualism Prevails, Despite the Urduization Policy

As a result of the 1981 census, which contained a question about the language 'normally spoken in the home', we can quote some figures on language distribution.

Table 12.1 Languages spoken, 1981 census (%)

Punjabi	48.17
Pashto	13.14
Sindi	11.77
Seraiki	9.83
Urdu	7.6
Baluchi	3.02
Hindko	2.43
Brahui	1.21
Others*	2.81

* This category includes fifty languages and dialects, mostly non-written.

The census does not ask about English, Arabic or Persian, since these languages are not widely spoken in private life. English is above all the key to responsible jobs in both the public and the private sector. Twenty years earlier, according to the 1960 census, only 2.7 per cent of Pakistanis had some knowledge of that language. No doubt such a figure would be an underestimation today, if we go by the expansion of the middle class – or, more precisely, of the salaried classes and other fields of employment which entail a knowledge of English.[2] In 1981, according to matriculation results – an examination in which English is compulsory – 19.56 per cent of the population spoke English. In practice, most of those who qualified could barely read the English textbooks, which they often tried to learn by heart. The total proportion of the population of Pakistan who really speak English is probably about 3 to 4 per cent.

Urdu is much more widely spoken – not only by those who have matriculated but also by *madrasah* pupils, the military (whatever their rank), and unskilled workers who can learn the language on the job. Another reason for the development of Urdu is that it is the language of communication between the provinces, and the language of television, the radio and the press. It is widely spoken by the middle classes, except in Sind (with the exception of the major towns).

Urdu is the most ideologically significant language in Pakistani society. It is an 'Islamic' language *par excellence*, for it was adopted in colonial times by the ulemas (doctors of Islamic law) and clerks [*maulvi*] to disseminate Islam.[3] It is also the language of examinations taken in *madrasahs* recognized by the national Ministry of Education, like those affiliated to the Deobandi, Barelwi, Ahl-i Hadith and Shi'a schools.[4] Finally, it is the language of religious tracts and sermons, and of the most reactionary newspapers. Most of the literature urging people to fight in Kashmir, to combat 'Western hegemony' or to support Islamic fundamentalism is in Urdu. Thus an educated person is much more exposed than the average Pakistani to such literature, which is aimed at encouraging antidemocratic, pro-militaristic attitudes.

Classical Arabic is understood only by a handful of men of religion in the *madrasahs*, and by a few university academics and researchers who practise Islam. Although all Muslims are supposed to have a knowledge of the Kuran, according to the 1981 census only 18.37 per cent of the population could read it. The rest are barely able to understand modern Arabic, even though the Arabic alphabet is virtually the same as that of Urdu. As for Persian, only experts understand it. A few students choose this language when they study for government competitive examinations, thinking they are taking the easy option, but for the most part they simply memorize certain passages.

In colonial times, the vernacular languages of the territories that became Pakistan in 1947 were not official teaching languages, but books in Punjabi, Sindi, Pashto, Baluchi and Brahui were used in academic establishments. These books glorified the Prophet of Islam, the saints, and purification rituals, but some of them also told of legendary lovers like Heer and Ranjha. Most of these books were read until the end of the eighteenth century; this proves that these languages, despite their lack of official recognition, had their own literary tradition. This tradition continues today in chapbooks in the vernacular languages which also speak of religion, of legends or stories of love, or of astrology, magic and sorcerers.

Since 1947, these regional languages have undergone several changes of fortune: they are not taught at all (like Punjabi, which has been sacrificed to Urdu on the altar of national integration; this means that the Punjabis can claim to be highly patriotic, and to justify their domination[5]); they are taught to some extent (like Pashto, which is used up to fifth grade in certain schools, then relegated to an option in higher grades); or they are taught only in some regions (Sindi, for example, is taught in Sind). Whatever the case, some people learn these languages on their own initiative, because the chapbooks are available in all Pakistan's major towns. William Hanaway and Mumtaz Nazir reckon that there are 940 chapbooks in Punjabi, Seraiki, Hindko (Hindi), Khowar, Pashto, Sindi, Persian and Urdu.[6] Films and songs in Punjabi and Pashto are especially popular.

Thus Pakistan is still a multilingual country. It is true that English dominates the national elite, and the Urduization policy is beginning to have an effect. But the vernacular languages are in good shape – including Punjabi, which – even if it is no longer taught – is still the majority language. Nonetheless, the influence of the education system is very strong.

The Education System: The Rise of the *Madrasahs*

English-language schools – that is, schools where the teachers really teach in English, and the pupils are from privileged Anglophone backgrounds – are too expensive for middle- and working-class families. Most Pakistani families, however, can afford public schools where the teaching is in Urdu and Sindi, and the few which teach Pashto to younger pupils. But the *madrasahs* are even more attractive, because board and education are free. Moreover, these Koranic schools have established national bodies to assess their pupils' knowledge of Urdu and Arabic. Nevertheless, in Pashto-speaking regions they teach in Pashto; while in Sindi-speaking regions they teach in Sindi. In the Punjab and Baluchistan, teachers often use the local languages in the classroom even though Urdu is the traditional language of education.

We do not know exactly how many *madrasahs* there are. Some very precise figures are given in the press: the periodical *Nawa-i-waqt* suggests that there are 6,761 Koranic schools (October 1999); while in 1995 the government was talking about 3,906. The *madrasahs* teach Islamic Arabic as a symbol of continuity with the past, and of Islamic identity, but most of their graduates cannot speak it properly.

Language and Power: The Ethnic Dimension

Urdu, heavily influenced by Persian, introduced into the education system by the British,[7] became a symbol of the Muslim elite in nineteenth-century India.[8] Thanks to the support of the British, it has become the language of government, law, education and business in regions once dominated by Muslims (particularly in Uttar Pradesh). As the struggle for work and power between Muslim and Hindu white-collar workers intensified, each community identified with its language, and 'cleansed' it of outside influences.[9] The battle between Urdu and Hindi in British India therefore followed, for the most part, the pattern of the power struggles between Hindus and Muslims.[10] Urdu was an essential feature of Muslim separatist ideology in India, and immediately after Partition the government sought to make this language a force for national integration. Since the federal government was in western Pakistan, and the administration and the army were dominated by Punjabis and Muhajirs, it came to be associated with central government hegemony. Nationalists in East Bengal, Sind, Baluchistan and the NWFP reacted by setting up ethnic affirmation movements based mainly on the defence of their languages. The most powerful linguistic movement, Bhasha Andolan – literally 'linguistic agitation' (that is, for the defence of Bengali) – was active between 1948 and 1951,[11] but it remained very influential until the second Partition in 1971. It rose up against the official ideology, and sought to make Bengali the symbol of a counterideology (see Chapter 2 above).

As for the pro-Pashto movement, it declined as the Pashtuns climbed the social ladder. Their business network has spread through the whole country, and they have joined the salaried classes in their thousands, especially the army. Nevertheless, the Awami National Party continues to criticize Punjabi hegemony in the name of a specific Pashtun identity, and wants Pashto taught at every level of the education system.

The Punjab, too, is riven with linguistic tensions which have socioeconomic origins. The Seraiki movement is a response to the economic underdevelopment of the southern Punjab. It may be limited to the region's intelligentsia, but the Seraiki label tends to bring together linguistic groups which have hitherto identified with different local idioms: Multani, Dereweli or Riasati. This movement shows very clearly how a local (Multani or Riasati) identity can become a wider ethnic identity (Seraiki).[12] In Baluchistan, Baluchi and Brahui are the languages of a literature of resistance against the domination of Urdu, the Punjabi elite, and the Mughlai culture (in the Indo-Gangetic plain).

Language and Social Status

The wish to learn a language is linked with the desire to climb the social ladder. People who speak minority languages are especially eager to learn another language if it is a prerequisite for a government job.

Some classes – landowners, for example, or so-called 'tribal leaders' in Baluchistan or the NWFP – enjoy a social influence that has nothing to do with their linguistic abilities. This also applies to political or religious leaders who need speak only a local language, since their power is based on the loyalty of their supporters and their own charisma. However, the greater part of the population – particularly in the towns – derive at least part of their power from their ability to write English and Urdu. No one who cannot read English or Urdu can get a white-collar job – except in Sind, where native-born Sindis have had their idiom recognized as the official language. In every province of Pakistan, anyone who can write Urdu, but not English, can get only menial jobs.

This situation is a legacy of colonial history. When the Great Mughals ruled India, Persian was the language of power; this forced the Hindus to learn it and to 'islamize' their culture.[13] Later, when the British launched an attack on the supremacy of Persian and installed English in the corridors of power, both Hindus and Muslims learned English, and the influence of Persian declined.[14] Still later, leading strata of the intelligentsia, who were also the most Westernized, were unwilling to substitute either Urdu or any other Pakistani language for English. Thus the supremacy of English is a reflection of very specific social interests.

Contrary to popular belief, Persian and English were never imposed by the government – quite the opposite: ordinary people were not allowed to learn them. Government mechanisms for learning the languages of power are highly discriminatory. Although most teaching is in Urdu, Sindi is used in primary schools in Sindi-speaking regions, and Pashto in the NWFP. These vernacular schools are mainly for the poor. For military and civil service elites, the state has created a parallel system where all subjects (or sometimes only scientific subjects) are taught in English. The military schools, which are directly or indirectly controlled by the army, are even more prestigious. There are also schools run by charitable military institutions like the Fauji Foundation (the army), the Bahria Foundation (the navy) and the Shaheen Foundation (the air force).

Other public services – the railways, Customs, telecommunications, the police, et cetera – run their own schools. The federal government also runs 'experimental' English-speaking schools. These establishments, their teachers and their facilities are of a much higher calibre than ordinary public schools, but they are cheaper for the sons and daughters of civil servants than for children from outside. Thus Pakistan's elite betray their declared commitment to provide state-financed teaching in vernacular languages.

As well as these public institutions, there is a network of private schools called 'English Medium' schools which provide an education in English. They are often extremely expensive: a place at a Froebel, Beaconhouse or City School System school can cost from 1,500 to 3,500 rupees a month. Families with modest means who know how important English is often make huge sacrifices to send their children to an English Medium school – hence the proliferation throughout Pakistan of schools which claim to teach in English. They cost between 50 and 100 rupees a month, and the quality of their teaching varies enormously. A number of these schools are run by religious organizations which claim to want to combine Islamic culture, modern technical subjects, and English. The wealthiest families send their children to study abroad or at the International American School, where a year's school fees are 10,000 dollars.

So Pakistan's elite maintains an education system where the majority of the population are either left in ignorance, or educated in the vernacular and thus at a disadvantage compared with those who control the government or the business world. Moreover, not only does this elite make no investment in its own education system, it subverts it by spending its money on a parallel model of education which is entirely for its own benefit.

Language Textbooks and Ideology

It is a well-known fact that there is an ideological dimension to language,[15] and the state's promotion of Urdu is a first indication of this. A second is the way languages have developed in Pakistan. The modernization process has entailed the invention of new terms to express new concepts – scientific facts, for example. These new terms are being created in accordance with very specific ideological criteria. The state uses Arabic and Persian roots, for instance, to make up new Urdu words, because it wants ordinary people to feel a sense of Pakistani (rather than ethnic) and Muslim (rather than secular) identity. At the same time, ethnic nationalists are creating new words on the basis of the ancient roots of their vernacular languages.

Language textbooks make their own contribution towards indoctrinating students. Although this indoctrination is mainly the province of books on history and sociology, it is furthered by books on linguistics. This propaganda – which can be subtle or blatant – is predominantly on behalf of Islam, nationalism and militarism. It finds expression in poems, essays, exercises, and so on, and appears equally in Urdu, English and Arabic books, and in textbooks in regional languages.

Religious education revolves around the fundamental principles of Islam, and around the illustrious personalities or events in its history. Lessons on nationalism, where the leaders of the movement for the creation of Pakistan are praised and revered, are aimed at strengthening a sense of nationhood and Pakistani identity. Language textbooks glorify war, and celebrate the heroes of conflicts between India and Pakistan. These three ideological themes complement one another: Islam encourages nationalism, and the most profound expression of nationalism happens to be militarism. The principal aim of this indoctrination process is to create a favourable climate for the state's anti-Indian policy.[16]

The state saw Urdu as a mark of Pakistani identity and a force for national integration in a country with five major ethnic groups, each with its own language and literary tradition. These groups, in turn, have endeavoured to resist this 'colonialism from the inside'. In this struggle, the elites of the ethnic groups have used their languages as symbols of an identity under threat.

As well as ethnic identity, social class plays an important part. English is associated with the upper middle classes and the elite; Urdu with the lower middle classes; while the vernacular languages are spoken mainly by farmers, unskilled workers, and the working class in general. This is borne out by relations with officialdom, especially in the towns. Nevertheless, there are places in Sind where Sindi is the accepted formal language in contexts where Urdu would be used in other regions of Pakistan. Moreover, in Sind and in certain parts of the Pashto-speaking area, ethnic pride is strong enough to curb the advance of Urdu, which is used purely for pragmatic purposes.

English is still thought of as the mouthpiece of Western liberal values, and Urdu as the Islamic and nationalist language *par excellence*; whereas the vernacular languages are associated with ethnic identity and nationalism. Nonetheless, Islamists and members of less powerful social classes are increasingly eager to learn English, because they see it as a way of climbing the social ladder in the modern world. Thus language is a key to understanding such complex political matters as the distribution of power within ethnic groups, between social classes, and even between individuals.

CONCLUSION

A Country in Crisis

Pakistan is not merely an artificial construction. There is not much risk that the country will break up, since the secession of East Bengal, the region where it was most difficult to achieve integration. But the country is still in pursuit of a national identity on which it can build to counter that of India – just at the very moment when it is going through a time of crisis on several fronts.

The coup of October 1999 plunged the country into an increasingly claustrophic and anachronistic spiral of military dictatorships. Like his predecessors Ayub Khan, Yahya Khan and Zia ul-Haq, the putschist General Pervez Musharraf put himself forward as someone who would be capable of restoring order and dignity in his country. In his first public speech, he announced that his aim was not to implement martial law, but 'only another path towards democracy. The armed forces have no intention to stay in charge any longer than is absolutely necessary to pave the way for true democracy to flourish in Pakistan . . .'[1]

Six months later, he announced that between December 2000 and July 2001 there would be local elections which would bring about the reestablishment of town and village councils that were no longer appointed but elected,[2] albeit without any participation by political parties. Thus Musharraf repeated Zia's tactics: in 1985 Zia organized 'non-partisan' elections as part of the move towards democracy, which was short-lived. Moreover, Musharraf took care to point out that he was implementing the Supreme Court ruling that general elections must be held between now and 2002, but that he retained the right to postpone them if he had not fulfilled his objectives.[3] Now, the seven-point programme which the regime set itself the day after the coup is – to say the least – ambitious: to restore the nation's confidence; strengthen its cohesion; stimulate the economy; reestablish law and order; depoliticize the country's institutions; decentralize power; and fight corruption.

Putting the economy of Pakistan to rights is no easy matter. The country's foreign debt rose to 38 thousand million dollars; about 50 per cent of the national budget goes on debt servicing. Even though Musharraf has announced a freeze on military expenditure – still 45 per cent of total expenditure in 1999–2000 – he is unlikely to make substantial cuts in the army's budget at a time when relations with India are still extremely tense.[4] Since he cannot cut costs, he is forced to bring in more revenue by fighting fraud. He averred that the guiding principle behind his coup was the battle against parasitism and corruption, announced that 22,000 civil servants would be dismissed – a purge reminiscent of those of his predecessors – and declared war on borrowers who 'neglected' to repay their bank loans. This operation recovered only about 15 to 20 per cent of the 211 thousand million rupees owed to the banks.[5] Musharraf attached even more importance to fighting tax fraud. Noting that only 1.2 million of his fellow citizens paid their taxes, he decided to get an idea of the value of undeclared income in the black economy – the estimate was 60 thousand million dollars (that is, equivalent to GNP) – by conducting a draconian investigation into the assets and income of tradesmen and industrialists. This somewhat demagogic measure immediately aroused the hostility of the All Pakistan Organization of Small Trade and Cottage Industries. 'Close down the town' campaigns paralysed the country in May–June 2000. The improved tax revenues hoped for as a result of better information about the employers' resources could still not be relied upon, and in any case would not be enough to solve the short-term financial problem.

So Pakistan has been forced to seek the support of international lenders – notably the IMF, whose decisions are strongly influenced by US foreign policy. The Americans will not let their former ally go to the wall, if only because they want to avoid further instability in a part of the world where there is already trouble enough. The IMF, which has suspended payments, will no doubt end up bailing Pakistan out; Paris and London reschedule the country's debts at regular intervals. In exchange for this support, however, Washington is putting strong pressure on Islamabad to rethink its regional policy. Not only does the US administration want to see Pakistan distance itself from the Taliban (while continuing to ask them to hand over Bin Laden); it is also worried about its activities in Kashmir at a time when the USA itself is forging a stronger relationship with New Delhi, epitomized by Bill Clinton's visit to India in March 2000 and A B Vajpayee's visit to Washington in September of that same year. Musharraf does not have much room for manoeuvre, because the army will not readily give up on Kashmir, nor will it willingly sacrifice the 'strategic depth' it gains from its presence in Afghanistan.

By way of compromise, the government has asked the Taliban to close training camps for Pakistani jihadists in Afghanistan, and to discourage *madrasah* students from crossing the border.[6] It has also decided to disarm Pakistani society, especially *madrasahs* which have close links with Islamist groups. In spring 2000, Moiuddin Haider, Interior Minister, suspended the issuing of gun licences.[7] This operation, whose effects were limited, was designed not only to oblige Washington but also to show that Pakistan was willing to act against undercover groups involved in innumerable shady deals, including smuggling consumer goods – the value of this alone is 2.5 thousand million dollars, a considerable loss to Pakistan's Customs service. It is therefore very much in the country's economic interest to take a harder line on the Taliban and on Islamists with links to the Afghan government.

The struggle against criminal groups also reveals the anxiety caused by the increasing violence throughout the country. This phenomenon is not confined to

Karachi, nor even to Sind, because today it is the Punjab which has the worst record: more and more clashes between Shi'a and Sunni (they caused 79 deaths in 1998 as against 57 in Sind) and frequent murders put Lahore ahead of Karachi (998 as against 662 in 1998) and the Punjab ahead of Sind (4,358 as against 3,562), with an average of 15 deaths a day.[8] This violence is a symptom of a serious social crisis, in addition to the country's political and economic failures. It has become so commonplace that it is now a 'legitimate way of settling disputes',[9] as a result of intensifying social inequalities.

Pakistan's economic crisis has impoverished ordinary people: a third of the population now live below the poverty threshold.[10] Their feelings of resentment are all the stronger by virtue of the fact that at the same time, *nouveaux riches* who have often come by their fortune through dubious means make ostentatious display of their opulence. 'Society has lost its value system' because of the rise of materialism and the corrodification of social relationships today 'Pakistanis often compare their country to France before 1789'.[11]

This comparison is even more apt in that the 'feudal lords' are not prepared to loosen their stranglehold on their country estates. But is Pakistan really in a prerevolutionary situation?

There are three leading actors in the political arena: the army faces some momentous challenges; the political parties lack leadership, and have been discredited by their frequent involvement in corruption; the Islamists – whether they belong to traditional organizations like the Jamaat-i Islami or to militant groups like the Lashkar-i Tayyiba – form the third point of the triangle. Their popularity has risen as a result of the Kargil war in spring 2000, and they put themselves forward as the revolutionary alternative to a military regime with undesirable Kemalist tendencies.[12] According to Ahmed Rashid, one of the leading experts in this field:

> 'some 80,000 militants have trained and fought with the Taliban since their emergence in 1994, providing a huge militant fundmentalist base for a Taliban-style Islamic revolution in Pakistan.'[13]

Is this the harbinger of an even more radical political shift than the 1999 coup – one which could set the seal on the failure of a military government embroiled in crisis?

EPILOGUE

Musharraf and the Islamists: From Support to Opposition after September 11

Since autumn 2000, when the first French edition of this book was published, both the internal political situation in Pakistan and the country's international position have changed dramatically. In both cases, the impact of September 11 was decisive: from the moment when Islamic networks – especially those linked to the Taliban, like Al-Qaeda – became the prime target of the antiterrorist coalition, Pakistan could no longer either retain its links with Afghanistan or remain indifferent to the growth of Islamist movements on its own territory.

This impression of a break, however, belies a certain element of continuity: General Musharraf was fully aware of the potential danger of these movements, even though he failed to translate this awareness into action. September 11 was a climactic catalyst whose impact on Pakistan's position in the world may be summed up in two courses of action: withdrawal from Afghanistan (even, to a much lesser extent, from Kashmir); and a return to the international fold; while its impact within the country itself has been – to put it briefly – a clampdown on Islamists (how effective this is we do not yet know) and the consolidation of Musharraf's power base.

Challenging Jihadist Strategy

Awareness and ambivalence

From the moment he came to power, Musharraf worried about the problems the Islamists were causing in his country – especially public order disruptions resulting from clashes between Shi'a and Sunni groups. Between his coup on 12 October 1999 and August 2001, sectarian violence – 83 riots involving 30 towns – left 220 dead and 2,000 wounded. Most seriously affected were the Federally Administered Tribal Areas (FATA), especially the Pashtun Tribal Areas (61 dead), followed by Karachi (54 dead).[2] These outbreaks of violence were fomented mainly by two militant Sunni organizations: the Lashkar-i-Jhangvi (LJ) and the Sipah-i Sahaba Pakistan (SSP).[3]

In February 2001, when the execution of an SSP militant condemned to death for murdering the Iranian consul general in 1990 provoked a violent reaction from his comrades-in-arms – eight people died after the perpetrators had launched a heavily armed anti-Shi'a attack – the Musharraf government decided to take repressive measures. In Jhang, a part of the Punjab known for violent confrontations between Sunni and Shi'a, the army arrested several SSP militants. Significantly, on 14 August – that is to say, about a month before September 11 – Musharraf decided to ban the Lashkar-i-Jhangvi and, for good measure, the Sipah-i-Muhammad Pakistan, a Shi'a movement. At the same time, however, he freed Azam Tariq, the SSP leader, who had been arrested during the violence in February. This proved that Musharraf had no appetite for a head-on confrontation with the Sunni party.

Musharraf was equally careful to handle the Islamists tactfully over the controversy surrounding the blasphemy law. This law, introduced by Zia, is often invoked against Christians who are accused – usually without any real grounds – of showing the Prophet insufficient respect and, as a result, are liable to imprisonment. In April 2000, Musharraf had decided to reform this law by ruling that charges of blasphemy had to be substantiated by a Deputy Commissioner before the police could be called in. The Islamist movements went into action, and Musharraf had to backtrack. The Islamists hailed his retreat as another victory to add to the one they had enjoyed six months earlier, in December 1999, when the Supreme Court had declared interest-bearing loans [*riba'*] 'non-Islamic'.

At the request of the Islamist parties, Musharraf also promulgated a Provisional Constitution (Amendment) Order, 2000, which included in the Provisional Constitutional Order of 14 October 1999 – Pakistan's temporary written Constitution – the Islamic measures which featured in the 1973 Constitution, which had been suspended since his coup. This Order restored the validity of Articles 203A and 203J (on the Federal Shari'ah Court) and Articles 260(a) and (b) (which laid down definitions of a 'Muslim' and a 'Non-Muslim'.

Musharraf's ambivalent attitude towards the Islamists was partly a reflection of his own deep personal ambiguity. He is quite happy to be seen as a 'Kemalist' – not only because he has the modernizing approach of an Atatürk who wants to make the 'sick man of Europe' (a diagnosis that could be transposed to Pakistan within South Asia) into a nation worthy of respect, but also because he has seen himself from the outset as the defender of the state – and that includes defending it against Islamists who threaten public order. At the same time, he had a distinguished career as an artillery officer under Zia, whose Islamization policy and strategy of forming links with the Islamists exerted a certain influence over him. The Jamaat-i Islami mentioned his name to Zia in the 1980s, and the strong man of Pakistan immediately entrusted him with the task of recruiting and training mujaheddin for the war against the Soviets in Afghanistan. He subsequently won considerable fame for suppressing a Shi'a uprising in Gilgit in 1988; during this operation his men acted with exceptional cruelty.[4] Not only had the army he led cooperated with the Islamists eleven years later, in the Kargil war in Indian Kashmir, but this collusion was even more in evidence in December 1999, when supporters of Maulana Masood Azhar, a Harkat-ul Ansar leader whom the Indians had detained in prison in Kashmir, hijacked an Indian Airlines plane from Katmandu to Kandahar in order to obtain his release. As soon as he was free, Azhar settled in Pakistan and set up a new movement to pursue the *jihad* in Kashmir, Jaish-i Muhammad (the Army of Mohammed), with the support – and this was common knowledge – of the ISI, headed by one of Musharraf's close collaborators, Lieutenant-General Mahmood, who had been among the officers who helped him to seize power in October 1999.

Quite apart from their common interests in Kashmir, Musharraf found that the Islamists were his allies against the political parties – including the MQM in Karachi, which saw the growth of the *madrasahs* as a power mechanism aimed against the Muhajir movement. Musharraf allowed the Islamists to take to the streets, while PPP or PML(N) demonstrations were crushed. The tone was set on 3 November 1999, when Musharraf allowed the Lashkar-i-Tayyiba to hold a meeting at Lahore attended by about half a million people. There was a comparable show of force in spring 2001, at the Aalmi Deoband Conference organized by Maulana Fazlur Rahman, leader of the Jamiyyat-ul Ulama-i-Islam (JUI), in the NWFP: again, 500,000 people were present – a sign that the Islamists were well and truly part of public life, with Musharraf's blessing. Rahman took advantage of this platform to confirm his support for the Taliban and their leader, Mullah Muhammad Omar, whose words were relayed on tape.[5]

Musharraf's attitude towards the Jihadists hardened a few weeks before September 11, after the resurgence of sectarian violence mentioned above, because the Jihadists and the sectarian groups appeared to have developed close relations. In these circumstances he promulgated an Anti-Terrorism Amendment Ordinance 2001, which included measures against jihadist organizations like the Jaish-i Muhammad and the Lashkar-i-Tayyiba, whose offices were boarded up; these measures, however, were mainly confined to Karachi.

At the same time – summer 2001 – there was severe controversy over the *madrasah* issue. These Koranic schools, the birthplace of some of the most violent Islamic movements – the Taliban, of course, but also the Harkat-ul Mujahiddin in Kashmir, and the Sipah-i Sahaba – had proliferated rapidly since the time of Zia, whose Islamization policy had allowed them to receive official recognition: in 1947 there had been 150; by 1950 there were 210. By 1971 there were 563, but today there are between 10,000 and 15,000, at least a tenth of which train militant jihadists. This success is due in no small measure to the 'charitable strategy' of these schools, which educate pupils free, and provide board and lodging for a very modest sum. After vacillating for some time, Musharraf took the decision to promulgate a law affecting the *madrasahs* on 18 June 2001: the Pakistan Madrasah Education (Establishment and Affiliation of Model Deeni Madaris) Board Ordinance 2001 allows for these schools to be brought into the public education system – not only must their curriculum conform to official standards, but from now on their sources of finance must be revealed to the state; this is one way of identifying foreign sponsors. Immediately, senior *madrasah* staff – and all the Islamic groups in general – rejected this measure, which has mainly remained a dead letter: one more indication of Musharraf's reluctance to confront the Islamist movement.

The consolidation of his government's power should have enabled him to disarm *madrasahs* which are in league with Islamist groups. It is true that in spring 2000 Moiuddin Haider, Minister of the Interior, froze the issuing of weapons licences, with a view to preventing sectarian groups from being able to lay their hands too readily on weapons of all kinds. However, the government did not enforce this policy with any great consistency either.

Musharraf himself has admitted that his *madrasah* reforms are being implemented slowly: 'There are about 10,000 of them [*madrasahs*] and there are about 1 million poor students getting free board and lodging. These *madrasahs* are doing a welfare service to the poor. The negative side is that most of them are only teaching religion, so my belief is that we need to carry out reforms to reinforce their strengths and eliminate their weaknesses.'[6]

Everything changed during the war in Afghanistan in autumn 2001, which marked Musharraf's break with the Islamists, and the simultaneous ending of the partnership between the army and paramilitary Islamists in Afghanistan and Kashmir.

Pakistan after September 11

After the attacks of September 11, the Bush administration quickly realized that it could not pursue its campaign in Afghanistan – both to break up Bin Laden's terrorist networks and to put an end to the Taliban regime – without Pakistan: not only because of the country's key geopolitical position, but also because it could provide information. Perhaps Musharraf thought at the beginning that cooperating with the USA against 'Islamic terrorism' would not necessarily mean that he had to stop supporting the Taliban and jihadist movements in Kashmir, but Pakistan's weak economy and diplomatic isolation did not give him much room for manoeuvre.

A Vulnerable Economy

As soon as he had taken power, General Musharraf put the economic crisis at the top of his agenda, accusing 'the politicians' – not without some justification – of ensnaring the country in a spiral of debt: between 1995–96 and 1999–2000, its total debt rose from 1,877 billion rupees to 3,096 billion – 97.5 per cent of GDP. As for foreign debt (48.4 per cent of the total in 2000), over the course of a veritable 'lost decade' from 1990–91 to 1999–2000, it went from 20.66 billion dollars to 37 billion.[7] As a result, debt servicing represented 45 per cent of budget spending (and 63 per cent of receipts) in 2000. At the Development Forum organized by the World Bank in 2000, the president of the committee on debt management and reduction presented his report and its conclusions: the level of Pakistan's debt was unsustainable; its value corresponded to 293 per cent of Pakistan's annual receipts of foreign currency, whereas the sustainable level as defined by the IMF is 150 per cent. As far as the World Bank was concerned, the stock of this debt, and its servicing, represented 610 per cent and 60 per cent respectively of state revenue. The report put this debt down to a chronic shortage of current and public accounts: notably because of the level of military expenditure, which has certainly fallen – from 26 per cent of budget spending in 1996–97 to 21 per cent in 2001–02, if we can believe the Finance Act passed in June – but is still very substantial.[8] The World Bank spokesman considered that in order to get out of the debt trap – and, quite simply, to continue to service its debt – Pakistan would need international financial assistance to the tune of 6 billion dollars until the year 2004.

Musharraf therefore set himself the task of reducing public debt and reassuring international lenders. He took some painful measures which every government before him had refused to take because they would be unpopular: he brought in an oil-price mechanism which led to significant price rises of 7.5 to 22.5 per cent, depending on the product in question; he abolished fuel subsidies; he imposed a General Sales Tax on electricity and abolished some wheat subsidies. He announced that 40,000 public-sector jobs would go: 12 per cent of the total. He also turned his attention to the defaulting borrowers who were becoming a greater and greater burden on the economy. The Finance Minister estimated the value of dubious loans – that is, loans where payment of interest or principal was more than ninety days late – at more than 4 billion dollars. Musharraf allowed tardy borrowers time to put their affairs on a legal footing, promising them an amnesty, but once the 16 November deadline had passed, the police made some spectacular arrests involving not only prominent businessmen but politicians – nine of those imprisoned had served in Nawaz Sharif's Cabinet, or belonged to his family. On 17 November, through President Tarar, Musharraf promulgated an ordinance to set up a National Accountability Bureau to oversee the legal proceedings already begun against the guilty parties. The Bureau had the power to conduct an accelerated investigation over a maximum of 75 days, after which the files had to be passed to special courts in each province; these courts, in turn, had only 30 days in which to give a ruling. For Musharraf, these people were 'white-collar criminals', because although they were often caught red-handed avoiding their financial obligations, they had substantial savings: paying one's debts featured in the civic code of ethics which Musharraf intended to restore. His first target was corrupt politicians, but he also had in his sights tradesmen and industrialists, who often had political connections – in a word, it was 'racketeering', embodied for several years by Nawaz Sharif, that was in the firing line.

Finally, and most importantly, Musharraf tackled the tax problem. Many sections of the population in Pakistan evaded tax by more or less legal means – in agriculture, in service industries and in business. The number of taxpayers is put at 1.2 million out of a population of 140 million. Musharraf brought in a tax on agricultural income and a Sales Tax on services. He came down especially hard on tradesmen who were suspected of large-scale tax fraud, when in fact they were already undertaxed. In May 2000 he launched a tax investigation which began with tradesmen in thirteen towns; the idea was to subject them to a 2 per cent turnover tax. This decision immediately prompted a tradesmen's strike which led to a spate of 'Close down the town' campaigns. Emotions ran even higher by virtue of the fact that this investigation was conducted in tandem with anticorruption inquiries which were also aimed at industrialists and tradesmen. In the face of this opposition, Musharraf made a partial retreat, pointing out significantly that files on defaulting borrowers – those who, quite simply, were not paying their debts – would be submitted to the Central Bank before (possibly) being passed on to the anticorruption unit.

All in all, the tax take for the whole year 2000–01 increased by only about 14 per cent, against a forecast of 25 per cent, taking the 'tax revenue/GDP' ratio from 10.9 per cent to 11.7 per cent. This represented some progress, but did not reduce the budget deficit significantly; moreover, other engines of economic policy were at a standstill. The privatization programme, for example, seemed to be incapable of getting under way, first and foremost because potential buyers have proved reluctant to take on concerns with huge deficits.

Thus the budget deficit was reduced by only about one percentage point – from 6.5 per cent to 5.4 per cent of GDP – between 1999–2000 and 2000–01; another factor was the terrible drought which hindered growth. The growth rate fell from 3.9 per cent to 2.6 per cent (below the growth rate of the population) over the same period, because of the poor performance of the agricultural sector:[9] a negative growth rate of 2.5 per cent, while industry achieved 6.8 per cent. Nevertheless, Musharraf succeeded in convincing Pakistan's financial backers of his determination, and so began to establish normal relations with them. At the end of the 1990s, Pakistan had in fact been penalized by the IMF through international sanctions which followed the nuclear weapons tests of 1998 and the military coup of 1999. For example, the IMF had frozen the final instalment of the 1.56 billion dollars' worth of credit which had been allocated to Pakistan in 1997. In late 2000, the IMF Administrative Council, in recognition of Musharraf's efforts, voted a 'standby' allocation of 596 million dollars – unanimously, except for the USA, which was still suspicious of Pakistan. This paved the way for the Club of Paris to sign an agreement to reschedule Pakistan's external public debt on 22 January 2001. In August of that same year, the Finance Minister, Shaukat Aziz, was assured by Christina Rocca, Undersecretary of State responsible for South Asia, that from then on the United States would support Pakistan at IMF meetings but things really changed after September 11.

Pakistan in diplomatic isolation

Despite all this, Pakistan was still very isolated indeed on the international front. By the end of the 1990s it had become a pariah nation. The nuclear weapons tests in spring 1998, which followed those of India, had prompted both the USA and Japan to impose draconian sanctions. The attacks on American embassies in Dar es Salaam and Nairobi the following summer, for which Osama bin Laden was held responsible, had tarnished Pakistan's image even further, since it was one of the three states which had recognized the regime of the Taliban, self-appointed protectors of the man who was known at that time as 'the Saudi millionaire'. Finally, General Musharraf's military coup on 12 October 1999 had added to the country's isolation: he had been subjected to further American sanctions and suspended from the ex-British Empire club, the Commonwealth. In effect, Pakistan had only two important allies left: China and Saudi Arabia.[10] Musharraf had only a few talks with the Western leaders who attended the UN's Millennium Summit. In March 2000 Bill Clinton spent only five hours in Pakistan – whereas he had spent five days in India, the first visit to India by an American President for twenty-two years – and the main purpose of that flying visit was to ask Musharraf to spare Nawaz Sharif's life. The European troika paid him a visit on 20 and 21 November 2000, just to show that the states of the European Union were eager to keep the dialogue going, but their main purpose was to drive home the fact that they wanted to see a return to democracy in Pakistan.

All Musharraf did to mollify the West was to visit India. The Americans were eager for the two countries to renew their discussions, because this might reduce the risk of nuclear escalation and further military conflict in Kashmir. Musharraf told the Indians on several occasions that he was ready to resume the dialogue. New Delhi, which had declared that it would have no dealings with the new regime in Pakistan on the morning after the military coup – to the extent of paralysing the SAARC, whose meetings were suspended – finally agreed to receive him. This was the moment Musharraf had been waiting for: he 'promoted' himself to the position of President, arguing that a general would be a less legitimate interlocutor for an Indian Prime Minister, and the discussions at the Agra Summit marked the beginning of his return to the international stage. He also derived some internal political advantage from them, because he had dared to put Kashmir at the heart of the agenda – to the great displeasure of the Indians who wanted him simply to condemn cross-border terrorism. This, however, was a very modest success for Musharraf in his efforts to reduce country's diplomatic isolation, a development which occurred only after 11 September 2001.

Pakistan withdraws from Afghanistan

Musharraf's lack of room for manoeuvre because of the economic crisis, and his diplomatic isolation, explain the fact that the day after September 11 he pledged himself to help the USA in its fight against Bin Laden and the regime of Mullah Omar, even if that meant shelving his alliance with the Taliban. On 12 September, he assured the USA of his 'unstinted cooperation in the fight against terrorism' But Musharraf probably still thought that he could play a double game: be rewarded for his good conduct by the antiterrorist coalition *and* keep some kind of link with moderate Taliban who might take power once the Americans had left.

Musharraf wanted to maximise his benefits, just as General Zia ul-Haq before him had gained the maximum financial and strategic advantages from supporting the Americans against the Soviet invasion of Afghanistan, while he played his own pawns on the region's political chessboard. Like Zia, Musharraf immediately put a price on his support – opening up Pakistan's airspace; providing 'information' and logistical backup – in both financial and political terms.

The diplomatic dividends for Pakistan's good conduct did not take long to materialize. The British and Dutch Prime Ministers, the German Chancellor, the President of Turkey, the American Secretary of State and Defense Secretary, and the Foreign Ministers of France, the Federal Arab Republic and Saudi Arabia came to Islamabad in rapid succession. As for Musharraf, he made a tour which took him to (not necessarily in this order) Tehran, Istanbul, Paris, London and New York, where the General-President addressed the UN and had his hour of glory on 12

November, by George W Bush's side, as the two men issued a joint communiqué which emphasized the strength of the friendship which had united their countries 'for fifty years'. Pakistan's return to the UN's favour had been heralded a little earlier by a joint statement by 54 Asian countries to the effect that the country would acquire a seat in the Security Council when the next rotation of nonpermanent members takes place in 2003.

At every stage of this readmission into the international community, Musharraf has reminded the world of the price his country is paying for the crisis in Afghanistan, emphasizing that this burden has a significant humanitarian element which was imposed on him by the influx of refugees – in mid-October 2001, the HCR estimated that 2,000 Afghans were crossing the border every day – and that it was dealing a body blow to an economy that was already in a very poor state of health.[11]

Musharraf's speeches prompted the richest partners in the antiterrorist coalition to rally round with financial support: some new rescheduling plans were negotiated under the aegis of the Clubs of Paris and London; Britain and the Netherlands have cancelled debts totalling £20 million and 14 million euros respectively; Canada has converted 282 million dollars' worth of credits into development aid; Germany has done the same to the tune of 51 million euros. On 14 November 2001, Pakistan's creditors promised to fill the financial gap to the tune of 3.2 billion dollars for the year 2000–01. As for bilateral aid, that exceeds a billion dollars; the USA heads the list, with 673 million dollars – in the context of a global project that could reach a billion dollars – followed by the United Kingdom (170 million dollars), Germany (75 million euros) and Japan (300 million dollars, preceded by 6 million dollars' worth of emergency aid). On the multilateral front, the European Union has offered – quite apart from 50 million euros' worth of aid – commercial concessions on textile exports: Customs duties on such exports (which account for 60 per cent of Pakistan's exports to the European Union) have been abolished, and import quotas have been raised to 15 per cent. As for the IMF, it has allocated Pakistan funds from the Facility for the Reduction of Poverty and for Growth, including 1.3 billion dollars' worth of credit and 300 million dollars from the World Bank. All in all, in three months international support went up to 6 billion dollars of promises, if we take into account direct aid, economic support programmes, and commercial deals. What remains to be seen is whether this support remains immaterial or is effectively delivered. But it is very important to note that it was agreed unconditionally: both structural reforms and democracy went out of the window.

Moreover, the USA lifted its sanctions on Pakistan. The first sanctions to go were those connected with nuclear weapons: from the 1978 Symington Amendment to the Pressler Amendment in 1990 and the Glenn Amendment in 1998. The sanctions imposed after the military coup were also reconsidered after a visit to Islamabad by a military delegation from the Pentagon and an emergency debate in the Senate during which Pakistan had to be awarded a certificate of democracy. The lifting of these sanctions means that soon Pakistan will not only be able to obtain loans from America, but also send soldiers to the USA for military training – something that has been impossible since 1990.[12]

However, Pakistan's establishment certainly did not think that the country's return to international favour would be incompatible with the continuation of its policy in Afghanistan – albeit in a different form.

On 16 September 2001, Musharraf sent Mullah Omar a delegation whose mission was to obtain the handing over of Osama bin Laden. It included the director of the Inter Services Intelligence (the secret services which have supervised Pakistan's Afghanistan policy since the early days), Lieutenant-General Mahmud, and Mufti Nizamuddin Shamzai, head of the most eminent Deobandi *madrasah* in Pakistan, Binori Town in Karachi, who at that time was very close to Bin Laden. However, this man, far from encouraging Mullah Omar – and he must have been one of the last Pakistani visitors to see him – to hand over Bin Laden, fuelled his anti-Americanism: a sentiment which he himself had expressed a week earlier, when he had exhorted all Muslims to start a *jihad* against the USA if it attacked Afghanistan.[13] However once the American air strikes began, on 7 October, Musharraf and his army could no longer hope to retain their privileged links with a country ruled by the Taliban, but some officers found this difficult to accept, as we saw from the fact that provisions, fuel, and maybe even weapons continued to be taken across the border and delivered to Mullah Omar's followers; and, moreover, from the fact that everyone was still keen on including 'moderate Taliban' in a government of national unity which would thus elude the clutches of their deadly enemy, the Northern Alliance.

For some time, the USA gave the impression that it was receptive to Pakistan's approach, and, above all, that it would keep the Northern Alliance at bay. On 12 November, during their famous meeting in New York, President Bush, in Musharraf's presence, asked the Northern Alliance forces not to enter Kabul, even if that meant leaving the Afghan capital alone when they took over the rest of the country. The next day, the town fell into the Alliance's hands, and people watching television in Pakistan saw that special American forces on the ground were advising their fighters on survival strategies. To add to Pakistan's frustration, at the very same moment the USA was failing to support Islamabad's efforts to find a Pashtun alternative to the Taliban, whose fate seemed to be sealed. It was as if the United States, behind its apparently friendly attitude to Musharraf, did not trust him further than it could throw him.[14] In a sense, the Pakistanis had met their masters in the art of doublespeak – unless (and this seems quite plausible) the decision to take Kabul was part of the Pentagon's strategy: the American strategists wanted a military victory at any price, while Colin Powell, the Secretary of State, was more inclined to fall in with Pakistan's wishes. Whatever the truth of the matter, the Pakistanis saw the seizure of Kabul as an American betrayal, considering that the USA had used them just as it had used them in the 1980s, when it needed them to drive out the Soviets, then lost all interest in their problems – especially the problem of refugees from Afghanistan.

When the Taliban fell, Pakistan lost its famous 'strategic depth' in Afghanistan: its rear base which, in theory, gave the country more clout in its dealings with India. This marked the complete failure of Pakistan's strategy in the region, as implemented by Zia and pursued by his successors. It is true that relations between Islamabad and Kabul became more difficult once the Taliban came under the

influence of the 'Arabs' and Bin Laden, weakening Pakistan's grip on a movement
which was largely its own creation. Islamabad's inability to persuade the Taliban not
to destroy the Bamiyan Buddhas, and above all its failure to secure the handing over
of the Laskhar-i-Jhangvi commandos who were crossing the Durand Line to cause
trouble in Pakistan, had borne witness to this loss of control, and the radicalization
of the Taliban which had led to it. But even if the Taliban were discarding their
Pakistani connections – mainly, we must stress, because of their military victories
over the Northern Alliance, which led them to think that they could do without
Islamabad's support – as far as Pakistan was concerned, they were still valuable allies:
even more so in view of the fact that Kabul's fall at the hands of Commander
Massoud's forces had allowed Islamabad's enemies to take power in the region.
Since the Northern Alliance enjoyed Delhi's support, Pakistan even felt that it had
good grounds for developing an 'encirclement syndrome'.

The process of putting new institutions in place in Afghanistan – which began at
the Bonn conference, but dragged on for months – did not augur well for Pakistan.
It had no powerful, reliable allies among the delegates facing each other at the
negotiating table. The United Front was dominated by Tajiks, Uzbeks and Hazaras
from the Northern Alliance; the group from Cyprus was made up of exiled Afghans,
and was closer to Iran; the Pashtuns from the Loya Pakhtia movement supported the
king; the only pro-Pakistan group was that of Pir Sayed Gailani, a Pashtun based in
Peshawar. Gailani, son of a mujaheddin commander who led the struggle against the
Russians, chose to settle in Peshawar, where he formed the National Islamic Front of
Afghanistan. In October 2001 he tried to establish a Pashtun alternative to the
Taliban, with Pakistan's support, by creating an Association for Peace and National
Unity in Afghanistan. In this context, he set up a meeting on 24–25 October 2001
attended by 1,500 Pashtun delegates, including several Afghan tribal chiefs: the
Pakistani authorities not only allowed them into the country, but also provided them
with an official vehicle. Islamabad wanted Gailani to have an important position in
the next Afghan government – maybe even to be Prime Minister.

But the Bonn conference established an interim authority in which the Peshawar
group were given only three ministerial posts out of twenty-nine, and there was no
Pashtun majority. It is true that the President, Hamid Karzai, is a Pashtun, but he is
no friend of Pakistan.[15] India, on the other hand, has allies in this government, starting with Dr Abdullah, Minister for Foreign Affairs, whose family live in exile in
Delhi.

So Pakistan, a prime mover in the Afghan crisis, has emerged battered and
bruised from the most recent war in the region. Musharraf has implied that he real-
izes he should have ditched the policy initiated by Zia in the 1970s. On 7 October
2001, when the American air strikes began, he ousted the members of his junta who
had collaborated most closely with the Taliban, despite the fact that these men had
supported his coup: Lieutenant-General Usmani and Lieutenant-General Mahmud
(head of the ISI) left the presidential entourage; while General Mohammad Aziz
Khan, who is also close to Musharraf, was promoted to the largely honorary post of
President of the Committee of the Armed Forces Chief of Army Staff.

Before reaching this decision, Musharraf took care to consult all the important officers. A considerable part of his power lay in the fact that he was close to his 'corps commanders', and liked to think of himself simply as 'primus inter pares'. This very collegiate course of action meant that his policy was backed by the most influential and senior military men, who probably shared his 'Kemalist' attitudes.

However, among officers further down the ranks there were probably people who were more in tune with the Islamist message, as a result both of the Islamization policy that started in General Zia's time, and of increasing army recruitment from the rural middle classes in the Punjab and the NWFP, whose conservative social attitudes are all of a piece with a certain predilection for Islamist thinking. It might be one m ore reason explaining why today Musharraf's chief political preoccupation is to bring the Islamists into line.

Bringing the Islamists into line

Musharraf's decision to support the USA against the Taliban put the final seal on his break with the Islamists. This break was more or less on the cards, if we remember the government's harder line with sectarian movements and the *madrasahs* in summer 2001 (see above): the Islamists were too popular with the general public, and indulged in violent activities which jeopardized public order; they threatened to become too powerful, and the military government – with some justification – feared for its own survival. The war in autumn 2001 precipitated Musharraf's break with the Islamists. At first, the General-President tried to placate the USA by putting the most anti-American leaders – like Maulana Fazlur Rahman, leader of the Jamiyyat-ul Ulama-i Islam, one of the most pro-Taliban parties – under house arrest; he then turned his attention to those who were against not only the Americans but himself as well – like Qazi Hussain Ahmed, leader of the Jamaat-i Islami, who was sentenced to a month in prison on 5 November for making an antigovernment speech. The government then stepped up the repression by arresting militants on their return from Afghanistan – they had gone there to fight alongside the Taliban.

The Islamists' reaction was weak, partly because of their lack of unity.[16] The Jamaat-i Islami and the various JUI factions, for example, have been longstanding rivals, and have been eager to emphasize their ideological differences. Qazi Hussain Ahmed always said that he did not model himself on the Taliban, whereas the JUI had always been close to this school of thought, which it had been instrumental in creating: in 1999, eight ministers in the Kabul government had been trained at the Darul Uloom Haqqania school run by Sami ul-Haq, one of the party's leaders. During the weeks when the Afghan war was going on – weeks of heightened emotions in Pakistan – the best-attended Islamist demonstrations took place only when all the different groups made common cause. They even set up a movement for this purpose: the Pakistan–Afghanistan Defence Council (PADC), which brought together twenty-two Islamist movements. However, it was only able to mobilize about 40,000 people in Karachi in October 2001, for what remains the largest pro-Taliban demonstration.

Even when they were united, the Islamists did not seem to constitute much of a threat to Musharraf, given that they had been traumatized by the shock of the Taliban's military defeat. This rout, which was more thorough than anyone had expected, had an immediate effect on Pakistan's Islamists: completely demoralized, they gave up demonstrating, even for the release of their leaders. Had they done so, they would have seen that they had little capacity for mobilization. The Islamists' reputation was damaged by this crisis: not only because they lost, but because the Pakistani people believed – rightly or wrongly – that the Afghans had betrayed them: the volunteers who went to help the Taliban fought alone, while the Afghans surrendered or went over to the enemy according to a logic that no longer had anything to do with Islamic ideology, but everything to do with the Pashtun tribal ethos. In this state of defeat, the Islamist project lost a great deal of its prestige, especially since large numbers of Pakistani militants died on Afghan soil.

There, the TSNM's seedbed for growth is by no means insignificant, especially in the famous Tribal Agencies of the FATA, the Federally Administered Tribal Areas, whose culture is Pashtun, although they are not under the control of Peshawar; they are administered directly by Islamabad, but in practice they enjoy considerable autonomy and even a special legal system, in so far as the FATA are divided up into several 'agencies' controlled by discrete clans. This area has constituted a refuge for the Taliban and become a new sanctuary for the Arabs of al-Qaeda – even more so in view of the fact that the TSNM militants immediately made common cause with their Pashtun brothers in Afghanistan during the war. As soon as the Anglo–American air strikes began, thousands of militants – some plausible estimates put the figure at 10,000 – crossed the border to come to the aid of the Taliban. Pakistani and Afghan Pashtuns came together on the terrain of an ethnic nationalism tinged with Islamism – the Pashtun ethos has obvious affinities with Taliban-style Islam, notably over the question of a woman's place in society.[17]

The TSNM militants and the Pashtuns in general, however, did not escape the demoralization suffered by other Islamists: they were the first to be affected by the collapse – indeed, the defection – of the Afghan Taliban. In the Pakistani press, many parents of young militants accused the Taliban of being responsible for the death of their sons because they did not fight fiercely enough: their 'irresponsible attitude' at Mazar-i-Sharif and Kunduz caused a lot of resentment.

Moreover, the ANP completely dissociated itself from the Taliban during the crisis, believing that they were paying the price for their extremism and their unnatural alliance with Bin Laden. The party declared itself in favour of an Afghan policy based on noninterference, and gave implicit approval to Musharraf's policy after September 11. The ANP even left the Alliance for the Restoration of Democracy, and agreed with the Bonn compromise. In Baluchistan, a province where the Pashtuns constitute a sizeable proportion of the population as a result of the influx of Afghan refugees, the Pakhtoonkwa Mili Awami Party also backed the Bonn agreement, and decided to support King Zahir Shah.

In this context, Musharraf can see his way towards clipping the wings of the Islamists in Pashtun areas without having to face a united front of opponents. Indeed, the fact that the TSNM leader has been sentenced to three years in prison has not caused much of a stir.

The generally weakened state of the Pakistani Islamists opened the way for forceful government action. The Americans urged Musharraf to finish them off once and for all. The head of the CIA, George Tenet, went to Islamabad in early December 2001 to encourage him to do this, and even to put a name to the most dangerous people, who should be placed under close surveillance. Musharraf remained very cautious, however, till the attack in New Delhi on 13 December, just as the conflict between India and Pakistan over Kashmir came to the fore again, in the wake of the Afghan crisis.

Towards a break with the Kashmir 'jihadists'?

In the 1980s and 1990s Indian Kashmir had become a favoured theatre of operations for 'jihadist' groups, prominent among which were the Hizbul Mujahideen, the Al Badr Mujahideen, the Harkat-ul Mujahiddin (also known as the Harkat-ul Ansar) and the Lashkar-i-Tayyiba, a movement formed under the auspices of the Dawat-ul-Irshad *madrasahs* (an organization set up in 1987 by two Punjabi teachers and an Arab preacher). These groups of 'mujaheddin' (the Indians call them 'mercenaries'), most of whom acquired their paramilitary skills in training camps in Pakistan, were in the habit of crossing the Kashmir line of control as soon as winter was over in order to continue their campaign.

For a long time it has been public knowledge that there are links between the main jihadist movements in Kashmir and Afghanistan. The founders of the four movements mentioned above – Hizbul Mujaheddin, Al Badr Mujaheddin, Harkat-ul Mujahiddin and Lashkar-i-Tayyiba – are all 'Afghanistan veterans', mujaheddin who fought against the Russians. The fact is that Afghanistan and Kashmir were two favoured *jihad* areas. Once Afghanistan was neutralized, after autumn 2001, there was only Kashmir, whose symbolic and strategic significance – as if this needed repeating is much greater for the Pakistanis than that of Afghanistan. Taking action in Kashmir could, in effect, be a good way for Pakistan-based Jihadists to show what they were capable of, despite the disastrous effects of the defeat of the Taliban and the deaths of hundreds of Pakistani Islamists in Afghanistan. This hypothesis seems to have been borne out by the attacks in Srinagar, and especially in Delhi, in winter 2001.

On 1 October 2001, a suicide bomber attacked the Jammu and Kashmir Assembly in Srinagar, killing forty people. No one claimed responsibility, but the method used was in effect a signature, because only the Jaish-i Muhammad and the Lashkar-i-Tayyiba carry out this kind of suicide bombing. In late 1999–early 2000, Jaish-i Muhammad and Lashkar-i-Tayyiba militants had carried out similar attacks against the Indian army in Indian Kashmir. The attack in Delhi on 13 December 2001 may have killed fewer people – fifteen in all – but its impact was far greater because it was aimed at the Parliament in New Delhi, which was infiltrated with astounding audacity by five activists. They gained access to the premises in an official car, armed with explosives, grenades and assault rifles, while a debate involving several government ministers was about to take place. The security services frustrated their attempt to kill these ministers, who were almost certainly their main target, but they shot several people, and the very fact that activists were able to perpetrate a suicide attack in the National Assembly made the people of India – who were in a state of shock – realize that kamikazes like this could strike at the very highest offices of state. The Indian government quickly traced this 'terrorist network' – at least, so they claimed – back to the Lashkar-i-Tayyiba, the Jaish-i Muhammad and the ISI, acting in concert.[18]

Bolstered by the general climate of opinion in the wake of September 11, the Indian government reacted to the attacks in Srinagar and Delhi with unprecedented force. As far as the Indians were concerned, the attacks on New York were a windfall: the world's greatest superpower had been the victim of the same 'Islamic terrorism' as India: for ten years New Delhi had been applying this label to the troubles in Kashmir, but no one had listened.[19] After the Srinagar attack, the Indians pursued this line with even more determination. They insisted that Pakistan should extradite Maulana Masood Azhar, leader of the Jaish-i Mohammed, to India, and made stronger demands than ever on the Americans to add Islamist groups who are active in Kashmir, like the Lashkar-i-Tayyiba and the Jaish-i Mohammed, to the list of Foreign Terrorist Organizations drawn up in the aftermath of September 11. Initially, only the Harkat-ul Mujahiddin appeared on this list; as a result, its offices had been boarded up and its assets frozen from the end of September 2001. The USA agreed to consider this request, but took their time about it. On 1 November, the Justice Department recommended to the State Department that the LT and the JM should be added to the list of terrorist groups.

The attack of 13 December brought an even stronger Indian reaction. New Delhi arraigned Islamabad publicly, implying that the government of Pakistan had had a hand in it. The Indian government demanded the extradition of twenty terrorists, including Masood Azhar, Syed Salahuddin (leader of the Hizbul Mujahideen), and several of their henchmen, who had been responsible for the 1999 hijacking; but also the gangsters involved – according to New Delhi – in the attacks in Bombay in 1993, like Daud Ibrahim and the Sikh separatists whom Pakistan had supported at the height of the struggle for Khalistan in the 1990s. Islamabad replied that Pakistan's involvement in the 13 December attack had yet to be proved, and that in any case, none of the twenty people accused by New Delhi was in the country. In response to this totally foreseeable prevarication, India made a show of force, prompted by the international situation in the wake of September 11 and also by the situation in India itself: the governing Bharatiya Janata Party (BJP – Party of the People of India) could not risk looking weak, because it was preparing for important regional elections in Uttar Pradesh, one of the biggest States in the Indian Union. George Fernandes, the Indian Defence Minister, announced an unprecedented troop deployment – even greater than in 1971 – along the border with Pakistan. On 26 December he also announced that Indian missiles – except Agni II, the latest addition to the arsenal – were poised for attack.

It was in this extremely tense situation that the USA formally added the LT and the JM to the list of Foreign Terrorist Organizations. It now contains the names of five movements based in Pakistan – no other country is so 'well' represented in this list of thirty-nine names. At the same time, the USA put pressure on General

Musharraf to follow the same policy in his own country. Washington was eager for him to do so, in order to defuse the situation with New Delhi. The Americans were keen to avoid any conflict, however limited, between India and Pakistan, because such a conflict could lead Pakistan to remove its troops from the Afghan border, where their mission was to capture Taliban and Al-Qaeda people retreating to Pakistan – and, if possible, Osama bin Laden. The warlike noises coming from New Delhi strengthened Washington's pressure on Islamabad to the point where, on 12 January 2002, Musharraf made an hour-long speech to the Pakistani nation which was, in reality, aimed at the USA too. On the pretext of going back to the original ideology behind Pakistan, as expressed by Jinnah, he railed against the rise of intolerance and fundamentalism. He spoke in the Kemalist tones which he had already adopted in his attacks on sectarian movements in 2000 and 2001: 'Sectarian terrorism has been going on for years. Every one of us is fed up of it . . . Our peace-loving people are keen to get rid of the Kalashnikov and weapon culture . . . The day of reckoning has come. Do we want Pakistan to be a theocratic state? Do we believe that religious education alone is enough for governance or do we want Pakistan to emerge as a progressive and dynamic welfare state?' Of course, Musharraf had his own political reasons for making such a speech. He held that the Islamists had set up a 'state within a state', and he intended to act against the threat this constituted. On this point, he went so far as to say: 'Today Pakistan is not facing any real threat from outside. But the real threats are posed from within . . .'. Understandably, however, the nub of his speech concerned external affairs: 'I would request that we should stop interfering with the affairs of others . . .'.

This combination of domestic and foreign concerns explains the measures Musharraf announced on 12 January 2002: all *madrasahs* had to register with the authorities by 23 March, just as foreign students were obliged to; those suspected of involvement in terrorist acts or sectarian violence would be dealt with in so-called speedy trial courts; above all, the Jaish-i Mohammed, Lashkar-i-Tayyiba, Sipah-i Sahaba Pakistan, Tehrik-i Jafria Pakistan and Tanzim Nifaz-i Shari'ah-i Mohammadi were dissolved. Militant members of these movements were immediately targeted: according to Ministry of the Interior officials, 1,900 activists were arrested and 600 organizational headquarters closed down in four days. However, most of them were freed soon after and it remains to be seen how serious Musharraf is so far as the fight against Islamism is concerned.

Musharraf asked the ISI to stop supporting Islamist action in Kashmir. But he did not put into question Pakistan's involvement alongside their 'brothers in Kashmir'. On 10 January, two days before his speech, he had overseen the setting up of a National Kashmir Committee under the presidency of the moderate Muhammad Abdul Qayyum Khan, former President of Azad Kashmir; the purpose of this committee was to continue the struggle by new means. In his speech on 12 January, Musharraf not only ruled out the possibility of handing one single Pakistani citizen over to India, but also emphasized the fact that the Kashmiri cause was 'in his blood', and that he would support the Kashmiris under Indian control 'morally, diplomatically and politically'. So Pakistan will remain embroiled in this regional conflict for the foreseeable future.

Even if Kashmir is still a central plank in Pakistan's foreign policy, this policy can no longer include state collusion with jihadist groups: Islamism will no longer constitute part of Musharraf's regional policy in either Kashmir or Afghanistan as centrally as before. He also has to get a grip on the situation within his own country. The moment he came to power, he made Sunni and Shi'a groups a specific target for action; hitherto, however, he has not come down on them particularly hard, for two main reasons: they have been useful foreign policy tools, and they have been quite capable of fomenting trouble on the streets. In the altered circumstances after September 11, however, Musharraf was able to seize the opportunity to crack down on organizations that had set up a 'state within a state', and thus reinforce his power. Overall, September 11 has helped the General-President to consolidate his position and institutionalize his authoritarian regime.

Institutionalizing Authoritarianism

General Musharraf's political game plan

General Musharraf did not simply institute a military regime and leave it at that. It is true that he has proclaimed himself Chief Executive, and then President, of Pakistan, while remaining head of the army and has given several military men government posts: the heads of the air force and the navy are members of his National Security Council – that is to say, his government. But Musharraf is no Zia – notably in his reluctance to impose martial law: he allowed President Rafiq Tarar to remain in office until spring 2001. Above all – like Ayub Khan, who invented the concept of guided democracy, and brought in a system of indirect elections designed to keep himself in power – Musharraf has a plan: even, perhaps, a political vision. He subscribes to the mindset of the military men who governed Pakistan before him in the sense that he shares their aversion to 'the politicians', but he parts company with them insofar as he is eager to establish a new political order which is not totally dominated by the military. The previous Martial Law Administrators 'put a military superstructure over the civilian structure, when they left the [original] civil structure as it was. I do not want this.'[20]

In February 2000 he assumed control of the legal system, obliging judges to swear allegiance to the 14 October 1999 Provisional Constitutional Ordinance. On 12 May 2000 the Supreme Court put his coup on a legal footing, investing him with legislative and constitutional powers. Nevertheless, the façade of a separation of powers remained: Pakistan's Chief Executive agreed to abide by the Supreme Court ruling of 12 May which enjoined him to hold a general election within three years of his coup.

The rebuilding of the state to which Musharraf aspires entails a total rethink of all institutions; their channels of power would have to be both the army and a president directly linked to a network of local representatives in a decentralized political system. His plan also involves bringing the political parties into line: they would be under military supervision, and Musharraf would like them to compete with a new political class which he is trying to bring into existence. He has taken two steps towards putting his plan into practice:

1. First, he has implemented some local reforms: he has replaced the all-powerful district commissioners, who exercised both executive and judicial functions – a legacy of the colonial era – with district coordination officers, under the supervision of local representatives sitting on district and municipal councils. With a view to implementing this reform, Musharraf organized local elections, hoping that they would bring about a change of political actors, since he had decided that they would be non-partisan (the political parties could neither put forward candidates nor support any candidate officially).

2. Secondly, he proclaimed himself President of the Islamic Republic of Pakistan for an indefinite period in June 2001 – the Succession Order 2001 states: 'The Chief Executive will hold the office of President until his successor takes over that office.'

These two measures – Musharraf's elevation to the office of President and the appointment of local representatives who, as far as possible, are not connected with the old political parties – in effect constitute a system, because it is from the relationship between the military state superstructure and the popular (not party-political) base that a new state structure must emerge. In April 2001, Musharraf told the important English-language monthly *The Herald*: 'After October 2001, I will be dealing with 106 [district] nazims and I think I will motivate every one of them. I will take them forward to serve the nation.'[21] Musharraf is also calling on the army to play a role in his political game plan – simply because, he says, Pakistan's history shows that the country cannot be governed without it. He proposes that, rather than having to take part in regular coups, it should have its own place in the political system, acting as a kind of bodyguard – hence his concept of a National Security Council, 'which ought to address all possible issues, all possible political crises, all possible diplomatic, international and security issues . . . Maybe it is out of time and out of place in the developed world but certainly not in ours.'[22]

The local reforms in 2001 immediately revealed the army's separate role: their cantonments, which are a prominent feature of most towns in both spatial and financial terms, are not under the control of the municipal councils; they are autonomous.

One implicit aim of this reform was to short-circuit the traditional political personnel. This institutional plan was part and parcel of the marginalization of the political structures that had allowed the politicians to gain power.

Musharraf takes on the political parties and the politicians

One of Musharraf's primary objectives after his coup was, naturally, to bring the politicians into line, particularly those who constituted a threat to his government – beginning with Nawaz Sharif, the Prime Minister whom he had just overthrown.

In August 2000, an amendment to the 1962 Political Parties Act debarred from public office all those politicians who were in a legally compromising situation; at the top of this list was Nawaz Sharif. Nevertheless, Musharraf did not treat Sharif as Zia treated Bhutto, who was executed two years after being ousted. On 10 November 1999, the former Prime Minister faced a charge – lodged by a colonel in the Pakistani army – of treason and attempted assassination, because he had issued orders aimed at preventing the plane bringing General Musharraf from Colombo from landing at Karachi. He was arrested on 18 November, and formally charged on 19 January 2000. His trial started on 26 January and lasted until 6 April; he was sentenced to life imprisonment, and all his assets were confiscated. In the meantime, on 25 March, Bill Clinton had paid a brief visit to Islamabad to ask Musharraf to spare Sharif's life. Sharif also stood trial on a charge of corruption – especially tax evasion – in spring 2000, as part of a more general campaign of denouncing the political methods of former regimes. On 22 July he was given a fine of 20 million rupees and fourteen years in prison. In October these penalties were commuted on appeal: henceforth, there is a 500-million-rupee limit to the value of Sharif's assets that can be seized.

This legal soap opera, however, came to an unexpected end a few weeks later, when Musharraf decided to let Sharif out of prison. He did this partly because he was afraid that Sharif's party would come back into politics – a fear prompted by the fact that Sharif had recently joined the ARD (see below). Sharif's release was also the result of pressure from the USA – Bill Clinton, who was coming to the end of his presidency, had promised Sharif's family that he would secure his release – and Saudi Arabia: Sharif was particularly close to Prince Abdullah, especially since the 1998 nuclear weapons tests, which had gone down very well in Saudi Arabia. Sharif was allowed to go to Saudi Arabia with his family under an arrangement which stipulated that he would not leave that country, would stay out of politics for at least ten years, would make no statement against the military government, and that his assets would be confiscated, together with 300 million rupees' worth of bank deposits – this would prove difficult to achieve, for legal reasons. That rid Musharraf of the two political heavyweights of the 1990s, Nawaz Sharif and Benazir Bhutto. In view of the latter's entanglements with the law, she was liable to immediate arrest if she set foot in Pakistan again (her husband, Asif Zardari, is still in prison).

Musharraf, however, did not emerge from this business completely unscathed. It is true that he had rid himself of his former rival, who, had he stayed in prison in Pakistan, could in the long run have been hailed as a martyr, or at the very least fomented political action by the PML(N). Nonetheless, in asking President Tarar to 'pardon' Sharif, so that he could be released, Musharraf ran the risk of undermining his campaign against political corruption – it was clear from all those millions of confiscated rupees how profitable this could be. The effect on public opinion was not improved when Sajjad Ali Shah, former president of the Supreme Court, chose this moment to announce that the President did not have the right to exonerate Sharif without the sanction of this body, the highest court in Pakistan's legal system. Musharraf's decision had obviously been prompted by the fact that Sharif's PML and some other major political parties had come together to form the ARD, a united front which threatened to scupper the Chief Executive's carefully prepared plans for political reform, simply because it foreshadowed the lesson that was to be drawn from the local elections, namely that the political parties were down but not out.

Musharraf decided to call local elections in 2000 – partly to win favour with the international community (in fact the first wave of elections took place on 31 December of that year, in order to fulfil his promise that elections would be held during the year after the coup), and partly to prepare for the 2002 transition: he hoped that these elections would not only prepare the ground for a less centralized political–administrative system, but also – and above all – produce a new political group which would promote his regime in towns and villages throughout Pakistan. That is why these were non-partisan local elections. In reality, the president of the National Reconstruction Bureau, Tanvir Navi, had to admit that only '25 to 50% of elected people had never been involved in politics in the past'.[23] In actual fact, the political parties played a very active part in the election campaign, and got several of their members elected.

At the same time, seventeen political organizations combined to form a Grand Democratic Alliance, which became the Alliance for the Restoration of Democracy in December 2000, when Nawaz Sharif's PML(N) joined the seventeen parties that had already formed a coalition around the PPP, the MQM (which soon left), the ANP, and so on.

Then Musharraf attempted to divide the ARD by favouring a section of Nawaz Sharif's party, the Pakistan Muslim League (Nawaz).[24] In December 2000, he began by encouraging the rebellious stirrings of Mian Muhammad Azhar, a PML(N) leader who was hostile towards Nawaz Sharif. Then in February 2001, once Nawaz Sharif had gone off to Saudi Arabia, 'anti-Nawaz' elements close to Azhar took control of the Punjabi branch – that is, the main branch – of the party, with the approval of the junta. The following month, Mian Muhammad Azhar was powerful enough to form a new party, the PML (Like Minded), with the support of Ejaz ul-Haq, son of Zia ul-Haq. Both men supported Musharraf, who had played a key role in this split. In fact, all these events seemed to indicate that the General-President was trying to equip himself with a one-party political machine in view of the elections due in 2002.

Musharraf's idea of establishing a new political system where he would have direct relations with a network of locally elected representatives, without involving the political parties, could not stand the test of time. It is true that the parties remained weak, but they adapted to their new status, and Musharraf himself was obliged to come to terms with them. In August 2001 he promised that the 2002 general election would be on a 'partisan basis', thus allowing the political parties to expand their activities. However, the situation changed after September 11. Musharraf then thought that he was in a position to assert himself and forget about the subtleties of democracy, because national security and unity were at stake. He therefore explained that, given the circumstances, he would remain President of Pakistan whatever the results of the October 2002 elections. Interestingly, he made this announcement while he was on an official visit in the USA.

President Musharraf: with American blessing, but without popular support

If the Americans were keen on the idea of reestablishing democracy in Pakistan before September 11, they seemed to forget all about it thereafter.

There were no democratic strings attached to the financial support granted to Pakistan by the antiterrorist coalition led by the USA. When Musharraf himself pledged in late 2001 to hold elections in 2002, the Americans did not make their aid conditional upon respecting this promise – had they done so, this would have given some encouragement to an intelligentsia caught in a stranglehold between the military government and Islamist fundamentalism. One can understand the bitterness of the editor in chief of Pakistan's leading magazine, for whom 'the problems of democracy and human rights have very clearly been relegated to a lower level while the USA returns to its cold war philosophy, according to which "our dictator is a good dictator"'.[25]

The General-President took full advantage of this situation by declaring in New York, on 13 November, that he would remain in office whatever the result of the 2002 poll. Western countries made no reaction whatsoever to this announcement. So in actual fact it was General Musharraf, even more than Pakistan as a whole, who made his big comeback on to the international stage. *Newsweek* breathed a sigh of relief as it told us, in its own inimitable way: 'We should certainly be happy that Pakistan is run by a military dictator friendly towards us, rather than that the country be a democracy that could have been hostile'.[26]

The events of September 11 made a twofold impact on Pakistan. On the domestic front, they enabled Musharraf to consolidate his position institutionally but led him to move against the Islamists, using repressive measures which may be hard to implement. They have already triggered a series of bomb attacks against Western interests in Pakistan: 14 Frenchmen working on a submarine in Karachi were killed by suicide bombers on 8 May, 2002. Islamist groups related to Al-Qaeda have obviously tried to destabilize Musharraf and force him to give up his collaboration with the anti-terrorist coalition. On the external front, September 11 has been a watershed, not only because it enabled Pakistan to be readmitted into the international community, but also because it forced the country to withdraw from Afghanistan and, to a lesser extent, from Kashmir. However, the internal and external dimensions must not be looked at separately, especially because one of the strengths of Musharraf as a Pakistani leader stems from outside support and more specifically from the USA. Now, this support must be justified and may not be sufficient.

Musharraf pushed his advantage further by organizing a referendum recalling the one Zia had held in 1985. On 30 April, 2002, the citizens of Pakistan were asked whether they wanted to entrust President Musharraf with a fresh five-year mandate to implement fully the reforms (whatever these were) he had just started. According to the official results, Musharraf received a huge endorsement of 97% of the vote: even Musharraf himself had to admit that such an incredible figure had been possible only because of fraud, which he attributed to the Election Commission.

However, he was nevertheless responsible for the style of his referendum campaign, which was replete with populist slogans and highly personalized. This episode, in fact, alienated large sections of Pakistani society. The low turnout (not reflected in the official figures) was a clear indication of this new development.

The referendum results enabled Musharraf to claim that he had enough legitimacy to distort further the democratic agenda. During the summer of 2002 he prepared the October 2002 elections by restoring the spirit – if not the letter – of the infamous Eighth Amendment. Once again, the President was giving himself the right to dismiss the Prime Minister and to dissolve assemblies. History was indeed repeating itself, with the blessing of the USA and at the expense of democracy.

Conclusion

The Pakistani army was able to stomach the loss of Afghanistan in exchange for the lifting of American sanctions and financial largesse from the international community, because they hoped that these two things would lead to military collaboration with the USA and a supply of American arms. Washington, however, does not seem to see its cooperation with Pakistan in the same light. On 1 December 2001, during a visit to Islamabad, Donald Rumsfeld reaffirmed that the USA had every intention of reestablishing its military cooperation, but for the moment it was not particularly inclined to meet Musharraf's demands. It dodged the issue of his request for a delivery of F-16s – Pakistan had paid for them, but not yet received them, and in the end the money was refunded, because of the sanctions – by simply agreeing to provide spare parts for the F-16s Pakistan already had. At the same time, the USA was discussing strategy closely with India. On 3 and 4 December 2001, the Defense Policy Group – of which Douglas Feith, American Under Secretary for Defense, was a member – announced joint military exercises, especially by the respective navies; this development worried Islamabad.[27] Should the USA pursue a pro-Indian policy – which was highly probable, given that they were already moving in that direction, and that the Americans probably considered India a stabilizing force in South Asia – Musharraf might be accused by some of his officers of bungling his support for Washington during the war in Afghanistan, and the joint anti-Al-Qaeda operations with the FBI in Pakistan. These operations, which enabled the Americans to capture one of Bin Laden's lieutenants, Zubaydah, in Faisalabad, are indeed resented because of the encroachment on national sovereignty they represent.

The consolidation of Musharraf's power and the pursuit of his policy also depends on the fact that the foreign aid that had been promised to Pakistan would materialize, saving the country's failing economy at a stroke: the war has stopped Pakistan's industry in its tracks, just as it was heading for recovery, and international aid, totalling only 1.7 billion dollars to date, will not go far towards covering the cost of the conflict: about 2.5 billion dollars. It will take more money than that to defuse resentful feelings in Pakistan, where 34 per cent of the population already live below the poverty threshold, while the wealthiest 10 per cent get 28 per cent of the (declared) income, and social spending fell from a meagre 9.2 per cent of GDP in 1979–80 to a microscopic 3.1 per cent in 1998–99.

Economic aid is even more necessary in view of the fact that Pakistan is afraid that it will be left to its own devices once the war is over: should such feelings of abandonment take root in Islamabad, not only would Musharraf's regime be weakened, but the entire Pakistani establishment – including Musharraf himself – could fall under the spell of an extremely dangerous campaign to go it alone, in Kashmir or elsewhere – by way of revenge, but also in protest against marginalization. Musharraf himself remains convinced that his main assets are his geostrategic position and his nuclear arsenal.[30]

GLOSSARY

Ahmadi or **Ahmadiyya**   heterodox Muslim sect founded by Mirza Ghulam Ahmad in about 1890.

Ahrar   literally 'free': an Islamic group with socialist tendencies formed in the Punjab in 1930 by Mazhar Ali Khan and Maulana Ataullah Shah Bukhari.

anjuman   meeting or assembly.

ashraf   literally 'nobles'; a generic term used in India to describe all Muslims of foreign origin – Arabs, Turks and Afghans – who, with high-caste converts, constitute a social stratum that is superior to the *ashlaf*, or low-caste converts.

barani   land that is dependent on rainwater irrigation.

biradari or **biraderi**   literally 'fraternity'; clan, community.

Bohra   a Muslim group from Indian Gujarat, mostly members of the Mustali wing of Isma'ili Shi'a.

Brahmans   the highest caste in the Hindu social system. Traditionally, they have a monopoly on the teaching of sacred texts and religious practices.

chela   pupil or disciple of a Hindu guru.

cipaye   Frenchified form of *sipahi*; soldier or person entrusted with the maintenance of order.

da'î   literally 'missionary'; spiritual leader of the Bohra.

dargah   literally 'door' or 'threshold'; sanctuary of a Muslim saint.

dini madari   religious school.

diya   literally 'price of blood'; monetary compensation paid by the guilty party to stave off vengeance. See *qisas*.

hajj   pilgrimage to Mecca.

hijra   literally 'migration'; the Prophet's Hegira, or migration, from Mecca to Medina in 622. It marked the official beginning of the Muslim religion

Hindko   an Indo-European language spoken in the north of Pakistan, especially in the Kaghan and Indus valleys. *Hindko* could mean 'Indian language' as opposed to Pashto, which belongs to the Iranian group.

ijma   literally 'consensus'; this is the third source of Muslim law after the Koran and the Sunna, normally the result of a consensus among the ulemas. For modernists, this consensus is that of the people's elected representatives.

Islamayyat or **Islamayat**   literally 'Islamity'; the name given to religious education courses after Zulfikar Ali Bhutto's regime.

jagirdar the beneficiary of a remuneration system for government and military executives in Muslim states and their vassal states since the time of the Delhi sultanate. Instead of a salary, the *jagirdar* are given an estate on which they can levy tax (and keep a portion of it). The erosion of the authority of the Mughal Empire allowed the *jagirdar* to establish hereditary fiefs where they dispensed justice and functioned as police. This system lasted throughout colonial times, especially in the Princely States.

Jat a large middle caste of farmers in the Punjab.

jirgah a meeting of tribal leaders [*sardar*].

kafir miscreant or infidel.

kashmiriat or **kashmiriyyat** 'Kashmirity'.

khan a title widely used among the Pashtuns. It is also a very common surname in the Indian subcontinent, in other communities as well. In the Afghan world it is generally applied to a landowner at the head of a large cognate or client group, whom he supports by providing food and other benefits; leader of a clan or tribe.

kharif autumn; autumn harvest.

khel clan, or subdivision of a Pashtun clan.

Khoja a Muslim group from Indian Gujarat, mostly members of the Nizari wing of Isma'ili Shi'a.

Kshatriya a high Hindu military caste. There are many *Kshatriya* among the landowning classes.

lambardar village chief.

maddhe sahaba a recitation in praise of the first three caliphs recognized by Sunni Muslims.

mansabdar literally 'a man of rank'; traditionally, a dignitary of the Mughal Empire. A local leader in the Tribal Areas.

mazhab a law school. Sunni Islam has four major law schools: the Hanafi school (to which most Muslims in the Indian subcontinent, together with the Muslims of Central Asia and the Turks, claim allegiance); the Hanbali school (in Saudi Arabia); the Maliki school (which predominates in Africa, apart from Egypt); and the Shafei school (represented in Arab countries, Southeast Asia and South India). The Twelver Shi'a also have a law school, called the Jafari school.

mehfil an assembly.

millat literally 'religious community'; by extension, nation. According to nationalist ulemas, a Muslim religious community within the Indian nation in the context of British India; in the Afghan context, the nation as opposed to the state.

Muhajir a Muslim of Indian origin who left India for Pakistan after Partition.

mujaddid reformer.

murid a disciple in a Sufi order.

musawat-i muhammadi literally 'Mohammedan equality'; the official name for Zulfikar Ali Bhutto's brand of Islamic socialism.

nawab honorific plural of *naib*, a provincial governor; more specifically, governors who became independent after the disintegration of the Mughal Empire.

parda or **purdah**   literally 'veil' or 'curtain'; a system that keeps women segregated in the traditional Muslim elite.

pir   a spiritual master in a Sufi brotherhood; a living or dead Muslim saint with miraculous powers.

pirzada   the son of a *pir*.

prasad   Hindu propitiatory dishes; food offered to an idol.

qaum   any subdivision of the universal Muslim community; in British India it was used more specifically to describe the Muslim community of the subcontinent as opposed to the Hindu community. The Muslim League considered this community to be a nation when it formed the movement for the creation of Pakistan. See *millat*.

qisas   private vengeance for a murder or a serious injury, which takes the form of inflicting the equivalent punishment on the guilty party.

Qureshi   an honorific title for people who are said to be descended from the Arab Qureish, the tribe of the Prophet Mohammed.

rabi   springtime; the spring harvest.

Rajput   a warrior class; members of the *Kshatriya* caste.

riba'   interest-bearing loans; usury.

safa'i   literally 'cleansing'; a word used at the time of Partition to describe the ethnic cleansing that took place on both sides of the new border between India and Pakistan.

sajjada nashin   literally 'he who sits on the prayer mat'; the guardian of a Sufi sanctuary.

sardar   the Persian word for commander; a tribal chief.

sayyid or **seyyed**   someone who is said to be descended from the Prophet.

Sunna   the Prophet's behavioural precepts, which lay down a code of conduct for Muslims. They are set out in the Traditions [*hadis*] passed down by the Companions of the Prophet, and constitute the second source of Muslim law after the Koran.

tabaruk   propitiatory dishes.

tahar   purity.

talaq al-ahsan   a man's repudiation of his wife by repeating the *talaq* phrase ('I repudiate thee') three times during the *tuhr* or 'clean' time (that is, the time when the woman is not menstruating), and abstaining completely from sexual intercourse during the *iddat* (the three-month period during which a widow or a divorced woman is not allowed to remarry). This form of divorce may be revoked during the *iddat*.

talaq al-bid'a   a man's instant and irrevocable repudiation of his wife by repeating the *talaq* phrase ('I repudiate thee') three times.

taliban   students of religion who are educated in seminaries or *madrasahs*.

tanzim   organization.

taqiyya   concealing one's religious faith as a means of self-protection (a Shi'a tradition).

taqlid   a passive acceptance of the law as taught in schools of jurisprudence. In the language of modernist Muslims, this word has pejorative connotations.

umma   the universal community of Muslims, as opposed to national communities (*qaum* and *millat*).

ushr   literally 'tithe'; a religious tax on harvests, in principle at a rate of 10 per cent.

wadera   major landowners in Sind.

walaya   submission to the hidden imam (among the Bohra).

waz   a sermon; preaching.

zahir   obvious; exoteric.

zakat   a religious tax on harvests, in principle paid annually at a rate of 2.5 per cent of capital.

zamindar   a Mughal Empire official, responsible for collecting land taxes in a given area. It has gradually acquired the wider meaning of 'landowner'.

zat   a term, of Arabic origin, used by Muslims as a name for the caste. See *Jat*.

ziyara   a (non-canonical) pilgrimage.

CHRONOLOGY

23 March 1940	In Lahore, the Muslim League pass a resolution demanding the formation of a country called Pakistan, which they intend to establish as a union of independent sovereign states.
14–15 August 1947	The Independence and Partition of British India. Regions with a Muslim majority (the western Punjab, the North West Frontier Province, Sind and Baluchistan to the west; East Bengal to the east) form Pakistan.
30 September 1947	Pakistan joins the United Nations Organization.
27 October 1947	Under attack from Pashtun tribes, the maharajah of Jammu and Kashmir asks India for help; this is provided on condition that his province becomes part of India.
29 January 1948	Under Indian pressure, the United Nations Security Council issues a recommendation that a referendum should be held in Kashmir.
11 September 1948	The death of Muhammad Ali Jinnah, Pakistan's founder and first head of state.
14 December 1948	Maulvi Tameezuddin is elected president of Pakistan's Constituent Assembly.
1 January 1949	Cease-fire in Kashmir.
6 January 1949	The Constituent Assembly passes a law authorizing the governor general to disqualify from public office anyone charged with corruption (the Public and Representation Office Disqualification Act, or PRODA.
22 February 1949	Rana Liaquat, wife of Prime Minister Liaquat Ali Khan, sets up the All Pakistan Women's Association (APWA).
27 July 1949	India and Pakistan sign a cease-fire agreement.
4 January 1950	Pakistan recognizes the People's Republic of China.
8 April 1950	Liaquat Ali Khan and Jawaharlal Nehru sign the Delhi Pact on the protection of minorities in their respective countries.
17 January 1951	General Ayub Khan replaces the British General Gracey as commander-in-chief of the armed forces.
16 October 1951	Assassination of Liaquat Ali Khan. He is succeeded by the governor general, Ghulam Muhammad.

26 January 1952	In Dhaka, Prime Minister Nazimuddin makes an announcement to the effect that Urdu will be Pakistan's national language. The Bengalis, who make up 54 per cent of the population, organize street protests. Three people die in a student protest on 21 February. On 7 May 1954, the Constituent Assembly declare Bengali the second national language.
6 March 1953	Anti-Ahmadi riots in Lahore lead to the imposition of martial law.
April 1953	Governor General Ghulam Muhammad dismisses Prime Minister Nazimuddin.
30 May 1953	Ghulam Muhammad dismisses Fazl ul-Huq, leader of the government of East Pakistan.
March 1954	The Awami League defeat the Muslim League in provincial elections in East Pakistan.
May 1954	Pakistan joins the Southeast Asia Treaty Organization (SEATO), a military alliance inspired by the USA.
24 July 1954	The Communist Party is declared an illegal organization.
24 October 1954	Ghulam Muhammad dissolves the Constituent Assembly.
3 January 1955	The Princely States of Baluchistan join the province of Baluchistan.
11 August 1955	Chaudhary Muhammad Ali becomes Prime Minister.
19 September 1955	Iskander Mirza succeeds Ghulam Muhammad as governor general.
23 September 1955	Pakistan joins CENTO, another strategic alliance inspired by the USA.
14 October 1955	Central government, dominated by Punjabis, decides to combine the provinces of West Pakistan (the Punjab, the NWFP, Sind and Baluchistan) into one entity, 'West Pakistan', in order to achieve a population that can rival East Pakistan in numerical terms. The 'small' provinces are not at all happy about this so-called 'One Unit Scheme'.
29 February 1956	The Constituent Assembly pass Pakistan's first Constitution.
4 March 1956	Mirza, the only candidate, is elected President of Pakistan.
23 March 1956	After nine years of debate, the Constitution is officially proclaimed. It establishes an Islamic republic and a political regime that is officially parliamentary and federal, but in fact highly centralized.
12 September 1956	Hussain Shaheed Suhrawady is appointed Prime Minister.
25 July 1957	The formation of the Pakistan National Party, an opposition party which subsequently became the National Awami Party (NAP).
18 October 1957	I I Chundrigar is appointed Prime Minister. On 16

	December he is forced to resign, and is succeeded by Feroz Khan Noon.

6 October 1958 — The *khan* of Kalat is deposed on a trumped-up charge of sedition.

7 October 1958 — President Iskander Mirza imposes martial law. Marshal Ayub Khan leads a military coup; he becomes chief administrator of martial law, then (on 24 October) Prime Minister. The National Assembly is dissolved; political parties are banned. On 27 October, Mirza is forced to resign. Politicians convicted of corruption are debarred from public office until 1 January 1966.

October 1959 — Introduction of a system called 'basic democracy', which in effect allows the President to select his own electoral body.

14 February 1960 — Ayub Khan is elected President of Pakistan.

2 March 1961 — The Family Law Ordinance outlaws polygamy and allows wives to ask for a divorce.

1 July 1961 — Rawalpindi becomes Pakistan's capital city. The former capital, Karachi, becomes part of the province of Sind. A new town, Islamabad, is to be built a few kilometres from Rawalpindi; it will become Pakistan's capital city in 1967.

28 April 1962 — The National Assembly is elected by the so-called 'basic democrats'. The ban on political parties is still in force.

8 June 1962 — Martial law is replaced by the second Constitution, drawn up under the auspices of the military, which establishes a presidential-style regime.

16 July 1962 — The National Assembly legalize political parties.

January 1963 — Zulfikar Ali Bhutto, former minister of 'basic democracy', takes over the Foreign Affairs portfolio.

7 January 1963 — Ayub Khan promulgates a Political Parties (Amendment) Ordinance, which threatens politicians convicted of corruption who try to regain public office with two years' imprisonment.

2 March 1963 — Pakistan signs a border agreement with China, which – in the context of the Sino-Indian war – marks a significant *rapprochement*.

20 April 1963 — Z A Bhutto lays the foundation stone for Pakistan's first nuclear reactor at Nilor, near Islamabad.

1 January 1964 — Protest demonstrations in Pakistan against the mysterious disappearance of the relic – one of the Prophet's hairs – from Srinagar's Hazrat Bal mosque.

18 September 1964 — An opposition alliance takes the form of the Combined Opposition Parties in order to fight the presidential election campaign. Its candidate is Fatima Jinnah, Qaid-i Azam's sister.

2 January 1965 — Ayub Khan is elected President.

4 January 1965	Ayub Khan's victory procession, which includes a number of Pashtuns, causes intercommunal riots.
21 March 1965	The 'basic democrats' elect the National Assembly.
April 1965	The second war between India and Pakistan breaks out; the first phase takes place in the Rann of Kutch, on the border between Gujarat and Sind. As a result of mediation by the British Prime Minister, a cease-fire is declared there on 30 June.
24 July 1965	Pakistan's military launch Operation Gibraltar, aimed at provoking an uprising by Indian Kashmiris around Srinagar. This aim was not achieved.
6 September 1965	The Indian army marches on Lahore, crossing the border without issuing a preliminary ultimatum.
19–20 September 1965	Ayub Khan pays a secret visit to China for talks with Zhou En Lai, who pledges to support him.
22 December 1965	Pakistan's first nuclear reactor comes on stream.
10 January 1966	Ayub Khan and Lal Bahadur Shastri sign a peace treaty at Tashkent.
5 February 1966	During a meeting in Lahore, Mujibur Rahman, president of the Awami League of East Pakistan, demands the implementation of the 1940 Lahore Resolution, and hence the formation of a genuinely federal Pakistan.
30 December 1966	Z A Bhutto forms the Pakistan People's Party (PPP).
1 January 1967	Politicians who were debarred from public office for corruption – which was not proved in every case – are free to resume political activity.
18 January 1967	Mujibar Rahman is arrested on a charge of conspiring with India against the national security of Pakistan (the so-called 'Agartala Conspiracy').
October 1967	The Planning Commission acknowledges that twenty-two families control 66 per cent of Pakistan's industrial assets and 87 per cent of the banking and insurance sector.
November 1967	Z A Bhutto and Wali Khan are arrested for criticizing Ayub Khan's regime after a student is killed by the police on 7 November.
17 February 1968	Bhutto and Wali Khan are released.
22 February 1968	Rahman is acquitted of the 'Agartala Conspiracy'.
24 March 1969	Ayub Khan resigns over the social unrest and violent demonstrations in East Bengal, abrogating the Constitution under whose terms he should be succeeded by the president of the National Assembly. He hands over to General Yahya Khan, who – rumour has it – brought about his resignation.
26 March 1969	Yahya Khan imposes martial law.

28 November 1969	Yahya Khan announces the winding-up of the One Unit Scheme, and cancels the elections.
28 March 1970	Yahya Khan promulgates the Legal Framework Order, which will be used as a framework for constitutional procedure. It stipulates that 169 out of the 313 seats in the National Assembly will be allotted to East Pakistan.
1 July 1970	The One Unit Scheme is wound up: Pakistan's western provinces regain their autonomy.
7 December 1970	Pakistan's first free elections are won by the Awami League, whose success in East Pakistan is overwhelming; in West Pakistan, on the other hand, Zulfikar Ali Bhutto's Pakistan People's Party (PPP) wins the most votes.
17 December 1970	Elections for the provincial assemblies.
14 February 1971	Yahya Khan announces that the Constituent Assembly will meet in Dhacca on 3 March to draw up a new constitution.
27 February 1971	Bhutto asks for this meeting to be postponed; Yahya Khan agrees.
3 March 1971	The Awami League organizes a week-long general strike.
25 March 1971	The army launches a large-scale military operation in East Pakistan; the Dhaka University campus is its main target.
6 December 1971	India recognizes Bangladesh's government-in-exile.
7–16 December 1971	The Indian offensive gets through the Pakistani army in a few days. With India's help, the Bengalis of Pakistan manage to secede and form Bangladesh (16 December).
20 December 1971	Yahya Khan hands over power to Bhutto, who becomes civilian martial law administrator.
2 January 1972	The Bhutto government announces that it will nationalize whole swathes of industry – from iron and steel to chemicals, including the electrical industry.
10 February 1972	It is made more difficult for bosses to sack their employees. Workers must be allowed some involvement in management.
1 March 1972	An agrarian reform measure stipulates that no one individual may own more than 150 acres of irrigated land and 300 acres of nonirrigated land.
19 March 1972	Insurance companies are nationalized.
20 April 1972	The interim Constitution is put into effect, and martial law is lifted.
1 May 1972	Sardar Ataullah Mengal becomes leader of the Baluchistan government.
2 July 1972	Indira Gandhi and Z A Bhutto sign the Simla Accords, which terminate the 1971 war.
8–16 July 1972	The vote on the Sindi Language Bill causes intercommunal riots in Sind.
24 December 1972	The Pashtun leader Khan Abdul Ghaffar Khan returns from eight years' exile in Kabul.

13 February 1973	Baluchistan's government collapses; this provokes civil disorder in the province. The NWFP government resigns in protest.
12 April 1973	The third Constitution is proclaimed, with the agreement of the major political forces.
July 1973	Daud deposes King Zahir Shah and takes power in Afghanistan.
22–24 February 1974	An Islamic Conference Summit in Lahore confirms Pakistan's full integration into the Arab–Muslim world.
18 May 1974	India carries out its first nuclear weapons test in Rajasthan, on the border with Pakistan.
June 1974	Fresh anti-Ahmadi riots in the Punjab – more violent than the 1953 riots.
10 February 1975	The National Awami Party is banned; Wali Khan is put in prison.
15 August 1975	Mujibur Rahman, founding president of Bangladesh, is assassinated.
1 March 1976	Bhutto appoints Zia ul-Haq Chief of Army Staff (COAS).
8 April 1976	The *sardar* system is abolished in Baluchistan, but the tribal chiefs retain their influence.
26–30 May 1976	Bhutto goes to China, where he strengthens the military ties between the two countries.
15 July 1976	Bhutto announces that cotton factories and flour mills are to be nationalized.
8 January 1977	Opposition parties join together to form the Pakistan National Alliance (PNA) in order to campaign for the 1977 elections.
8 March 1977	The PPP wins 155 of the 200 National Assembly seats.
28 March 1977	Bhutto becomes Prime Minister for the second time.
9 April 1977	The police open fire on Pakistan National Alliance demonstrators protesting against government ballot-rigging.
21 April 1977	Bhutto calls on the army to restore public order.
5 June 1977	The Punjabi court rules that it is illegal to maintain martial law; two days later martial law is lifted.
June 1977	Bhutto reaches a power-sharing agreement with the PNA.
4 July 1977	General Zia ul-Haq has Bhutto arrested.
5 July 1977	Zia suspends the 1973 Constitution and dissolves both central and provincial governments. He imposes martial law, claiming ballot-rigging by the PPP government. He promises new elections within ninety days.
3 September 1977	Z A Bhutto is accused of murdering a PPP dissident.
September 1977	The USA suspends military and economic aid to Pakistan because it suspects the country of having a nuclear weapons programme.
18 March 1978	Bhutto is condemned to death by the Punjabi court.

11 June 1978	Altaf Hussain, a pharmacy student at Karachi University, launches the All Pakistan Muhajir Student Organization.
6 February 1979	The Supreme Court confirms the Punjabi court's verdict and sentence on Z A Bhutto by four votes to three; all the four judges concerned are Punjabis.
10 February 1979	The Hudood Ordinance introduces 'Islamic' punishments for drinking alcohol, theft and adultery.
23 March 1979	Zia announces elections for 17 November; they are never held.
4 April 1979	Bhutto is executed. Many nations disown Pakistan, but not for long, because after the invasion of Afghanistan, Washington sees Pakistan as a bulwark against Soviet expansionism.
6 September 1979	Pakistan joins the Movement of Non-Aligned States.
25 September 1979	Non-partisan municipal elections.
27 December 1979	The Soviet army invades Afghanistan.
26 February 1980	Formation of a Federal Shari'ah Court.
20 June 1980	The Zakât and Ushr Ordinance brings in an Islamic taxation system.
4–5 July 1980	A Shi'a convention protests against the *zakat* because it is a Sunni tradition.
February 1981	The Movement for the Restoration of Democracy (MRD) is formed.
March 1981	Benazir Bhutto is put under house arrest.
September 1981	The USA gives Pakistan forty F-16s and 3.2 thousand million dollars' worth of military aid.
December 1981	Press censorship is relaxed.
July–August 1983	MRD demonstrations against the military regime and for more regional autonomy are suppressed by the army.
September 1983	More non-partisan political elections.
10 January 1984	Benazir Bhutto leaves Pakistan for Europe.
18 March 1984	The state breaks up the student organizations; Altaf Hussain launches the Muhajir Qaumi Movement (MQM).
October 1984	The Pakistani, Iranian and Turkish Ministers of Foreign Affairs form the ECO, which is launched officially on 28 January 1985.
19 December 1984	A 'yes' vote in a referendum on Islamization allows Zia to announce that he has been 'elected' President for a five-year term.
25 February 1985	Non-partisan legislative elections are organized.
24 March 1985	General Zia appoints Muhammad Khan Junejo Prime Minister.
March 1985	The 8th Amendment to the 1973 Constitution strengthens the President's powers; notably, he has the power to dismiss the Prime Minister.

8 December 1985	The South Asia Association for Economic Cooperation is formed.
30 December 1985	Martial law is lifted, and the 1973 Constitution – extensively amended – is reinstated.
10 April 1986	Benazir Bhutto returns to Pakistan after two years' exile in England.
15 October 1987	Qazi Hussain Ahmad is elected leader of the Jamaat-i Islami.
30 November 1987	Non-partisan municipal elections. Unofficial MQM candidates win most of the seats in Hyderabad and Karachi.
29 May 1988	Zia dismisses Junejo from his post and dissolves Parliament: all pretence of being a civilian government is dropped.
15 June 1988	Zia promulgates the Shari'ah Ordinance, which elevates the Mufti to the status of councillors in civil courts.
17 August 1988	Zia dies in a plane accident.
6 October 1988	Eight political parties, including M K Junejo's Pakistan Muslim League, combine to form the Islami Jamhoori Ittehad (IJI) coalition; the Jamaat-i Islami join on 10 October.
16 November 1988	The PPP wins the general election.
2 December 1988	Benazir Bhutto becomes Prime Minister.
12 December 1988	Ghulam Ishaq Khan is elected President of Pakistan.
5 February 1989	The last Soviet troops withdraw from Afghanistan.
June 1989	Wali Khan's National Awami Party joins the IJI.
1 October 1989	Pakistan becomes a member of the Commonwealth, from which Z A Bhutto had withdrawn it.
27 May 1990	The Muhajirs of Hyderabad's Pucca Qila district are victims of police violence – which they might have provoked – as a result of which about sixty people die.
6 August 1990	President Ghulam Ishaq Khan dismisses Benazir Bhutto's government. Ghulam Mustafa Jatoi becomes interim Prime Minister.
September 1990	Pakistan sends men to Saudi Arabia.
October 1990	The USA suspends aid to Pakistan.
24 October 1990	The IJI wins the general election.
27 October 1990	Fresh elections for the provincial assemblies.
6 November 1990	Nawaz Sharif becomes Prime Minister.
1 January 1991	Pakistan fights alongside the USA in the Gulf War.
7 February 1991	The Sharif government announces liberalizing economic reforms.
April 1991	Nawaz Sharif announces a National Finance Award Committee to share out national resources between the four provinces, and Indus Water Apportionment Awards to share the river water out between them.
1 January 1992	Altaf Hussain, leader of the MQM, goes into exile in London.

17 January 1992	G M Syed is arrested once more, at the age of eighty-nine, for acting as spokesman for an independent Sind.
May 1992	The army launches an offensive against the MQM in Karachi.
8 January 1993	General Asif Nawaf Janjua, army chief, dies suddenly and is replaced by General Abdul Waheed Kakar.
18 April 1993	President Ghulam Ishaq Khan dismisses Nawaz Sharif from his post.
25 April 1993	Nawaz Sharif appeals against this decision in the Supreme Court, which rules in his favour and restores him to his position on 26 May. On 27 May Sharif wins a vote of confidence in the National Assembly.
18 July 1993	General Kakar secures the resignation of Ghulam Ishaq Khan and Nawaz Sharif.
6 October 1993	The PPP wins the general election.
9 October 1993	Fresh elections for the provincial assemblies.
19 October 1993	Benazir Bhutto becomes Prime Minister again.
13 November 1993	Farooq Leghari is elected President of Pakistan.
5 December 1993	Benazir Bhutto takes over the leadership of the PPP from her mother, who now supports her son Murtaza in his bid to become Prime Minister.
October 1994	The Taliban take over Afghanistan.
November 1994	The Shi'a Sipah-i Muhammad movement is formed.
November 1994	Operation Clean-up fails and the army withdraw from Karachi, which is racked by intercommunal violence.
15 March 1995	Murtaza Bhutto launches the PPP (Shaheed Bhutto).
18 June 1995	The TSNM incites its supporters to civil disobedience.
11 February 1996	General Jahangir Khan becomes chief of army staff.
April 1996	The Pakistani government cannot manage to make the four provinces agree on a plan for allocating federal resources based on the National Finance Commission's proposed budget scheme. The three smaller provinces want 90 per cent of the money to be distributed on the basis of each region's population; this suggestion is rejected by the Punjab.
September 1996	Violent clashes between Sunni and Shi'a in the Parachinar leave about a hundred dead.
4 November 1996	President Leghari dismisses Benazir Bhutto.
12 December 1996	Leghari announces that the tribes of the FATA (Federally Administered Tribal Area) will be granted direct universal suffrage at the next elections.
6 January 1997	Leghari appoints a Council for Defence and National Security, composed of the head of Inter Services Intelligence (ISI) and the heads of all the armed forces, to supervise the political process.

19 January 1997	A plastic bomb is planted in Lahore's Iranian Cultural Centre, probably by Sunni extremists.
3 February 1997	The Pakistan Muslim League wins an overwhelming majority in the Assembly. Its leader, Nawaz Sharif, becomes Prime Minister on 17 February.
1 April 1997	The National Assembly pass the 13th Amendment to the Constitution, which removes the presidential powers granted by the 8th Amendment, thus reinstating a parliamentary system.
25 May 1997	Pakistan recognizes the Taliban government in Afghanistan.
2 December 1997	The chief justice of the Supreme Court, Sajjad Ali Shah, is forced to leave office. President Leghari resigns.
1 January 1998	Rafiq Ahmed Tarar becomes President.
6 April 1998	Experimental launch of a missile with a 1,500-kilometre range.
11–13 May 1998	India carries out fresh nuclear weapons tests, twenty-four years after its first test.
June 1998	Pakistan carries out nuclear weapons tests which give rise to economic sanctions, especially by the USA.
28 August 1998	Nawaz Sharif announces the introduction of the Shari'ah Bill.
7 October 1998	General Jahangir Karamat resigns from his post as chief of army staff. He is succeeded by General Pervez Musharraf.
February 1999	Atal Bihari Vajpayee, the Indian Prime Minister, goes to Lahore to meet his Pakistani counterpart.
May–July 1999	War in Kargil, in Indian Kashmir.
4 July 1999	Nawaz Sharif goes to Washington, where Bill Clinton puts pressure on him to withdraw Pakistani troops from Kargil.
12 October 1999	General Musharraf's *coup d'état*.

NOTES

INTRODUCTION

1. This expression was used by a British official in a work relating to the Partition (P Moon, *Divide and Quit*, Berkeley and Los Angeles, CA, University of California Press, 1962). For a general survey of the official position of the Congress Party, see the book by Rajendra Prasad, one of Gandhi's lieutenants who presided over the Constituent Assembly of Independent India, later the Indian Union, as President of the Republic (R. Prasad, *India Divided*, Bombay, Hind Kitab, 1947).
2. For more details about Partition, see C Markovits (ed.), *Histoire de l'Inde moderne*, Paris, Fayard, 1994, ch. xxv.
3. This idea is still alive, even in the Pakistani press. In May 2000, Mubarak Ali wrote in Dawn, the newspaper started by Jinnah: 'Since the beginning Pakistan has been confronted with the monumental task of formulating a national identity distinct from India. Born out of a schism of the old civilization of India, Pakistan has debated over the construction of a culture of its own, a culture which will not only be different from that of India but one that the rest of the world can understand' (M Ali, 'In Search of Identity, *Dawn Magazine*, 7 May 2000).
4. New Delhi had settled this matter as early as 1950, whereas five years later Pakistan still recognized the States of Bahawalpur and Khairpur, and those of Baluchistan, grouped together as the Baluchistan States Union. Karachi, too, enjoyed a separate establishment. All these administrative entities were welded together under the single organization *One Unit Scheme* in 1955, but the Princely States of Dir, Swat and Chitral were not amalgamated within the North-West Frontier Province until 1969; in 1973 they were regrouped in a collective body bearing the name PATA (the Provincially Administered Tribal Areas) – not to be confused with FATA (the Federally Administered Tribal Areas), which were themselves a regrouping of the Tribal Agencies, that portion of Kashmir conquered by Pakistan in 1948–49 (Azad Kashmir – Free Kashmir) and the Northern Territories.
5. See, for example, A Hussain, 'Ethnicity, National Identity and Praetorianism: The Case of Pakistan', *Asian Survey*, no. 16 (10), October 1976, p. 919.
6. S J Burki, *Pakistan*, Boulder, CO, Westview Press, 1999, p. 14.
7. Some Pakistani authors say that this movement harks back to Shah Walihullah (1703–63), a theologian who spent his time reestablishing the purity of orthodox Islam, as opposed to the cult of the saints, and reconquering the lands won by the Marathas with the help of the Afghan sovereign, Ahmad Shah Abdali. Such an interpretation is, of course, improper. See, for example, S M J Zafar, *Founders of Pakistan*, Lahore, Publishers United, 1968.
8. G Étienne, *Le Pakistan, don de l'Indus: Économie et Politique*, Paris, PUF, 1989.
9. P. Lafrance, 'And yet, Pakistan exists', in C Jaffrelot (ed.), *Pakistan: Nationalism without a Nation?*, London, Zed Books, 2002, pp. 337–348..
10. The military chiefs head a powerful 520,000-strong army.

1 ISLAMIC IDENTITY AND ETHNIC TENSIONS

1. T Amin, *Ethno-National Movements of Pakistan's Domestic and International Factors*, Islamabad, Institute of Political Studies, 1993, p. 73.
2. Cited in R Raza (ed.), 'Constitutional Development and Political Consequences', in *Pakistan in Perspective, 1947–1997*, Karachi, Oxford University Press, 1997, p. 4.
3. F Robinson, *Separatism among Indian Muslims*, Cambridge, Cambridge University Press, 1974.
4. This mistrust cost the Muslims dear: for example, whereas they occupied 72 per cent of the posts in the judicial system in 1850, they occupied no more than 46 per cent in 1885.
5. The Muslim elite had already suffered the replacement of Persian by the Indian vernacular languages in 1837, a measure which applied throughout British India. T Rahman, *Language and Politics in Pakistan*, Karachi, Oxford University Press, 1998, pp. 37, 69.
6. In what was called 'the uncovenanted civil service', which covered those parts of the administration not subject to contract. On these matters, see P Brass, *Language, Religion and Politics*, Cambridge, Cambridge University Press, 1974.
7. This report, published in 1871, marked the beginning of a change in the British analysis of the situations of the Muslims in India. Hunter describes with some emotion how, through the fault of the English, they lost the virtual monopoly they had enjoyed in the administration and the country, thus finding themselves in a pitiable position.
8. D Lelyveld, *Aligarh's First Generation: Muslim Solidarity in British India*, Princeton, NJ, Princeton University Press, 1978.
9. This social coalition is not surprising, since the Muslim intelligentsia of the United Provinces is to a large extent descended from the dignitaries of the Mughal Empire and of the states which succeeded it – like Sayyid Ahmad Khan himself.
10. G Minault, *The Khalifat Movement: Religious Symbolism and Political Mobilization in India*, New York, Columbia University Press, 1982.
11. He was besides little concerned about Islamic prohibitions, particularly those of a dietary nature.
12. Extract from a speech by Jinnah, President of the Muslim League, during a session in Lahore in March 1940, quoted in Syad Sharifuddin Pirzada (ed.), *Foundations of Pakistan – All India Muslim League documents: 1906–1947*, Karachi, National Publishing House, 1970, pp. 337–8.
13. Neither Iqbal nor Rehmat included Bengal in their plans. This was the first sign of the marginalization of this province.
14. Pirzada (ed.), *Foundations of Pakistan*, p. 341.
15. I Talbot, *Punjab and the Raj, 1849–1947*, Delhi, Manohar, 1988, p. 89.
16. Y Samad, *A Nation in Turmoil: Nationalism and Ethnicity in Pakistan, 1937–1958*, New Delhi, Sage, 1995, p. 72.
17. D Gilmartin, *Empire and Islam: Punjab and the Making of Pakistan*, Berkeley, CA, California University Press, 1988.
18. I Talbot, *Pakistan: A Modern History*, London, Hurst, 1999, p. 78.
19. M S Korejo, *G M Syed: An Analysis of his Political Perspectives*, Karachi, Oxford University Press, 2000.
20. Cited in Harun-or Rashid, *The Foreshadowing of Bangladesh: Bengal Muslim League and Muslim League Politics, 1936–1947*, Dhaka, Asiatic Society of Bengal, 1987, p. 181.
21. The trading communities (particularly of Gujarat), the Memons, the Bohras, the Khojas – from which Jinnah is descended – and the Chiniotis, saw Pakistan as a means of escape from their Hindu competitors. In the 1940s they embarked on a massive financing of the Muslim League (S A Kochanek, *Interest Groups and Development: Business and Politics in Pakistan*, Karachi, Oxford University Press, 1983, ch. 1).
22. Having failed to make his voice heard during the Round Table conferences, Jinnah remained in England on a political semi-retirement which ended only on his return to India in the mid-1930s.

23. Jinnah ordered this 'day of direct action' on 16 August 1946 to prove to Congress his ability to mobilize masses behind him. In Calcutta the demonstrations took a violent turn – to Jinnah's great surprise, it seems – under pressure from Hussain Shaheed Suhrawardy, head of the government of Bengal and leader of the Muslim League, who hoped thereby to establish his influence within the party.

24. Samad, *A Nation in Turmoil*, pp. 90–125.

25. Pirzada (ed.), *Foundations of Pakistan*, p. 341. By deliberately sounding ambiguous, Jinnah managed for a long time to avoid saying whether he foresaw two states or a single Pakistan. For the debate about the 'Lahore Resolution', see I A Malik (ed.), *Muslim League Session 1940 and the Lahore Resolution*, Islamabad, National Institute of Historical and Cultural Research, 1990.

26. Noted that it was at that very moment that the idea of an independent Bengal, advocated by H S Suhrawardy, received Jinnah's assent (Samad, *A Nation in Turmoil*, p. 95).

27. After the 1938 reform, Punjab had 90 representatives, Bengal 100, the United Provinces 70 and the Bombay Presidency 30. Added together, the two first regions mustered only 40 per cent of the voters.

28. H Khuhro, 'The Capital of Pakistan', in H Khuhro and A Mooraj (eds), *Karachi: Megacity of our Times*, Karachi, Oxford University Press, 1997, pp. 95–111.

29. F Ahmed, *Ethnicity and Politics in Pakistan*, Karachi, Oxford University Press, 1998, p. 95.

30. K B Sayeed, *The Political System of Pakistan*, Boston, MA, Houghton Mifflin, 1967, p. 132. Although they represented only 3.5 per cent of the population in 1947, the Muhajirs of Sind occupied 21 per cent of the posts in the Pakistan Civil Service (R Braibanti, *Asian Bureaucratic Traditions Emergent from the British Imperial Tradition*, Durham, NC, Duke University Press, 1966, p. 263).

31. See the personal testimony of Afak Maydar, 'The Muhajirs in Sind: A Critical Essay', in J Henry Korsen (ed.), *Contemporary Problems of Pakistan*, Boulder, CO, Westview Press, 1993, p. 117.

32. Rahman, *Language and Politics*, pp. 230–31.

33. S P Cohen, 'State Building in Pakistan', in A Banuazizi and M Weiner (eds), *The State Religion and Ethnic Politics: Pakistan, Iran and Afghanistan*, Syracuse, NY, Syracuse University Press, 1986, p. 318.

34. C Dewey, 'The Rural Roots of Pakistani Militarism', in D A Low (ed.), *Political Inheritance of Pakistan*, Basingstoke, Macmillan, 1991, pp. 255–83.

35. C H Kennedy, *Bureaucracy in Pakistan*, Karachi, Oxford University Press, 1987, p. 194.

36. I Talbot, 'Le poids du Punjab', in C Jaffrelot (dir.), *Le Pakistan, carrefour de tensions régionales*, Brussels, Éditions Complexes, 1999, p. 92.

37. L Binder, *Religion and Politics in Pakistan*, Berkeley, CA, University of California Press, 1961, p. 205.

38. Liaquat Ali Khan has stressed elsewhere that establishing a theocracy was out of the question. He draws a radical difference between such a regime and the necessity for the Muslims of Pakistan to follow 'the Islamic way of life' (Liaquat Ali Khan, *Pakistan: The Heart of Asia*, Cambridge, MA, Harvard University Press, 1950, pp. 6, 10).

39. In promulgating the Land Alienation Act (1901) the British Raj had protected the indebted farmers of the Punjab from the covetousness of merchant-insurers who were ready to take their land in repayment. Only farmers could purchase agricultural land.

40. Shahid Javed Burki, *Pakistan: Fifty Years of Nationhood*, Boulder, CO, Westview Press, 1999, p. 29.

41. There seems to have been no plot behind this murder. The killer was a civil servant from the NWFP who had been employed to propagate an anti-Afghan tract among the Pashtuns. He thought himself badly paid for his services, and his act may have been prompted by a desire for vengeance.

42. In other cases, particularly in East Pakistan, the property of 'departing' Hindus was given to 'arriving' Muslims, and the same transaction occurred on the Indian side after the value had been decided and the migrants' agreement had been obtained.

43. R Raza, 'Constitutional Development and Political Consequences', in *Pakistan in Perspective, 1947–1997*, pp. 1–60.

44. The 1961 census revealed that the population of East Pakistan was 50.8 million, while that of West Pakistan was 42.9 million. The quotas were therefore not proportional to the demographic figures.

45. M Rashiduzzamun, 'East–West Conflicts in Pakistan: Bengali Regionalism, 1947–1970', in A Jeyaratnam Wilson and D Dalton (eds), *The States of South Asia: Problems of National Integration*, London, Hurst, 1982, p. 117.

46. Raza, 'Constitutional Developments and Political Consequences', p. 18.

47. S Wolpert, *Zulfi Bhutto of Pakistan: His Life and Times*, New York, Oxford University Press, 1993, pp. 145–6.

48. R Sisson and Leo E. Rose, *War and Secession: Pakistan, India and the Creation of Bangladesh*, Berkeley, CA, University of California Press, 1990.

49. A Jalal, *Democracy and Authoritarianism in South Asia*, Cambridge, Cambridge University Press, 1985, p. 188.

50. Ibid., pp. 188–199.

51. M G Chitkara, *Jiy-e Sind G.M. Syed*, New Delhi, APH Publishing Corporation, 1996; M S Korejo, *G.M. Syed: An Analysis of his Political Perspectives*, Karachi, Oxford University Press, 2000.

52. S P Cohen, *The Pakistan Army*, Karachi, Oxford University Press, 1988, p. 44; Khalid B Sayeed, 'The Role of the Military in Pakistan', in J van Doorn (ed.), *Armed Forces and Society*, The Hague/Paris, Mouton, 1968.

53. Quoted in Wolpert, *Zulfi Bhutto of Pakistan: His Life and Times, op. cit.*, p. 139.

54. The four Punjabi judges of the Supreme Court found him guilty, while the others, all originating from a different province, acquitted him (O Noman, *Pakistan: Political and Economic History since 1947*, London, Kegan Paul International, 1992, p. 193).

55. As for the senior national civil service, it contained 55.8 per cent Punjabis, 11.6 per cent NWFP, 20.2 per cent urban Sindis (mostly Muhajirs), 5.1 per cent Sindis from rural areas and 3.1 per cent Baluchis in 1983. In public-sector enterprises the proportion of Punjabis was estimated at 41 per cent, and that of urban Sindis at 47 per cent, against 6 per cent from the NWFP, 3.5 per cent from rural Sind and 1 per cent of Baluchis (Jalal, *Democracy and Authoritarianism*, pp. 190 and 195).

56. Noman, *Pakistan*, p. 196.

57. S S Harrison, 'Ethnicity and the Political Stalemate in Pakistan', in A. Banuazizi and M. Weiner (eds), *The State Religion and Ethnic Politics*, pp. 281–2.

58. For more details, see K B Sayeed, *Politics in Pakistan: The Nature and Direction of Change*, (n.d.), in particular in the excellent Chapter 6, entitled 'Pakistan's Central Government versus Baluchi and Pashtun Aspirations', pp. 113–38.

59. Tehran – which perhaps incited Bhutto to launch this scheme – also tried to persuade the Afghan authorities to recognize the Durand Line, at the very moment when Daud, who in 1973 had just seized power in Kabul, was supporting Pakistanis revolting in the name of a free 'Baluchistan'. (See C Jaffrelot, 'Interpreting Ethnic Movements in Pakistan', *The Pakistan Development Review*, 37 [4], Winter 1998, pp. 153–75; Rasul Bakhsh Rais, 'Comments', ibid., pp. 176–9.)

60. U Phadnis, *Ethnicity and Nation-Building in South Asia*, Delhi, Sage, 1989, p. 183; Harrison, 'Ethnicity and the Political Stalemate in Pakistan', p. 274.

61. Ibid., pp. 274–5.

62. In 1975 the government even passed a law envisaging a seven-year prison sentence for any Pakistani maintaining that more than one nationality existed in the country.

63. A 1999 study showed that the level of literacy among Baluchi women does not exceed 2 per cent (*The News*, 3 May 1999).

64. *Economic Survey 1996–1997*, Islamabad, Government of Pakistan, 1997, p. 107.

65. *The News*, 20 February 1997, p. 1.

66. At the moment of his resignation, Mengal had declared that he was doing this to defend Baluchi identity.

67. The size of the 'yes' vote – 99 per cent – bears witness to the popularity of the Pakistani project, but Khan's boycott prevents us from drawing definite conclusions. As everywhere else, the exacerbation of the conflict between Hindus and Muslims, and Muslim League propaganda on the Islam-in-danger theme, had rallied the Muslims of the NWFP enthusiastically to Jinnah's plan (I Talbot, *Provincial Politics and the Pakistan Movement: The Growth of the Muslim League in North-West and North-East India, 1937–1947*, Karachi, Oxford University Press, 1999, p. 110).

68. They represented a fifth of the effective strength immediately after Independence (Cohen, *The Pakistani Army*, p. 44).

69. This amounts to slightly more than the PPP at 14 per cent and less than the Jamiyyat-ul Ulama-i Islam at 23 per cent.

70. Daud had already set himself up as the champion of Pashtun irredentism when he was Prime Minister of Afghanistan (1953–63). See Chapter 6.

71. Noman, *Pakistan*, p. 198. Wali Khan considered that the Durand line had disappeared during the war in Afghanistan (*Frontier*, 21 February 1998).

72. Y Samad, 'Pakistan on Punjabistan: Crisis of National Identity', *International Journal of Punjab Studies*, 2 (1), 1995, p. 30.

73. M G Weinbaum, 'The Impact and Legacy of the Afghan Refugees in Pakistan', in J H Korson (ed.), *Contemporary Problems of Pakistan*, pp. 133–9.

74. M Waseem, *Politics and the State in Pakistan*, p. 437.

75. *The News*, 29 April 1999.

76. If 70 per cent of the inhabitants of the NWFP speak Pashto, those in the Nowshera and Kohat regions speak Hindko, those in Mazra the Harazwal and Kohistani dialects, those in Chitral use Khwar and those in Dera Ismail Khan speak Seraïki.

77. The recognized leader of the ANP, Wali Khan's wife Begum Nasim Wali, justified the split from the PLM (Nawaz or N) on an emotional basis: 'I want an identity – I want a name change so that the Pashtuns may be identified on the map of Pakistan' (*The News*, 1 March 1998). This militant speech shows that the Pashtuns are no longer motivated merely by separatist sentiments, since they claim territorial recognition within the borders of Pakistan.

78. Muhajirs were close to the JI not only because they saw themselves as part of its Islamic ideology but because the JI has also given humanitarian aid to the victims of the 1947 Partition (S V R Nasr, *The Vanguard of Islamic Revolution: The Jama'at-i Islami of Pakistan*, Berkeley, CA, University of California Press, 1994, pp. 00–9).

79. Samad, 'Le Problème mohajir', in Jaffrelot (dir.), *Le Pakistan, carrefour de tensions régionales*, p. 77.

80. S Akbar Zaidi, 'Sindi vs Muhajir in Pakistan: Contradiction, Conflict, Compromise', *Economic and Political Weekly*, 18 May 1991.

81. They have, it would seem, benefited from the support of Zia, whose politics of Islamization policy was appreciated by the Muhajirs. He saw in the MQM as a means of countering the strong return of the PPP in Sind, where the movement for the restoration of democracy was then at its height.

82. F Shaheed, 'The Pashtun–Muhajir Conflicts, 1985–1986: A National Perspective', in V Das (ed.), *Mirrors of Violence: Communities, Riots and Survivors in South Asia*, Delhi, Oxford University Press, 1990, pp. 194–214.

83. J Rehman, 'Self-determination, State-building and the Muhajirs: An International Legal Perspective of the Role of the Indian Muslim Refugees in the Constitutional Development of Pakistan', *Contemporary South Asia*, 3 (2), 1994, pp. 122–3.

84. Altaf Hussain has also used means of communication like the telephone in conjunction with loudspeakers to hold mass meetings at a distance, thus introducing a new form of transnational mobilization.

85. Interview with Altaf Hussain in *India Today*, 15 July 1995, p. 42.

86. An opinion poll conducted at the end of 1996 suggests that fewer than half of Karachi's inhabitants, 46.7 per cent, are in favour of the creation of new Pakistani regions (leaving 53.3 per cent against). All the same this is far higher than the number of favourable opinions obtained in other towns: Lahore 15 per cent, Islamabad 16.1 per cent, Peshawar 21.7 per cent, Quetta 25.6 per cent, Multan 26.7 per cent and Sukkur (no doubt due to the high proportion of Muhajirs) 34.4 per cent. *The Herald Annual,* January 1997, p. 160.

87. Sharif's government was composed of over 85 per cent Punjabis *(The News,* 24 October 1999).

88. M Abou Zahab, 'Islamabad: L'armée du salut?', *Politique internationale,* 86, Winter 1999–2000, p. 379.

89. *Dawn,* 13 July 1998.

90. The Seraiki movement, at first linguistic and literary, took shape in the 1970s, when the speakers of Riasti at Bahawalpur, of Multani at Multan and of Derajati at Dera Ghazi Khan considered that they all spoke the same language.

91. *Dawn,* 3 October 1998.

92. S Minhaz, *The Friday Times,* 11 August 2000.

93. The religious minorities protest regularly against the system of separate electorates, a legacy of the colonial era which exacerbates their political marginalisation by denying them the right to vote for candidates from outside their community.

94. See C Jaffrelot (ed.), *Pakistan: Nationalism without a Nation?* op. cit.

2 EAST BENGAL

1. R Ahmed, *The Bengal Muslims, 1871–1906: A Quest for Identity,* New Delhi, Oxford University Press, 1981, pp. 5–27.

2. R Ray, *Change in Bengal Agrarian Society circa 1760–1850,* New Delhi, Manohar, 1979, pp. 27–9.

3. R Ahmed, *The Bengal Muslims, 1871–1906,* pp. 39 *ff.*

4. Ibid., pp. 101–5.

5. T Maniruzzaman, *The Bangladesh Revolution and its Aftermath,* Dhaka, University Press Ltd, 1980, 2nd edn, 1988, pp. 36–52.

6. M Nurul Islam, *Bengali Muslim Public Opinion as Reflected in the Bengali Press (1901–1930),* Dhaka, Bangla Academy, 1973, pp. 218–47.

7. *Amader bhasa samasya,* Dhaka, Renaissance Publications, 1947, pp. 34–5.

8. S Sen, *Muslim Politics in Bengal, 1937–1947,* New Delhi, Impex India, 1976, p. 251.

9. M S Qureshi, *Étude sur l'évolution intellectualle chez les musulmans du Bengale, 1857–1947,* Paris/The Hague, Mouton, 1971, p. 116.

10. Harun-or-Rashid, *The Foreshadowing of Bangladesh: Bengal Muslim League and Muslim Politics, 1936–1947.* Dhaka, 1987, pp. 386–406; Sen, *Muslim Politics in Bengal,* pp. 238–9.

11. B Umar, *Purba Banglar Bhasa Andolan o Tatkalin Rajniti,* Dhaka, 1968, pp. 437–73.

12. Ibid., p. 439.

13. R Jahan in *Pakistan: Failure in National Integration,* New York, Columbia University Press, 1972, pp. 38–40.

14. Ibid., p. 12.

15. M Ansari, *Bangladeser Itihas,* Sirajul Islam (ed.), Dhaka, Asiatic Society of Bangladesh, 1993, vol. 1, p. 504.

16. Jahan, *Pakistan: Failure in National Integration,* p. 12.

17. On the movement for the language, see Umar, *Purba Banglar Bhasa Andelan o Tatkalin Rajniti.*

18. Ibid., pp. 38–48.

19. Ibid., pp. 23–38; K B Sayeed, *Politics in Pakistan: The Nature and Direction of Change,* New York, Praeger, 1980, p. 40.

20. H Zaheer, *The Separation of East Pakistan: the Rise and Realization of Bengali Muslim Nationalism,* Karachi/New York, Oxford University Press, 1994, pp. 49–57; Rehman

Sobhan, *History of Bangladesh*, Sirajul Islam (ed.), Dhaka, Asiatic Society of Bangladesh, 1st edn 1992, 2nd edn 1997, vol. 2, pp. 722–94.

21. Enayetur Rahim, *History of Bangladesh*, Sirajul Islam (ed.), p. 583.
22. Jahan, *Pakistan: Failure in National Integration*, p. 62.
23. Ibid., pp. 85–6.
24. Rahim, *History of Bangladesh*, p. 592.
25. Ibid., p. 527.
26. Jahan, *Pakistan: Failure in National Integration*, p. 173.
27. Sobhan, *History of Bangladesh*, pp. 722–94.
28. Rahim, *History of Bangladesh*, p. 603.
29. Ibid., pp. 604–5.
30. Maniruzzaman, *The Bangladesh Revolution and its Aftermath*, p. 79.
31. Jahan, *Pakistan: Failure in National Integration*, p. 193.
32. Ibid., p. 195; T. Maniruzzaman, The Bangladesh Revolution, p. 80.
33. Rahim, *History of Bangladesh*, p. 615.
34. Ibid., p. 620.
35. Zaheer, *The Separation of East Pakistan*, p. 157.
36. Rahim, *History of Bangladesh*, p. 622; Jahan, *Pakistan: Failure in National Integration*, p. 197.
37. Maniruzzaman, *The Bangladesh Revolution*, p. 31.
38. Ibid., p. 124.
39. Jahan, *Pakistan: Failure in National Integration*, p. 204.
40. 'The Lessons of February 21', *The Wave*, 1969, quoted by Maksud, *History of Bangladesh*, vol. 3, p. 335.
41. *The News International, Pakistan*, 19 December 1999.

3 A FRUITLESS SEARCH FOR DEMOCRACY

1. See, for example, L. Ziring, *Pakistan: The Enigma of Political Development*, Boulder, CO, Westview Press, 1980, p. 97.
2. The theory according to which Jinnah embodied the viceregal tradition of British colonialism was first put forward by Khalid Bin Sayeed.
3. A McGrath, *The Destruction of Pakistan's Democracy*, Karachi, Oxford University Press, 1998, p. 42.
4. Ibid., p. 43
5. Ibid., p. 35
6. The Muslim League had a majority in the Constituent Assembly which served as the Parliament, but constitutional debates went on unceasingly, in particular over ethnic community issues.
7. He also served as a minister in the government of Liaquat Ali Khan, his Prime Minister, whose members he chose himself. He held the portfolios designated Evacuation and Refugees Rehabilitation, and State and Frontier Regions.
8. From his real name, Abdul Jabbar Khan, Dr Khan Sahib can be identified as the brother of Abdul Gaffar Khan.
9. One day Jinnah said these words about the newly born Pakistan: (quoted in K B Sayeed, 'The Heart of the Pakistan Crisis', *Dawn*, 14 August 1998).
10. As early as July 1948 Liaquat Ali Khan had obtained an amendment to the Government of India Act authorizing central government to dismiss a provincial government, on the model of the prerogative enjoyed by the Viceroy of India by virtue of Section 93.
11. K B Sayeed stresses that they 'were not courageous enough to take a stand against the bureaucracy or the government of the day when some of their leaders were removed from office arbitrarily by the government' (quoted in K B Sayeed, *The Political System of Pakistan*, Boston, MA, Houghton Mifflin, 1967, p. 83).
12. McGrath, *The Destruction of Pakistan's Democracy*, p. 67.

13. S V R Nasr, *Mawdudi and the Making of Islamic Revivalism*, New York, Oxford University Press, 1996.

14. See C Jaffrelot, *La Démocratie en Inde: Religion, caste et politique*, Paris, Fayard, 1998, chs I and II.

15. A Jalal, *The State of Martial Rule: The Origins of Pakistan's Political Economy of Defence*, Cambridge, Cambridge University Press, 1990, p. 300.

16. K Callard, *Pakistan: A Political Study*, London, G Allen & Unwin, 1957, ch. VII.

17. C Jaffrelot, *La Démocratie en Inde, op. cit.*, ch. I.

18. Moreover, the British created the province of Baluchistan during the Second Afghan War (1878–80) and the North-West Frontier Province in 1901 the better to assure the defence of their colonial territory.

19. P R Newberg, *Judging the State: Courts and Constitutional Politics in Pakistan*, Cambridge, Cambridge University Press, 1995, p. 43.

20. P R Newberg, *Judging the State: Courts and Constitutional Politics in Pakistan*, Cambridge, Cambridge University Press, 1995, pp. 66–7.

21. Sind, the rural notables benefited in 1947 from the exodus of the Hindus, who, though they were mostly city-dwellers, owned considerable estates. They helped themselves to 800,000 out of the 1,345,000 acres abandoned.

22. Although 20 out of 40 of those elected in the eastern part of the country were lawyers – yet another indication of the East–West divide (Mushtaq Ahmad, *Government and Politics in Pakistan*, Karachi, Pakistan Publication House, 1959, p. 115).

23. Deprived of victory by central government intervention in 1954, the United Front was once more invited to form a government in September 1956, but its members soon pulled it to pieces; thus the Awami League was reduced to a sort of government which appeared and disappeared depending on whether the two chiefs, Huq and Suhrawardy, came to an understanding.

24. Isabelle Cordonnier, *The Military and Political Order in Pakistan*, Geneva, Programme for Strategic and International Security Studies, 1999, p. 16.

25. Jalal, *The State of Martial Rule: The Origins of Pakistan's Political Economy of Defence*, p. 42.

26. That year the defence budget absorbed practically the whole of the state revenue (ibid., p. 99).

27. H A Rizvi, *The Military and Politics in Pakistan (1947–1986)*, New Delhi, Foundation Books, 1988, pp. 44–5.

28. Abdul Sattar, 'Foreign Policy', in Rafi Raza (ed.), *Pakistan in Perspective, 1947–1997*, Karachi, Oxford University Press, 1997, p. 74. At the end of the 1950s the military aid received by virtue of the different alliances concluded by Pakistan represented $500 million and the economic aid $750 million (Y Samad, *A Nation in Turmoil*, p. 169).

29. S Cohen considers that in the years 1950 to 1960 an 'American generation' succeeded the 'British generation' which sprang from colonization (S Cohen, *The Pakistan Army*, Karachi, Oxford University Press, 1998, pp. 55–70).

30. Today, an overwhelming majority of the military come from just three districts of the Punjab (Rawalpindi, Jhelum and Campbellpur), and two of the NWFP (Kohat and Mardan): Cohen, *The Pakistan Army*, p. 44.

31. J Rosselli, 'The Self-Image of Effeteness: Physical Education and Nationalism in Nineteenth Century Bengal', *Past and Present*, no. 86, 1980.

32. I Talbot, *Pakistan: A Modern History*, London, Hurst, 1999, p. 149.

33. He wrote a circular on these lines when he was appointed to this post in 1951 (H Feldman, *Revolution in Pakistan: A Study of the Martial Law Administration*, London, Oxford University Press, 1967, p. 35).

34. Ibid., p. 74.

35. M Waseem, *Politics and the State in Pakistan*, Islamabad, National Institute of Historical and Cultural Research, 1994 (2nd edn), p. 149.

36. A Weiss, *Culture, Class and Development in Pakistan: The Emergence of an Industrial Bourgeoisie in Punjab*, Boulder, CO, Westview Press, 1991, p. 34.

37. Jalal, *The State of Martial Rule,* p. 306.
38. Ayub Khan eliminated the epithet 'Islamic' – hitherto added to the word 'Republic' – from the 1962 Constitution, and erased the references to the Koran and the Sunna which featured in the 1956 text. He was, however, forced to retract the first of these decisions after 1963, when the First Amendment to the Constitution reestablished the designation 'Islamic Republic of Pakistan'.
39. The organization also served, perhaps, as a model for the establishment, under the 1962 Constitution, of an Advisory Council on Islamic Ideology, whose members, all nominated by the President, had the job of advising those in power, at regional as much as at the national level, how they might make it possible for Muslims to live according to the requirements of the Koran, and to check the conformity to Islamic principles of laws passed prior to 1962. Ayub Khan was careful to appoint modernists to the Advisory Council. This aroused indignation among the Jamaat-i Islami, in whose opinion it was the ulemas' vocation in life to supervise the Council (J Malik, *Colonization of Islam: Dissolution of Traditional Institutions in Pakistan,* Delhi, Manohar, 1996, p. 35).
40. His autobiography – Ayub Khan, *Friends not Masters: A Political Autobiography,* New York, Oxford University Press, 1967 – gives us an excellent insight into his political style.
41. However, the Assembly was called upon to vote only on new public expenditure; existing funding was renewed automatically.
42. Sayeed, *The Political System of Pakistan,* p. 106.
43. In 1963, Ayub Khan even had an amendment to the Constitution – the first – voted which reduced the judges' control over laws, the conformity to the Fundamental Principles of the Constitution. The courts nonetheless struggled to resist pressure. In October 1964 the High Court of West Pakistan ordered the immediate release of Maududi, the leader of Jamaat-i Islami, who had been arrested ten months earlier with 43 other party officials when the party had been declared illegal. The press had been submitted to an iron law contained in two presidential regulations of 1963, which gave the executive the power to take control of newspapers and printrooms considered guilty of publications likely 'to arouse hatred or bring the government into contempt', or liable to stir up rivalry or hatred between the two halves of the country.
44. Z A Bhutto, *The Myth of Independence,* Karachi, Oxford University Press, 1969.
45. On the two years of his reign, see H Feldman, *The End of the Beginning: Pakistan 1969–1971,* Karachi, Oxford University Press, 1976.
46. H Zaheer, *The Separation of East Pakistan: The Rise and Realization of Bengali Muslim Nationalism,* Karachi, Oxford University Press, 1995.
47. Talbot, *Pakistan: A Modern History, op. cit.,* p. 195.
48. His slogan was 'Islam is our faith. Democracy is our polity. Socialism is our economy' (Z A Bhutto, *Pakistan and the Alliances,* Lahore, Pakistan People's Party, 1969).
49. R W Jackson, *South Asia Crisis: India, Pakistan and Bangladesh: A Political and Historical Analysis of the 1971 War,* New York, Praeger, 1975.
50. S Wolpert, *Zulfi Bhutto of Pakistan: His Life and Times,* New York, Oxford University Press, 1993; S Taseer, *Bhutto: A Political Biography,* London, Ithaca Press, 1979.
51. Rizvi, *The Military and Politics in Pakistan, 1947–1986,* Lahore, Progressive, 1986, pp. 198–9.
52. He explains this himself in *If I am assassinated . . .,* New Delhi, Vikas Publishing House, 1979.
53. Cohen, *The Pakistan Army, op. cit.,* p. 73.
54. Cordonnier, *The Military and Political Order in Pakistan,* p. 32.
55. C Kennedy, *Bureaucracy in Pakistan,* Karachi, Oxford University Press, 1987, p. 89.
56. Malik, *Colonization of Islam,* p. 37.
57. These measures brought numerous communists to Bhutto's ranks, but he alienated them soon after by his repressive measures in Baluchistan and against the workers' demonstrations in Sind during the summer of 1972 (F Sulehria, 'Past, Present and Future of the Left Movement in Pakistan', *South Asia Citizens Web Dispatch,* 26 May 2000).

58. M G Weinbaum, 'The March 1977 Elections in Pakistan', *Asian Survey*, no. 17(7), July 1977, pp. 599–618.
59. Talbot, *Pakistan: A Modern History*, p. 255.
60. In 1982, of 42 Pakistani ambassadors in post abroad, 18 were retired military men. See K L Kamal, *Pakistan: The Garrison State*, New Delhi, Intellectual Publishing House, 1982.
61. F Grare, *Le Pakistan face au conflit afghan (1979–1985)*, Paris, L'Harmattan, 1997, p. 180.
62. Bhutto also considered that the Americans slackened their guard to Zia's benefit for just this reason (Z A Bhutto, *From My Death Cell*, New Delhi, Orient Paperback, n.d., p. 65).
63. In the long term, the war in Afghanistan weakened the democratic process by giving new clout to the Pakistani secret services within the Inter Service Intelligence (ISI). This institution was, in effect, charged with distributing Western aid to the Afghan resistance, and even with playing up to Pakistan's Afghan policy. The ISI's hostility towards the return to civilian power postponed liberalization of the regime (I H Malik, *State and Civil Society in Pakistan: Politics of Authority, Ideology and Ethnicity*, Basingstoke, Macmillan, 1997, ch. 5).
64. A M Weiss (ed.), *Islamic Reassertion in Pakistan: The Application of Islamic Laws in a Modern State*, Syracuse, NY, Syracuse University Press, 1986.
65. Talbot, *Pakistan: A Modern History, op. cit.*, p. 279.
66. This was the case with the blind servant girl Safia Bibi, who received 15 strokes of the cane for falling pregnant after being raped by a man who escaped any sentence for lack of proof.
67. In fact this decree was applied only to financial transactions, not to every area of the law, following the establishment of feminist movements (A M Weiss, 'Women's Position in Pakistan: Sociocultural Effects of Islamization', *Asian Survey*, no. 25 (8), August 1985, p. 870).
68. Cohen, *The Pakistan Army*, p. 90.
69. W L Richter, 'Domestic Politics in the 1980s', in Craig Baxter and Syed Razi Wasti (eds), *Pakistan Authoritarianism in the 1980s*, Lahore, Vanguard, 1991, p. 79.
70. S Huntington, *The Third Wave: Democratization in the Twentieth Century*, Norman, University of Oklahoma Press, 1991.
71. C Jaffrelot, 'Comment expliquer la démocratie hors d'Occident', in C Jaffrelot (dir.), *Démocraties d'ailleurs: Démocratie et démocratisation hors d'Occident*, Paris, Karthala, 2000.
72. Sayyed Vali Reza Nasr, 'Democracy and the Crisis of Governability in Pakistan', *Asian Survey*, no. 32 (6), June 1992, p. 523.
73. M Waseem, 'Pakistan's Lingering Crisis of Dyarchy', *Asian Survey*, no. 32 (7), July 1992, pp. 612–34.
74. On that day, some Sindi police officers, who were carrying out investigations in search of arms, opened fire on civilians killing some 40 Muhajirs, including women and children; they explained their action by alleging sniper attacks – an allegation which could not be substantiated since there was no independent inquiry. Several times the army demanded full powers to restore public order in Sind (by this method they would have been able to bypass the power of the judges). Benazir Bhutto refused to set up such an arrangement, which could have given rise to a veritable parallel government.
75. After 6 October 1989, 'the night of the jackals' had united two senior official of the ISI, IJI deputies and PPP dissidents in a conspiracy to overthrow the Prime Minister. Benazir Bhutto replaced the leader of the ISI, General Hamid Gul, by General Shamsur Rahman Kallue, but his organization more or less boycotted him.
76. The JI's unease was also caused by its rivalry with another member of the coalition, the MQM, which also held Islam to be the symbol of the nation and found a foothold in the Muhajir middle class, among whom the JI had already enjoyed solid support.
77. Malik, *State and Civil Society in Pakistan*, p. 36.
78. This party then withdrew from the IJI, thereby reducing its parliamentary majority.
79. M Waseem, 'Dix ans de démocratie au Pakistan?' in Jaffrelot (dir.), *Démocratie d'ailleurs*, p. 477, M Waseem, *The 1993 Elections in Pakistan*, Lahore, Vanguard, 1994.
80. In 1991, the IJI government had already been accused of guaranteeing borrowing

amounting to 1,200 million rupees, illegally agreed by state cooperatives, in favour of the Ittifaq Industrial Group, owned by the Sharif family. This group, just like that of the Minister of the Interior, had borrowed millions of rupees from the National Industrial Credit Financial Corporation (NICFC), although the Cooperative Societies Act 1925 forbade such loans to limited companies. This diversion of funds was at the bottom of the successive bankruptcies of numerous cooperatives, and losses amounting to 17,000 million rupees, not to mention the problems of two million shareholders.

81. Khalid Bin Sayeed, 'The Three Worlds of Democracy in Pakistan', *Contemporary South Asia*, no. 1 (1), 1992, p. 62.

82. Muhammad Qasim Zaman, 'Sectarianism in Pakistan: the Radicalization of Shia and Sunni Identities', *Modern Asian Studies*, no. 32 (3), 1998, p. 707; S V R Nasr, 'The Rise of Sunni Militancy in Pakistan: The Changing Role of Islamism and the Ulama in Society and Politics', *Modern Asian Studies*, no. 34 (1), 2000, pp. 139–80.

83. Mariam Abou Zahab, 'The Regional Dimension of Sectarian Conflicts in Pakistan', in C Jaffrelot (dir.), *Pakistan: Nationalism without a Nation?* London, Zed Books, 2002, pp. 115–30.

84. The only Islamic party to confront the electorate, the JUI, won just two seats in the National Assembly.

85. The turnout had continued to fall from 54 per cent in 1970 (in East Pakistan) to 43.07 per cent in 1988, 45.46 per cent in 1990, 40.92 per cent in 1993 and 35.92 per cent in 1997.

86. Mohammad Waseem, 'Pakistan Elections 1997: One Step Forward', in C Baxter and G H Kennedy (eds), *Pakistan: 1997*, Boulder, CO, Westview Press, 1999.

87. Conscious of the fact that all his power emanated from his parliamentary majority, Sharif tried hard after the spring to have a law voted to prevent deputies from crossing the floor in the course of a legislative term, a standard practice with the potential to alter power relations significantly. President Leghari refused to promulgate such a law, but Sharif achieved his ends thanks to the 14th Amendment.

88. Asif Ali Zardari, Benazir Bhutto's husband, was arrested as soon as she was out of power in November 1996. His trial began in gaol, where he was accused – among other things – of the murder of Murtaza Bhutto.

89. Sharif had no compunction about having the PPP leader harassed by the police, especially in Sind (Human Rights Commission of Pakistan, *States of Human Rights in 1997*, Lahore, 1998, p. 174).

90. This operation lasted until July 1999 (*The News*, 26 July 1999).

91. Talbot, *Pakistan: A Modern History*, p. 364.

92. Meanwhile, the press had dubbed him 'Emperor Shah Jahan II' because of his luxurious lifestyle, which was, particularly noticeable during his numerous trips abroad in his special Boeing 'on loan' from the national airline (*The News*, 24 October 1999).

93. This choice, which he lived to regret, was made twice, since he appointed Musharraf head of the Joint Chiefs of Staff Committee only in April 1999.

94. Cordonnier, *The Military and Political Order in Pakistan*, p. 50.

95. See the heated reaction of Maleeha Lodhi, ambassador to the USA under Benazir Bhutto, who agreed to accept the same post again under Musharraf (M Lodhi, 'Back to the Future', *The World Today*, November 1999, pp. 4–7).

96. The Swiss government, which has also made some legal moves in her direction, froze her bank accounts and those of her husband.

97. Jean-Luc Racine, 'Le Pakistan après le coup d'État militaire', *Critique Internationale*, no. 7, April 2000, p. 25.

98. To these must to be added four civilians whose nomination on 25 October 1999 disappointed Pakistanis who had been hoping to see some new faces in positions of authority: Sharifuddin Pirzada, serving as Minister of Justice, had previously worked with Zia.

99. Ayesha Jalal's thesis according to which India – a 'formal democracy' tending towards political centralization – and Pakistan were on the path to convergence has remained unsubstantiated by facts (Jalal, *Democracy and Authoritarianism*).

100. On this point see P Schmitter and T L Karl, 'What Democracy is . . . and is not', in L Diamond and M Plattner (eds), *The Global Resurgence of Democracy*, Baltimore, MD, Johns Hopkins University Press, 1993, p. 45.

101. S Shafqat, 'Political Culture of Pakistan: A Case of Disharmony between Democratic Creed and Autocratic Reality', in S Shafqat (ed.), *Contemporary Issues in Pakistan Studies*, Lahore, Gautam, 1995, p. 71.

102. In May 1999 the Punjabi government dissolved 1,941 NGO groups, accusing them of having no other aim but to accumulate grants (*The News*, 10 May 1999). At that very moment, Nawaz Sharif was preparing an NGO Bill which was never submitted to the deputies.

4 PAKISTAN AND THE POWER GAME

1. Government of Pakistan, Minister of Foreign Affairs website, *Pakistan and the Major Powers*, 1999.

2. The other member states are Thailand, the Philippines, Australia, New Zealand, France, Great Britain and the United States.

3. S M Burke, in S M Burke and L Ziring, *Pakistan's Foreign Policy: An Historical Analysis*, Karachi, Oxford University Press, 1990, p. 241.

4. The crushing of the communist uprising by the Indonesian army in 1965 caused China to abandon the idea of a new Afro-Asiatic conference.

5. Ayub Khan used this as the title of his autobiography, *Friends not Masters*, published in 1967.

6. Leaders of Pakistan preferred the word 'bilateralism' as a description of their bilateral relations on all fronts.

7. The *Kissinger Transcripts*, published in 1999, revealed how Henry Kissinger warned China about a possible Indian victory in East Pakistan within two or three weeks of the 1971 victory (W Burr, *The Kissinger Transcripts*, New York, The New Press, 1999).

8. The Symington Amendment, passed in 1977, gave the White House the power to impose sanctions on any state that Congress suspected of buying or selling nuclear weapons technology. The Pressler Amendment (1985) required assurances from the American President that Pakistan had no nuclear missiles as a precondition for continued aid to Islamabad. For the duration of the war in Afghanistan, the White House affirmed without batting an eyelid that Pakistan was not a nuclear power; however, Zia had let it be understood since 1987 that Pakistan had the atomic bomb.

9. Benazir Bhutto, leader of the PPP (Pakistan People's Party), was in semi-exile in London in order to escape corruption charges by the Sharif government. Nawaz Sharif himself, leader of the PML(N) (Pakistan Muslim League [Nawaz]), was sentenced to life imprisonment in April 2000.

10. The Organization for Economic Cooperation (OEC), founded in 1985 but not fully operational until 1991, took over from the Association for Regional Cooperation, a not particularly active development project involving Pakistan, Iran and Turkey (1964–79). The OEC changed – without necessarily becoming more effective – with the entry of the five Central Asian republics (Kazakhstan, Uzbekistan, Turkmenistan, Kirghizstan and Tajikistan) and Azerbaijan, rapidly followed by Afghanistan. The SAARC members were Pakistan, India, Nepal, Bangladesh, Bhutan, Sri Lanka and the Maldives.

11. Several thousand Pakistani troops were indeed sent out to the Gulf, but they played no part in the liberation of Kuwait.

12. One of these groups, Harkat ul-Mujahiddin, is labelled 'terrorist' by Washington. The latest American government report (*Patterns of Global Terrorism: 1999*, Washington, Department of State, 2000) took a firm stance on this question, clearly calling on Islamabad to stop supporting groups that trained in Afghanistan and operated in Kashmir, and to close 'certain *madrasahs* or religious schools, that actually serve for conduits for terrorism'.

13. R Chase, E Hill and P Kennedy (eds), *The Pivotal States: A New Framework for US Policy in the Developing World*, New York, Norton, 1998, p. 4.

5 LIVING WITH INDIA

1. India: 3.2 million square kilometres; a thousand million inhabitants; GNP: 1,500 thousand million dollars; armed forces: 1.1 million men. Pakistan: 803,000 square kilometres; 135 million inhabitants; GNP: 215 thousand million dollars; armed forces: 590,000 men. The only thing they have in common is the baseline indicator of human development, which puts the two neighbours in the same area in relation to the world community: Pakistan 138th, India 139th. The fact that Pakistan has a better per capita GNP does not make up for this asymmetry.

2. In India, secularism is defined as the characteristic of a state with no religious preference. This principle does not by any means preclude the protection of specific minority religions. Organizations opposed to Nehru's secularist line – the Great Hindu Assembly (Hindu Mahasabha), which no longer exists. the Association of Servants of the Nation (Rashtriya Swayamsevak Sangh, or RSS), the Universal Hindu Assembly (Vishva Hindu Parishad) and its political wing, the Bharatiya Janata Party – are, on the contrary, organizations which affirm the Hinduness of the Indian identity. This identitarian affiliation, which verges on communalism, sees other communities as a potential or real threat which must be limited or fought.

3. In the South Asian context, the concept of 'religious communities' applieds to the major generic affiliations: Hindus, Muslims, Christians, Sikhs, and so on.

4. K K Aziz, *The Making of Pakistan: A Study in Nationalism*, London, Chatto & Windus, 1967, p. 143.

5. Ibid., p. 151.

6. Ibid.

7. Ibid., p. 153.

8. On this important matter of images of the other, which leads to what Stephen Cohen calls 'the grotesquely inflated belief of the superiority of Pakistani martial classes over "Hindu India"' (S.P. Cohen, *The Pakistan Army*, Karachi, Oxford University Press, 1988, pp. 41–2).

9. The Muslim sovereign of the little principality of Junagadh, where there was a Hindu majority, had chosen to join Pakistan. India was opposed to this, on the basis of the dominant religion, but did not put forward the same argument in the case of Kashmir, since this would have legitimized its union with Pakistan.

10. This did not prevent the majority of television viewers in Pakistan from avidly watching films on Indian channels.

11. K K Aziz, *The Murder of History: A Critique of History Textbooks Used in Pakistan*, Lahore, Vanguard Books, 1993. The fact that this criticism of school textbooks is the work of an author who defended the two-nations theory in an earlier book does not detract from its importance.

12. The Radcliffe Commission was under urgent instructions to set the borders between India and Pakistan on the eve of Partition.

13. V P Menon, *The Transfer of Power in India*, Princeton, NJ, Princeton University Press, 1957, p. 134.

14. There are still important places of Hindu pilgrimage in Kashmir – Amarnath, for example.

15. Powerful people in the Congress Party brought her to power – provisionally, as they thought – after Shastri's sudden death during the Tashkent Conference. After 1969, Indira Gandhi got rid of her advisers. When she faced the uprising in East Pakistan, she was in complete control.

16. For the events leading up to the war of secession – following the 1970 elections and the refusal of the elites in eastern Pakistan to give power to Mujibur Rahman's Awami League, which won those elections, see Chapter 2.

17. S M Burke and L Ziring, *Pakistan's Foreign Policy: An Historical Analysis*, Karachi, Oxford University Press, 1990, p. 401. Burke, trained by the Indian Civil Service before Partition, was a Pakistani diplomat – and ambassador – before becoming a respected historian.

18. The Indian army went into Pakistan on 21 November 1971. The Pakistan army went into Dhaka on 16 December. India then proclaimed a unilateral cease-fire, ratified the next day by General Yahya Khan, Pakistan's chief of army staff, who left his post on 20 December.

19. The arrival of the US aircraft carrier *Enterprise* in the Gulf of Bengal simply intensified Indian nationalist feeling. The Indians saw this intrusion as a pro-Pakistan act of intimidation.

20. The joint declaration of 4 July 1999 by the American President and the Prime Minister of Pakistan mentions the Simla Accord twice in a dozen lines and states that 'it was vital for the peace in South Asia that the Line of Control in Kashmir be respected by both parties in accordance with their 1972 Simla Accord.'

21. Z A Bhutto, *Reshaping Foreign Policy: Articles, Statements and Speeches*, Lahore, Classic, 1979, p. 130.

22. Abdul Saltar, 'Simla Agreement: Negotiation under Duress', *Regional Studies*, Islamabad, 1995, 13:4, pp. 28–55.

23. This is the theme developed by William Burrows and Robert Windrem in their famous book *Critical Mass: The Dangerous Race for Superweapons in a Fragmenting World*, New York, Simon & Schuster, 1994, challenged in India by Jagjit Singh, director of the Institute for Defence and Strategic Analysis.

24. For an example of a Washington think-tank that was especially active in this context, see M Krepon and A Sevak (eds), *Crisis Prevention, Confidence Building and Reconciliation in South Asia*, Washington, DC, Henry L Stimson Center, 1996.

6 ISLAM AND FOREIGN POLICY

1. These names have been given to the nuclear missiles Pakistan has developed.
2. Gait Minault, *The Khalifat Movement*, New York, Columbia University Press, 1982.
3. For the Deobandi school, see B Metcalf, *Islamic Revival in British India*, Princeton, NJ, Princeton University Press, 1982.
4. Hafeez Malik, *Moslem Nationalism in India and Pakistan*, Lahore, People's Publishing House, 1980, p. 255.
5. This is how Pakistan organized raids into the interior of a still-Soviet Tajikistan in 1987; see a book by a member of the Pakistani services at the time: M Yousaf and A Mark, *The Bear Trap: Afghanistan's Untold Story*, London, Mark Cooper, 1992.
6. For an analysis and critical appraisal of Pakistan's policy on the Taliban, see A Rashid, *Taliban*, London, Tauris, 2000. For an overall analysis of the Taliban, see W Maley (ed.), *Fundamentalism Reborn: Afghanistan and the Taliban*, London, Hurst, 1998.
7. See Metcalf, *Islamic Revival in British India*.
8. See O Roy, *L'Afghanistan. Islam et modernité politique*, Paris, Le Seuil, 1985.
9. On this slide from revolutionary Islamism into conservative neofundamentalism, see O Roy, *L'échec de l'Islam politique*, Paris, Le Seuil, 1992.
10. O Roy, *La Nouvelle Asie centrale*, Paris, Le Seuil, 1997.
11. Azadi Afghan Radio News Release, 30 May 2000.

7 THE COUNTRY AND ITS PEOPLE

1. Under Ranjit Singh (1780–1839), the Punjab was a powerful kingdom which eventually annexed Kashmir and Peshawar, which it seized from the emir of Kabul. Several French officers who fought in the Napoleonic Wars helped Ranjit Singh to establish a modern army which would make life difficult for the conquering British. See J-M Laffont, *La*

Présence française dans le royaume sikh du Pendjab, 1822–1849, Paris, École française d'Extrême-Orient, 1992.

2. G R Elsmie, *Thirty-Five Years in the Punjab*, Lahore, Al-Biruni, 1975 edn, p. 168.
3. See the analysis by A R Omran of Al-Azhar University, *Family Planning in the Legacy of Islam*, London, Routledge, 1992.
4. *Newsline* inquiry, March 2000.
5. A Mohammad, *Salam New York*, Paris, Presses du CNRS, 2000.
6. *Dawn*, 12 June 1997, 25 June 1998, 28 August 1999.
7. *Dawn*, 15 September 1998.

8 ECONOMIC DEVELOPMENT

1. As early as 1968, Mahabub ul-Haq, Chief Economist of the Planning Commission, revealed the fact that twenty-two families dominated 66 per cent of modern industry, 79 per cent of insurance companies and 80 per cent of assets in private banks. See I Talbot, *Pakistan: A Modern History*, London, Hurst, 1998, p. 181.
2. Here in the sense of the English word barrage: a dyke with sluicegates which holds the water in order to release it into the canal.
3. This time I mean a dam – that is, a barrage which creates a vast basin full of water.
4. Akbar Zaidi disputes the increasing use of the word 'feudal' to refer to what he calls 'capitalist agriculture'. See his *Issues in Pakistan's Economy*, Karachi, Oxford University Press, 1999.
5. See, for example, *Dawn*, 11 April 1999, 8 February 2000.
6. *Dawn*, 13 June 1999.
7. *Dawn*, 22 December 1999.
8. *Dawn*, 20 May 1997.
9. Arjmand Zahra, *Dawn*, 12 January 2000.
10. Ibid.

9 BETWEEN CASTE AND TRIBE

1. L Dumont, *Homo hierarchicus.*,Paris, Gallimard, 1966.
2. J-F Jarrige, *Mehrgarh*, Karachi, Government of Sind Culture Department, 1995.
3. Sir Denzil Ibbertson, a British administrator, was one of the most acute analysts of Punjabi society. See his *The Punjab Castes*, Lahore, Sang-e-meel Publications, 1997 edn.
4. Saharan and Sahelian West Africa show that in practice, if not in law, Muslim societies can include castes. See Abdul Wedoud Oul Cheikh, *Nomadisme, islam et pouvoir politique dans la société maure*, sociology thesis, Paris-V, 1985; C Hamès, *Les Maures ou le système des castes hors de l'Inde*, Paris, Cahiers internationaux de sociologie, vol. 46, 1969; Y Wane, *Toucouleurs, stratification sociale*, Dakar, IFAN, 1969.
5. This is different from the Urdu term *biradari*, which describes a villa with three arches on each façade.
6. Azam Chaudhary, *Justice in Practice*, Karachi, Oxford University Press, 1999.
7. This was still going on recently, especially in the west of the country, according to a system also known by a Persian name, *hamsayagui*. A foreign element, by placing itself under the protection of a given community, attained the status of *hamsaya* or 'neighbour' (that is, sharing the same shade). This element could be a small group that had broken away from its tribe of origin, or a community that belonged to a different ethnic group. After several generations – but sometimes fairly rapidly – the *hamsaya* were assimilated, especially if their ties with the protecting tribe had been reinforced by marriage. Thanks to some inventive genealogists, a shared ancestry was unearthed and this integration became complete.
8. A Lefebvre, *Kinship, Honour and Money in Rural Pakistan*, London, Curzon Press, 1999.
9. This name is oddly reminiscent of Tumen, the name of a Mongol legion. Perhaps the Baluchis came under Mongol influence during the Ilkhanid era.

10. Ibbertson, *The Punjab Castes.*
11. L Duprée, *Afghanistan*, Princeton, NJ, Princeton University Press, 19973.
12. This language belongs to the Iranian group which includes Kurdish, Persian and Baluchi.
13. The word *khan* is Mongol; the word *malik* is Arab; *jirgah*, however, is a genuine Pashto word. This leads us to speculate that 'chiefhood' had been established for only a few centuries, whereas the deliberative council was part of a more deeply rooted tradition.
14. Lefebvre, *Kinship, Honour and Money in Rural Pakistan.*
15. Ibid.
16. This was noted on more than one occasion by Mariam Abou Zahab, a teacher in Inalco and one of the keenest observers of Pakistani society.
17. This should not be confused with the socioethnic category of the same name, made up of Urdu-speaking immigrants.
18. Mariam Abou Zahab made a special note of this.
19. C Jaffrelot, *Dr Ambedkar*, Presses de la Fondation nationale des Sciences politiques, 2000.
20. Ibid.

10 THE DIVERSITY OF ISLAM

1. The word 'Wahhabi' derives from the name of the group's founder, Muhammad ibn Abdulwahhab (1703–92); inspired by the work of the Damascene theologian Ibn Taimiyya (1263–1328), he condemned any act of veneration which was not directed towards Allah (this is the monotheist doctrine).
2. S Shafqat, 'Religious Groups: Rise of Dawat-ul-Irshad/Lashkar-e-Tayyaba and the Problem of Democratic Framework in Pakistan', paper presented at the 'Islam and Politics in Pakistan' conference, Paris, CERI, December 1999.
3. D Matringe, 'L'Islam au Pakistan', in F Lenoir and Y Masquelier (eds), *Encyclopédie des religions*, Paris, Bayard, 1997, p. 808.
4. J Malik, *Colonization of Islam: Dissolution of Traditional Institutions of Learning*, Delhi, Manohar, 1996, pp. 235–44.
5. A Schimmel, *Islam in the Indian Subcontinent*, Leyden, Brill, 1980.
6. M Gaborieau, 'Renouveau de l'Islam ou stratégie politique occulte? La Tablighi Jamaat dans le sous-continent indien et dans le monde', in C. Clémentin-Ojha (dir.), *Renouveau religieux en Asie*, Paris, EFEO, 1997.
7. M Gaborieau, 'Le néo-fondamentalisme au Pakistan: Maududi et la Jamâ'at-i Islami', in O Carré and P Dumont (dirs), *Radicalismes islamiques*, Paris, L'Harmattan, 1986, p. 72.
8. There is still, however, a branch of the Jamaat-i Islami in India There are also branches in Bangladesh, Kashmir, England and the USA. They are all officially independent of one another.
9. Twelver Shiism was established in several regions of India; in the Deccan it founded kingdoms which were strongly influenced by the Iranian Safavids from the sixteenth century onwards. However, it was in the north of India, after the collapse of the Mughal Empire, that the Shi'a became a powerful minority. In 1722 they established a Shi'a state in the Awadh principality, between Delhi and Benares; its capital city was Lucknow.
10. The word *khoja* – from the Persian *khwâja* (lord or master) – is equivalent to the Hindu *thâkur*, which also means master. Members of the Lohana caste, who converted to Isma'ilism in large numbers, were known by this name. After their conversion they took the name Khoja.
11. According to Nizari tradition, the first *da'i* – Nuruddin, who is known in India as Satgur Nur – was sent to Gujarat.
12. Literally 'veil' or 'curtain'. This term now implies the segregation of women, because they are obliged to wear the veil, especially among the Indo-Muslim upper classes.
13. The Hafizi, who spread their message through Egypt and Syria by means of the official Fatimid *da'wa*, did not survive the dynasty's fall in 1171.

14. *Da'i*: literally, 'the one who calls', 'summons' people to the one true faith. In its wider sense it means a missionary or preacher, but the word does refer specifically to Isma'ilian propagandists.

15. According to the classic etymological explanation, this term comes from the Gujarati word *vohorvu*, meaning 'trade'. In fact most Isma'ili converts were urban tradesmen or merchants. A less common explanation holds that the Bohra took this name from their original Hindu caste, the 'Vohrâ'. See F Daftary, *The Ismâ'ilîs: Their History and Doctrine*, Cambridge, Cambridge University Press, 1990, p. 299.

16. For men, a *lungî* (a long loincloth), a white muslin *kurtâ* (tunic), and a skullcap woven from gold thread and cotton. Women traditionally wore a *lehangâ* (a long gathered skirt), a *blouse* and an *aurhnî* (a veil worn round the shoulders or over the head). See AA Engineer, *The Bohras*, Delhi, Vikas Publishing House, 1993 [1980], pp. 150–51.

17. A *nabî* is a prophet who does not make law, as opposed to a *rasûl*, a legislating prophet (that is to say, one who lays down a new law).

18. It was in Lahore that two future members of this branch of the Ahmadiyya, Kamaluddin and Ahmad Husain, launched their daily, *Paygham-i sulh* ('Message of Peace'), in 1913 – that is, a year before the definitive break with the Qadiani. Their leader, Muhammad Ali, left Qadian for Lahore with his supporters; in that city he established the headquarters of his breakaway branch, known from then on as the Lahori. See Y Friedmann, *Prophecy Continuous: Aspects of Ahmadi Religious Thought and its Medieval Background*, Berkeley, University of California Press, 1989, pp. 20–22.

19. This word might come from the Arabic *sûf*, 'wool', referring to the coarse woollen robe worn by the first ascetics as a token of simplicity.

20. D Matringe, 'Les dargâh dans les pays de l'Indus', in M A Amir-Moezzi (dir.), *Lieux d'islam: cultes et cultures de l'Afrique à Java*, Paris, Éditions Autrement, 1996, pp. 255–73.

21. Here this term includes both the Qadiani and the Lahori, since the latter were as much objects of Islamist attacks as the former.

22. The Ahrar are an Islamic group with socialist tendencies, formed in 1930. They began their anti-Ahmadi activities in 1934.

23. See S V R Nasr, *The Vanguard of Islamic Revolution: The Jama'at-i Islami of Pakistan*, London and New York, Tauris, 1994, pp. 131–2.

24. See M Q Zaman, 'Sectarianism in Pakistan: The Radicalization of Shi'i and Sunni Identities', *Modern Asian Studies*, 32 (3), 1998, p. 692.

25. Here I mean Twelver Shi'a only. Hitherto the Isma'ilians have not been subjected to violence (although one of their leaders was murdered in Karachi in December 1998). Nonetheless, even though they direct their attacks at the Twelvers, the Sunni Islamists, who want the Shi'a to be pronounced a non-Muslim minority, want – according to this same logic – to see all non-Sunni Muslims, including the Isma'ilians, considered as non-Muslims.

26. In the nineteenth century there were mixed marriages, especially in the more elevated echelons of Muslim society; Shi'a and Sunni came together to celebrate the commemoration of Hussain's martyrdom.

27. Teaching methods in the *madrasahs* vary according to the school of thought with which they are affiliated. The Barelwi and the Deobandi, for example, use more or less the same textbooks, but have different ways of teaching: the Barelwi favour discussion, while the Deobandi lay stress on following the teacher's instructions to the letter. There is a further difference: the Barelwi tend to accept the status quo, and are willing to submit to earthly authority, while the Deobandi are more inclined to oppose the government. See Malik, *Colonization of Islam*, p. 173.

28. *The News*, 10 October 1999.

29. The SSP was originally called the Anjuman-i Sipah-i Sahaba (the Organization of the Army of the Companions of the Prophet); the TJP used to be called the Tahrik Nifaz Fiqh-i Jafaria (the Movement for the Protection of the Shi'a Law). In the 1990s, the bloodiest exploits of these two parties were supported by the Lashkar-i Jhangvi (the Jhangvi

Army, founded in 1990) (for the SSP); and the Sipah-i Muhammad (Muhammad's Army) (for the TJP).

30. S V R Nasr, 'Islam, the State, and the Rise of Sectarian Militancy in Pakistan', paper presented at the 'Islam and Politics in Pakistan' conference.
31. A jihadist organization is an organization which considers that *jihad* is an essential and integral prerequisite for an Islamic revival. See Shafqat, 'Religious Groups'.
32. *Herald*, November–December 1998.
33. B Picquard, 'Efficacité symbolique et effets pervers de la politique d'islamisation au Pakistan', in G Heuzé and M Sélim (dirs), *Politique et religion en Asie du Sud*, Paris, Karthala, 1998, pp. 223–50.
34. Zaman, 'Sectarianism in Pakistan', p. 701.
35. Ibid., pp. 708–9.

11 ISLAM AND POLITICS

1. For more about the Ahmadiyya, see Chapter 10.
2. Quoted in L Binder, *Religion and Politics in Pakistan*, Berkeley, University of California Press, 1961, p. 100.
3. The 1937 Shari'ah Act, which provided for Islamic rulings to prevail over normal customs in matters of personal law, had explicitly excluded the passing on of farmland from these provisions: women were still not allowed to inherit land. See M. Gaborieau, 'Islamic Law, Hindu Law and Caste Customs: A Daughter's Share of Inheritance in the Indian Subcontinent', *Annales islamologiques*, vol. XXVII, Cairo, Institut français d'archéologie orientale, 1993, pp. 157–68.
4. The famous Munir Report, whose full title is *Report of the Court of Enquiry into the Punjab Disturbances of 1953,*, Lahore, West Punjab Government Press, 1954.
5. See K Callard, *Pakistan: A Political Study*, London, Allen & Unwin, 1957, p. 230.
6. This reformist seminary, which was against populist devotions and the worship of saints, was established in 1867 in the town of Deoband. After 1919 it was in the vanguard of the Muslims' struggle against the British.
7. A theological school established at the end of the nineteenth century, which followed the teachings of Ahmad Riza Khan Barelwi (1856–1921): unlike the Deobandi school, it encouraged populist veneration of the Prophet and the saints. For more details, see Chapter 10.
8. *The Political Theory of Islam*, Pashtunkot, Dar-ul-Islam, 1939.
9. Binder, *Religion and Politics in Pakistan*, pp. 70 ff.
10. For more about these sectarian clashes, see Chapter 10.

12 LANGUAGES AND EDUCATION

1. T Rahman, *Language and Politics in Pakistan*, Karachi, Oxford University Press, 1996.
2. H Alavi, 'Politics of Ethnicity in India and Pakistan', *Pakistan Progressive*, 9, 1 (Summer 1987); reprinted in H Alavi and J Hariss (eds), *Sociology of Developing Countries*, London, Macmillan Education Ltd, 1987, pp. 222–46.
3. B Metcalf, *Islamic Revival in British India: Deoband 1860–1900*, Karachi, Royal Book Company, 1989 (first published 1982).
4. A H Nayyar, 'Madrasah Education: Frozen in Time', in P Hoodbhoy (ed.), *Education and the State: Fifty Years of Pakistan*, Karachi, Oxford University Press, 1998, pp. 215–50; T Rahman, *Language, Education and Culture*, Karachi, Oxford University Press, 1999, ch. 5.
5. Hence the development of a small movement for the defence of Punjabi, confined to intellectual circles, especially in Lahore. These intellectuals maintain that the state uses Urdu and English so that the Punjabi elites can retain their power, to the detriment of the cultural integrity of the Punjabi people.
6. W Hanaway and M Nasir, 'Chapbook Publishing in Pakistan', in W Hanaway and W

Heston (eds), *Studies in Pakistani Popular Culture*, Lahore, Sang-e-Meel, 1996, Appendix A, pp. 441–615.

7. Metcalf, *Islamic Revival in British India*.

8. A Rai, *A House Divided: The Origin and Development of Hindi-Urdu*, New Delhi, Oxford University Press, 1991 (first published 1984).

9. C R King, *One Language, Two Scripts: The Hindi Movement in Nineteenth-Century North India*, Bombay, Oxford University Press, 1994.

10. Rahman, *Language and Politics in Pakistan*, ch. 4; P R Brass, *Language, Religion and Politics in North India*, Cambridge, Cambridge University Press, 1974, pp. 119–81; J D Gupta, *Language Conflict and National Development: Group Politics and National Language*, Berkeley and London, University of California Press, 1970.

11. S Alam, 'Language as Political Articulation: East Bengal in 1952', *Journal of Contemporary Asia*, 21, 4, 1991, pp. 469–87.

12. C Shackle, 'Siraiki: A Language Movement in Pakistan', *Modern Asian Studies*, 11, 3, 1977, pp. 379–403.

13. R Faruqi, 'Unprivileged Power: The Strange Case of Persian (and Urdu) in Nineteenth-Century India', *The Annual of Urdu Studies*, no. 13, 1998, pp. 3–30.

14. Ibid.; T Rahman, 'Decline of Persian in British India', *South Asia*, vol. 22, no. 2, June 1999, pp. 47–62.

15. B L Whorf, *Language, Thought and Reality*, ed. John B de Coroll, Cambridge, MA, MIT Press, 1956.

16. R Saigol, *Knowledge and Identity: Articulation of Gender in Educational Discourse in Pakistan*, Lahore, ASR Publications, 1995.

CONCLUSION

1. General Musharraf's address to the nation, 17 October 1999, reprinted in *The Herald*, November 1999, p. 25.

2. In 1998, the government of the Punjab – which had been democratically elected – followed the country's centralizing tradition by appointing the members of village councils in accordance with a new Punjab Local Government (Amendment) Ordinance.

3. *The News*, 26 May 2000.

4. A Rashid, 'Pakistan's Coup: Planting the Seeds of Democracy?', *Current History*, December 1999, p. 414. The 2000–2001 Budget envisaged continuing the 44.35 per cent expenditure on foreign debt servicing and 19.4 per cent on defence, but these were underestimations, mainly because they were based on over-restrictive definitions of these items.

5. M Abou Zahab, 'Islamabad: l'armée du salut?', *Politique internationale*, no. 86, Winter 1999–2000, p. 371.

6. *The Nation*, 6 February 2000.

7. *The News*, 28 March 2000.

8. *The News*, 11 January 1999.

9. Abou Zahab, 'Islamabad: l'armée du salut?', p. 368.

10. As for members of the middle class, who have also suffered a reduction in income exacerbated by the continuing depreciation of the rupee, they want to leave the country – the long queues outside the consulates of Western countries bear witness to this. Among them are many tradesmen and industrialists; their departure could weaken the country's economic potential (I am grateful to Mariam Abou Zahab for this information).

11. Abou Zahab, 'Islamabad: l'armée du salut?', p. 369.

12. On 20 October 1999 – that is to say, a week after General Musharraf's coup – Qazi Hussain Ahmad, leader of the Jamaat-i Islami, declared that he was against the new government's 'Kemalism or secularism' (*Dawn*, 21 October 1999).

13. Rashid, 'Pakistan's Coup', p. 413.

EPILOGUE

1. See Saeed Shafqat, 'From Official Islam to Islamism: The Rise of Dawat-ul-Irshad and Lashkar-i-Tayyiba', in C Jaffrelot (ed.), *Pakistan: Nationalism without a Nation*, New Delhi, Manohar, 2002, pp. 131–47.
2. These figures are taken from a remarkable inquiry whose results were published in *The Herald*.
3. The LJ is an offshoot of the SSP, but it has adopted a strategy of violence, whereas the SSP has taken a different path, becoming a political party (see Chapter 10).
4. M Beletski, 'Pervez Moucharraf: un itinéraire trouble', *Moskovie Novosti*, reprinted in *Courrier international*, no. 576, 21 November 2001, p. 42.
5. It is true that Qazi Hussain Ahmad's Jamaat-i Islami was in the forefront (with the tradesmen) of the protests against the tax inquiries mooted in 2000, but it was an isolated element within the Islamist organizations. Other parties, such as the JUI, did not obey Qazi Hussain Ahmed's calls for antigovernment protests in late 2000. They had realized that the struggle against the traditional political parties was one of Musharraf's priorities, and that he would handle the Islamists carefully.
6. Interview in the *Financial Times Survey*, 6 March 2001.
7. The country's main creditors at the time were Japan (4,827 million dollars), the USA (2,702 million), Germany (1,280 million) and France (1,276 million).
8. In fact, the 6.9 per cent reduction in military expenditure in the 2000–01 budget – and their subsequent stabilization – was achieved by transferring military pensions to a section called 'General Administration'. In reality, military expenditure rose by 11.4 per cent in 2000–01.
9. The drought which affected Sind and Baluchistan spread to the whole country in 2001, reducing the flow of the major watercourses to 18 per cent below the average between 1980 and 1997; this also severely affected the production of hydroelectric power.
10. The diplomatic links between the two countries went hand in hand with transnational relations, largely because of the many Pakistanis who emigrated to Saudi Arabia: in 1999–2000, Saudi Arabia was Pakistan's main external source of finance – mostly expatriate workers sending money home: 310 million dollars; followed by the United Arab Emirates (148 million) and Kuwait (135 million).
11. Musharraf set out four main demands for economic support:

   1. A substantial part of Pakistan's debt should be wiped out, so that it could reduce its debt service from 1.6 billion dollars to 400–500 million.
   2. The country should be given easier access to Western markets, especially textile markets.
   3. The Facility for the Reduction of Poverty and for Development (FRPC), a programme devised by the IMF and the World Bank, should be implemented, allowing Pakistan to receive long-term loans at low interest rates.
   4. The expenses of the war in Afghanistan should be covered.

12. During a visit to Islamabad in October 2001, Colin Powell assured Musharraf of America's intention to resume military cooperation, probably seeing it as a way of eventually turning Pakistan's officers away from the Islamist path.
13. S Hussain, 'Clerics Violated Official Brief during Visit to Afghanistan', *The Friday Times*, 7 October 2001. This is confirmed by a former ISI agent who, under cover of anonymity, revealed in an interview with *The Herald* that the delegation had simply asked Mullah Omar to bear in mind the gravity of the situation (*The Herald*, November 2001, p. 25).
14. See Ahmed Rashid's excellent analysis, 'Post-Taliban Order is a Source of Concern for Pakistan', eurasianet.org, 25 October 2001.
15. One must recall that his father had been murdered by the Taliban.

16. The first thing to stress is the extent of the divide between Deobandi and non-Deobandi, even within jihadist movements which claim to be fighting in the name of Islam. To take just one example: the Harkat-ul Mujahiddin explicitly bans non-Deobandi from its ranks. Even among the Deobandi there are deep divisions. During last spring's Aalmi Deoband Conference, Maulana Fazlur Rahman did all the talking, although leaders of other Deobandi movements – from Qazi Hussain Ahmed to Maulana Fazlur Rahman Khalil; from the Harkat-ul Mujahiddin to Hamid Gul, former chief of the ISI – were present. Moreover, the prospect of elections could rekindle the tensions between rival groups.

17. The American air strikes and the Northern Alliance artillery caused numerous casualties among the Pashtuns – especially in Kunduz, where there were some 1,300 Pashtuns. So the TSNM fighters tried to withdraw to their home territory. Musharraf attempted to close the border, making them even angrier, but in vain. These groups are capable of imposing their own law in this region, and thus challenging the state's authority in part of the country. Pashtun tribes, obeying orders from the PADC, blocked the strategic Karakorum Highway, which links Pakistan to China and the Siachen glacier, at about ten points. These 'insurgents' then freed about fifty common-law criminals. The inhabitants of Gilgit, cut off from the rest of Pakistan, called on the Pakistani state for help; the fact that it made haste slowly is an indication of the importance of these Islamists, who could also step up the conflict with the Shi'a, their 'enemy within', especially in the Punjab.

18. According to the authorities in New Delhi, the leader of the Fidayeen – a word which appeared in the Indian press on several occasions after the attacks – was one of those responsible for the hijacking of the Indian Airlines plane in December 1999. These same authorities hold that Pakistan's involvement was proved by the brand name of the explosives (Wah Nobel): the detonator was found at the scene.

19. According to Indian government statistics, 884 of the 1,027 mercenaries killed in Kashmir over the last twelve years were Pakistanis.

20. Interview with Musharraf, *Financial Times Survey*, 6 March 2001.

21. Interview with Musharraf, *The Herald*, April 2001, p. 57.

22. Ibid., p. 54.

23. *The Herald*, August 2001, p. 55.

24. Musharraf told Raja Zafar, one of the dissidents: 'You are the horse; sideline Nawaz and take away the party', but only a small minority followed him (*The News*, 13 February 2001).

25. Zaffar Abbas, 'Pakistan's Great Gamble', *The Herald*, October 2001, p. 22.

26. Quoted in Robert Fisk, 'Farewell to Democracy in Pakistan', *The Independent*, 26 October 2001.

27. It is probably Pakistan's apprehensiveness about India – notably its fear of being encircled, now that Afghanistan is no longer the ally it once was, and India has begun negotiations with Iran – that explains the Pakistani military's early dialogue with the Iranian authorities: on 4 December 2001, Musharraf held meetings with the Iranian Foreign Minister and Deputy Defence Minister, with a view to developing military links.

28. www.eurasianet.org, 8 November 2001.

29. [all this is duplicated verbatim in the text, on the same page as this note]

30. In March 2001, he declared: 'India's strategy is certainly to isolate us. But I have faith in this country. This is a country of 140 million people; we are a nuclear power; we have a geostrategic importance; we lie at the crossroads of the Middle East, Central Asia and South Asia. Nobody can ignore us; we cannot be sidelined' (interview with the *Financial Times Survey*, 6 March 2001).

INDEX

Abdullah, Sheikh 120, 121, 122, 127, 130
Abdurrahman, Sheikh Omar 140
Achaemenids 5
Action Committee for the National Language 44, 47
Afghanistan
  post-Taliban 268
  relations with Pakistan 4–5, 79–80, 106–7, 138–41, 265–9
  resistance movements 139–40
  Soviet invasion (1979) 79–80, 106
Aga Khans 226–7, 237
'Agartala trial' 24, 52
Agricultural Research Council 180
agriculture
  Punjab 18, 168
  Sind 168
Ahl-i Hadith 134, 139, 222
Ahl-i Sunnat wa Jamaat 222–3
Ahmad, Abdul Mansur 15
Ahmad, Hazrat Mirza Tahir 230
Ahmad Khan, Sayyid 10, 223
Ahmad Shah Abdali 195, 198
Ahmad Shah Durrani 198
Ahmadi 37, 137, 224, 228–9, 236
  anti-Ahmadi movement 230–1, 241, 243, 245
Ahmed, Qazi Hussain 140, 269
Ahrar 230, 241, 243
Ahsan, Admiral 54
Akbar 136
Akhand Bharat 118
Aksai Chin 122
al-Azad, Alauddin 58
Al-Badar 146
Al Badr Mujahideen 271
al-Mulk, Muhsin 11
Alexander the Great 5
Ali, Jam Mashooq 215
Ali, Maulana Ataha 47

Ali, Chaudri Rehmat 13
Ali, Muhammad and Shaukat 11, 12
Ali Khan, Liaquat
  anti-communism 99
  assassination 65
  Islamization policy 242
  and language question 44
  and Mujahirs 17, 19
  as prime minister 63–4
Ali Khan, Yakub 84
Ali Shah, Sajjad 89
Aligarh, Muslims in 10–11
Aligarh Muslim University 223
Aligarh Scientific Society 10
All-Pakistan Muhajir Student Organisation (APMSO) 33, 34
All-Pakistan Organization of Small Trade and Cottage Industries 257
All-Pakistani Women's Association 81
All-Parties National Language Action Committee 47
All Parties Students' Action Committee 52
All-Party Hurriyat Conference (APHC) 128, 133
All-Party Muslim Conference 12
Alliance for the Restoration of Democracy 277
Amar Sonar Bangla 55
Ambedkar, Dr 216
Amin, Nurul 47, 48, 52, 54
Amritsar 127
Anjuman-i Taraqi-i Urdu 18
ANP see Awami National Party
Ansari 204
Anti-Terrorism Amendment Ordinance 2001 261
APHC see All-Party Hurriyat Conference
APMSO see All-Pakistan Muhajir Student Organisation

Arabic 251
Arains 154, 206
Arora, General A S 57
Arya Samaj Hindu 228
Asad, Muhammad (Leopold Weiss) 240–1,
    243
Association for Peace and National Unity in
    Afghanistan 268
Association of Ulemas of India 12
Attlee, Clement 2
Auchinleck, General Claude 117
Awami League (League of the People)
    arrest of leaders 50
    and East Bengal 56, 57, 60, 63, 75
    foundation 23
    and language question 47
    six-point programme (1966) 24, 51, 52, 53
    tendencies 49
    see also National Awami Party
Awami Muslim League 46, 47
Awami National Party (ANP) 32, 253, 270
Awan 203
Ayodhya mosque 38
Ayub Khan, General Muhammad
    agricultural policy 170
    birth control policy 158–9
    centralism 23
    and the constitution 71–2
    coup (October 1958) 50
    and divorce laws 71
    and East Bengal 50, 51, 52, 53, 58
    economic policy 164, 187
    foreign policy 100–1, 102
    industrial policy 70
    Islamization policy 9, 137, 238
    land policy 70
    modernism 244–5
    resignation (1969) 73, 104, 123
    support for Punjabis 19
    and war with India (1965) 72
Azad Kashmir 120, 122, 123, 128
Azhar, Maulana Masood 260–1, 272
Azhar, Mian Muhammad 277
Azhar, Muhammad Masud 92
Aziz, K K 114
Aziz, Sartaz 89
Aziz, Shaukat 264
Aziz Khan, General 268
Azzam, Abdullah 140

Babar, General 142
Babur 135
Badauni, Abdul Hamid 240
Baghdad Pact (1955) 100, 105
Baha ul-Haqq 204

Bahria Foundation 254
Baluchi People's Liberation Front (BPLF)
    29
Baluchi Students' Organization (BSO) 29
Baluchis 194–6
Baluchistan
    insurrection 29
    languages 253
    nationalism 28–30
    refugees in 30
Baluchistan National Alliance 30
Baluchistan National Movement 30
Baluchistan National Party (BNP) 30
Bamiyan Buddhas 268
Bandung Conference (1955) 100
Bang-i Islam 41–3
Bangladesh
    foundation 4, 25, 123–5
    independence 56, 59–60
    see also East Bengal
Bangladesh Nationalist Party (BNP) 60
Banya 207
Barelwi 222–3, 240
Barelwi JUP 74
Barnard, C E 153
Basic Democracies Order (1959) 71
Basic Principles Committee (BPC) 21
Beg, General Mirza Aslam 83, 86
Bengal
    independence 41–3
    Muslim League in 14–15, 39, 40
    Muslims in 39–41
    proposed division of 2
    under the Raj 153
    see also East Bengal
Bengali 4, 41, 43–6, 47, 49, 58
Bharatiya Janata Party (BJP) 114, 131, 272
Bhasani, Maulana Abdul Hamid Khan 46,
    47, 49, 53, 54, 59
Bhasha Andolan 253
Bhutto, Benazir
    and corruption 87, 88, 185
    dismissal 85, 88
    exile 276
    and Muhajir nationalism 34
    and PPP 83
    as prime minister 84, 86–8
    and Sindi nationalism 27
Bhutto, Mumtaz 27, 29
Bhutto, Murtaza 87, 88
Bhutto, Shah Nawas 14
Bhutto, Begum Nusrat 79
Bhutto, Zulfikar Ali
    agricultural policy 170
    and Ahmadi question 230

Bhutto, Zulfikar Ali – *continued*
  and army 76
  and Baluchistan 29
  and Bengal 54
  and civil service 76
  economic policy 164–5
  and elections (1977) 78
  execution (1979) 79
  foreign policy 106
  Islamization policy 9, 137, 245–6
  and PPP 24, 73, 74
  and Sindi nationalism 26
Biharis 34, 35, 60, 84
bin Laden, Osama
  and Afghan war 140, 144
  'handing over' of 267
  and September 11, 2001 265
  and Taliban 135, 145, 147, 175, 268
  and US embassy bombings (August 1998)
    91, 264
Binori Town, Karachi 267
biradari 190, 191, 194, 201, 202, 216, 217
Bizenjo, Ghaus Bux 29
BJP *see* Bharatiya Janata Party
BNP *see* Baluchistan National Party;
  Bangladesh Nationalist Party
Board of Talimat-i Islamia 242
Bogra, Muhammad Ali 19, 49, 66, 99–100,
  102, 243
Bohra 207, 214
Bohra Ismailism 227–8, 237
Bose, Sarat Chandra 42
BPC *see* Basic Principles Committee
BPLF *see* Baluchi People's Liberation Front
Brahmans 191, 192
Brahui language 28, 251, 253
Brahuis 194
British East India Company 65
British government
  Afghan policy 18
  plan for Indian federation 1
Brohi, A K 238
BSO *see* Baluchi Students' Organization
Bugti, Nawal Akbar 30
Bush, George W 266, 267

Carter, Jimmy 106
CDNS *see* Committee for Defence and
  National Security
Central Committee for the Caliphate 12
Central Treaty Organization (CENTO) 69,
  100
chapbooks 252
Chaudhary, Muhammad Azam 217
Chechen wars (1999) 144

China
  and Kashmir question 122
  relations with India 121–2
  relations with Pakistan 102, 107, 175
Chinioti 213, 214
Chistiyya 229
Chitral 156
Chowdhury, Moffazal Haider 59
Chowdhury, Munier 59
Chundrigar, I I 19, 68
Clinton, Bill 92, 175, 257, 264, 276
Committee for Defence and National Security
  (CDNS) 88
Committee for the Official Language 18
Committee of Fundamental Principles 64, 66
Communist Party of India 40
Complete Test Ban Treaty (1996) (CTBT)
  109, 126
Congress Party
  and elections (1937) 12
  and elections (September 1945) 1
  Muslims in 11
Constituent Assembly 1–2, 21, 64, 66
Consultative Commission on Islamic Ideology
  243, 245
Council of Common Interests 25
CTBT *see* Complete Test Ban Treaty

Daud, Prince 139
Daudi Bohras 227–8
Dar ul-Ulum Ashrafabad 222
dargah 229–30
Darling, Sir Malcolm 153
Darul Uloom Haqqania 269
Data Ganji Bakhsh 229
Daultana, Miam Mumtaz 68, 70, 243
Dawat-ul-Irshad 271
Declaration of Objectives (1949) 242, 243
Defense Policy Group 279
Delhi, suicide bombing (December 2001) 271
Deobandi JUI 74
Deobandi *madrasah* (1867) 136
Deobandi school 134, 139, 146, 221–2, 232,
  240, 248
Dera Ghazi Khan 196
Dera Ismail Khan 196
Derajat 196
Dir 156
Dixon, Owen 121
Dulles, John Foster 99
Dumont, Louis 189
Duodeciman Shi'a 225–6, 237
Durand Line 15, 28, 138, 197, 268
Durrani 198
Dustom, Rashid 109, 143

East Bengal
    administration 21, 23
    armed struggle 56–8, 104
    culture and literature 58–9
    defence 51
    economic autonomy 50
    elections (1954) 47–50
    elections (1970) 53–4, 75
    foundation 43
    language movement 43–6, 47
    non-cooperation movement 54
    and Six-Point Programme (1966) 51–5
    see also Bangladesh
East Bengal Regiment 56
East Pakistan
    economy 23
    foundation 21
    military operation against (March 1971) 25,
        164
    population 20
    self-government movement 24
East Pakistan Rifles 56
East Pakistan Students' League 51
East Pakistan Youth League 47
Ejaz, Manzur 180
Ejaz ul-Haq 277
Elective Bodies (Disqualification) Order (1959)
    (EBDO) 70
Elsmie, G R 153
English language 251, 253–4, 255
English Medium schools 254
Ershad, General H M 59, 60
Ettefaq group 214

Farakka Dam 60
Faruki, Kemal 239
Fauji Foundation 254
Fazl-i-Hussain, Miam 13, 18
Federal Shari'ah Court 80, 247, 260
Federally Administered Tribal Areas (FATA)
    259, 270
Feith, Douglas 279
Ferghana valley 143
Fernandes, George 272
'feudal lords' 67–8, 258
Frere, Sir Bartle 155

Gaborieau, Marc 224
Gailani, Pir Sayed 268
Ganatantri Dal 47–8
Gandhara civilization 5
Gandhi, Indira
    and East Bengal 57
    and Punjabi regionalism 127
Gandhi, Mohandas K 1

Gandhi, Rajiv 131
Gangohi, Rashid Ahmad 221
Ghaffar Khan, Abdul 15, 31, 63
Ghakkar 203
Ghazali, Imam 159
Ghaznevids 135, 198
Ghilzai 198
Ghorid empire 135
Ghulam Ahmad, Mirza 228, 236
Glenn Amendment (1998) 266
Golden Temple, Amritsar 127
Goldsmid Line 28
Government of India Act (1935) 12, 61, 62
Green Revolution 18, 33, 167–9, 170, 180
Gujjar 203
Gujral, I K 60, 118, 131, 132
Gul, General Hamid 146
Gulf War (1991) 109, 141
Gurdaspur 117

Haider, Moiuddin 257–8, 261
Hakim, Khalifa Abdul 239
Hamidullah, Muhammad 240
Hanaway, William 252
Hari Singh (Maharaja of Kashmir) 120,
    121
Harkat ul-Ansar (HUA) 142, 146, 233, 271
Harkat-i Inqilab Islami 140
Harkat-ul Mujaheddin (HUM) 91, 92, 128,
    146, 233, 261, 271, 272
Hashim, Abul 40
Hassan Khan, General Gul 76
Hayat Khan, Sikander 13
Hekmatyar, Gulbuddin 108, 140
Herodotus 196
Hizbollah 146
Hindu Mahasabha 11, 42, 113
hissa 201
Hizb-i Islami 108, 140, 141
Hizbul Mujaheddin 128, 271
Houmayoun, Emperor 196
HUA see Harkat ul-Ansar
HUM see Harkat-ul Mujaheddin
Hunter Report (1871) 10, 14
Huq, A K Fazlul 15, 23, 24, 41, 42, 47, 48, 49,
    63, 66
Hussain, Altaf 33, 34, 35
Hussain, Nazir 222, 226
Hussein, Chaudry Shujaat 215

Ibbertson, Sir Denzil 189
ICS see Indian Civil Service
IJI see Islami Jamhoori Ittehad
IJT see Islami Jamiat-i Tulaba
Ilyas, Muhammad 224

Imad, Colonel 142
imamate 225–6
Independent Power Projects (IPP) 185
India
    economic growth 166
    Hindu nationalism 114, 118
    Muslims 10
    as nuclear power 125
    partition 1–2, 116–18, 156–7, 235–8
    relations with China 121–2
    relations with Pakistan 112–33, 175
    relations with USSR 101
    war with China (October 1962) 102
    war with Pakistan (1948) 120
    war with Pakistan (September 1965) 72,
        103, 115, 122–3
    war with Pakistan (November 1971) 25,
        57–9, 75–6, 104
'India-Occupied Kashmir' (IOK) 120
Indian Civil Service (ICS) 21, 153
Indian Independence Act (1947) 61
Indian Mutiny (1857) 10
Indus civilization 189
Indus River 5, 117, 151, 167
Indus Treaty (1958) 117, 121, 130
Inter Services Intelligence (ISI) 107, 127, 140,
    141, 146, 261
'Interim Report' (September 1950) 64–5
International American School 254
IOK see 'India-Occupied Kashmir'
IPP see Independent Power Projects
Iqbal, Mohammad 13, 223, 239
Iran, relations with Pakistan 144, 175
Ishaq Khan, Ghulam 34, 83, 84, 85, 86
ISI see Inter Services Intelligence
Islam
    arrival in Sind 5
    Islamic groups 221–34
    and Pakistan 4, 6, 9, 16–17, 98–9, 104–5,
        134–47, 235–49
    see also Muslims
Islam, Kazi Nasrul 58
Islamabad, becomes capital 20
Islamabad–Lahore motorway 36, 186
Islami Jamhoori Ittehad (IJI) 32, 34, 83, 85
Islami Jamiat-i Tulaba (IJT) 225, 244
Islamic Chhatra Sangha 56
Islamic Development Bank 106
Islamic Jihad 140
Ismailism 226–8, 237
Ispahani 40

Jacob, John 155
Jafa al-Sadiq, Imam 226
Jafarey, Vasim 166

jagirdar 193
Jahan, Rounaq 50
Jaish-i Muhammad 260–1, 271, 272, 273
Jamaat-i Islami (JI)
    and East Bengal 56
    and elections (1970) 74
    and elections (1997) 249
    Islamism 136, 139, 140, 141, 146, 224–5,
        231, 241, 243, 244, 246, 269
    and Muhajirs 33
    and Musharraf 258
    repression of 63
Jamhoori Watan Party (JWP) 30
Jamiyyat-ul Ulama-i Hind (JUH) 136, 222,
    240
Jamiyyat-ul Ulama-i Islam (JUI) 28, 134,
    136, 141, 146, 222, 240, 243, 249, 261,
    269
Jamiyyat-ul Ulama-i Pakistan (JUP) 56, 223,
    240, 243
Jammu and Kashmir Liberation Front (JKLF)
    127
Janjua, General Asif Nawaz 86
Jats 154, 192, 197, 205–6, 215
Jhang Group 89
JI see Jamaat-i Islami
Jinnah, Fatima 50, 72
Jinnah, Muhammad Ali
    background and early career 11
    centralism 62
    death 19
    Islamness 137, 237–8
    and language question 45
    and liberal democracy 62
    and Muslim independence 1, 9, 13
    religion 237
    two-nations theory 114, 223
    sees Congress Party as threat to Muslims
        12–13, 16
jirgahs 197
JKLF see Jammu and Kashmir Liberation
    Front
JUH see Jamiyyat-ul Ulama-i Hind
JUI see Jamiyyat-ul Ulama-i Islam
Junagadh 116, 121
Junejo, Muhammad Khan 79, 82
JUP see Jamiyyat-ul Ulama-i Pakistan
JWP see Jamhoori Watan Party

Kabor (Munier Chowdhury) 59
Kalabagh barrage project 33, 180, 186
'kalashnikov culture' 35, 233
Kalat 28
Kamboh 206–7
kammi 201, 202

Karachi
  industry 184
  migration to 33, 160
  population 17
  university 162
  violence 176
Karachi Electricity Supply Corporation
  (KESC) 185
'Karachisuba' 34
Karakorum road 122
Karamat, Jahangir 36, 89, 90
Kargil war 90–1, 110, 115, 129, 258
Karim, Abdul (Prince of Kalat) 28
Karzai, Hamid 268
Kashmir
  and Indo-Pakistan war (1965) 122–3
  origins of dispute 117, 120
  relations with Pakistan 97–8, 102, 103, 104,
    110, 115, 257, 265
  and terrorism 127–8, 271–4
  UN resolutions on 121
  war over (1948) 120
KESC see Karachi Electricity Supply
  Corporation
Khalistan 127
Khan, Ahmad Riza 223
Khan, Ismail 142
khans 193, 194, 197–8
Kharral, Khalid Ahmed 215
Khatris 155
Khattab, Commander 144
Khattak, Ajmal 31, 37
Khattak, Habibullah 214
Khoja 207, 213–14
Khoja Ismailism 227, 237
Khokar, Nawaz 215
Khudai Khidmatgar ('Red Shirts') 15, 31
Khuhro M A 62, 70
Kipling, Rudyard 189
Kotri barrage 167
Krishak Proja Party 14–15
Krishak Sramik Party 23, 47, 63
kshatriya 191

Ladakh 122
Lahore Declaration (1999) 131
Lahore Resolution (23 March 1940) 16, 28,
  41–2, 235
Lahori 228–9
lambardar 193
Lashkar-i-Jhangvi (LJ) 259, 260, 268
Lashkar-i Tayyiba 146, 258, 261, 271, 272, 273
League of Sind 14
League of the Muslim Students of East
  Pakistan 47

Leghari, Farooq 86–7, 88, 89
Loya Pakhtia 268
Lyall, Alfred 153

madrasahs 136, 139–40, 142, 143, 175, 222,
  231–2, 233–4, 248, 251, 252, 261–2,
  273
Magsi, Zulfiqar Ali Khan 30
Mahboob ul-Haq 215
Mahmud, Lieutenant-General 267, 268
Mahmud of Ghazni 198
Majlis-i Shura 79
Malik, Kauser Abdulla 180
Mangla barrage 167
Manila Pact (1954) 100
Manzilgarh 14
Marri, Khair Buksh 29
Massoud, Commander 109, 142, 143, 144,
  268
Maududi, Abul Ala 224–5, 230, 235, 241,
  242, 243
Mauss, Marcel 201
Mektal-ul Khadamat 140
Mellor, John 180
Memon 212, 214
Mengal, Akhtar 30
Mengal, Attaullah Khan 29
Meo 203
MFLO see Muslim Family Laws Ordinance
Minto, Lord 11
Mir Chakar 196
Mir Wais 198
Mirza, Iskander 19, 49, 67, 68, 70, 238, 239
Mogul Empire 5, 39, 135, 136
Mohenjo-Daro 5, 26
Monem Khan, Abdul 52
Mookerjee, Shyamprasad 42
Mountbatten, Lord Louis 2, 120
Movement for Pakistan 222, 223, 225, 227
Movement for the Defence of the Bengali
  Language 58
Movement for the Oppressed Nationalities of
  Pakistan (PONM) 37
Movement for the Restoration of Democracy
  27, 32, 81–2
MQM see Muhajir Qaumi Mahaz
MQM Haqiqi 35
Muhajir Qaumi Mahaz (MQM) 34–6, 83, 84,
  86, 214
Muhajirs 17–18, 19–20, 25–6, 33–6, 116, 156,
  204, 214, 236, 250
Muhammad, Ghulam 19, 21, 63, 65–7, 238,
  243
Muhammad Ali, Chandri 19
Muhammad Shah (Aga Khan III) 226, 227

Muhammedan Anglo-Oriental College 10, 223
Muhammedan Educational Conference 11
Mukti Bahini 56, 57, 60, 75
Munir, Judge Muhammad 238, 243
Musharraf, General Pervez
  domestic policy 274–5
  early career 260
  economic policy 263–4
  and elections 277, 278
  foreign policy 110, 264–6, 278
  and Islamist groups 259–62, 269–71, 273
  Islamism 147
  and Kashmir 129
  and *madrasahs* 261–2, 273
  and political parties 275–7
  and referendum (2002) 278–9
  and regional minorities 37
  seizure of power (October 1999) 36, 91–2, 93
  seven-point programme 256–7
Muslim Brothers 140, 146, 224
Muslim Conference 120
Muslim Convention League 72
Muslim Family Laws Ordinance (1961) (MFLO) 71, 245
Muslim League
  in Bengal 14–15, 39, 40
  and 'day of direct action' (16 August 1946) 2, 16, 41
  decline 67
  and elections (1937) 12
  and elections (1945–46) 1, 235–6
  foundation 11
  Islamism 137
  Lahore Resolution (23 March 1940) 16, 28, 41–2, 235
  and Liaquat Ali Khan 63
  and Muslim 'homeland' 9, 13
  in North-West Frontier Province 15
  in Punjab 13–14
  in Sind 14
Muslims
  in Congress Party 11
  desire for independent territory 1
  in Punjab 18–20
  in United Provinces 10
  see also Islam
Mustali Ismailism 227
Mutahedea Qaumi Mahaz 35

Nabi Mohammedi 140
Nadwi, Sulaiman 240
Naik, Niaz 132
Namangani, Joma 143

Nanautawi, Muhammad Qasim 221
Naqshabandiyya 229
Nassir Khan 195
National Accountability Bureau 263
National Awami Party (NAP) 28, 31, 49, 63
National Conference (Sheikh Abdullah) 120, 121
National Democratic Front 72
National Islamic Front of Afghanistan 268
National Kashmir Committee 273
National Reconstruction Bureau 277
National Security Council 92
Navi, Tanvir 277
Nazimuddin, Khwaja 19, 39, 42, 43, 44–5, 47, 63, 65–6
Nazir, Mumtaz 252
Neemrana Initiative 132
Nehru, Jawaharlal
  becomes prime minister (September 1946) 2
  and Constituent Assembly 1–2
  and Kashmir 120
  non-alignment policy 99
Nestlé 182, 188
Niazi, General A A K 57
Nimitz, Admiral Chester 121
Nixon, Richard 99
Nizam-i Islami 47, 56
Nizari Ismailism 227
Noon, Malik Firoz Khan 19, 68, 70
Non-Proliferation Treaty (1968) 109, 126
Northern Alliance 267, 268
Northern Territories 120, 122
North-West Frontier Province (NWFP)
  economy 31–2
  Muslim League in 15
  under the Raj 155
Nouri, Mullah 143
Novartis 188
NWFP *see* North-West Frontier Province

Omar, Mullah Muhammad 261, 265, 267
'One Unit Scheme' 21, 28, 63, 66, 73
Operation Brass Tacks 127, 131
Operation Clean-up 34, 35, 36, 86
Operation Gibraltar 72, 123
Operation Kargil 90, 110, 115
Operation Searchlight 56, 75
Osman, Saukat 58
Osmany, Colonel M A G 56
Ottoman caliphate 11, 12, 136

PADC *see* Pakistan–Afghanistan Defence Council
Pakhtunkhwa 33

Pakhtunkhwa Milli Awami Party 30, 270
Pakhtunwali 189, 197
Pakistan
  and Afghan resistance movements
    139–40
  agriculture 165, 166, 167–71, 180–3
  anti-communism 99
  Arab communities 204
  arms trafficking 176
  army 69, 90
  'artificiality' of 2, 4
  banking system 172
  Bengali/Punjabi relations 64–7, 73
  birth control 158–9
  blood ties 190–1
  borders 138
  budget deficit 264
  business community 212–16
  caste system 192, 236
  censuses 36, 157–8
  child labour 172
  Christians 202, 236
  constitution 9, 20–1, 64–5, 67, 82, 83–4,
    86, 88–9, 137, 235, 238–49
  contraband goods 178–9
  crises 256–8
  crops 151, 181
  cultures 4
  debt 177–8, 256–7, 262–3
  democracy 93–4, 177
  deregulation 174–5
  diplomatic isolation (1990s) 264–5
  diplomatic relations with India 130–1
  economic development 163–6
  economic growth 161, 176
  economic prospects 187–8
  economic wastage 179–80, 187
  education 162, 254
  elections (1970) 73–5
  elections (1977) 78
  elections (1984) 82
  elections (1988) 83
  elections (1990) 85
  elections (1993) 86
  elections (1997) 88
  emigration 134, 159–60, 165
  employment 160–1
  energy sector 184–6
  exports 173, 178
  'feudalism' 67–8, 258
  financial system 177–9
  foreign aid 164, 165, 173–4, 177, 264, 266,
    279–80
  foreign investment 178
  foundation 1–2
  fundamentalist organizations 128, 145–7,
    175–6
  gardeners 206–7
  and Gulf War (1991) 109
  health care 162
  heroin trade 176
  history 5, 135–6
  immigration to 2, 17–18
  industrial ownership 70, 171
  industry 163–4, 171–3, 174, 183–4
  infrastructure 172
  internal migration 160
  irrigation 151, 167, 180
  Islam 4, 6, 9, 16–17, 98–9, 104–5, 134–47,
    235–49
  Islamic groups 221–34, 259–62, 269–71
  and Kashmir question 97–8, 102, 103,
    104, 110, 115, 120–3, 128, 130, 133,
    257, 265
  land ownership 170
  languages 4, 6, 9, 18, 21, 26, 26–7, 37,
    43–6, 47, 64, 134, 156, 193, 250–5
  legal system 247–8, 249
  loans, interest on 178, 263
  merchants 207
  military expenditure 166
  mineral resources 153
  multinationals 188
  as nuclear power 5, 106, 109, 125–7
  origin of name 13
  pedlars 208
  persecutions of 'others' 37–8, 247–8
  pole communities 212
  population 20, 37, 157–8, 162
  poverty 258
  professions 208–10
  public services 176
  Punjabi hegemony 18–20, 36
  relations with Afghanistan 4–5, 79–80,
    106–7, 138–41, 265–9
  relations with China 102, 107, 175
  relations with India 112–33, 175
  relations with Iran 144, 175
  relations with Turkmenistan 144
  relations with USA 93, 94, 99–100, 101,
    102, 104, 107, 109, 110, 125–6, 175,
    257, 265–6, 278
  relations with USSR 101
  religious groups 193
  religious students, unemployment of
    248
  and September 11, 2001 278
  shopkeepers 207
  Sindis rise to power 25–8
  social structures 192–4, 216–18

Pakistan – *continued*
  Sunni/Shi'a conflict 81, 87–8, 135, 144,
    176, 231–2, 233–4, 248, 258, 259–60
  and the Taliban 4, 91, 141–2, 257–8,
    267–8, 269, 270
  taxation 166, 257, 263–4
  terrain 151
  trade with India 132
  tradesmen 208–10
  transport 186
  transport workers 208
  tribes 194–203
  Turkish communities 204–5
  urban communities 211–16
  urbanization 158, 234
  violence 162, 258
  wandering communities 210–11
  war with India (1948) 120
  war with India (September 1965) 72, 103,
    115, 122–3
  war with India (November 1971) 25, 57–9,
    75–6, 104
  Western alliances 99–100
  see also East Pakistan; West Pakistan
Pakistan–Afghanistan Defence Council
  (PADC) 269
Pakistan Armed Forces Ordinance (1998)
  90
Pakistan Democratic Alliance (PDA) 85
Pakistan–India People's Forum for Peace and
  Democracy 132
Pakistan Madrasah Education Board
  Ordinance (2001) 261
Pakistan Muslim League (PML) 32, 86, 88,
  223, 261, 276, 277
Pakistan National Alliance (PNA) 78
Pakistan National Party 29
'Pakistan-Occupied Kashmir' 120
Pakistan People's Party (PPP) 24, 26, 27, 54,
  73, 74, 83, 84, 223, 261
Pakistani Communist Party 44
panchayat 217
Parsees 215
Pasha, Anwar 59
Pashto language 15, 251, 252, 253
Pashtun Tribal Areas 259
Pashtunistan 31, 62, 138, 139
Pashtuns 4, 15, 29–30, 32, 197
Pathans 4, 15, 31, 156, 196 200, 222
PDA *see* Pakistan Democratic Alliance
People's Party (Baluchistan) 28
Persian language 251, 253–4
Piracha 207
PML *see* Pakistan Muslim League
PNA *see* Pakistan National Alliance

Political Parties Act (1962) 72
PONM *see* Movement for the Oppressed
  Nationalities of Pakistan
Powell, Colin 267
PPP *see* Pakistan People's Party
Pressler Amendment (1985) 126, 266
Principles of Policy (1956) 243
Public and Representative Officers
  (Disqualification) Act (1950) (PRODA)
  64
Punjab
  agriculture 18, 168
  and Barelwi 223
  castes 154–5
  and Deobandi 222
  linguistic tensions 253
  Muslim League in 13–14
  Muslims in 18–20
  proposed division of 2
  under the Raj 65, 153–4
  University 154, 162
  wheat shortages 164
Punjabi 4, 251, 252

Qadiani 228–9
Qadirriyya 229
Qaid-i Azam 163
Qasim Shahi 226
qaum 190–1, 192, 200, 216, 217
Qayyum Khan, Abdul 73
Qayyum Khan, Muhammad Abdul 273
'Qazi courts' 80
Qureshi 204
Qutb, Sayyid 241

Rabbani, Borhanuddin 142
Radcliffe Commission 117
Rahman, Fazlur 239, 261, 269
Rahman, Mujibur
  assassination 59
  and East Bengal 46, 49, 52, 54, 55, 56
  as prime minister 58
  and six-point programme (1966) 24, 25, 51,
    53, 75
Rahman, Ziaur 56, 59, 106
Rahman Khan, Ataur 49, 54
Rajagopalichariar, C 62
Rajputs 191–3, 202–3, 205, 215
Ram, Chhotu 13
Rann of Kutch 122
Rashid, Ahmed 258
Rashtriya Swayamsevak Sangh 113
Rawalpindi 20
Reagan, Ronald 107, 126
'Red Shirts' *see* Khudai Khidmatgar

Refah 146
Regional Development Cooperation Association 105
Republican Democratic Party 52
Rocca, Christina 264
Round Table Conference (1930) 12
Round Table Conference (1969) 24
Roy, Kiran Shankar 42
Roy, Tridiv 54
Rumsfeld, Donald 279
Rushdie, Salman 134

SAARC *see* South Asia Association for Regional Cooperation
Saeed, Hakim 36
Safavids 135
Sahib, Dr Khan 62, 63, 66
Salahuddin, Syed 272
Samad, Yunas 16
Sami ul-Haq 142, 269
sardar 28, 29, 30, 67, 156, 193
Sayyedna 237
Sayyid 204
SEATO *see* Southeast Asia Treaty Organization
Seifullah family 214
Septiman Shiism 226–7
Seraiki movement 253
Seraiki province 37
Sethi, Naja 89–90
seypi 201, 202, 216
Shafi, Mufti Muhammad 240
Shahab ud-Din 198
Shaheen Foundation 254
Shahidullah, Muhammad 41, 45, 46
Shamzai, Mufti Nizamuddin 267
sharia law 138, 223, 224, 246, 247
Sharif, Nawaz
    background 85
    and Baluchistan 30
    economic policy 174
    and Islamic groups 91
    Islamization policy 9, 85, 249
    and Kashmir 110
    and Muhajir nationalism 35–6
    opposition to Benazir Bhutto 84, 185
    and Pashtun nationalism 32–3
    as prime minister 85–6, 88–92
    resignation 86
    trial and imprisonment 276
    and tribal law 138
Sharif, Shabhaz 89
Sharif family 214
Shastri, Lal Bahadur 123
Shaybanids 135

Sheikhs 204
Sherpao, H M 31
Shi'a
    conflict with Sunni 81, 87–8, 135, 144, 176, 231–2, 233–4, 248, 258, 259–60
    tendencies 225–9, 237
Siachen 127
Simla Accords (1972) 104, 124–5
Simon Commission 12
Sind
    agriculture 168
    arrival of Islam in 5
    and Deobandi 222
    language 26–7, 251, 252
    Muslim League in 14
    nationalism 25–8
    under the Raj 154, 155
Sind Baluch Pashtun Front 29
Sind National Front 27
Sind United Party (SUP) 14
Sindi Desh 27
Singh, Ranjit 153
Sipah-i-Muhammad Pakistan 260
Sipah-i Sahaba 146
Sipah-i Sahaba Pakistan (SSP) 232, 233, 234, 259–60, 261, 273
Six-Point Programme (1966) 24, 51–5, 75
South Asia Association for Regional Cooperation (SAARC) 4, 108, 131
South Asia Preferential Trade Association 132
Southeast Asia Treaty Organization (SEATO) 69, 100
Srinagar 120, 121, 127, 271
SSP *see* Sipah-i Sahaba Pakistan
Suez Crisis (1956) 100
Sufism 229–30, 234
Suhrawardiyya 229
Suhrawardy Hussain Shaheed 23, 24, 39–40, 41, 42, 46, 49, 50, 63, 68, 72, 100
Sulaymani Bohra 228
Sunni
    conflict with Shi'a 81, 87–8, 135–6, 144, 176, 231–2, 233–4, 248, 258, 259–60
    dominance in Pakistan 236
    extremism 145
    tendencies 221–5
SUP *see* Sind United Party
Swat 156
Syed, G M 14, 25–6, 63
Symington Amendment (1978) 107, 125–6, 266

Tablighi Jamaat 134, 136, 142, 224, 225
Tagore, Rabindranath 55, 58
Tahrik Nifaz Fiqh-i Jafaria (TNFJ) 81

Tahrik-i Jafaria Pakistan 232, 273
Tahrik-i Nifaz-i Shari'ah Muhammadi
    (TNSM) 87, 270
Tajikistan, refugees 142–3
Taliban
    American support for 145
    and contraband 178
    and heroin production 176
    Islamism 146
    relations with Pakistan 4, 91, 141–2, 257–8,
        267–8, 269, 270
    rise to power 143
    training 108, 134, 140
Tamaddun Majlis 43–4
Tanzim Nifaz-i Shari'ah-i Mohammadi
    273
Tarar, Rafiq 36, 89, 274, 276
Tarbela barrage 167, 180, 186
Tariq, Azam 260
Tashkent, peace of (1966) 72, 73, 123
Task Force on Energy 185
Tebhaga movement 44, 48
Tenet, George 271
Thaka 203
thakka 201
Thanavi, Ihtishamul Haqq 240
Tibet 122
Tikka Khan, General 54, 56, 76
TNFJ see Tahrik Nifaz Fiqh-i Jafaria
TNSM see Tahrik-i Nifaz-i Shari'ah
    Muhammadi
Turkmenistan, relations with Pakistan 144
two-economy theory 23

Uigurs 141
Umar, Badruddin 58
umma 134, 136, 225
Unionist Party 13–14
United Front 23, 48, 67
United Front (Afghanistan) 268
United Nations, and Kashmir 121
United Provinces (Uttar Pradesh)
    Muslims in 10–11
Unocal 144
Urdu 4, 6, 9, 18, 21, 27, 31, 41, 43, 44, 45, 46,
    47, 64, 134, 137, 250–1, 252–3, 255
USA
    relations with Pakistan 93, 94, 99–100, 101,
        102, 104, 107, 109, 110, 125–6, 175,
        257, 265–6, 278
Usmani, Lieutenant-General 268
Usmani, Shabbir Ahmad 222, 240, 242
Uzbekistan
    Islamic groups 143
    refugees 142

Vajpayee, Atal Behari 118, 131, 257
Vartan Bhanji 201, 202

wadera 155, 157, 168
Wahhabi 136, 140, 145, 222
Wajed, Sheikh Hasina 60
Wali Khan 31, 32, 63
Waliullah, Syed 58
Water and Power Agency 90
Water & Power Development Authority
    (WAPDA) 185
Watto, Manzoor 215
Wavell, Lord 2
West Pakistan
    economy 23, 157
    population 20
Women Lawyers Association 81
Women's Action Forum 81
World Islamic Conference 104, 105, 135, 245

Yahya Khan, General Agha 24–5, 53, 54, 55,
    56
    and East Bengal 104
    and elections (1970) 73–4
    and Operation Searchlight 75
    resignation 76
Yoldashev, Taher 143
Younous Khales 140
Yusuf, Muhammad 224

Xinjiang 122, 140, 175

Zahir Shah 270
zakat 80, 81, 89, 231, 232, 246
zamindars 15, 39, 193, 201, 202
Zardari, Asif Ali 87, 276
Zhou En Lai 101, 102
Zia ul-Haq, General
    and Afghanistan 79–80, 106–7, 126, 136,
        138–9
    and Ahmadi question 231
    death (1988) 82
    economic policy 165
    hostility to India 78–9
    Islamization policy 9, 79, 80–1, 137–8, 225,
        231–2, 235, 246–7
    and referendum (1984) 82
    and Sikh separatists 127
    support for Pashtuns 32
    support for Punjabis 27
Ziaduddin, Lieutenant General Kwaja 90, 91
Zoroastrians 215